FEMINIST FRAMEWORKS AND THE BIBLE

LIBRARY OF HEBREW BIBLE/
OLD TESTAMENT STUDIES

630

Formerly Journal for the Study of the Old Testament Supplement Series

Editors
Claudia V. Camp, Texas Christian University
Andrew Mein, Westcott House, Cambridge

Founding Editors
David J. A. Clines, Philip R. Davies and David M. Gunn

FEMINIST FRAMEWORKS AND THE BIBLE

Power, Ambiguity, and Intersectionality

Edited by

L. Juliana Claassens and Carolyn J. Sharp

t&tclark

LONDON · NEW YORK · OXFORD · NEW DELHI · SYDNEY

T&T CLARK
Bloomsbury Publishing Plc
50 Bedford Square, London, WC1B 3DP, UK
1385 Broadway, New York, NY 10018, USA

BLOOMSBURY, T&T CLARK and the T&T Clark logo
are trademarks of Bloomsbury Publishing Plc

First published 2017
Paperback edition first published in 2019

ISBN: HB: 978-0-5676-7157-8
PB: 978-0-5676-8808-8
ePDF: 978-0-5676-7158-5
ePub: 978-0-5676-8006-8

Series: Library of Hebrew Bible/ Old Testament Studies, volume 630

Typeset by Newgen Knowledge Works Pvt. Ltd., Chennai, India

To find out more about our authors and books visit
www.bloomsbury.com and sign up for our newsletters.

CONTENTS

Part III
INTERROGATING POWER

Part IV
EMBRACING AMBIGUITY

Part V
POSTSCRIPT

ACKNOWLEDGMENTS

We would like to thank the Alexander von Humboldt Foundation as well as the Vice Rector of Research, Eugene Cloete of Stellenbosch University for the funding that made the original Feminist Frameworks conference possible, bringing a number of international and local scholars together in Stellenbosch, South Africa, in March 2015. We are thankful also for the dedicated efforts of Estelle Muller and Helette van der Westhuizen before and during this stimulating conference.

We wish to express our gratitude to Bloomsbury T&T Clark for being willing to publish *Feminist Frameworks and the Bible*, which is a result of expanding the initial Stellenbosch conversation by inviting more colleagues from far and wide to share their frameworks for feminist interpretation. A sincere word of appreciation goes to Ria Smit, who spent many hours copyediting and checking references.

Feminist Frameworks and the Bible brings together a number of feminist scholars from around the world. Each of us has many people to thank: family, friends, colleagues, and allies who make our feminist interpretive efforts possible. Without these respective communities of care, this book would not have come to fruition.

ABBREVIATIONS

AB	Anchor Bible
AJBS	*African Journal of Biblical Studies*
ANEM	Ancient Near East Monographs
AOTC	Abingdon Old Testament Commentaries
ASV	American Standard Version
BETL	Bibliotheca Ephemeridum Theologicarum Lovaniensium
BHS	Biblia Hebraica Stuttgartensia
BibInt	*Biblical Interpretation*
BibInt	Biblical Interpretation Series
BKAT	Biblischer Kommentar, Altes Testament
BLS	Bible and Literature Studies
BMW	Bible in the Modern World
BN	*Biblische Notizen*
BWA(N)T	Beiträge zur Wissenschaft vom Alten (und Neuen) Testament
BZABR	Beihefte zur Zeitschrift für Altorientalische und Biblische Rechtsgeschichte
CBET	Contributions to Biblical Exegesis and Theology
CBQ	*Catholic Biblical Quarterly*
CC	Continental Commentaries
CurTM	*Currents in Theology and Mission*
DCLS	Deuterocanonical and Cognate Literature Studies
ESV	English Standard Version
FB	Forschung zur Bibel
FCB	Feminist Companion to the Bible
GCT	Gender, Culture, Theory
GPBS	Global Perspectives on Biblical Scholarship
HALOT	*The Hebrew and Aramaic Lexicon of the Old Testament*. Ludwig Koehler, Walter Baumgartner, and Johann J. Stamm. Translated and edited under the supervision of Mervyn E. J. Richardson. 4 vols. Leiden: Brill, 1994–1999
HBM	Hebrew Bible Monographs
HR	*History of Religions*
HSHR	Hermeneutics: Studies in the History of Religions
HThKAT	Herders Theologischer Kommentar zum Alten Testament
HUCA	*Hebrew Union College Annual*
IBC	Interpretation: A Bible Commentary for Teaching and Preaching
IEJ	*Israel Exploration Journal*
Int	*Interpretation*
ISBL	Indiana Studies in Biblical Literature

ITC	International Theological Commentary
JAAR	*Journal of the American Academy of Religion*
JBL	*Journal of Biblical Literature*
JBQ	*Jewish Bible Quarterly*
JETS	*Journal of the Evangelical Theological Society*
JFSR	*Journal of Feminist Studies in Religion*
JHebS	*Journal of Hebrew Scriptures*
JPS	Jewish Publication Society
JPSTC	Jewish Publication Society Torah Commentary
JR	*Journal of Religion*
JSOT	*Journal for the Study of the Old Testament*
JSOTSup	Journal for the Study of the Old Testament Supplement Series
LHBOTS	Library of Hebrew Bible/Old Testament Studies
NAC	New American Commentary
NIB	The New Interpreter's Bible
NJPS	New Jewish Publication Society
NKJV	New King James Version
NRSV	New Revised Standard Version
OBO	Orbis Biblicus et Orientalis
OBT	Overtures to Biblical Theology
OTE	*Old Testament Essays*
OTL	Old Testament Library
PRSt	*Perspectives in Religious Studies*
PSB	*The Princeton Seminary Bulletin*
RBL	*Review of Biblical Literature*
SBL	Society of Biblical Literature
SBLDS	Society of Biblical Literature Dissertation Series
SBLStBL	Society of Biblical Literature Studies in Biblical Literature
SemeiaSt	Semeia Studies
SJOT	*Scandinavian Journal of the Old Testament*
Th Viat	*Theologia Viatorum*
TS	*Theological Studies*
VT	*Vetus Testamentum*
WBC	Word Biblical Commentary
WW	*Word and World*
ZAW	*Zeitschrift für die alttestamentliche Wissenschaft*

Chapter 1

INTRODUCTION:
CELEBRATING INTERSECTIONALITY, INTERROGATING POWER, AND EMBRACING AMBIGUITY AS FEMINIST CRITICAL PRACTICES

L. Juliana Claassens and Carolyn J. Sharp

The Color Picker at paint stores is remarkable in its ability to give the most poetic descriptions to the many different hues and tints within a single color: Sprout Green, Leaf Green, Forest Green, Precious Emerald, Bold Avocado, Sugared Lime, Caterpillar, Frog. And that is just for green. Warm colors. Cool colors. Midtone colors. Bright tints. More subdued hues. Light and dark shades. Nevertheless, despite the wide selection of variations for the color green, most everyone who is not color-blind may well recognize green as the color of plants, grass, and foliage, with its connotations of new life, lusciousness, and flourishing.

It is Alice Walker who famously acknowledged the difference between *feminist* and *womanist* in terms of color when she said, "Womanist is to feminist as purple is to lavender."[1] Similar. But different.

Indeed, the study of gender in the Hebrew Bible has come a long way since its inception, with our foremothers claiming their voices, naming systems of oppression, breaking the silence regarding gender-based violence, and celebrating women's gifts by reading the Hebrew Bible in critical, constructive, and creative ways. We have come to learn that race matters, class matters, sexual orientation matters, and social location matters.

Since the inception of feminist biblical interpretation in the early 1980s, feminist interpreters[2] were joined by womanist,[3] *mujerista*,[4] and Asian feminist[5] interpreters, as well as interpreters from Latin America[6] and Africa,[7] who all reflected on their feminist identities in terms of their unique experiences, leading one to indeed speak of "feminisms" in the plural. Womanist biblical interpretation has grown quite multifaceted and richly shaded, as is evident in Nyasha Junior's recent full-length monograph on womanist biblical interpretation.[8] And in (South) Africa, where one of the editors lives, there are vibrant conversations about which term to use, with some scholars choosing to be known as African feminists, and others as womanist scholars. Someone like Madipoane Masenya (one of the contributors to this book) has coined the term *bosadi*, which is a Sesotho word for the term womanist, to describe her unique expression of feminist biblical interpretation (cf. also her contribution in this volume).

To make things even more interesting and richly shaded, feminist biblical interpretation increasingly occurs at the intersection of methods such as postcolonial[9] and queer[10] biblical interpretation, broadening the original definition of what is meant by feminist biblical interpretation. Both editors of this volume over the years have come to embrace and utilize approaches that attend to these variations in terms of queer and postcolonial biblical interpretation, as is evident in a previous book on which some of the contributors to this volume worked together, entitled *Prophecy and Power*.[11] This volume, edited by two of the contributors to *Feminist Frameworks and the Bible*, Christl Maier and Carolyn Sharp, intentionally sought to bring together scholars who have been dedicated to cultivating gender, postcolonial, queer, and trauma perspectives with regard to the interpretation of the book of Jeremiah.

One could thus say that *Feminist Frameworks and the Bible* on the one hand wants to celebrate the rich colors making up the feminist biblical interpretation landscape today, but on the other hand takes the time to explain our different places on the Color Picker to one another. And what better way to do this than to not merely speak in theoretical terms about our respective understandings of feminist biblical interpretation, but to demonstrate this approach by applying it to a biblical text of our choice—which interestingly enough reveals what we are interested in now, and how we see ourselves at this particular moment in time.

The origin of this project was the celebration of the inaugural lecture of one of the editors, Juliana Claassens, who, after studying at Princeton Theological Seminary, taught at a number of institutions in the United States (St. Norbert College in Green Bay, Wisconsin; Baptist Theological Seminary in Richmond, Virginia; Wesley Theological Seminary in Washington, DC) before moving back in 2010 to teach at her alma mater, Stellenbosch University in South Africa. In 2014 she became only the second female full professor in the Faculty of Theology's 159-year existence. Thanks to generous support from the Alexander von Humboldt Foundation, she hosted the Feminist Frameworks conference in March 2015 in conjunction with her inaugural lecture ("An Abigail Optic: Reading the Old Testament at the Intersections," which appears in a revised format in this volume). This rich conference brought together scholars from five countries to reflect on this one question: "What constitutes the feminist framework with which you read the Hebrew Bible?" Contributors were asked, first, to reflect theoretically on their definition of feminism and how it relates to the various intersections at which they read the Hebrew Bible and, second, to choose one Hebrew Bible text to illustrate the framework/prism/optic that governs their interpretive practices.

The original group of contributors was expanded to include additional authors who have distinguished themselves as feminist and postcolonial biblical scholars in different parts of the world. In the essays included in this volume, it will be evident that our feminist frameworks are as diverse and richly shaded as the different tints and hues represented on the Color Picker. We see the world from different vantage points, causing us to regard the topics and issues we are studying in quite different ways, depending on which metaphorical prism, optic, telescope, or microscope each one uses to examine the biblical text, as well as the world in which one is reading this text.

The example of the various shades of green cited in the beginning of this introduction serves the function of demonstrating that, in spite of the diversity, there still exists general agreement regarding the associations green might evoke, which are markedly different from, for example, those of red or yellow. Similarly, it is evident from the contributions included in this volume that there is general agreement in terms of key themes and core values that are important for feminist biblical scholars everywhere, such as justice, peace, equality, inclusion, reconciliation, and transformation. These are values and themes that bind us together, even though we might still be divided as to the details or the definitions of what is meant by justice, inclusion, or transformation. It is these values that also guide our search for common ground, which, in the spirit of Judith Butler's notion of precarity, includes an understanding of a shared sense of vulnerability, and which is dedicated to forging alliances across barriers of race, gender, class, and sexual orientation.[12] In this regard, *Feminist Frameworks and the Bible* embodies our commitment to create counter-communities of care rooted in feminist inquiry and practice—islands and oases where all voices are heard, where we are honest about power relationships (cf. Sharp's definition in this volume), and where creativity is rewarded and justice and joy are embraced.

The notion of the rich shades and colors evoked by the metaphor of the Color Picker also stands for the creativity and ingenuity reflected in the work of the feminist biblical interpreters included in this volume as well as elsewhere in the guild. The essays in *Feminist Frameworks and the Bible* are a good example of new interpretive perspectives that might emerge by bringing divergent texts and contexts together, as well as by introducing new hermeneutical lenses that open up a whole new line of inquiry regarding biblical texts of which one might have thought the last word had been spoken. For instance, one might imagine that one cannot say anything fresh about the book of Ruth, which has been an important book for feminist biblical interpreters. And yet this volume contains two quite different, new interpretations of Ruth and Naomi (cf. the contributions by Sharp and Masenya). Also included among the contributions are a creative encounter between the biblical narrative of Jael killing the enemy leader Sisera (Judges 4); a discussion of Winnie Madikizela-Mandela, whose transformation from innocent girl to militant icon is told in the film *Mandela: A Long Walk to Freedom* (Van der Walt); and a postcolonial interpretation of "Dinah at the Contact Zone" (Dube).

What is quite special about this collection of essays is that it not only includes voices from six different countries but also reflects an intergenerational conversation. With regard to the international nature of this volume, in addition to feminist and postcolonial scholars from the United States, Germany, and New Zealand, *Feminist Frameworks and the Bible* also includes some striking voices from the African continent (Botswana, Nigeria, South Africa) who over the years have not only shaped African biblical interpretation but also had an impact on the global conversation regarding feminist and postcolonial biblical interpretation.

Concerning the intergenerational aspect of this volume, it is wonderful to hear the wise voices of those seasoned feminist biblical scholars who have retired or are getting close to retirement—feminist pioneers in very different parts of the world, ranging from Fort Worth, Texas to Princeton, New Jersey and from Münster, Germany to Otago, New Zealand and Stellenbosch, South Africa (Camp, Sakenfeld, Wacker, McKinlay, Mouton), who have sought to find their feminist voice and also have helped generations of female scholars to do the same. As editors of this volume, we feel obliged to continue this task, doing what we can to create space for younger colleagues and students to help keep the feminist flame alive.

The stories of how these women in very different parts of the world are helping to define the field of feminist and postcolonial biblical interpretation are invaluable, as they give us some sense of how far we have come, yet on the other hand also remind us, in the words of Ecclesiastes, that there is nothing new under the sun (Eccl 1:9). Amid our own struggles for space to do what we love, it is good to remember that the battles facing those of us who are midcareer, or just starting our professional lives, are sadly still the same. The cross-cultural conversation spanning continents also serves as a reminder that though the names, faces, and details of our respective battles for recognition differ, much is eerily familiar.

Finally, one should also note that regardless of the fact that we have gathered a rich diversity of voices from different social locations, there are of course many more life stories and frameworks worthy of inclusion. The selection of essays included in *Feminist Frameworks and the Bible* is limited in terms of the social locatedness of the two editors and their networks of feminist scholars cultivated over the years. This *Feminist Frameworks and the Bible* project can and ought to be supplemented by other voices joining the conversation that reflect even further colors, tints, and hues regarding the nature and significance of feminist biblical interpretation.

This collection of essays is divided into three main subsections reflecting the subtitle of this book: *Power, Ambiguity, and Intersectionality*. The actual categories are not so neatly to be divided, though. Most of the contributions to *Feminist Frameworks and the Bible* touch on several of these themes.

In the introductory essay, Katharine Doob Sakenfield offers a retrospective on how far we as feminist scholars have come. Close readings of biblical texts and sociocultural research have been amplified, in more recent feminist interpretive praxis, by contextually situated modes of analysis, engagement of intersectional approaches, and attention to gender as a dimension of reception history. The next main section of essays, "Celebrating Intersectionality," considers the importance of intersectionality, a notion in critical theory that has become vitally important to feminist biblical interpretation. Intersectional thinking proposes that one cannot focus on gender in isolation but needs to understand it as part of a complex constellation of factors that include, among other things, race, class, sexual orientation, social location, geography, and disability. Here, contributors intentionally explore the intersections between feminist and postcolonial biblical interpretation, recognizing the importance of reading, as Judith McKinlay has proposed, in more than one key.[13] L. Juliana Claassens's essay, "An Abigail

Optic: Agency, Resistance, and Discernment in 1 Samuel 25," explores 1 Samuel 25 to illumine ways in which Abigail's praxis of hospitality and persuasive discourse may be understood as means of resistance to ancient Israelite patriarchal norms and the explicit threat of militarized violence. Musa W. Dube's essay, "Dinah (Genesis 34) at the Contact Zone: 'Shall Our Sister Become a Whore?," utilizes an 1850s Cape Colony judicial case involving sexual violence, racism, classism, and colonial prejudice to frame her reading of Genesis 34 in terms of gender oppression and the discursive imperialism of those seeking to displace the indigenous Other. Judith E. McKinlay's piece, "Jezebel and the Feminine Divine in Feminist Postcolonial Focus," brings into contrapuntal dialogue two polarizing ideologies—seen in Deuteronomistic representations of Jezebel and Protestant missionary attitudes toward Maori views of the sacred—to frame a response of resistance to cultural practices of Othering. Christl M. Maier's essay, "The 'Foreign' Women in Ezra-Nehemiah: Intersectional Perspectives on Ethnicity," considers issues of ethnic difference, gender, and separatist religious praxis in Persian-era Yehud, using postcolonial notions of ambivalence and hybridity to frame representations of the agency of non-Israelite women in Ezra-Nehemiah.

Essays in the next main section, "Interrogating Power," show that feminist biblical interpreters, regardless of their social locations, have in common the realization that power is important in their daily lives, in their scholarly pursuits, in their respective work environments, in church politics, and at home. Many of us have felt the effects of abuses of power on our own bodies and psyches, something that compels us to find ways to subvert or transform operations of power that cause harm, and to use power for good. Moreover, intersectional thinking helps us to understand that one cannot speak in simple binary categories of unilateral power relations that turn men into perpetrators and women into helpless victims. As the contributions to this volume indicate, it is more complex as women, who increasingly enter positions of power and influence, are challenged to be cognizant not to mimic those expressions of force that have been so detrimental to our own well-being. The following essays include an honest interrogation of biblical stories regarding power wielded by female protagonists, and a searching examination of the association between power and violence more generally. Marie-Theres Wacker's essay, "The Violence of Power and the Power of Violence: Hybrid, Contextual Perspectives on the Book of Esther," examines operations of power within the plot of Esther in its Masoretic and Septuagintal versions, considering the effects of tropes of violence for the characterization of Esther, then suggesting some implications for readers in contemporary post-Shoah, post-apartheid, and diaspora contexts. Charlene van der Walt's piece, "'Is There a Man Here?' The Iron Fist in the Velvet Glove in Judges 4," reads the biblical story of Jael in relation to a 2013 film about South African political leader Winnie Mandela, exploring ways in which a narrative ethics framework might help readers navigate complex social circumstances of violence and dehumanization with compassion and moral imagination. Funlola Olojede's essay, "Miriam and Moses's Cushite Wife: Sisterhood in Jeopardy?," examines Miriam's outburst against Moses's Cushite wife in light of ancient Israelite social norms, using the Numbers 12 story to engage political discourses about race in contemporary South African conflicts involving interracial/interethnic intimacy.

In the next main section, "Embracing Ambiguity," contributors' interpretations show what we as feminist biblical scholars know well: biblical texts, as life itself, are complex, ambiguous, and contested. For instance, this section includes reflections on the all-important question that is pressing these days: who is an insider and who is not? Also, how does one assess power within contexts in which individuals have few options to act to the best of their ability? The capacity to engage complexity is quite a valuable life skill when it comes to reading biblical texts but also for merely considering life in our glocal (globalized as well as local) contexts, which are becoming increasingly complex and ambiguous by the day. Carolyn J. Sharp's piece, "Is This Naomi? A Feminist Reading of the Ambiguity of Naomi in the Book of Ruth," considers ambiguity in the literary characterization of Naomi as a narratological strategy that foregrounds ways in which diaspora threatens to change the indigene to the detriment of the postexilic Judean social body. The essay of Madipoane Masenya (ngwan'a Mphahlele), "Stuck between the Waiting Room and the Reconfigured Levirate Entity? Reading Ruth in Marriage-Obsessed African Christian Contexts," uses a *bosadi* reading of Ruth to address challenges experienced by African Pentecostal women pressured toward heterosexual monogamy in social contexts in which men regularly choose polygyny. Claudia V. Camp's essay, "Daughters, Priests, and Patrilineage: A Feminist and Gender-Critical Interpretation of the End of the Book of Numbers," considers issues of priestly authority, masculinity, and political geography articulated in Numbers, focusing on ways in which the story of the daughters of Zelophehad may be seen to frame postexilic identity via gendered ideologies about boundaries and the threat of disunity. Jacqueline E. Lapsley's piece, "'I Will Take No Bull from Your House': Feminist Biblical Theology in a Creational Context," reads Psalm 50 through a feminist hermeneutic that de-emphasizes anthropocentrism in favor of advocacy for the flourishing of all creatures within a cosmocentric theology.

Concluding this collection is a postscript by another feminist pioneer, Elna Mouton, who was the first female professor in the Faculty of Theology at Stellenbosch University. Highlighting the importance of female agency, resistance, and discernment as key capacities for the larger feminist project, Mouton suggests in "Feminist Biblical Interpretation: How Far Do We Yet Have to Go?" that a posture informed by intersectional thinking will engage processes and systems that perpetuate oppression. She asserts the vital importance of liminality and challenges theological systems that purvey essentialist or domineering images of God, noting that biblical conceptions of compassion and *shalom* may be mobilized to address contemporary contexts of alienation, vulnerability, dehumanization, and violence. Mouton calls for moral and ethical stances that can embrace both wonder and discomfort as we move toward justice, reconciliation, and peace.

Feminist Frameworks and the Bible is a volume that seeks to move forward the conversation on the nature and significance of feminist biblical interpretation by creating the space for a number of exciting feminist and postcolonial interpreters from around the world to showcase their craft. Our contributors read biblical texts in creative and constructive ways that can contribute to a world in which gender justice and equality are a reality and not merely an elusive dream. In this ongoing quest, feminist efforts to celebrate intersectionality, interrogate power, and embrace ambiguity will be imperative as we strive to open our interpretive traditions to emancipatory visions of community.

Notes

1. Alice Walker, *In Search of Our Mothers' Gardens* (San Diego: Harcourt Brace Jovanovich, 1983), xi–xii.
2. Cf., e.g., the 1998 and 2012 editions of the *Women's Bible Commentary* for a collection of these feminist voices: Carol A. Newsom and Sharon H. Ringe, eds., *Women's Bible Commentary: Expanded Edition with Apocrypha* (Louisville, KY: Westminster John Knox, 1998); and Carol A. Newsom, Sharon H. Ringe, and Jacqueline E. Lapsley, eds., *Women's Bible Commentary: Revised and Updated* (Louisville, KY: Westminster John Knox, 2012). Cf. also Ilana Pardes, *Countertraditions in the Bible: A Feminist Approach* (Cambridge, MA: Harvard University Press, 1992).
3. Renita J. Weems, "Re-Reading for Liberation: African American Women and the Bible," in *Voices from the Margin: Interpreting the Bible in the Third World*, Revised and expanded Third Edition, ed. R. S. Sugirtharajah (Maryknoll, NY: Orbis, 2006), 27–39; Dolores Williams, "Hagar in African American Appropriation," in *Hagar, Sarah, and Their Children: Jewish, Christian, and Muslim Perspectives*, ed. Phyllis Trible and Letty M. Russell (Louisville, KY: Westminster John Knox, 2006), 171–84.
4. Ada María Isasi-Díaz, "The Bible and *Mujerista* Theology," in *Lift Every Voice: Constructing Christian Theologies from the Underside*, ed. Susan Brooks Thistlethwaite and Mary Potter Engel (Maryknoll, NY: Orbis, 1998), 261–9; cf. also Letty M. Russell et al., eds., *Inheriting Our Mothers' Gardens: Feminist Theology in Third World Perspective* (Louisville, KY: Westminster, 1988).
5. Gale A. Yee, "Yin/Yang Is Not Me: An Exploration into Asian American Biblical Hermeneutics," in *Ways of Being, Ways of Reading: Asian American Biblical Interpretation*, ed. Mary F. Foskett and Jeffrey Kah-Jin Kuan (St. Louis, MO: Chalice, 2006), 152–63. Cf. also Oo Chung Lee, ed., *Women of Courage: Asian Women Reading the Bible* (Seoul: Asian Women's Resource Center for Culture and Theology, 1992).
6. Elsa Tamez, ed., *Through Her Eyes: Women's Theology from Latin America* (Maryknoll, NY: Orbis, 1989).
7. Mercy Amba Oduyoye, *Introducing African Women's Theology* (Sheffield: Sheffield Academic, 2001); Musa W. Dube, ed., *Other Ways of Reading: African Women and the Bible* (Atlanta, GA: SBL, 2001).
8. Nyasha Junior, *An Introduction to Womanist Biblical Interpretation* (Louisville, KY: Westminster John Knox, 2015).
9. Musa W. Dube, *Postcolonial Feminist Interpretation of the Bible* (St. Louis, MO: Chalice, 2000); Musa W. Dube, "Rahab says Hello to Judith: A Decolonizing Feminist Reading," in *The Postcolonial Biblical Reader*, ed. R. S. Sugirtharajah (Oxford: Blackwell, 2006), 142–58; Kwok Pui-lan, "Making the Connections: Postcolonial Studies and Feminist Biblical Interpretation," in *The Postcolonial Biblical Reader*, ed. R. S. Sugirtharajah; Oxford: Blackwell, 2006, 45–64; Kwok Pui-lan, *Postcolonial Imagination and Feminist Theology* (Louisville, KY: Westminster John Knox, 2005); Laura E. Donaldson,

"The Sign of Orpah: Reading Ruth through Native Eyes," in *The Postcolonial Biblical Reader*, ed. R. S. Sugirtharajah (Oxford: Blackwell; 2006), 159–70.

10. Teresa J. Hornsby and Ken Stone, eds., *Bible Trouble: Queer Reading at the Boundaries of Biblical Scholarship*, SemeiaSt 67 (Atlanta, GA: SBL, 2011).

11. Christl M. Maier and Carolyn J. Sharp, eds., *Prophecy and Power: Jeremiah in Feminist and Postcolonial Perspective*, LHBOTS 577 (London: Bloomsbury T&T Clark, 2013).

12. Judith Butler, *Precarious Life: The Powers of Mourning and Violence* (London: Verso, 2004), 43–9.

13. Judith E. McKinlay, "Challenges and Opportunities for Feminist and Postcolonial Biblical Criticism," in *Prophecy and Power: Jeremiah in Feminist and Postcolonial Perspective*, ed. Christl M. Maier and Carolyn J. Sharp, LHBOTS 577 (London: Bloomsbury T&T Clark, 2013), 19–20.

PART I
RETROSPECT

Chapter 2

FEMINIST BIBLICAL INTERPRETATION: HOW FAR HAVE WE COME?

Katharine Doob Sakenfeld

The burgeoning of contemporary feminist biblical interpretation began in the 1970s and has grown exponentially over the ensuing forty-five years. Although feminist interpretation covers the whole of the Christian Bible, illustrations for this introductory essay will focus on Hebrew Bible/Old Testament/First Testament contributions, in keeping with the focus of the essays in the volume as a whole.

Let me begin with a personal word about my own journey. My love affair with the Bible began in my childhood church school, learning stories and memorizing verses and even chapters. In an undergraduate course I was captivated by the strangeness of Old Testament narratives and the prophetic calls for justice, and I took first steps on a long road toward an academic vocation. When I applied to graduate school I was committed to the church and dreamed of becoming an undergraduate religion teacher, so I became a candidate for commissioned church worker (a non-ordained category) in my Presbyterian denomination. I remember thinking that this action might also convince an admissions committee that I was not just seeking a "MRS" degree. I never imagined becoming ordained, certainly not teaching in a theological seminary. It was the 1960s, when contemporary feminist biblical interpretation was not yet on the horizon; questions at the heart of this book and of my life today were nowhere in my graduate school world. When eight years later I did pursue ordination and then accepted a call to seminary teaching, I still had never met another ordained woman, nor had I met a female seminary professor. Somehow, it never occurred to me that I was doing anything unusual; that was fortunate, because I am generally a timid person and would not have deliberately stepped into unfamiliar roles.

Methodologically, I was immersed in the positivistic academic worldview of my graduate school program, and I began my teaching career at Princeton Theological Seminary still without any awareness of feminist ferment. All that changed in 1972 during a gathering with the only other woman faculty member and half a dozen women students. I experienced a conscientization moment, still etched in my memory as if it were yesterday. Yet even when I turned to feminist inquiry, positivism at first prevailed; I assumed that "right" exegetical answers could trump past wrong ones. This view fit well with the traditionally conservative Protestant view of Scripture of my upbringing: Scripture, if carefully enough studied, would give Christians the correct warrant for women's proper place in church and society. Ambiguity and frameworks were not relevant categories in that context. Then, through the work of legendary American feminist theologian Letty Russell, the concept of authority in community gave me theological space for ambiguity and multiple frameworks. I came to realize that no exegetical strategy could guarantee an unassailable interpretation, and that texts themselves, not just their interpreters, can sometimes be harmful rather than beneficial to one's health. I began to explore tensions and disagreements among interpretations in a fresh way. Traveling in Asia and engaging in Bible studies with women in contexts far different from my own deepened my commitment to this exploration and provided me insights to share with my North American community. I am grateful that, over the decades, encounters with an ever-broadening range of feminist interpreters of Scripture, among them many of the contributors to this volume, have continued to expand my horizons. This introductory essay, focused especially on my own North American context, can mention only highlights of the astonishing development of new perspectives and frameworks that I have been privileged to witness.

Phyllis Trible's *God and the Rhetoric of Sexuality*[1] is often regarded as the pioneering volume that demonstrated how close reading of texts from the Hebrew Bible could yield interpretations radically different from those familiar in traditional exegesis. Trible's work focused on a literary approach to the text, giving attention to its "interlocking structure of words and motifs" rather than to questions of historical context,[2] and that focus on the text itself remains central to much continuing feminist research and publication.

Yet from early on, scholars have also been curious about women's actual daily life in biblical times, and have resisted any assumption that the biblical text provides full or even accurate insight into women's existence. To contextualize and supplement the text, scholars have turned to sociocultural inquiry into the various periods of the world in which the texts were formed, including the use of archaeology, comparative Near Eastern textual investigations, sociology, and economic theory, among other disciplines, that may illumine cultural underpinnings of texts composed, edited, and finalized by elite urban males. Archaeological remains have provided important indicators of village agricultural and familial life; social sciences have offered clues into the participation of women in aspects of the domestic economy in various periods, and these insights are supplemented, supported, or qualified through attention to legal and other texts from surrounding cultures. Early pioneers in these areas include Carol Meyers[3] and Phyllis Bird,[4] each of whom, like Trible, continues to update and expand her work.

The work of these representative pioneers and countless others raises questions that continue to be contested. Do narratives about women in the Hebrew Bible give us any reliable insight into the status, role, and life experience of ordinary Israelite women? If so, of which period(s)? How has the perspective of the male elite biblical writers colored, idealized, denigrated, or otherwise obscured the actual situation of the ancient women? How should archaeological and cross-cultural evidence be properly used in relation to the biblical text in assessing such questions? The resulting literature is by now almost impossible for any one reader to review, much less assimilate, and it often seems cacophonous, with deep disagreements among interpreters not only about exegetical details, but more generally about whether individual female biblical characters should be read positively or negatively. Eve, Sarah, and Bathsheba are prominent among traditionally "negative" characters who have been reread positively, but with significant dissenting feminist readings. Conversely, Ruth and Esther, who are frequently viewed as "positive" characters, have been reread negatively. Often the interpretive differences arise not only or even primarily from disagreements about ancient cultural or textual issues but also from differing contemporary lenses or perspectives brought to the text.

As feminist scholars asked new questions, they recognized themselves as part of a larger perspectival movement that encompassed especially liberation theology in the early period and then global perspectives, most recently postcolonial perspectives (or optics, as they are called in some essays in this volume). The assumption that biblical scholarship was objective was rapidly crumbling, as interpreters realized that not only the questions asked but also the range of answers arrived at were closely connected to the interpreters' own and quite varied contexts. In North America, the emergence of womanist (African-American) and *mujerista* (or Latina) readings quickly showed the significance of cultural context. Renita J. Weems's *Just a Sister Away: A Womanist Vision of Women's Relationships in the Bible*[5] is a classic early example. Strikingly, still today more than twenty-five years later, many students—whether white or African-American, male or female—who are assigned this text are surprised to learn of Weems's connection between the slave girl Hagar and African-American women's experience. We have come far, but there is still a long way to go. The contributions of women from underrepresented constituencies in North America are increasing as their numbers in the field increase, albeit more slowly than one would wish. One may note in particular the work of Nyasha Junior,[6] the essay collection edited by Mitzi J. Smith[7] with its superb introduction to the key figures and their contribution to womanist scholarship since Weems, and the recently published volume of womanist essays edited by Gay L. Byron and Vanessa Lovelace.[8]

Of course, recognition of the significance of interpreters' varied situational, geographical, and cultural perspectives has developed globally as well, perhaps even more so than in North America. Among the pioneers of special note in this area have been Kwok Pui-lan,[9] Musa Dube,[10] and Musimbi Kanyoro.[11] Essays by women from every continent have proliferated and bear testimony to ever-increasing participation in feminist interpretation (typically with descriptors specific to the geographical/cultural context of the writer). These contributions relate not just to the historic cultures of different parts of the globe but also, and significantly, to the development of questions focused around colonialism and postcolonialism: how biblical texts were produced in colonial contexts (Babylonian, Persian, and Greco-Roman) and how the Bible remains deeply implicated in the legacy of modern global colonialism and its aftermath. Feminist essays on these themes, with particular focus on biblical and contemporary women, continue to appear in many journals and collections focused on marginalized or postcolonial voices. Computerized cataloging continues to increase awareness of such voices beyond their immediate regions, although access to many important resources still remains limited, especially for the considerable majority in all parts of the world who are not connected to affluent academic institutions that offer access to costly database search engines.

With increasing attention to interpreters' particular contexts, contemporary interpretive lenses have proliferated more and more, leading at times to a sense of fragmentation. Individual interpreters frequently share their personal stories as the lens through which they analyze a particular biblical character or passage. To what extent and in what ways may other readers then respond to such analyses? What are the possible bases for conversation among interpreters who have very different experience-based views of the same text? Once there is a self-conscious effort to state one's personal context and approach, how can conversation move beyond "I see where you're coming from"? Indeed, many of the contributions in this volume wrestle with the question: how do interpreters seek fresh ground beyond the old right/wrong objectivist model or the cacophony of "everyone is right"?

It is at this juncture that several moves in the more recent literature, all well illustrated in this volume, come to the fore: textual constraints, points of mutual contact, and intersectionality. The first of these, renewed attention to constraints, is provided by renewed attention to close reading of the text and its ancient context. Such attention was never absent, as seen in the pioneering examples discussed earlier in this chapter, but it sometimes took a backseat as contemporary perspectival questions emerged. While the text does not and cannot provide definitive answers to many feminist questions, it is possible to debate whether readings are fundamentally with or against the grain of the text, and to consider criteria for determining the grain. Even if the answer is unclear in a specific case, construing the question in this way may offer common ground for pointing to features in the text itself and in the world out of which it arose. Contemporary context is certainly not ignored, but can be set more intentionally in comparison or contrast to the ancient setting. In addition, there appears to be a renewed concern for degrees of generalization about contemporary perspectives. Interpreters' personal contexts may still sometimes be described individualistically, but even in such cases more general features of context are highlighted in such a way that their transferability to related contexts, or their contrast to other contexts, is more readily visible. The importance of the personal is not erased nor are local geographies, but the relationships between local and broader contexts are problematized.

Closely related to both of these shifts is a third and key feature of recent feminist literature, namely its emphasis on intersectionality. Scholars, especially of minoritized groups, long ago noted the relationship among race/ethnicity, sex/gender, and class/economic status, and global scholars added the political (especially postcolonialism) to the mix. Alongside and intertwined with these longer-standing intersectional categories are newer cross-disciplinary studies, notably queer theory and trauma theory. Recent literature suggests that the theorizing of intersectionality as a feminist analytical tool is taking hold more broadly. The plural word "frameworks" in the title of this volume signals the effort of many contributors to develop this dimension of recent feminist conversation.

This essay began with the pioneering developments of the 1970s and early 1980s. Recent research, however, has revealed that many "new" feminist readings and discoveries are not so new after all. Attention was drawn early on to *The Woman's Bible*,[12] but that has turned out to be only the tip of the iceberg. The history of interpretation has arisen as a new subdiscipline in biblical studies generally, as biblical scholars have joined with historians of Judaism, Christianity, and, in some instances, Islam to gather and analyze interpretations of the Bible by early modern and premodern scholars. With the computerization of library records many texts beyond those generally known have come to light, particularly writings by women interpreters of Scripture. Pioneering discoveries were gathered and published by Marion Ann Taylor and Heather E. Weir[13] in 2006. The creative strategies for finding printed books and pamphlets by women included database searches using "Bible" as subject heading and "Mrs." or typical nineteenth-century female first names as the author heading.[14] Perusing the ninety excerpts on women in Genesis included in this anthology reveals a mix of perspectives, with some authors finding biblical precedent for nineteenth-century traditional British and American values of the feminine, while others challenge aspects of this same worldview. Taylor expanded her purview chronologically and geographically in a subsequent volume with an alphabetically arranged dictionary/handbook format.[15] Here, well more than one hundred scholars have contributed brief biographical and analytical essays on 180 women who over the centuries wrote about the Bible, focusing almost entirely on pre-twentieth-century authors; each entry includes a bibliography of the woman's own publications, as well as relevant secondary literature. The introduction provides an excellent overview of the range of women writers geographically, religiously, and educationally, as well as summarizing insights into patterns of focal texts and perspectives discernible in this collection covering many centuries. Research into the history of early women's interpretation of Scripture continues, among other venues, in an established unit at the annual meetings of the Society of Biblical Literature, where presenters continue to add new names as well as new analyses that serve as clear reminders that feminist "discoveries" of the 1970s and beyond have a long prehistory.

The recovery of women interpreters from earlier eras draws attention to another dimension of modern work, that of contributions by so-called ordinary readers. Taylor notes that although many women included in her volumes were clearly educated, and even in some cases had knowledge of biblical languages and access to academic studies of the Bible, many did not have much "expertise." In referring to interpreters of our own time, the term ordinary is sometimes used to describe biblical interpreters (male or female) who interpret biblical texts without the usual academic credentials of "expert" interpreters. Much of my own work has been with such so-called ordinary readers, whether in local congregations in the United States or in gatherings in various parts of Asia.[16] Yet, I as well as others have problematized this designation, recognizing that every reader brings some kind of expertise to the text, the expertise of particular life experience, and often it is the questions asked and interpretations offered by non-academics that open new horizons for academic inquiry. Here the interconnectedness of various features noted in this essay becomes apparent: everyone brings perspectives, as described earlier in this chapter, and the introduction of new perspectives, regardless of source or context, helps to move the conversation forward.

Although only Christian communities regard the Christian Bible as foundational for faith and practice, the Bible's cultural influence has extended far beyond Christian circles, especially because of its use (misuse) in Euro-American global colonization. It has been used historically to circumscribe and control the place of women in the family, in the religious sphere, and in society generally. Much of early modern feminist interpretation focused on rereading texts that were key to arguments for such limitations on women's roles, and in some faith communities these exegetical debates continue, still clinging to the old "objectivity" presuppositions. Where such arguments for so-called complementarianism continue to flourish, some feminists continue trying to challenge traditionalists within the old framework, reiterating alternative readings of supposedly anti-woman texts and lifting up competing texts that suggest different roles for women.

At the same time, the area traditionally called biblical theology remains a tantalizing future horizon for feminist biblical study. Phyllis Trible pointed to the silence of feminists in this area in a key 1989 essay; she proposed a way forward focused on the constructive and hermeneutical aspects of such an enterprise that would use gender as a primary lens but would not result in a single, comprehensive theology.[17] Phyllis Bird, distinguishing her viewpoint from that of Trible, has proposed a different way forward, arguing for the need of a synthetic theology of the Old Testament/Hebrew Bible, but one that is descriptive and historical rather than constructive.[18] Such a feminist descriptive project, in Bird's view, understands gender through and through as a theological category, a theology shaped by feminist recognition of the pervasive perspectival limitations (male, elite, generally urban, and generally well-off) of the biblical text. A different response to Trible's concern has recently appeared in *After Exegesis: Feminist Biblical Theology*.[19] Building on a dialogic approach proposed by Carol A. Newsom,[20] each of the contributions to this feminist essay collection honoring Newsom is focused on a different theological theme (creation, sin, justice, suffering, hope, salvation, and so on), and each intentionally sets two or more Old Testament/Hebrew Bible passages in dialogue, seeking points of intersection among sometimes contrasting voices within the text.

Finally, the development of feminist biblical interpretation is evidenced bibliographically by the continuing appearance of reference works, notably the Feminist Companion series begun in 1993 and edited principally by Athalya Brenner, now totaling more than two dozen volumes of collected feminist essays on individual biblical books; by the appearance of *Women in Scripture*[21] in 2000; and also by the twentieth-anniversary edition of the *Women's Bible Commentary*[22] in 2012. Are such resources comparable to specialized reference works in other areas, or are they evidence that feminist interpretation still is relegated to an "adjectival" niche? Students on every continent continue to arrive in introductory college or graduate level courses on the Bible with no idea that the feminist frameworks conversation is even taking place. Some more traditional academic colleagues still view the conversation as an add-on or optional. The last half-century has indeed seen significant strides in increased attention to feminist work as well as in more nuanced and sophisticated categories of analysis, but the task must continue. The essays in the present volume further this work, demonstrating convincingly that fresh methods and frameworks offered from around the globe do indeed open new interpretive vistas.

Notes

1. Phyllis Trible, *God and the Rhetoric of Sexuality*, OBT 2 (Philadelphia: Fortress, 1978).
2. Trible, *God and the Rhetoric of Sexuality*, 8.
3. See Carol Meyers, *Discovering Eve: Ancient Israelite Women in Context* (New York: Oxford University Press, 1988), and her recent work *Rediscovering Eve: Ancient Israelite Women in Context* (New York: Oxford University Press, 2013).
4. See Phyllis A. Bird, *Missing Persons and Mistaken Identities: Women and Gender in Ancient Israel*, OBT (Minneapolis: Fortress, 1997), a collection of essays published over the previous two decades, and *Faith, Feminism, and the Forum of Scripture: Essays on Biblical Theology and Hermeneutics* (Eugene, OR: Cascade, 2015).
5. Renita J. Weems, *Just a Sister Away: A Womanist Vision of Women's Relationships in the Bible* (San Diego: LuraMedia, 1988).
6. Nyasha Junior, *An Introduction to Womanist Biblical Interpretation* (Louisville, KY: Westminster John Knox, 2015).
7. Mitzi J. Smith, ed., *I Found God in Me: A Womanist Biblical Hermeneutics Reader* (Eugene, OR: Cascade, 2015).
8. Gay L. Byron and Vanessa Lovelace, eds., *Womanist Interpretations of the Bible: Expanding the Discourse* (Atlanta: SBL, 2016).
9. Note the early work of Kwok Pui-lan, *Discovering the Bible in the Non-Biblical World* (Maryknoll, NY: Orbis, 1995), as well as many edited volumes and essays.
10. Musa W. Dube, *Postcolonial Feminist Interpretation of the Bible* (St. Louis: Chalice, 2000); see also work by Dube and other members of the Circle of Concerned African Women Theologians in Musa W. Dube's edited volume, *Other Ways of Reading: African Women and the Bible* (Atlanta: SBL, 2001).
11. Musimbi R. A. Kanyoro, *Introducing Feminist Cultural Hermeneutics: An African Perspective* (Sheffield: Sheffield Academic, 2002).
12. Elizabeth Cady Stanton and the Revising Committee, *The Woman's Bible* (New York: The European Publishing Co., 1895–1898).
13. Marion Ann Taylor and Heather E. Weir, eds., *Let Her Speak for Herself: Nineteenth-Century Women Writing on Women in Genesis* (Waco, TX: Baylor University Press, 2006).
14. Taylor and Weir, *Let Her Speak for Herself*, xvi.
15. Marion Ann Taylor, ed., *Handbook of Women Biblical Interpreters: A Historical and Biographical Guide* (Grand Rapids, MI: Baker Academic, 2012).

16. For examples of such "ordinary" readings, cf. my book, Katharine Doob Sakenfeld, *Just Wives? Stories of Power and Survival in the Old Testament and Today* (Louisville, KY: Westminster John Knox, 2003).
17. Phyllis Trible, "Five Loaves and Two Fishes: Feminist Hermeneutics and Biblical Theology," *TS* 50 (1989): 279–95.
18. Phyllis Bird, "Old Testament Theology and the God of the Fathers: Reflections on Biblical Theology from a North American Perspective," in *Biblische Theologie: Beiträge des Symposiums "Das Alte Testament und die Kultur der Moderne,"* ed. B. Janowski et al., Altes Testament und Moderne 14 (Münster: LIT, 2005), 69–107. Reprinted in Phyllis A. Bird, *Faith, Feminism, and the Forum of Scripture: Essays on Biblical Theology and Hermeneutics* (Eugene, OR: Cascade, 2015), 1–44.
19. Patricia K. Tull and Jacqueline E. Lapsley, eds., *After Exegesis: Feminist Biblical Theology* (Waco, TX: Baylor University Press, 2015).
20. Carol A. Newsom, "Bakhtin, the Bible, and Dialogic Truth," *JR* 76 (1996): 290–306.
21. Carol Meyers, ed., *Women in Scripture: A Dictionary of Named and Unnamed Women in the Hebrew Bible, the Apocryphal/Deuterocanonical Books, and the New Testament* (Boston: Houghton Mifflin, 2000).
22. Carol A. Newsom et al., eds., *Women's Bible Commentary: Revised and Updated* (Louisville, KY: Westminster John Knox, 2012).

PART II
CELEBRATING INTERSECTIONALITY

Chapter 3

AN ABIGAIL OPTIC: AGENCY, RESISTANCE, AND DISCERNMENT IN 1 SAMUEL 25

L. Juliana Claassens

Embracing Intersectionality

In March 2015, I had the privilege to give my inaugural lecture as Professor of Old Testament at Stellenbosch University. This lecture coincided with the Feminist Frameworks conference that forms the basis of the current volume of essays and that brought together a number of international and national feminist scholars reflecting on the feminist framework that shapes their reading of the Old Testament.

If I have to summarize my own feminist framework that over the years has been shaped to inform the way I read the Old Testament, it would involve the ongoing quest of embracing intersectionality. In this regard, I have been very much informed by the work of Judith McKinlay, who argues in the introductory essay to a collection of essays on recent approaches to the book of Jeremiah, edited by Christl Maier and Carolyn Sharp, *Prophecy and Power: Jeremiah in Feminist and Postcolonial Perspective*, that as a feminist biblical interpreter who lives and works in a country plagued by its postcolonial past, it is necessary for her to approach the Old Testament in more than one key. Drawing on gender as well as postcolonial perspectives, she calls her approach to reading the Old Testament a "Rahab prism," so taking her cue from Rahab, the Canaanite woman whose story in the book of Joshua has been quite significant for both feminist and postcolonial scholars.[1]

This idea of multiple, intersecting reading lenses resonates with my own work as is also evident in my contribution to this particular volume, in which I explored gender, postcolonial, queer, and trauma perspectives on the metaphor of a woman in labor that is used throughout the book of Jeremiah.[2] Actually, taking stock of my work of these past 15 years or so, I have always considered it important to read the Old Testament at the intersections, that is, a multidimensional approach that helps one to uncover new levels of meaning in the text as well as allows one to be attentive to the hermeneutical issues underlying shifting interpretive contexts.

In addition to these multiple intersecting reading lenses that have shaped my engagement with the text over the years, I can identify three further intersections that have been quite formative in my own feminist framework. First, I find myself reading the Old Testament at the unique intersection of the United States, Europe, and (South) Africa. Having obtained my PhD from Princeton Theological Seminary, I spent the first eight years of my teaching career at various institutions in the United States[3] before moving back to South Africa, where I am currently teaching at my alma mater, Stellenbosch University. Since then, I increasingly have been exposed to the European conversation due to my connections with our Dutch colleagues at the Protestant Theological University[4] and the time I spent in Germany thanks to the Alexander von Humboldt Foundation.[5]

In terms of the helpful notion of hybridity offered to us by postcolonialism,[6] I continue to be shaped, changed, and transformed by these divergent contexts. For instance, in the course of my physical and intellectual travels between countries, I have come to understand the distinct effect of teaching in the African context on the way in which I read the Old Testament. In terms of my interest in gender, the constant awareness of the challenges facing especially the women of this continent in terms of poverty, education, health care, and violence, as have compellingly been raised in the growing body of work done by the Circle of Concerned African Women Theologians,[7] changes the way I come to the text, what I notice in the text, and what I end up doing with the text. Not only can I not help noticing the marginalized voices in Scripture, but I am also more cognizant of the fact that race and class do matter deeply. At the same time, moving between contexts also has instilled in me the awareness that, despite some of the marked differences, women from these widely different contexts have in common that they quite often have succeeded against great odds, "making a way out of no way," to quote my professor Katharine Sakenfeld's interpretation of the book of Ruth.[8]

Second, a particularly significant intersection that has shaped my feminist framework ever since my doctoral work is that I find great joy in engaging with scholars from beyond the field of biblical studies. From the Russian literary theorist Mikhail Bakhtin, whom I have employed as theorist for my doctoral dissertation,[9] to trauma theorists[10] and, most recently, the feminist philosophers Judith Butler and Martha Nussbaum, theorists from other disciplines have contributed to shaping the way in which I look at texts. Granted, the interdisciplinary enterprise is full of risks, as one never can be an expert in all fields. And yet, it is exactly this vulnerability of moving outside our safe disciplinary categories that may open up new and exciting interpretive possibilities that prevent the field from stagnating. Hence I have found that the study of the Old Testament is greatly enriched by these interdisciplinary perspectives—the unique voices of theorists from other fields kindling the creative spark to see something new in the text that one would not necessarily have seen on one's own. For instance, I have found Martha Nussbaum's work on emotions particularly helpful as she contemplates the question of what it will take for individuals and societies to become compassionate in nature, moving beyond disgust to truly seeing the face of the Other.[11] And Judith Butler asks questions that are most important for a conversation on human dignity, such as: who counts as a human being? What constitutes "a livable and grievable life?"[12] And particularly crucial for the violent world in which we live: by what means can "the frames by which war is wrought time and [time] again" be broken?[13]

Third, I typically describe myself as a feminist biblical *theologian* with the emphasis on the theological nature of the interpretive endeavor. Methodologically, I thus find myself at the intersection of focusing on the literary and theological dimensions of the text while also maintaining a sense of the historical embeddedness of the ancient texts.[14] With regard to this intersection, I consider it important to contemplate the link between texts from ages past and contemporary reading communities. In this regard, Martha Nussbaum has been helpful with her explanation of using ancient narratives in thinking through the issues that haunt us in the present. For instance, with reference to the ancient Greek tragedies, she argues that tragedy offers a bridge between the particularity of ancient narratives and the universality of human experience.[15] As she writes about the act of reading tragic narratives: "Tragic spectatorship cultivates emotional awareness of shared human possibilities, rooted in bodily vulnerability."[16] An important part of my feminist framework hence relates to the approach of using Old Testament texts as a means for the reader to engage his/her own context more deeply.

In the rest of this essay, I use the intriguing story of Abigail as it is narrated in 1 Samuel 25 to illustrate something of what I mean by "reading the Old Testament at the intersections." In what I call an "Abigail Optic," I hope to illustrate my feminist framework that has been shaped by some of the intersections outlined earlier in this essay.

Seeing Abigail

In 1 Samuel 25, one encounters the fascinating story of Abigail, whose act of providing a lavish feast to David and his band of hungry men prevents a terrible tragedy from happening. Abigail is the wife of Nabal, whose name in Hebrew literally means fool. Her act of hospitality is set in the context of David fleeing for his life from King Saul, who in the preceding chapters has been doing his utmost best to remove this threat to his power. At this stage in the narrative David thus is a fugitive and, as noted in 1 Samuel 22:2, surrounded by a group of landless, disenfranchised cohorts who are finding themselves on the fringes of society ("Everyone who was in distress and everyone who was in debt, and everyone who was discontented gathered to him; and he became captain over them" (1 Sam 22:2, NRSV)). The narrative starts with David sending some men to the wealthy landowner Nabal, asking for something to eat, saying three times that they seek peace and have done no harm while dwelling in Nabal's land (vv. 5–8), an assertion that is later corroborated by the testimony of Nabal's servant to Abigail (vv. 15–16). However, Nabal—who in verse 36 is depicted as eating and drinking the feast of a king—refuses, treating David with absolute disdain by asking, "Who is David? Who is the son of Jesse?" (v. 10) and hurling slurs at David according to the later testimony from Nabal's servant (v. 14). An angry David vows to wipe out Nabal's whole household by morning, which most likely would have happened were it not for one of Nabal's servants who turned to Abigail for help. Abigail's initiative, which includes her providing David and his men with generous provisions and delivering an extensive speech in which she convinces David to refrain from violence, ends up not only saving all the members of her household but also preventing the future king from having blood on his hands. Indeed, her actions live up to the designation bestowed upon her by the narrator in verse 3 that she was both clever and beautiful.

Now a feminist framework for this narrative implies that one focuses one's attention on Abigail. As a feminist biblical interpreter, I am interested in what we can glean from the text regarding Abigail's own story, thus bringing her narrative portrayal into conversation with women's realities then and now. However, such an objective is not self-evident. Abigail could quite easily disappear amid the battles among men, her story relegated to a mere footnote in the rise of David or the decline of Saul, depending on one's point of view. In fact, some literary interpretations of 1 Samuel 25 end up making Abigail's story about something else than her encounter with David. So it has been argued that the story of Abigail and Nabal really is symbolic of David's conflicted relationship with Saul.[17] Or that 1 Samuel 25 contains allusions to the ancestral narratives with Nabal/David/Abigail being associated with respectively Laban/Jacob/Rebekah or Esau/Jacob.[18] While such interpretations are compelling, the problem is that Abigail disappears back into the shadows of oblivion.[19] Even feminist interpretations that read Abigail in conjunction with David's other wives (Michal, Bathsheba, and Abishag) tend to turn her into a mere stock character who serves the patriarchal agenda of the text.[20]

However, an alternative (feminist) framework may yield a different reading. In light of my objective to identify the feminist framework that I typically use to read Old Testament narratives such as the one told of Abigail in 1 Samuel 25, I will now introduce three perspectives that have been generated from my reading this text at the intersections, as outlined in the first part of this essay. These perspectives will not only highlight different aspects of my own feminist framework but also may reveal different hues of this fascinating story.

First, one should not overlook the fact that this narrative is set in a context of trauma that actually includes multiple levels of trauma. So this story begins in 1 Samuel 25:1 with the reference to the death of Samuel, the prophet of God who was instrumental in instituting the institution of kingship. The narrative is thus set in the context of the traumatic loss of a revered leader, which suggests a sense of great insecurity. This leadership vacuum is further exacerbated in terms of the weakened position of the current King Saul, whose increasingly erratic behavior is causing him to hunt down his rival David, who, as the reader knows from 1 Samuel 16:1–13, actually has been anointed king by Samuel.[21]

Moreover, as mentioned before, the story is set against the backdrop of a near tragedy in which Abigail's whole family could have been wiped out by morning. In verse 13, the threat of violence is graphically depicted when David tells 400 of his men to strap on their swords—the reference to sword repeated three times to heighten the sense of imminent violence. What is more, even as Abigail is hurrying to intervene, a slighted David is fuming in verses 21–22 that he has done only good to Nabal, who has only "returned [him] evil for good," hence vowing that by morning there will be not one male (literally in Hebrew "no wall-pisser") left in Nabal's house. The narrative thus assumes a fearfully traumatic time when violence and vengeance threaten to destroy the community.

In terms of reading this narrative at the intersection of history and theology, one can imagine how the book of Samuel, which most likely saw its final form in the context of the aftermath of the Babylonian exile, seeks to come to terms with far too much violence.[22] In terms of trauma theory, (tragic) narratives serve as a means of making sense of trauma. Kathleen Sands is right in asserting that the stories one tells in times of trauma are significant: "Tragedies mark off trauma and in so doing wrench back from trauma the rest of life, during which time does not stand still and from which swaths of meaning can be made."[23] As will be evident later in this essay, it may be that a story such as the one of Abigail that is told in a context of real trauma seeks to imagine a different way, perhaps as it considers measures that actually could offer a way out of violence.

Second, reading the story of Abigail in terms of a feminist framework helps one to identify a remarkable portrait of female agency. In verse 18, a series of active verbs are used in quick succession when Abigail is said to hurry, taking 200 loaves, two wineskins, five prepared sheep, five measures of parched grain, 100 clusters of raisins, and 200 cakes of dried figs, and loading it all on presumably more than one donkey! She immediately sends these provisions to David and his men, saying that she will follow soon after. The sense of urgency surrounding her actions is further communicated by the threefold repetition of the term to hurry (vv. 18, 23, and 34). However, in all her hurried activity, the narrator informs us that Abigail did not tell her husband anything (v. 19). Abigail is portrayed in this narrative as a woman in control—a woman who acts independently, so resisting the patriarchal strongholds of her society.

In addition, Abigail's speech to David contributes to this portrayal of female agency. Abigail's speech, which is quite lengthy (the longest single prose speech by a woman in all of the Old Testament),[24] speaks of David as the future king and thus can rightly be described as prophetic. In this regard Ellen van Wolde argues that, in the absence of the prophet Samuel, Abigail acts as the spokesperson of God who shows in her speech remarkable insight, emerging as a model of wisdom and discernment. At this point in the narrative, David is running for his life, a homeless, landless fugitive who is easily dismissed by Nabal. And yet Abigail recognizes him as the future king, thus showing keen insight and understanding. Indeed it is a sign of wisdom to recognize greatness in the most unlikely places or persons.[25] Moreover, Abigail's words and actions have a pronounced effect. Ellen van Wolde outlines how Abigail's speech, which she calls a "rhetorical tour de force," has a transformative effect on the future king, causing David's eyes to be opened.[26] As David himself admits in verses 32–34, it is Abigail's swift actions in addition to her persuasive words that saved her household from a violent massacre.

I find compelling indeed the notion of a woman acting in distinctive ways to resist the violence that threatens her household. This theme is particularly interesting when one takes into consideration what Judith Butler writes about the possibility of individuals stepping outside of their predetermined roles and resisting the frameworks within which war is waged. She argues that "the singular 'one' who struggles with non-violence is in the process of avowing its own social ontology."[27] According to Butler, individuals are profoundly shaped by violence as behavioral and societal norms are inscribed and reinscribed upon people. Thus, for an individual to step out of a mold and—as in the case of Abigail—to resist the reality of violence that permeates her world, this individual has to be compelled by some kind of understanding of human beings and the world at large that makes nonviolence possible. For Butler, this alternative frame of reference that serves the purpose of breaking the "frames of war" is in the first instance the conviction that the individual is " … less as an 'ego' than … a being bound up with others in inextricable and irreversible ways, existing in a generalized condition of precariousness and interdependency"[28] and, secondly, the realization that potential victims of violence are human beings, which Butler's poignant quote cited in the introduction to this essay characterizes as "lives that count as livable and grievable."[29]

What is interesting, though, about Abigail's story is that this act of transcending the violence that marks her community comes through acts of hospitality, by offering a feast of food to the hungry, to the landless, to the marginalized. The story of Abigail's provision of food offers an interesting point of connection to my first book, namely, an exposition of the metaphor of the God who provides food in the Old Testament, which extends in significant ways into the New Testament.[30] In the introduction to this book, I describe the special link that has existed throughout the ages between women and food, using the following marvelous quote by Kim Chernin:

> For food, in fact, preserves the silenced history of women's power. From infancy and through all the stages of our later development, women have exhibited in their relation to food capacities and qualities they have surrendered in many other aspects of their lives. Adept at the mysteries of creating bread from a cup of water, a handful of flour, a pinch of salt, a woman serves up the loaf that is the bread of life—exhibiting in the bowls and retorts of her domestic alchemy the awesome power of transforming matter into nurturance. Skilled in the preparation of those healing infusions of chamomile tea to relieve a belly ache, soft gelatine for a flu, cranberries without sugar to help with nausea, she all along was the mother-magician, adept at the healing arts.[31]

In the case of Abigail, this "mother-magician" in her own right uses her abundant gifts of food to powerful effect. Alice Bach calls her the "mother provider of transformation," noting that she turns "raw material" into "salvific nourishment." Indeed, she offers prepared food such as "dressed sheep" and loaves of bread.[32] What is more, this life-giving sustenance not only saves David and his men from hunger, but by providing food, Abigail also saves her family. As Judith McKinlay rightly notes, Abigail's act of providing food brings life in a context where the denial of food is deadly.[33] In this regard, one could perhaps pause a moment to ask just whom it is that Abigail is seeking to save. Her husband, Nabal? But he is a fool and is called one by Abigail when in verse 25 she tells David to disregard Nabal, "an ill-natured fellow ... for as his name is, so is he; Nabal is his name, and folly is with him." So why save Nabal if she knows that his foolishness—in terms of the theological understanding of the day—will bring an end to him?[34]

In this regard, it is important to note that the threat of violence in this context is directed to multiple male members of Nabal's house. But who is the mother of these presumably multiple sons of Nabal's house whom David vows to eradicate by morning? The text does not say. Despite calling Abigail the "mother provider," Alice Bach presumes that Abigail has no children, that she is childless—like David's other wife, Michal, of whom it is said explicitly that she had no child to the day of her death (2 Sam 6:23).[35] However, one later reads about Abigail having a son, Chileab, with David (2 Sam 3:3; cf. 1 Chr 3:1), so she is obviously not barren, as so many other significant female characters in the biblical text. So, is Abigail perhaps speaking up for the lives of her sons? Particularly in a cultural context in which children form a natural part of marriage, one might assume that this woman is acting on behalf of her children. If so, Abigail's story offers a sharp contrast to that of another mother in 2 Samuel 21, whose life also has been marred by violence: Saul's wife Rizpah, who could do little to save her sons from being brutally executed by the Gibeonites. The only thing left for Rizpah to do is to mourn the deaths of her sons publically—an act of mourning that continues until David grants them a proper burial.[36] This contrast makes the case of Abigail all the more remarkable; this mother, whether biological or performing the role of a mother, saves her household by offering gifts of food and drink to avert violence.

The idea of Abigail acting as a mother, yet at the same time resisting the patriarchal norms of her society, is worth considering. In an article that explores the performativity of motherhood, Irene Oh engages with both Judith Butler and Martha Nussbaum to consider female agency in terms of motherhood.[37] Oh argues that motherhood should be understood as performative; that is to say, "women who willingly become mothers and assume the care of children ... need not necessarily be seen as succumbing to patriarchal stereotypes of domestic femininity."[38] Drawing on the work of Butler, Oh argues that "motherhood emerges as a social institution that both reinforces and potentially subverts dominant gendered paradigms of family and society."[39] She points out that, for Butler, "possibilities for agency lie not outside of but within existing power structures."[40]

Therefore one can say that Abigail performs as a mother and simultaneously transcends the sociocultural norms of her day, which would have relegated her to a position of submissive domesticity. In fact, the idea of employing skills and values of mothering within a broader sphere that involves peacemaking relates to the work of Sarah Ruddick, who contemplates the ethical implications embedded in the act of mothering in the broad sense of the word (she calls her husband her "co-mother"), which she defines as "a sustained response to the promise embedded" in the creation of a new life.[41] This commitment to "mothering" includes, among other things, a desire to preserve life and to foster growth, which may naturally be extended, according to Ruddick, into "a commitment to protect the lives of 'other' children, to resist on behalf of children assaults on body or spirit that violate the promise of birth."[42] In light of such an understanding, Abigail's peacemaking efforts, which center on her actions and words that are intent on resisting violence, are a natural extension of her commitment as a mother to preserve life—whether her own or that of another mother—embodied in the act of providing food.

Third, reading the Old Testament at the intersections prevents one from reading in only one key. Even though I find compelling a feminist framework that focuses on Abigail's agency, the model of peacemaking and resisting violence that her wise example offers, nonetheless, a gendered and a postcolonial interpretation of the text compels one to dig deeper, to look at the text from more than one angle.

For instance, several elements in this text worry me in terms of a gendered interpretation of this text. For example, Abigail's use of subservient language causes the feminist in me to cringe, when she repeatedly uses the term "my lord" (eight times in vv. 25–31) and calls herself "your servant girl" (vv. 28 and 31), a designation suggesting a lower-class woman who holds no power,[43] despite the fact that she is the wife of a landowner who probably was quite affluent, judged by her access to abundant food supplies that include luxury goods such as meat. Moreover, Abigail literally throws herself at King David's feet: in verses 23–24 she falls on her face and at his feet (cf. also the reference to "prostrating herself" in v. 23). And in verses 30–31 Abigail asks David to remember her when he becomes king (cf. the reference in the ESV, "when the LORD has done to my lord according to all the good that he has spoken concerning you, and has appointed you prince over Israel," in v. 31), which David honors at the end of the narrative when he woos her in verses 39–40 and takes her to be his wife.

What is more, this is most certainly not some kind of Hollywood romance as the story ends with the reference in verse 43 that David took another wife, Ahinoam of Jezreel, at the same time as Abigail. But probably most disturbingly from a feminist point of view is that, after this striking portrayal of female agency that relates Abigail's redemptive actions and poignant speech, she all but disappears from the story. Alice Bach rightly notes, "We do not hear her wise voice again."[44] After all her take-charge activity throughout the narrative that had such a profound effect on the lives of her family and community and the life of the future king, Abigail's story ends in silence. She is featured only one more time—when she and her "sister-wife" Ahinoam are caught in a violent hostage drama with the Amalekites that most certainly left them threatened if not violated sexually (1 Sam 30).[45]

In light of Judith Butler's proposition that in terms of gender we are "bound up with the continuing actions of norms, the continuing action of the past in the present, and so the impossibility of marking the origin and end of gender formation as such,"[46] it no surprise that the text reinscribes traditional gender perspectives toward the end of the narrative. But what does one do with these elements in the ancient text that may be troubling to contemporary (Western) feminists? On the one hand, such concerns may help readers of today to recognize that, in different sociocultural contexts, different gender realities are at work. In this regard, Judith Butler has been quite sensitive to the fact there is no one-size-fits-all feminism that applies to all communities everywhere. One is reminded of the complex conversation among women of different cultural and religious contexts today; for instance, whether the burka is a symbol of oppression or exemplifies a woman's right to choose within her particular cultural and religious context.[47] Or with regard to the controversy whether the best way to characterize the controversial cultural practice that still is quite widespread in Africa today is female genital *circumcision*, female genital *mutilation*, or female genital *surgery*—the latter term communicating that this practice is an elective procedure similar to the West's fascination with plastic surgery.[48] Such divergent viewpoints thus offer an important conversation starter in which women from different contexts may voice their respective understandings of female agency and female well-being.[49]

Conversely, gender perspectives on this narrative in 1 Samuel 25 highlight certain gender realities that still haunt us today. For instance, the threat of sexual violence experienced by Abigail and Ahinoam calls to mind the vulnerability of the female condition according to which women around the world continue to be susceptible to violence.[50] With regard to Abigail's disappearance from the text one could well ask what this unfortunate situation tells us about women's gifts today? It may challenge us to reflect on the numerous ways in which women's gifts are not recognized. It draws our attention to those instances in which women in the professional realm make a strong entrance and show incredible creativity and resolve, only to disappear through what has come to be known as the *leaky pipeline* phenomenon.[51]

And yet this narrative about a woman who even amid a very patriarchal culture transcends the script her culture has written for her helps us to appreciate modern-day instances in which women step outside of the molds created for them in the many patriarchal societies around the world, which also make up the realities of many communities on the African continent, where I live and work.[52] This resistance is quite often complex and imperfect, but it is true to life. It is also a reminder that women's ways in the world are seldom straightforward or easygoing.

Looking at the text from a postcolonial point of view, one finds several intriguing elements that would warrant a postcolonial reading. For instance, the image of Abigail meeting the future King David and his band of brothers with the best of the land's produce, which amounts to a feast fit for a king and probably could feed a small village, calls to mind the intercultural encounters that have marked much of the Western entry into colonial Africa whereby the foreign visitors/invaders (missionaries/explorers/mercenaries) robbed countries of their resources (or, in the form of ever-new manifestations of the colonial enterprise, continue to rob them).[53] Abigail's lavish feast may be read in terms of the indigenous population "voluntarily" extending their gifts of hospitality to newcomers. However, one does not need to look too far to find that, more often than not, local resources were obtained by force or coercion.

Moreover, the image posed by Abigail saving her people from a sure death, only to disappear at the end of the narrative, shows similarities to Rahab the Canaanite (Joshua 2 and 6), who, according to Laura Donaldson, may be understood in terms of what she calls the "Pocahontas complex," that is, an indigenous woman portrayed as the "good native" who "saves" the colonizers, allows them to colonize her native land, and then is assimilated into the colonizing group.[54] Lori Rowlett, who continues along the same line of thinking, argues that both Pocahontas and Rahab are co-opted by the colonizing powers when words that praise the colonizers as conquering heroes are put into the mouths of these female characters by their respective authors—in the case of Rahab serving as a means of ventriloquizing Deuteronomistic ideology: "She [Rahab, but also Pocahontas] becomes the medium for transmitting the colonizing power's arrogance in its representation of itself to itself."[55] Indeed, reading the Old Testament at the intersection of Africa, the United States, and Germany as well as at the intersection of gender and postcolonial criticism impacts what one sees in the text.

Seeing as Abigail

I mentioned earlier that the narratives that are told in times of trauma are significant. Such narratives contain important values that may play a powerful role in shaping the moral imagination. For instance, Kathleen Sands argues that tragedies—or near tragedies, as in the case of Abigail—may constitute "the birth trauma of moral consciousness." Tragedies impart to the reader the understanding that "life is not as it should be; *we* are not as we should be."[56] In this regard, Abigail's actions that prevent a near tragedy offer the current community—as well as later generations who are themselves in situations of violence, hovering on the brink of annihilation—the opportunity to reflect on questions such as, How does one survive in a hostile world? How may one go about transcending violence?

In this regard, an interesting angle to Abigail's story is the close association with wisdom when the Wise Abigail and the Foolish Nabal are contrasted throughout the narrative. Abigail's act of generosity stands in a sharp contrast to that of her husband, Nabal, who treats David and his men with contempt, refusing them food while this fool of a man is depicted as feasting on his own (cf. v. 36, "like the feast of a king"). The contrasting perspectives of wisdom and folly in this text are highlighted by Judith McKinlay, who sees in Abigail's act of providing food allusions to the figure of Woman Wisdom who in Proverbs 9:1–6 holds a banquet of meat and wine, inviting all to participate.[57] This portrayal relates to the broader theme in the book of Proverbs, according to which the Way of Wisdom is sharply contrasted with the Way of Folly—the latter leading to certain death.[58]

In the immediate literary context, it has been argued that Abigail's story serves as an object lesson, teaching David restraint in violence or bloodguilt.[59] Considering the later court history, it may be debatable whether David did learn, but at least in the immediate context David is twice in a position of killing his nemesis, Saul, but refrains from doing so (1 Sam 24 and 26). Indeed, Woman Wisdom professes in Proverbs 8:15, "By me kings reign, and rulers decree what is just." Wise kings reign in wisdom, which—as Abigail's story illustrates—implies refraining from violence and sharing goods; the act of hoarding resources is portrayed in this context as leading to death—in Nabal's case, literally.[60]

It is a question, though, whether the example of this Wise Woman in 1 Samuel 25 continues to speak across the chasm of space and time. In terms of an Abigail Optic, is it possible to see as Abigail sees? And what does such a way of seeing mean for feminist biblical interpretation that is committed to reading the Old Testament at the intersections? In conclusion, I would like to identify three characteristics of an Abigail Optic that reveal something of the feminist framework that shapes the way in which I look at the text as well as at the world.

First, an Abigail Optic implies that female agency is recognized both in the patriarchal context of the Old Testament world as well as in the contemporary interpretive contexts that make up our respective realities. Each of the feminist scholars represented in this *Feminist Frameworks and the Bible* volume over the years has presented us with rich examples of feminist and postcolonial biblical interpretation, attending to the voices on the margins, confusing categories such as margin and center, and making issues of race, sexual orientation, and class central to the act of reading the Old Testament. In addition, each of these women has rich stories to share about their respective journeys of becoming a voice, of taking a stand, of showing resolve—often in very trying circumstances. As I was only the second woman to become Full Professor in the Faculty of Theology of Stellenbosch University's 159 years of existence, my inaugural lecture gave me the opportunity to not only reflect on my own journey to this place, but doing so by means of reflecting on Abigail, whose agency, as the preceding portrayal illustrates, is complex, but whose speech and actions had a life-giving and transformative effect indeed.

Second, an Abigail Optic is deeply committed to resisting all conditions that hamper the human ability to flourish. Abigail's act of resisting violence by offering gifts of food fits in well with my most recent project, which explores narratives in the Old Testament that depict instances of female resistance. This project, as also my life and work in general, is deeply rooted in the belief that an integral part of being human is to resist dehumanizing circumstances. My hope is that, in my teaching, scholarship, and community interaction, I may continue to find ways to challenge dignity-defying situations and also to encourage women, men, and children whose human dignity is jeopardized to find ways to reclaim their dignity.[61]

Third, a key aspect of an Abigail Optic is the important theme of discernment, that is, the wisdom to understand that survival is rooted in the ability to share goods rather than to hoard them for oneself, to show solidarity with other individuals and groups who find themselves in a situation of precarity,[62] to create a space where others may flourish, and, finally, to recognize royalty clothed in a pauper's clothes.

Values such as these, which we have seen emerge from the act of reading Abigail's story at the intersections, ultimately may also mean for us today the difference between life and death. Particularly in a context in which violence, greed, power struggles, and selfishness threaten the well-being of our individual and corporate lives, the ability to embrace wisdom and grow in discernment may be what makes it possible for us not only to survive but also to thrive.

Notes

1. Judith E. McKinlay, "Challenges and Opportunities for Feminist and Postcolonial Biblical Criticism," in *Prophecy and Power: Jeremiah in Feminist and Postcolonial Perspective*, ed. Christl M. Maier and Carolyn J. Sharp, LHBOTS 577 (London: Bloomsbury T & T Clark, 2013), 19–37.

2. L. Juliana M. Claassens, "Like a Woman in Labor: Gender, Queer, Postcolonial and Trauma Perspectives on Jeremiah," in Maier and Sharp, *Prophecy and Power*, 117–32.

3. After graduating in 2001 from Princeton Theological Seminary under direction of Katharine Sakenfeld, Dennis Olson, and Don Juel, I spent a year working as a pastor in a Presbyterian congregation half an hour outside New York City before teaching for the next eight years at St. Norbert College, Green Bay, Wisconsin; Baptist Theological Seminary at Richmond, Virginia; and Wesley Theological Seminary, Washington, DC, before returning to South Africa in 2010.

4. For the past nine years, the Protestant Theological University of the Netherlands (first in Kampen, now in Amsterdam and Groningen) and the Faculty of Theology at Stellenbosch University, South Africa have collaborated in yearly conferences alternating between the two institutions and focusing on various aspects pertaining to the theme of human dignity. In 2013, some of the fruits of this rich collaboration were published in the collection of essays *Fragile Dignity: Intercontextual Conversations on Scriptures, Family, and Violence*, ed. L. Juliana M. Claassens and Klaas Spronk, SemeiaSt 72 (Atlanta: SBL, 2013).

5. Courtesy of the Alexander von Humboldt Foundation, I spent twelve months (between 2012 and 2015) in Münster, Germany with my host Marie-Theres Wacker of the Katholisch-Theologische Fakultät, Westfälische Wilhelms-Universität Münster, whose contribution is also included in this volume.

6. Drawing on Homi Bhabha's definition of hybridity as the "'in-between space' in which the colonialized translate or undo the binaries imposed by the colonial project," R. S. Sugirtharajah continues to describe postcolonial criticism as a product of hybridity: "It is an inevitable growth of an interaction between colonizing countries and the colonized. It owes its origin neither to the First or the Third World, but is a product of the contentious reciprocation between the two," "Charting the Aftermath: A Review of Postcolonial Criticism," in *Postcolonial Biblical Reader*, ed. R. S. Sugirtharajah (Malden, MA: Blackwell, 2006), 7–32 (15–6).

7. Isabel Apawo Phiri outlines the Circle's objectives well: "The Circle is a community of African women theologians who come together to reflect on what it means to them to be women of faith within their experiences of religion, culture, politics and social-economic structures in Africa." Phiri continues to cite the Circle's 2007 draft constitution: "The Circle seeks to build the capacity of African women to contribute their critical thinking and analysis to advance current knowledge using a theoretical framework based on theology, religion and culture. It empowers African women to actively work for social justice in their communities and reflect on their actions in their publications," "Major Challenges for African Women Theologians in Theological Education (1989–2008)," *Studia Historiae Ecclesiasticae* 34 (2008): 63–81 (67). Various publications have appeared under the auspices of the Circle, including *The Will to Arise: Women, Tradition, and the Church in Africa*, ed. Mercy Amba Oduyoye (Maryknoll, NY: Orbis, 1992); *Talitha Cum! Theologies of African Women*, ed. Nyambura J. Njoroge and Musa W. Dube (Pietermaritzburg: Cluster Publications,

2001); and *African Women, Religion, and Health: Essays in Honor of Mercy Amba Ewudiziwa Oduyoye*, ed. Isabel Phiri and Sarojini Nadar (Pietermaritzburg: Cluster Publications, 2000).

8. Katharine Doob Sakenfeld, *Ruth*, IBC (Louisville, KY: John Knox, 1999), 87.

9. Cf. the methodological chapter in my dissertation (L. Juliana M. Claassens, "The God Who Feeds: A Feminist Theological Analysis of Key Pentateuchal and Intertestamental Texts," PhD dissertation, Princeton Theological Seminary, 2001) that was later published in L. Juliana M. Claassens, "Biblical Theology as Dialogue: Continuing the Conversation on Bakhtin and Biblical Theology," *JBL* 122 (2003): 127–44.

10. Cf., e.g., L. Juliana M. Claassens, "Calling the Keeners: The Image of the Wailing Woman as Symbol of Survival in a Traumatized World," *JFSR* 26 (2010): 63–78 and my recent article "Trauma and Recovery: A New Hermeneutical Framework for the Rape of Tamar (2 Samuel 13)," in *Bible Through the Lens of Trauma*, ed. Christopher Frechette and Elizabeth Boase (Atlanta: SBL, 2016), 177–92. In my work I have been influenced by the work of, among others, Judith Herman, *Trauma and Recovery: The Aftermath of Violence—from Domestic Abuse to Political Terror* (New York: Basic Books, 1997) and Kai Erickson, "Notes on Trauma and Community," in *Trauma: Explorations in Memory*, ed. Cathy Caruth (Baltimore: Johns Hopkins University Press, 1995), 183–99. In biblical studies, Daniel L. Smith-Christopher, *A Biblical Theology of Exile*, OBT (Minneapolis: Fortress, 2001) and Kathleen M. O'Connor, *Jeremiah: Pain and Promise* (Minneapolis: Fortress, 2011) were instrumental in sparking the growing interest in a hermeneutics of trauma.

11. Martha C. Nussbaum, *Upheavals of Thought: The Intelligence of Emotions* (Cambridge: Cambridge University Press, 2001). Cf. her most recent book, *Political Emotions: Why Love Matters for Justice* (Cambridge: Harvard University Press, 2013).

12. Judith Butler, *Frames of War: When Is Life Grievable?* (London: Verso, 2009), 180–1. Cf. also Judith Butler, *Precarious Life: The Powers of Mourning and Violence* (London: Verso, 2004).

13. Butler, *Frames of War*, 184.

14. Cf., e.g., my contribution to the *Theological Commentary of the Bible*, L. Juliana M. Claassens, "Isaiah," in *Theological Commentary of the Bible*, ed. Gail R. O'Day and David L. Petersen (Louisville, KY: Westminster John Knox, 2009), 209–22. Cf. also my books *The God Who Provides: Biblical Images of Divine Nourishment* (Nashville: Abingdon, 2004) and *Mourner, Mother, Midwife: Reimagining God's Delivering Presence in the Old Testament.* (Louisville, KY: Westminster John Knox, 2012) as examples of reading the Old Testament at this particular intersection between theology and history.

15. Nussbaum, *Political Emotions*, 265.

16. Nussbaum, *Political Emotions*, 258, 201–2.

17. Robert Polzin, *Samuel and the Deuteronomist: A Literary Study of the Deuteronomic History. Part Two: 1 Samuel* (San Francisco: Harper & Row, 1989), 205–15. Cf. Barbara Green, "Enacting Imaginatively the Unthinkable: 1 Samuel 25 and the Story of Saul," *BibInt* 11 (2003): 1–23.

18. Mark E. Biddle, "Ancestral Motifs in 1 Samuel 25: Intertextuality and Characterization," *JBL* 121 (2002): 617–38.

19. Much of the feminist enterprise has been dedicated to bringing female characters out from the shadows; Johanna Bos's article is classic in this regard: "Out of the Shadows: Genesis 38; Judges 4:17–22; Ruth 3," *Semeia* 42 (1988): 37–67.

Judith E. McKinlay rightly states that we are in great debt to these early feminist foremothers' work. Feminists since then have sought to take the conversation further, reading the stories through more than one lens. Cf. an excellent exposition of this in McKinlay's introduction to her collected essays on women and land read through a postcolonial lens, *Troubling Women and Land: Reading Biblical Texts in Aoteara New Zealand*, BMW 59 (Sheffield: Sheffield Phoenix, 2014), xiii–xv.

20. Adele Berlin calls Abigail "much more a type than an individual; she represents the perfect wife." David's other wives, Bathsheba and Abishag, she calls "agents," arguing that "they are not important for themselves, and nothing of themselves, their feelings etc., is revealed to the reader. The reader cannot relate to them as people. They are there for the effect they have on the plot or its characters," *Poetics and the Interpretation of Biblical Narrative* (Winona Lake, IN: Eisenbrauns, 1999), 32. Cf. also the work of Melissa A. Jackson, who reads David's women through a comedic framework, *Comedy and Feminist Interpretation of the Hebrew Bible: A Subversive Collaboration*, Oxford Theological Monographs (Oxford: Oxford University Press, 2012), 142–70.

21. 1 Samuel 25 is set in the context of David fleeing for his life; it is sandwiched between Chapters 24 and 26, in which David twice has the opportunity to kill King Saul, before whom he is fleeing. This particular framework offers some intriguing interpretive possibilities explored in the essay L. Juliana M. Claassens, "Cultivating Compassion?: Abigail's Story (1 Samuel 25) as Space for Teaching Concern for Others," in *Considering Compassion: Global Ethics, Human Dignity, and the Compassionate God*, ed. Frits de Lange and L. Juliana M. Claassens (Eugene, OR: Wipf and Stock, forthcoming).

22. See David Jobling's chapter "The Dead Father: A Tragic Reading of 1 Samuel," which seeks to relate the tragic elements in the text with "the tragedy in the circumstances of its creation," in *Berit Olam: Studies in Hebrew Narrative & Poetry: 1 Samuel* (Collegeville, MN: The Liturgical Press, 1998), 250–81.

23. Kathleen M. Sands, "Tragedy, Theology, and Feminism in the Time after Time," *New Literary History* 34 (2004): 41–61 (42).

24. Mary Shields notes that Abigail's speech is 131 words long; only Deborah's song in Judges 5 contains more words: "A Feast Fit for a King: Food and Drink in the Abigail Story," in *The Fate of King David: The Past and Present of a Biblical Icon*, ed. Tod Linafelt, Timothy Beal, and Claudia V. Camp, LHBOTS 500 (London: T&T Clark, 2010), 38–54 (44).

25. Cf. Judith E. McKinlay, "To Eat or Not to Eat: Where Is Wisdom in This Choice?," *Semeia* 86 (1999): 73–84 (80–81). Cf. also Alice Bach, "The Pleasure of Her Text," in *The Pleasure of Her Text: Feminist Readings of Biblical and Historical Texts*, ed. Alice Bach (Philadelphia: Trinity Press International, 1990), 25–44.

26. Ellen von Wolde, "A Leader Led by a Lady: David and Abigail in 1 Samuel 25," *ZAW* 114 (2002): 355–75 (374).

27. Butler, *Frames of War*, 166.

28. Butler, *Frames of War*, 181.

29. Butler, *Frames of War*, 180.

30. Claassens, *The God Who Provides*.

31. Kim Chernin, *The Hungry Self: Women, Eating, and Identity* (New York: Harper & Row, 1985), 200.

32. Bach, *The Pleasure of Her Text*, 49.

33. McKinlay, "To Eat or Not to Eat," 79–80. Cf. also Shields, "A Feast Fit for a King," 54.

34. Cf. also Abigail's prediction that God will eliminate David's enemies, which turns out to be true when Nabal is struck down by God in verse 38. In terms of the larger literary context, this prediction may also refer to the demise of Saul. Cf. also the reference to the lives of David's enemies being like a pebble being flung out of a sling that calls to mind David's earlier encounter with Goliath (1 Sam 17).
35. Bach, *The Pleasure of Her Text*, 49.
36. Cf. L. Juliana M. Claassens, "Violence, Mourning, Politics: Rizpah's Lament in Conversation with Judith Butler," in *Restorative Readings: The Old Testament, Ethics, and Human Dignity*, ed. L. Juliana M. Claassens and Bruce C. Birch (Eugene, OR: Wipf & Stock, 2015), 19–36.
37. Irene Oh, "The Performativity of Motherhood: Embodying Theology and Political Agency," *Journal of the Society of Christian Ethics* 29/2 (2009): 3–17.
38. Oh, "The Performativity of Motherhood," 4.
39. Oh, "The Performativity of Motherhood," 5.
40. Oh, "The Performativity of Motherhood," 6.
41. Sara Ruddick, *Maternal Thinking: Toward a Politics of Peace* (New York: Ballantine Books, 1989), 49.
42. Ruddick, *Maternal Thinking*, 57, 81. For Ruddick, "the effort of world protection may come to seem a 'natural' extension of maternal work," which explains the subtitle of her book: *Toward a Politics of Peace*.
43. Bach, *The Pleasure of Her Text*, 42.
44. Bach, *The Pleasure of Her Text*, 55. Bach links Abigail's voicelessness to her status as widow: "In spite of her marriage to David, Abigail remains a widow, that is, she survives without speech in the text," 55.
45. David Jobling points out that Abigail and Ahinoam were in enemy hands for quite a few days (1 Sam 30:13), which included a drunken orgy (v. 16). He suggests evocatively that presumably they were raped: *1 Samuel*, 184.
46. Butler, *Frames of War*, 168.
47. Butler refers to the work of Chandra Mohanty in her essay "Under Western Eyes" in which she argues that a First World feminist framework that focuses on the "ostensible lack of agency signified by the veil or the burka, not only misunderstands the various cultural meanings that the burka might carry for women who wear it, but also denies the very idioms of agency that are relevant for such women," *Precarious Life*, 47. Cf. also Martha C. Nussbaum's insightful analysis that challenges five arguments typically employed for banning the burka, *The New Religious Intolerance: Overcoming the Politics of Fear in an Anxious Age* (Cambridge: Harvard University Press, 2012), 105–32.
48. Hilary Charlesworth, "Martha Nussbaum's Feminist Internationalism," *Ethics* 111 (2000): 64–78 (73). Charlesworth rightly points out that, for Nussbaum, a key concept within a feminist internationalism is a woman's right to choose, which is an essential element in liberal philosophy that underlies Nussbaum's thought. However, as Charlesworth poignantly asks, "Can a woman authentically choose to accept discriminatory practices that reduce her human capabilities?" Or is there the underlying "implication that the choice of inequality would be irrational in some way?" (72).
49. To avoid that the "views of well-educated Western white women" will be projected "onto women of diverse backgrounds and cultures," Martha C. Nussbaum seeks to create a space "which lets the voices of many women speak and which seeks collaboration with women and men from many different regions in the process of

forming a view," *Sex and Social Justice* (Oxford: Oxford University Press, 1999), 8–9. Cf. Butler, who hopes for an "international feminist coalition" in which, she argues, "we could have several engaged debates going on at the same time and find ourselves joined in the fight against violence, without having to agree on many epistemological issues," *Precarious Life*, 48–9.

50. Louise du Toit points out that South African rape statistics are equal to and even exceed those of countries that are at war. For instance, in 2012–2013 there were approximately 65,000 reported instances of rape per year (according to statistics from the South African Police Service, available at: http://www.saps.gov.za/resource_centre/publications/statistics/crimestats/2014/crime_stats.php, accessed January 27, 2015). This number typically is multiplied by 20 to account for a global low reporting rate, translating into an estimated 1.6 million rapes per year; "Rumours of Rape: A Critical Consideration of Interpretations of Sexual Violence in South Africa," Stellenbosch Forum Lecture, February 25, 2013.

51. The leaky pipeline phenomenon refers to the notion that, even though many women start out a career in academia, they somehow disappear; only a small percentage of women end up becoming full professors. This is a global phenomenon outlined, e.g., by Judith S. White in her article "Pipeline to Pathways: New Directions for Improving the Status of Women on Campus," *Liberal Education* 91 (2005): 22–7. At Stellenbosch University the figures are equally grim. Statistics compiled by the Women's Forum show that women make up 73 percent of all junior lecturers, with only 21 percent of women reaching the rank of full professor.

52. Cf. the wonderful examples of African women sharing their respective journeys of surviving, often amid very difficult circumstances, in the numerous publications that have appeared from the various chapters of the Circle of Concerned African Women Theologians. For instance, in her contribution to one of the Circle publications, Nyambura J. Njoroge writes how the story of Rizpah as told in 2 Samuel 21 has helped her to notice the "African woman's inner strength and spirit that, despite of death or because of it, continues to fight for life," "A Spirituality of Resistance and Transformation," in *Talitha Cum!: Theologies of African Women*, ed. Nyambura J. Njoroge and Musa W. Dube (Pietermaritzburg: Cluster, 2001), 67–76.

53. Cf. Musa W. Dube's description of a postcolonial approach to interpreting both ancient and modern imperializing texts that contain helpful examples of the types of issues that one can look for in a postcolonial (feminist) reading of the text, *Postcolonial Feminist Interpretation of the Bible* (St. Louis: Chalice Press, 2000). Cf. also the wonderful collection of essays that displays the rich variety of scholars engaging in postcolonial biblical interpretation, *Postcolonial Perspectives in African Biblical Interpretations*, ed. Musa W. Dube, Andrew M. Mbuvi, and Dora Mbuwayesango (Atlanta: SBL, 2012).

54. Laura Donaldson, "The Sign of Orpah: Reading Ruth through Native Eyes," in *Ruth and Esther: A Feminist Companion to the Bible*, Second Series, ed. Athalya Brenner (Sheffield: Sheffield Academic, 1999), 130–44. Lori Rowlett expands on Donaldson's argument, arguing that Rahab, like Pocahontas, fits the "pattern of the way that female characters are used in accounts of conquest: she represents the 'good native' who acquiesces almost immediately to the conquerors, as though she from the start recognizes an innate superiority in them and in the colonizing culture," "Disney's Pocahontas and Joshua's Rahab in Postcolonial Perspective," in *Culture, Entertainment and the Bible*, ed. George Aichele, JSOTSup 309 (Sheffield: Sheffield Academic, 2000), 68–75 (66).

55. Rowlett, "Disney's Pocahontas and Joshua's Rahab," 75.
56. Sands, "Tragedy, Theology, and Feminism in the Time after Time," 43.
57. McKinlay, "To Eat or Not to Eat," 73–84. Cf. Mary Shields, who identifies extensive further parallels between Abigail and Woman Wisdom in her intriguing article "A Feast Fit for a King," 38–54. For instance, she argues as follows: "Nabal, the fool, ate the feast that led to death while David accepted the feast leading to life," 51.
58. Cf., e.g., Christl M. Maier, "Conflicting Attractions: Parent Wisdom and the 'Strange Woman' in Proverbs 1–9," in *Wisdom and Psalms: A Feminist Companion to the Bible*, ed. Athalya Brenner and Carole Fontaine, Second Series (Sheffield: Sheffield Academic, 1998), 92–108.
59. Cf. Barbara Green's intriguing argument that 1 Samuel 25 features as a kind of dream sequence in which David contemplates the road not taken relating to his encounters with Saul in 1 Samuel 24 and 26; "Enacting Imaginatively the Unthinkable," 6–8. Cf. also Shields, "A Feast Fit for a King," 40.
60. Cf. Shields's comment that "David almost followed the way of folly, and it could have been the death of his ambitions." Thanks to Abigail's help he ends up choosing the way of life, leaving a clear path to the throne; "A Feast Fit for a King," 54.
61. Cf. L. Juliana Claassens, *Claiming Her Dignity: Female Resistance in the Old Testament*, Collegeville (MN: Liturgical Press, 2016).
62. Cf. Judith Butler's description of this term and her account of how she "moved from a focus on gender performativity to a more general concern with precarity" in "Performativity, Precarity and Sexual Politics," *AIBR. Revista de Antropología Iberoamericana* 4/3 (2009): i–xiii. Available at: http://www.aibr.org/antropologia/04v03/criticos/040301b.pdf, accessed January 27, 2015.

Chapter 4

Dinah (Genesis 34) at the Contact Zone: "Shall Our Sister Become a Whore?"

Musa W. Dube

Introduction: Colonial Contexts, Race, and Sexual Violence

In her article "Rape, Race and Colonial Culture: The Sexual Politics of Identity in the 19th Century Cape Colony" Pamela Scully discusses the case of Mrs. Anna Simpson versus Damon Booysen.[1] On April 2, 1850, Mrs. Simpson was reportedly raped by an 18-year-old laborer in George, a town about 200 miles from Cape Town, while her husband had gone to town. Scully establishes the racial identity of Booysen as Khoi, therefore black. Mrs. Simpson reported the case, which was heard by Judge Justice William Menzies on September 16, 1850. Booysen, who had confessed to the clerk that he indeed raped Mrs. Simpson, because he was drunk, was found guilty and sentenced to death (although not cross-examined by the judge). A deputation of about ten white men in the community later visited the judge and advised that Mrs. Simpson is not white, rather that "the woman and her husband are Bastard coloured persons, and that instead of her being a respectable woman, her character for chastity was very indifferent and that it was strongly suspected that she had on several occasions had connection with the prisoner."[2] Judge Menzies quickly wrote and sent a letter to Harry Smith, the governor of the Cape Colony, to the effect that he had made a terrible mistake by assuming that Mrs. Simpson was a white respectable woman, but that a deputation of reputable white men had since corrected him. He, therefore, wished the judgment of Booysen to be changed from a death sentence to "a term of imprisonment with hard labour." And Booysen's sentence was changed accordingly. In short, "once Anna Simpson's race had been proclaimed with certainty by members of the settler elite of George, Judge Menzies confidently proceeded along a different route of sentence in accordance with the logic of how to deal with the rape of a black woman"[3] in a colonial setting.

This case best highlights the interconnection of racism, gender, class, and sexual violence in colonial contexts.[4] As Scully points outs, the white men who came to the rescue of Booysen, a black man of low class, realized that they too were participants in the rape of black women of color. Should such a judgment be allowed to stand, then they too would be liable for their acts, since black women of color could use the court to protect themselves. Sexual violence against women was judged differently depending on the race of the woman and her status in the empire. If she was a colonized woman, her rape was not judged as a serious crime. The accused could serve a term with labor and be discharged, even if he was black. If the rapist was white and his crime was against a colonized woman, he was obviously not guilty of a rape offense. If a white colonizer woman was raped by a black man of color, or claimed to be raped, the sentence was death, as attested by the classic case of the lynching of black men in the United States and the mistaken identity of Mrs. Simpson that initially earned Booysen a death sentence.

The race- and gender-biased legal system is discussed and substantiated by Judge Menzies to George Napier, an earlier governor of the Cape Colony. Napier was of the position that it was unfair to black women of color, since it made them easy targets of sexual violence by men who knew that justice would be lenient on them. Defending the biased legal system to Governor George Napier, Judge Menzies held that

> it is certain that women in the lower ranks on whom rape has been committed suffer much less injury from degradation in the opinions of their associates than would be occasioned on women in a higher rank of life … Rape on their person [of high-class white women] would inflict the most poignant and permanent anguish and grief … and mar all their prospects of happiness in life … The population of this colony consists of half-civilized and uneducated persons of color whose passions and appetites are under no restraint except what rises of punishment … I am of the opinion that fear of punishment of death at present affords to virtuous females of this colony, particularly in the Country Districts, their only protection against violence of lust.[5]

This characterization of the colonized as people with hyper-sexual appetites meant that when black colonized women were raped, they were only being served what they had asked for, either by the men of their race or by white men. This, however, meant that white women were constructed as in need of protection from the extreme sexual appetites of black men. As intimated in the quote, the untamed passions of the "uncivilized" served the larger agenda of justifying the colonization of the Other as a service of civilizing, colonizing, or Christianizing them. Scully, thus, points out that "The Booysen case and other narratives of rape suggest the centrality of sexuality to the constitution of colonial identities and expose implicit assumptions about race, gender, and class that frequently guided colonial rule."[6]

The Cape Colony was a contact zone that had brought the initial Dutch colonizers and later British colonizers into contact with the indigenous people, such as the Khoi, the !Kung, the Bantu people, and indentured labor, exported from elsewhere. Contact zone is a term coined by Mary Louise Pratt "to refer to the space of colonial encounters, the space in which people geographically and historically separated come into contact with each other to establish ongoing relations, usually involving conditions of cohesion, radical inequality, and intractable conflict."[7] According to Pratt, contact zones are "social spaces where disparate cultures meet, clash, and grapple with each other, often in highly asymmetrical relations of domination and subordination—like colonialism, slavery, or their aftermaths as they are lived out across the globe today."[8]

The social, sexual, economic, and political intercourse in the colonial context is characterized by a dynamic tension. That is, while it is a contact zone, it is simultaneously dependent on the ideological claim of keeping races apart on the basis of racial, religious, or cultural superiority of the colonizer. It does not imply that there is no contact—be it sexual, social, economic, or political between the colonized and the colonizer. It follows that the contact zone is inevitably a hybrid space. Indeed, the fact that, two centuries after the first Dutch settlement of 1652, there was now an established community of mixed races is in itself an attestation that the sexualities of the colonized and the colonizer crossed many boundaries toward each other, and had never closed borders at any time. That is, existing boundaries had never been watertight. Yet for the purpose of oppressing, exploiting, and controlling the colonized, the colonizer always peddles an ideology of superiority, separation, and purity, when facts on the grounds attest to something else.[9] The dynamic tension of separation and interaction is consistently maintained in the contact zones by travelers harboring colonizing desires toward indigenous populations and lands.

In colonial contexts, the rape of colonized women becomes an act and a rhetorical discourse of desire and entitlement of the colonizer. Women's bodies, which are equated to their lands, symbolize the coveted targeted colony. The taking of the bodies of colonized women is a colonizer's script of articulating his desired entitlement to enter the foreign land, plant his seed, and possess the land as well. It is both the land and the women that are raped. The colonized woman's body is thus imagined and constructed as available for taking. The body of the colonizer woman, who represents the colonizing land, must, on the other hand, be constructed as totally unavailable to the colonized man, as Judge Menzies argued earlier in this essay.

From Cape Colony to Shechem

What happens if we read the story of Dinah's rape through a postcolonial lens? What would be the justification for reading Dinah through a postcolonial lens, apart from this reader's social location? Jacob arrives with his family into Shechem, following closely on the steps and dreams of Abraham: dreams of becoming a great nation; dreams of possessing the land of Canaan (Gen 12:1–3; 15:1–6; 17:1–10; 22:1–18), popularly known as the promised land. The promise consists of narrativized imperializing texts. Shechem, the prince of the land, sees Dinah, the daughter of Leah and Jacob, and rapes her (Gen 34:1–3). How would the family of Jacob respond and how does the response reflect the dynamics of the contact zone? In this essay, I would like to take up my earlier agenda of interrogating biblical texts for colonizing ideologies with the purpose of asking whether the text offers avenues of reading for liberating interdependence in our relations.[10] These are questions that I, as colonized subject, have found useful in interrogating ideological constructions of the Other that legitimize their subjugation. The questions I wish to put to Genesis 34 are as follows:

- Does Genesis 34 have a clear stance against the political imperialism of its time?
- Does Genesis 34 belong to the texts that encourage travel to distant and inhabited lands, and how does it justify itself?
- How does Genesis 34 construct difference? Are there dialogue and liberating interdependence, or are there condemnation and replacement of all that is foreign?
- Does Genesis 34 employ gender and divine representations to construct relationships of subordination and domination?

Before I can delve into these questions, it is important to briefly narrate the story of Dinah and to converse with other feminist readers. My postcolonial feminist approach will be discussed thereafter.

Genesis 34: Dinah, the Daughter of Leah and Jacob

Dinah, the daughter of Leah and Jacob, while living in Shechem, decided to visit the daughters of the land. Shechem, the son of Hamor and the prince of the land, sees her, rapes her, and then falls in love with her. He asks his father, Hamor, to meet Jacob, the father of Dinah, to request her hand in marriage. The matter is reported to Jacob, who keeps quiet, awaiting the return of his sons, who were out herding cattle. Just as they return, Hamor arrives to present his son's desire to marry Dinah, saying, "the heart of my son Shechem longs for your daughter: please give her to him in marriage. Make marriages with us: give your daughters to us, and take our daughters yourselves; and the land shall be open to you; live and trade in it and get property in it" (vv. 8–10). Shechem himself adds, "Put the marriage present and gift as high as you like, and I will give whatever you ask me; only give me the girl to be my wife" (v. 12).

The brothers are outraged that their sister has been defiled, but they deceitfully say they agree with the request and long-term proposal on condition that all Hivite men undergo circumcision. Hamor and Shechem happily oblige. All the men undergo circumcision. On the third day, while they are still in pain and recuperation, Dinah's brothers attack and kill all the males, including Hamor and Shechem the prince. They take Dinah from Shechem's house, and "they took their flocks and their herds, their donkeys, and whatever was in the city and in the field. All their wealth, all their little ones and their wives, all that was in the houses, they captured and made their prey" (vv. 28–29). It is at this point that Jacob's thoughts are verbally expressed, saying, "You have brought trouble on me by making me odious to the inhabitants of the land, the Canaanites and the Perizzites; my numbers are few" (v. 30). To his concern the sons respond, "Should our sister be treated like a whore?" (v. 31). Jacob moves to Bethel, 30 kilometers from Shechem. Dinah, the daughter of Jacob and Leah, never openly expresses her thoughts and feelings to Shechem, Hamor, Jacob, and the brothers. Indeed, we never hear again about Dinah in the Hebrew Bible.

The passage is an interpretation crux: due in part to its use of irony and trickery in the plot, scholars disagree about the meaning of the story. The first irony is characterized by a rapist who falls in love with his victim and seeks to marry her. This is followed by trickery of the brothers, who deliberately mislead Shechem and the whole city to murder them. Another irony lies in the fact that the enraged brothers who seek to correct the violence unleashed upon their sister end up becoming more violent by killing all the men of the city and capturing their wives, children, and property. One can also read as ironic that Dinah is never given any narrative opportunity to express herself. In fact, as many scholars have noted, the last we ever hear about her is in verse 31. Lastly, Jacob, who remained mute from the beginning of the report on Dinah's rape and during the proposed marriage, only speaks in relation to his own safety rather than Dinah's traumatic experience: "You have brought trouble on me … my numbers are few, and if they gather themselves against me and attack me, I shall be destroyed, both I and my household" (v. 30). The narrative devices that use irony and trickery demand extensive attention from the reader, for what is said and what is done or meant are two different things. As I have written elsewhere regarding tricksters: "What should be and what becomes are two different things. The trickster changes his/her views and stance several times, thereby changing the story and its outcome."[11]

Some Feminist Readings of Dinah's Story

As Cheryl Exum has pointed out, a feminist hermeneutic of suspicion asks the question: "Whose interests are served?"[12] The Dinah story has been read by several feminist scholars including Susan Niditch, Danna Nolan Fewell, David Gunn, Cheryl Exum, Susanne Scholz, Johanna Stiebert, and Janet Everhart, among many others, who investigated the patriarchal construction and possible rereadings.

To begin with Susan Niditch: her reading underlines that in Genesis Dinah is both "absent and present," for while she is central to the action of Shechem, Hamor, and her brothers, she nonetheless "has no dialogue, no voice."[13] Niditch notes that Genesis 34 features "the female victim as bait and [male] trickery as vengeance."[14] Niditch's reading thus pays attention to the trickery mode and its function in the story. She points out that Genesis 34, like most trickster stories, has the following pattern:

A problem in status, deception to improve status, and success of the plan. The rape lowers Dinah's status but also that of her father and brothers, and it is their status that occupies the author … their status is raised in turn by the success of their plan and the theft of other women, while Dinah's lowered status remains ... Men are the protagonists of the trickster pattern; the woman Dinah serves as an occasion for their contest, as the wives and daughter of Hamor mark its closure.[15]

Niditch thus holds that "the question of status that is addressed through trickery is not her status but that of her brothers, whose rightful territory—that is one of their women—has been breached by an outsider."[16] She further holds that the taking of daughters and wives of Hivites by Dinah's brothers most probably highlights that "wife stealing and rape was regularly associated with war in ancient Israel, even when the reason for the war had nothing to do with ownership of women."[17]

In their book *Gender, Power, and Promise: The Subject of the Bible's First Story* Danna Nolan Fewell and David Gunn make a thorough analysis of the characterization of women characters in Genesis as wives, mothers, daughters-in-law, and daughters, by interrogating their ideological function in a patriarchal narrative that harbors a sustained interest in the "promise" that was given to Abraham and his descendants (Gen 12:1–3; 15:1–6; 17:1–10; 22:1–18). The "promise" defines a sustained colonial desire that stretches from Genesis to Joshua. The promise held that YHWH said to Abraham, "Go from your country and your kindred and your father's house to the land that I will show you. I will make of you a great nation, and I will bless you, and make your name great" (Gen 12:1–3). Fewell and Gunn note that in the beginning God involved women directly in the plot toward fulfilling the promise, often through closing and opening their wombs, thus providing tension in the plot toward the desired destination. Consistent with Niditch's observation that the female functions as bait, Fewell and Gunn note that daughters, "when present at all are for the most part ignored or used as pawns in men's business dealings."[18] The story of Lot's daughters is a good example in this regard.

Turning to Dinah, Fewell and Gunn engage in a detailed analysis of the story, highlighting the marginal status of Dinah in a patriarchal family; both irony and trickery; and the rather problematic patriarchal voice of the narrator who manipulates the reader to sympathize with Shechem the rapist as a lover. Moreover, Fewell and Gunn problematize the motivation behind the brothers' response (namely, their honor, not Dinah's), which relates to the degree of violence experienced by the Hivites. Finally, Fewell and Gunn reflect on the options of a raped woman within the law of Israel as well as the striking similarities with Tamar's rape and Judah's taking of a Canaanite woman, which while not described as the use of force, also involves seeing a woman and taking her. They point out the following:

As a literary construct in a male-conditioned narrative, Dinah's options are limited indeed. As long as rape is seen as extension of sexual desire, or as breach of male honor, as long as restitution means marrying one's rapist, women's experiences, women's right, like the daughter Dinah, will never have a voice.

Justice can never be served, safety can never be assured in a society where men, men's rights, men's honor, and men's texts control women's lives.[19]

In her article "Through Whose Eyes? A 'Right' Reading of Genesis 34" Susanne Scholz's feminist reading seeks to have a dialogue with readers who have fallen for the narrator's lure to sympathize with Shechem as a lover rather than a rapist. Scholz points out that "biblical scholars mitigated the rape by dwelling on love. Rape could become love; love could incorporate rape. In biblical commentaries, love resulted from rape; in forensic medicine, libido resulted from rape."[20] Scholz begins by outlining what constitutes a feminist reading and the purposes of feminist interpretation. That is, a feminist reading interprets Genesis 34 from the perspective of the subjugated, the raped victim-survivor—a reading that sides with Dinah. Scholz reviews biblical commentaries on Genesis 34; reviews medical forensic books on rape; and assesses feminist understanding of rape, which insists on centering the victim-survivor. Lastly, Scholz undertakes a reading of the first three verses in Genesis 34 to exegete the word used for describing Shechem's violence against Dinah. She concludes that "several verbs describe the selfishness and disregard Shechem held for Dinah" and that "when rape is accentuated, love talk is not involved."[21]

In her book *Fathers and Daughters in the Hebrew Bible* Johanna Stiebert also reads Genesis 34. Three factors are highlighted in the relationship of fathers and daughters, namely that fathers have "a vested interest in their daughters' virginity"; that fathers have authority to broker marriages of their daughters; and that "the story alludes to the possibility of forming alliances between peoples through the exchange of daughters."[22] Stiebert, nonetheless, highlights how the younger generation disrupts this arrangement: Dinah's going out leads to her defilement, and the brothers take over the marriage negotiations. Echoing Niditch, as well as Fewell and Gunn, Stiebert states,

> Dinah is no more than a pawn in this story—a pawn, first, in the unsuccessful negotiations to unite Hivites and Israelites and secondly, in an inter-generational conflict between her father and brothers. Her brothers usurp their father's authority to either smooth over or avenge Shechem's sexual claim to Dinah. In calling Dinah, their sister, "daughter" (Gen. 34:17), they indicate their seizure of a control that is by rights their father's.[23]

Stiebert gives extended attention to the readings of Dinah's story by Julian Pitt-Rivers and Helena Zlotnick. As summarized by Stiebert, Pitt-Rivers's anthropological reading "argues for a gradual resolution of the question as to whether sisters should be kept and married within the patrilineage, or given away to foreigners for the sake of political advantage."[24] Closely following on Pitt-Rivers, Zlotnick underlines that Shechem's biggest crime, which led to his death, was that his acts threatened to have him (and Hivites) incorporated into Jacob's family, thus promoting exogamous marriage that was held to be a threat to unity.

In her article "Women Who Love Women Reading Hebrew Bible Texts: About a Lesbian Biblical Hermeneutics" Janet Everhart describes lesbian hermeneutics as diverse, depending on the social location of a particular reader. She links lesbian hermeneutics with feminist, LGBT, and queer theory. Everhart summarizes Deryn Guest's lesbian biblical hermeneutics and applies them to three texts: Genesis 34, Ezekiel 16 and 23, and the stories of Ruth and Naomi. According to Everhart, Guest offers four principles: first, commitment to a hermeneutic of hetero-suspicion; second, dedication to disruption of sex/gender binaries; third, loyalty to appropriation; and fourth, reengagement, which is the desire to make a difference.[25] On her reading of Genesis 34, Everhart focuses on the first three verses, underlining that the opening verse states that Dinah leaves her home to seek the women of the land. Although her efforts are frustrated by a violent man, Shechem, Everhart points out that, "From a Lesbian perspective, the possibility that Dinah is seeking a female partner seems obvious once someone suggests it. Failure to explore seriously this option highlights the heterosexual bias of most readers."[26] Everhart proposes that from contemporary lesbian understanding, that "went out" could be read as Dinah "coming out." She argues that the large compound of Jacob's four wives and their children must have consisted of many other women, but she goes out "to seek the women of the land," which suggests an erotic relationship.[27]

Anita Diamant's novel *The Red Tent* is in a league of its own in its reading of Dinah, for unlike most readers, her interpretation distinguishes itself by giving voice to the silenced daughter of Leah and Jacob. The whole novel is narrated through the eyes of Dinah. Diamant opens her novel as follows: "We have been lost to each other for so long … On those rare occasions when I was remembered, it was as a victim. Near the beginning of your holy book, there is a passage that seems to say I was raped and continues with a bloody tale of how my honor was avenged."[28] In *The Red Tent*, Dinah tells the story of the whole family, beginning with how Rachel met Jacob at the well to the time when Jacob died in Egypt, where Dinah had escaped, well before Joseph was sold into slavery to the same country. Diamant reconstructs Dinah and Shechem's relationship as a beautiful tale of mutual love at first sight, which is fully supported by Shechem's mother, who creates a space for their relationship to bloom. Jacob and the brothers reject it with violence, but Dinah and her mother-in-law escape to Egypt, where she gives birth to Shechem's son.

My Social Location and Reading Practices

Like most feminists in the guild, I am motivated in my reading by an attempt to understand how texts expound ideologies of oppression; how they have legitimized the oppression of the Other; and whether they can be reread for liberating interdependence. I subscribe to the assumption that biblical texts were written in patriarchal cultures, reflecting the views and interests of patriarchal authors, interpreters, translators, scholars, and institutions that have guarded how they are interpreted and used in cultures where biblical texts are read.

Together with the feminist guild, I subscribe to the paradigm that recognizes that gender oppression is always in tandem with other categories of oppression and domination such as class, caste, race, ethnicity, sexuality, physical ability, and religion, among others.

My feminist practice also takes a closer interest in understanding how and why biblical texts are linked to imperial and colonial domination, resistance, and collaboration. This is because, as a black African woman of southern Africa, I was born and bred in Botswana to parents whose diaspora status was a product of the Zimbabwean colonial history. For the past two decades the Zimbabwean postcolonial struggle for land has continued to rage in full view of the global community thirty-five years after independence. My parents, having been dispossessed of their land in the 1950s when it was declared a white man's farm, first chose to remain in their original village, thereby assuming the status of servants of the white farmer. On realizing that it was not a workable relationship, they chose to migrate to Botswana instead of settling in the reserves, which were crowded and infertile places, and where black indigenous populations of the then Rhodesia (now Zimbabwe) were relocated. Botswana was a country that did not attract settler colonizers given its semi-desert temperatures. As a child of first-generation diaspora parents, one remains standing between spaces, families, languages, cultures, nations, histories, and boundaries. Indeed, one remains perpetually unsettled, searching, and dislocated in outlook and practice.

In terms of textual analysis I often read on, between, and behind the texts, given that postcoloniality arises from histories of imperial domination, while heavily dependent on spinning texts of domination and provoking both resistance and collaboration, thus making narrative and ideological criticism an important part of my reading. As a postcolonial feminist, I enter the narrative attentive to both the construction of women and the colonized and how their construction links itself with various other social categories of oppression. Occupying an oppositional postcolonial space, and being ever so conscious of the West's claim to the center of knowledge, theory, and philosophy, I also employ indigenous and contextual ways of reading such as storytelling, divination, *mmutle* (trickster), and HIV and AIDS frameworks of reading, among others.[29] In sum, my feminist reading is, more often than not, multifaceted and multidisciplinary in engaging the colonial and patriarchal oppression and in relation to all forms of oppression. Given this social location, my postcolonial feminist practices have sought to highlight:

The literary-rhetorical methods by which colonizing narrative constructs and reproduces self-validating means of traveling to, entering into, and taking possession of foreign lands and people through intertextuality. Specifically, it highlights how the narrative methods of imperializing texts depend on intertextual reiteration of the following literary-rhetorical constructions:

- Authorizing travel through divine claims;
- Representing the targeted foreign lands and people as in need or desiring the colonizing heroes and their nations;

- Representing the colonizing nations as superior and exceptionally favored by divine powers to invade, help, or dispossess their victims;
- Using gender representations to construct their claims.

Because the exposition on empire and method finds "God" or divinely grounded claims central to the narratives' strategies of imperialism, it is crucial to carry out a postcolonial analysis of sacred texts.[30]

Historical and Discursive Imperialism

Scholars of Genesis date the compilation of the book to the exilic or postexilic times, although the context of its narration discusses the pre-monarchical period. According to Terence Fretheim, the narratives were most probably composed and compiled to assist the exilic or postexilic community "in coming to terms with their own past."[31] However, the narratives of Abraham and Sarah, Isaac and Rebekah, and Jacob and his four wives, the founding patriarchs and matriarchs of the nation of Israel, are hardly attested in other historical records. Barry Bandstra points out that "for years, historians and archaeologists have been looking for evidence to substantiate the biblical picture of Abraham. There is no specific mention of Abraham or his associates in any ancient extra-biblical text."[32] Niditch thus suggests that "rather than beginning with the assumptions about the historical reliability of a text and date when it was written down, one should ask what sort of literature this is in terms of its style, structure, content, and messages."[33] There is no particular scholarly consensus on the genre of Genesis, although it is largely accepted that it consists of myths, sagas, legends, folktales, and genealogies.[34] It is also recognized that the book of Genesis is unified by its structural and thematic organization, which consists of the first eleven chapters, featuring mythological stories, and the rest of the book, featuring circles of founding fathers and mothers; that is, Abraham and Sarah; Isaac and Rebekah; Jacob and his four wives; Judah and Tamar; and the Joseph stories. Among the stories of the founding fathers and mothers is the theme of the promise, namely, that God promises Abraham that he will become a great nation, promises him land, and promises that he will become a blessing to the nations. The narratives of the founding fathers and mothers are characterized by them moving from one place to another, but mostly around and toward the promised land, Canaan. As I have argued, the promise describes an imperial desire and dream that seek to dispossess and displace the Other, who is the indigenous native. The economy of "the promise consists of imperializing texts that are "characterized by literary constructions, representations, and uses that authorize taking possession of foreign geographical spaces and people."[35]

Divine Authorization to Travel to Foreign Lands

When it comes to divine authorization to travel to foreign lands and to take the targeted lands, there is no need for special pleading in Genesis 12–50, which is the context of Dinah's rape. God tells Abraham to leave his homeland and go to a land that God will show him (12:1–3). The identity of the land is not revealed. Abraham obeys. He moves with Sarah his wife, traveling from Haran to Canaan (Gen 12). Bandstra describes it as follows: "He stopped at two places, Shechem and the region of Bethel, before arriving in Negev. At both Shechem and Bethel he built an altar to Yahweh ... staking claim to these lands."[36] In Chapters 15 and 17, the targeted land is specified by the divine power. The verses read: "On that day Yʜᴡʜ made a covenant with Abram, saying: 'To your descendants I give this land, from the river of Egypt to the Great River, the Euphrates'" (15:18), "'and I will give to you, and to your offspring after you, the land where you are now an alien, all the land of Canaan, for a perpetual holding; and I will be their God'" (17:8). Moreover, the text describes the targeted/promised land as an occupied land, that is, "'the land of the Kenites, the Kenizzites, the Kadmonites, the Hittites, the Perizzites, the Rephaim, the Amorites, the Canaanites, the Girgashites, and the Jebusites'" (15:19–21).

Although the plot of Abraham's promised life is complicated by various encounters such as the barrenness of his wife (15:2–6); drought that forced him to move to Egypt (12:10); fear of foreigners who might desire his wife (12:10–20 and 20:1–18); God's demand of the sacrifice of Isaac (22:1–18), among others, the encounters never lose sight of the promise of greatness and possession of land, which keeps on being reiterated on several critical occasions (12:1–3; 15:2–18; 17:1–10; 22:16–18). When Sarah dies, Abraham finds Isaac a wife, Rebekah (Gen 24), who mothered two sons, Jacob and Esau. Jacob is central to the continuation and realization of the promise. Jacob becomes the father of twelve sons and one daughter, Dinah. He becomes Israel (32:28).

In the beginning of Chapter 28, Isaac blesses Jacob, although believing he is Esau. The narrator tells us:

> Then Isaac called Jacob and blessed him and charged him, "You shall not marry one of the Canaanite women. Go at once to Paddan-aram to the house of Bethuel, your mother's father; and take as wife from there one of the daughters of Laban, your mother's brother. May God Almighty bless you and make you fruitful and numerous, that you may become a company of peoples. May he give to you the blessing of Abraham, to you and to your offspring with you, so that you may take possession of the land where you now live as an alien—land that God gave to Abraham. (28:1–4)

Jacob flees from Canaan to Paddan-aram, after stealing his brother's hereditary rights, to seek a wife from his uncle's house. On his way to Paddan-aram, Jacob lies down to sleep and God reiterates the promise given to Abraham to him in a dream saying, "the land on which you lie, I will give to you and to your offspring, and your offspring shall be like dust of the earth, and you shall spread abroad to the west and to the east and to the north and to the south" (28:13–14). In the morning, he renames the place Bethel, the house of the Lord, and puts up a pillar. After fourteen years of labor, Jacob is married to Rachel, Leah, and two concubines; a few years later, he decides to return to Canaan, although scared of Esau. At Peniel he wrestles with God and his name is changed to Israel (Gen 32). Jacob has a happy reconciliation with Esau (Gen 33) and finally reaches the city Shechem, "which is in the land of Canaan"; buys some land; and "erect[s] an altar and call[s] it El-Elohe-Israel" (33:20). Abraham's entry into Canaan followed a similar route: he passed through Shechem and Bethel, where God appeared to him and gave him a promise (12:6–8) and he built an altar to God. In short, Jacob's life is also characterized by travel and God's promise, following closely on the path traveled by Abraham. Fretheim thus says, "the references to 28:10–22 and the notices of various journeys that take him the length of the promised land in a manner parallel to Abraham provide linear coherence."[37] For Bandstra, "the Abraham and Jacob cycles could be called albums, the episodes being similar snapshots."[38]

As said earlier in this essay, Fewell and Gunn analyze the role and matriarchs in the quest for the promise, noting,

> In the beginning God involves women directly: he insists that Sarah bear the child of the promise; he assures Hagar that she too will become a great nation; he explains to Rebekah that she will mother not one nation but two ... Taking her revealed knowledge to heart, Rebekah becomes the first voluntary guardian of the promise, ensuring, through whatever dubious means, that Jacob (Israel) inherits the choice land and prosperity rather than Esau (Edom) ... After Rebekah, however, God deigns not to speak to the other women of Genesis. Women, as mothers, are necessary, but the crisis is over. Israel (Jacob) has been born. From this point on women become unwittingly caretakers of the promise. Leah and Rachel (Genesis 29–30), together, "build up the house of Israel" ... Tamar (Genesis 38), in an effort to secure her own economic well-being, keeps Judah's line intact, holding in trust the future monarch David.[39]

The Characterization of the Other

The Other who occupies the coveted land in Dinah's story is often constructed negatively, but not exclusively so. The Other also appears as the good natives, who love/cling to/adore their potential colonizer (23:1–20; 34:8–10). Both constructions serve the interests of the colonizing power. In Genesis's promised-land ideology this is discerned in terms of several encounters and the construction of particular ethnic groups. For example, the cities of Sodom and Gomorrah are characterized as evil and worthy to be wiped out (Gen 18–19), and there is a constant disapproval of sons of the promise marrying Canaanites, as is evident from Isaac's counsel that Jacob seek a wife from his uncle's family, and from Esau's marriages to Hittite women, which cause bitterness to his parents (28:1–9; 26:34–35; 28:6–9; 36:1–14). The disapproval is driven home by Rebekah, who says if Jacob marries a Canaanite woman, as Esau has done, she would rather die than live (27:46). Nothing is explicitly stated on what made Canaanite people so repugnant, save for their ethnic difference. One of Jacob's sons, Judah, marries Shua's daughter, a Canaanite woman, and his family is notably characterized by frequent deaths (38:1–27).[40]

So far, nothing is said about daughters of the promise and their relationship to sons of the land, partly because they are narratively not born, and partly because Dinah's story in Chapter 34 answers the question.[41] Noting the absence of daughters, Fewell and Gunn assert that, "daughters neither exist, nor are they missed. It is the daughter-in-law who will make a difference in this family's story."[42] Otherness is also constructed through Abraham-related groups, which are nonetheless cleared away from the path of the promise and the blessing. Their origins are either constructed negatively, with some form of social stigma or disadvantage, or just written out of the plot of the promised-land and blessing mythology. This is clearly evident in the origins of Moab and Ammon (19:30), which are traced to the incest of Lot and his daughters, hence banned from association with Israel (Neh 13:1). In addition, even though Ishmael, the son of Hagar and Abraham, is said to be the father of nations (Gen 16:1–16; 21:8–21; 26:12–18), we are also informed that "he shall be an ass of a man, with his hand against everyone, and everyone's hand against him" (Gen 16:11). Finally, sons born from Abraham's second marriage (after Sarah's death) are also excluded from the descendants carrying the promise (25:1–6), just like Ishmael was separated from Isaac (21:10–14).

Reading Dinah's Body/Story

The literary context of Dinah's rape is, therefore, within a narrative context that weaves elaborate tales of divinely sanctioned travel authorizing the taking of lands of the Other who have always lived in the targeted lands, namely, the Canaanites. As Bandstra points out, "the God who was later identified as the God of Israel encountered Abraham and made a covenant with him that included promises of future well-being including the inheritance of Canaan as a family homeland and the growth of his family into an international empire."[43] In his article "A Native American Perspective: Canaanites, Cowboys, and Indians," Robert Allen Warrior has long stated that given their experience as colonized and dispossessed groups, Native Americans will read the biblical text from the perspective of the dispossessed Canaanites.[44] As a postcolonial feminist reader, I focus my attention on how the text constructs patriarchal and colonial oppression of the Other. This inevitably places me in in-between spaces—in the third space.

Current research is of the view that Genesis consists of sources that must have circulated separately as oral and written, that they were written by different authors at different times whose narrated time is different from its composition and historical time.[45] Nonetheless, scholarly reconstruction places the compilation, (some) composition, and redaction of the stories of matriarchs and patriarchs of Israel within the historical Babylonian exile experience, which was a traumatic national context that came to shape a wide range of literature in the Hebrew Bible. The Babylonian Empire's conquest consisted of the destruction of Jerusalem and the temple and enforced diaspora, leading to loss of independence, land, and king, and a massive crisis of faith and identity. The Genesis narrative is, therefore, written/compiled/edited to address the exilic crisis. The form of resistance adopted toward the encounter with imperial oppression is not a rejection of imperialism as an unacceptable evil. Rather, the writers/compilers/editors of Genesis set out to weave a narrative that constructs their own colonial dreams and desires, and that stretches into the whole Pentateuch: God will also make them a great nation; God will give them an occupied land; and God will make them a blessing to the world.

Accordingly, this colonizing dream constructs indigenous groups negatively and discourages intermarriages (26:34; 27:46; 28:1–5; 34). At the same time, indigenous populations and lands are constructed as desiring if not adoring their colonizing partner (see 23:1–20; 34:8–12). Both are faces of the same coin that are well represented in Dinah's story, as it shall be clear later in this essay. Since the contact zone defines the "presence, interaction, interlocking understandings, and practices, often within radically asymmetrical relations of power,"[46] the self-imagined separation of the colonizer, historic or discursive, is already inscribed within unavoidable interaction with the colonized or targeted people and lands, through sharing of space, which inevitably includes the intertwinement of economic, political, cultural, and social structures. This includes the interaction of bodies, sexually. A colonizing narrative constructs the relationships at the contact zones to serve the purposes of domination and subordination by narratively controlling, minimizing, and suppressing the virulent contact zone. Every colonial contact zone is thus characterized by a dynamic tension; that is, on the one hand, there is inevitable interaction; on the other, there is prohibited or shunned interaction between the desiring colonizer and the targeted indigenous people/lands.[47] Further, the shunned colonized groups are depicted as loving/desiring the colonizing group. This is reflected in the story of Dinah in Chapter 34, which I propose to read with two sets of women: a) women from the colonizing side (Sarah and Rebekah as sisters to their husbands), and b) indigenous women depicted as whores (Tamar and Rahab).

Now Enter Dinah and Shechem!

Shechem, a man whose land is targeted by colonial dreams and desires, does the unimaginable: he sees the daughter of Jacob and Leah, Dinah, and sexually forces himself on her (rapes her) and then asks for her hand in marriage. His act and response demonstrate the ideological construction of the colonized: he is a native with uncontrolled sexual passions, attested by his "seeing and taking" Dinah by force—rape. Second, he is a native who clings to and loves his colonizer, as the narrator repeatedly underlines that his heart was drawn to Dinah, the daughter of Jacob, and he "loved the girl" (Gen 34:3). He is willing to do anything to marry Dinah.[48] Divining the story of Shechem by the rape case of the Cape Colony cited in the introduction to this essay, Shechem is probably dead meat. Yes, he is. Unlike Booysen who was let off the death row when a group of white men came to testify that he did not rape a white woman, but a black woman (colonized woman) whose reputation was compromised due to her race, Shechem will not be so lucky.

Shechem has raped Dinah, the daughter of Jacob, Israel, the bearer of the promise, that is, a colonizing patriarch. Men are coming from Jacob's family, but they are not coming to save Shechem, the person, and the city. In addition, the response of the brothers reflects colonizing ideology in the contact zone—namely, their rejection of the proposed marriage that is demonstrated by the annihilation of all Hivite men.[49] The killing is the rejection of the proposed long-term relationships of social coexistence. The brothers go out killing Hivite men and retrieve their sister from Shechem's house, for they do not want their sister to be treated as a whore. Whoredom and loose sexual morals are often linked to the colonized in colonizing literature. The dynamic tension of colonial contact zone interactions that are simultaneously denied in their active presence is evident in the capture of Hivite women, children, and wealth, which attests to interaction rather than separation, even in its worst forms.

In his article "They're Nothing but Incestuous Bastards: The Polemical Use of Sex and Sexuality in Hebrew Canon Narratives," Randall Bailey has highlighted how the denigration of the Other often depends on characterizing the Other as sexually deviant or morally lacking, as some of the examples described earlier in this essay attest. Among the examples that he assesses are the cases where Abraham (12:10–20; 20:1–18) and Isaac (26:1–33) were traveling to foreign lands and disguised their wives as their sisters. Randall highlights that "in these narratives, the patriarch speculates that foreigners among whom the family is intending to reside are types of sexual deviants who will kill a man in order to marry his wife. Thus there is a plan of trickery devised in which the matriarch is to pose as the sister of the patriarch … and then profits from such deception."[50]

These stories of wives posing as sisters share in the ideology of colonial contact zone narratives that characterize the Dinah story. They depict natives as people with some sexual passions that are uncontrollable. The indigenous people are also depicted as desiring/loving traveling colonial heroes as attested by their yearning for their wives and the amount of wealth they give to the brother/husband. Consistent with the dynamic tension of the contact zone colonial ideology, their desire to have and to hold the body of the woman of the colonial travelers is denied. In the case of Abraham, God is the mighty warrior who extracts Sarah from the bosom of Pharaoh and Abimelech's harem, returning her back to Abraham. In Genesis 34, Dinah's brothers take up arms, murder all the men of Shechem, and return Dinah from the house of Hamor to the house of Jacob. In all three of these cases, Abraham, Isaac, and Jacob's sons gain great wealth from the events, signifying that colonizing traveling heroes imagine themselves as entitled to the resources of foreign lands, especially from the lands of their targets.

Dinah, Tamar, and Rahab

This entitlement to wealth of the targeted lands includes access to the native women. Although native women may be depicted negatively and intermarriages between the sons of colonizing heroes are seemingly discouraged, the interaction is nevertheless permitted. The native woman can and should cross the boundaries toward the colonizing heroes, for she represents the desires of the colonial dreams. She is the land that must exchange hands, from the natives to the colonizing heroes. And so Tamar the Canaanite (Genesis 38), the daughter-in-law of Judah, will take off her widowhood clothes and dress up as a prostitute to woo her father-in-law and to bear the great ancestor of David, Perez, and Zerah. She plays a prostitute just for Judah, presenting her body as available to him. Thereafter she ceases playing a whore and remains faithful to Judah and his family. Similarly, Rahab the sex worker receives Joshua's spies and entertains them overnight. But by the time they leave, she pleads to be aligned to the Israelites (Joshua 2). Once she and her family have been saved from the destruction of Jericho, her alliance belongs to her invaders, the Israelites. She ceases to be a whore and becomes the mother of Boaz, a great ancestor of David (Matt 1:5).

In Dinah's story, her brothers are firm that their sister should not cross the cultural boundaries. If she has crossed them, she must be returned. They ask their father a rhetorical question, "Should our sister be treated as a whore?" (Gen 34:31). This question serves to justify why all the Shechemites were killed: they were killed for proposing long-term relations of mutual interdependence that threatened to put the colonized and the colonizer in a relationship of equality (although not gender equality). A relationship of mutual interdependence is proposed by Hamor, when he comes to ask for Dinah's hand in marriage, saying, "Make marriages with us; give your daughters to us, and take our daughters for yourselves ... and the land shall be open to you; live and trade in it, and get property in it" (Gen 34:8–10). Note how women's bodies are linked to the land and property. Although Hamor's proposal was rejected, this does not stop Dinah's brothers from carrying off "all" the Shechemites' women and children to their camp, before moving to Bethel, 30 kilometers away from Shechem. Dinah, a woman from the colonizer's camp, notably crosses the guarded boundaries to visit the native women of the land. Why did she want to visit?[51] Her efforts are met with fierce resistance. First, by Shechem, whose sexual violence stops her from meeting the women of the land; second, by her brothers, who kill all Hivite men to return her to the colonizer's camp. The Shechemite women and children are forcefully brought to her camp. Ironically, the women finally meet! The voices of women from both camps remain unheard, awaiting our hearing.[52] They bring before us Gayatri Spivak's question: "Can the subaltern speak?"[53] It is in this broken landscape that the postcolonial feminist framework invites dialogue, storytelling, and the birthing of relationships of liberating interdependence from and among women, who are wounded by both patriarchal and colonial structures of oppression and domination.

Notes

1. Women and people of color are categories that are used more in the United States than in southern Africa, where there are separate categories of *black* (African) and *colored* (people of mixed race). Scully uses "people of color" in an inclusive way.

2. Pamela Scully, "Rape, Race, and Colonial Culture: The Sexual Politics of Identity in the 19th Century Cape Colony, South Africa," *The American Review* 100 (1995): 335–59 (335).

3. Scully, "Rape, Race, and Colonial Culture," 341.

4. See also Daniel J. Walther, "Sex, Race and Empire: White Male Sexuality and the 'Other' in Germany's Colonies, 1894–1914," *German Studies Review* 33 (2010): 45–71; and Daniela Baratieri, "'More than a Tree, Less than a Woman.' Sex and Empire: The Italian Case," *Australian Journal of Politics and History* 60 (2014): 360–72.

5. Cited in Scully, "Rape, Race, and Colonial Culture," 346–7.

6. Scully, "Rape, Race, and Colonial Culture," 338.

7. Mary Louise Pratt, *Imperial Eyes: Travel Writing and Transculturation* (New York: Routledge, 1992), 6.

8. Pratt, *Imperial Eyes*, 4.

9. For example, Pratt, *Imperial Eyes*, 55, finds that in the natural historians' documentation of *Anders Sparman's Voyage to the Cape of Good Hope*, published in 1783, and William Paterson's *Narrative of Four Voyages in the Land of the Hottentots and the Kaffirs*, published in 1781: "Both writers report on transracial sexual alliances and intermarriages—not just the common case of European men and African concubines, but also a tale of a European woman bearing a child by an African lover; of a European man who marries a tribal woman out of true love."

10. See Musa W. Dube, *Postcolonial Feminist Interpretation of the Bible* (St. Louis: Chalice Press 2000), 129.

11. Musa W. Dube, "The Subaltern Can Speak: Reading the Mmutle (Hare) Way," *Journal of Africana Religions* 4 (2016): 54–75 (64).

12. J. Cheryl Exum, "Feminist Criticism: Whose Interests Are Being Served?," in *Judges and Method: New Approaches in Biblical Studies*, ed. Gale A. Yee (Minneapolis: Fortress, 1995), 65–90.

13. Susan Niditch, "Genesis," in *The Women's Bible Commentary*, ed. Carol Newsom and Sharon H. Ringe (Louisville, KY: Westminster, 1992), 10–25 (23).

14. Niditch, "Genesis," 23.

15. Niditch, "Genesis," 24.

16. Niditch, "Genesis," 23.

17. Niditch, "Genesis," 24.

18. Danna Nolan Fewell and David M. Gunn, *Gender, Power, and Promise: The Subject of the Bible's First Story* (Nashville: Abingdon, 1993), 85.

19. Fewell and Gunn, *Gender, Power, and Promise*, 85.

20. Susanne Scholz, "Through Whose Eyes? A 'Right' Reading of Genesis 34," in *Genesis: A Feminist Companion to the Bible*, ed. Athalya Brenner, Second Series (Sheffield: Sheffield Academic, 1998), 150–71 (159).

21. Scholz, "Through Whose Eyes?," 171.

22. Johanna Stiebert, *Fathers and Daughters in the Hebrew Bible* (Oxford: Oxford University Press, 2013), 52–3.

23. Stiebert, *Fathers and Daughters*, 53.

24. Stiebert, *Fathers and Daughters*, 54.

25. Janet Everhart, "Women Who Love Women Reading Hebrew Bible Texts: About a Lesbian Biblical Hermeneutics," in *Feminist Interpretation of the Hebrew Bible in Retrospect. Volume II: Social Locations*, ed. Susanne Scholz (Sheffield: Sheffield Phoenix, 2014), 188–204 (195).

26. Everhart, "Women Who Love Women Reading," 200.

27. Daniel J. Walther, "Racializing Sex: Same Sex Relations, German Colonial Authority, and *Deutschtum*," *Journal of the History of Sexuality* 17 (2008): 11–24, shows that modern Europe banned all gay persons from the colonies, returning them to mother countries in an attempt to keep racial and sexual superiority over indigenous people.

28. Anita Diamant, *The Red Tent: A Novel* (New York: Picador, 1997), 1.

29. See Musa W. Dube, *Other Ways of Reading: African Women and the Bible* (Atlanta: SBL, 2001), one volume in which we attempted to present African frameworks of thinking and reading texts.

30. Dube, *Postcolonial Feminist Interpretation*, 117.

31. See Terence E. Fretheim, "Genesis," in *NIB: A Commentary in Twelve Volumes*, Volume 1, ed. Leander E. Keck (Nashville: Abingdon, 1994), 319–674; and R. N. Whybray, "Genesis," in *The Pentateuch*, ed. John Barton and John Muddiman (Oxford: Oxford University Press, 2010), 53–91.

32. Barry Bandstra, *Reading the Old Testament* (Belmont, CA: Thomson Wadsworth, 2004), 99.

33. Niditch, "Genesis," 12.

34. Fretheim, "Genesis," 324–5.

35. Musa W. Dube, "Reading for Decolonization (John 4:1–42)," *Semeia* 75 (1996): 37–59 (97).

36. Bandstra, *Reading the Old Testament*, 101.

37. Fretheim, "Genesis," 536.

38. Bandstra, *Reading the Old Testament*, 97.

39. Fewell and Gunn, *Gender, Power, and Promise*, 89–90.

40. Death haunts the family of Judah, as a tool that the story uses to deal with Judah's crossing of boundaries. One finds the same narrative strategy in the book of Ruth, in which an Israelite couple, Naomi and Elimelech, went to settle in Moab and their sons married Moabite women. All the men die, leaving three widows behind. Although Ruth is maintained and bore Obed, who becomes a great ancestor of David, it would seem that the narrative first has to try to purge the relationships that involved shunned ethnic groups. In Judah's case, his wife (a Canaanite) dies, and two sons within a short space of time. He becomes scared that the last one might also die. After these series of deaths, it becomes narratively permissible for Judah to sire Perez and Zerah through his daughter-in-law, Tamar.

41. Whybray, "Genesis," 82.

42. Fewell and Gunn, *Gender, Power, and Promise*, 71–2.

43. Bandstra, *Reading the Old Testament*, 23.

44. Robert Allen Warrior, "A Native American Perspective: Canaanites, Cowboys, and Indians," in *Voices from the Margin: Interpreting the Bible in the Third World*, Revised and Expanded Third Edition, ed. R. S. Sugirtharajah (Maryknoll, NY: Orbis, 2006), 235–41. See also George E. Tinker, "Reading the Bible as Native Americans," in *NIB: A Commentary in Twelve Volumes*, Volume 1, ed. Leander E. Keck (Nashville: Abingdon Press, 1994), 174–80, who points out that "the closest analogy to Native American history in the Old Testament seems to be the experience of the Canaanites, dispossessed of their land and annihilated by foreign invader," 174. Similarly, Laura Donaldson, "The Sign of Orpah: Reading Ruth through Native Eyes," in *Ruth and Esther: A Feminist Companion to the Bible*, Second Series, ed. Athalya Brenner (Sheffield: Sheffield Academic, 1999), 130–44, reads the book of Ruth from the perspective of the Moabites who returned to

her mother's house, rather than Ruth who leaves and becomes integrated in the narratives of David.

45. See Niditch, "Genesis," 10–11; Bandstra, *Reading the Old Testament*, 38–51; and W. G. Plaut, "Genesis, Book of," in *Dictionary of Biblical Interpretation*, ed. John Hayes (Nashville: Abingdon, 1999), 436–42 (440–1).

46. Pratt, *Imperial Eyes*, 7.

47. See Daniel J. Walther, "Sex, Race and Empire," and Daniela Baratieri, "More than a Tree, Less than a Woman."

48. Shechem's deep yearning for Dinah can also be analyzed using Frantz Fanon's *Black Skin, White Masks*, trans. Charles Lam Markmann (New York: Grove Press, 1967), in which he elaborates the crisis of masculinities that are created by the colonial context, which devalues native people's humanity while constructing the colonizer as the epitome of humanity.

49. The voice of Jacob that speaks critically toward the sons' violence, which is repeated in Genesis 49:5–7, is an "anti-conquest" narrative device (term by Louise Pratt, *Imperial Eyes*, 39), which is the capacity of the colonizing characters to speak critically about their project without abandoning it.

50. Randall Bailey, "They're Nothing but Incestuous Bastards: The Polemical Use of Sex and Sexuality in Hebrew Canon Narratives," in *Reading From This Place: Social Location in the USA*, Vol .1, ed. Fernando Segovia and Mary Ann Tolbert (Minneapolis: Fortress, 1994), 121–38 (125).

51. Some reasons are provided above by the interpretations of Danna Nolan Fewell and David Gunn, and Janet Everhart.

52. The retelling of Dinah's story and the women of Shechem needs a whole new article—more than I can pursue in this essay. In addition, Diamant, *The Red Tent*, 189–204, gives a creative retelling of what transpired between Shechem and Dinah, contributing to this feminist rereading. She presents them as self-chosen lovers. However, with the murder of Shechem, she returns to the silenced Dinah, documenting Dinah's internal thoughts as follows: "All the way back up the hillside to the tents of Jacob, I screamed in silence," 205.

53. Gayatri Chakravorty Spivak, "Can the Subaltern Speak?," in *Marxism and the Interpretation of Culture*, ed. Cary Nelson and Lawrence Grossberg (Urbana: University of Illinois Press, 1988), 271–313.

Chapter 5

JEZEBEL AND THE FEMININE DIVINE IN FEMINIST POSTCOLONIAL FOCUS

Judith E. McKinlay

I have become very interested in the processes of Othering, so often linked with the imposition and maintenance of opposing orthodoxies. I begin with the I, for my interest is personal. As a woman, and a feminist, I know a little about Othering from the underside, but, as a white New Zealander (a Pakeha) belonging to the dominant culture in a postcolonial society, I am also aware of its binary opposite. It is a matter of power and power imbalance. I recognize, too, that, as a woman, I view the world from my place within it; for while our genes play a significant role in who we are, Simone de Beauvoir's much-quoted saying still stands: "One is not born, but rather becomes a woman."[1] It is societies, and communities within societies, that order the ways in which we live. Gender expectations and the accepted norms are conveyed in such subtle ways that we tend to comply without realizing the extent of our enculturation.[2] This applies to ancient societies as much as to our own. While 1 and 2 Kings make it very clear that Jezebel did not comply with established gender norms, I am curious about this text that so damningly Others her. Who was responsible and why? I recognize the complexity, for there is more to this Othering than the ways of an ancient Israelite woman. The judgment also concerns the matter of a feminine representation of the divine. These are, of course, textual prescriptions. As Esther Fuchs writes, "biblical narrative universalizes and legislates its male-centered epistemology."[3] I have long found her insistence that we ask the question *cui bono* a guiding point, to be asked both of the text and of our own work.[4]

So I begin, as a feminist reader. What does that mean for how I proceed? This is a significant question, for as Stephen Moore observes, feminist criticism is "a radically eclectic enterprise." We work in different ways, viewing through different lenses. What Moore sees us sharing in common is "a critical sensibility, an encompassing angle of vision that, in a more fundamental fashion than a methodological framework, brings previously unperceived or disavowed data into focus."[5] This is always the hope. Cheryl Exum likewise recognizes that "feminist biblical criticism is neither a discipline nor a method, but more a variety of approaches." What she sees linking them together are "the interests and concerns of feminism as a world view and political enterprise."[6] So while I will be working with a feminist hermeneutic, I will have a choice of whatever analytical tools I consider best suit the purpose of probing this Jezebel narrative. For it is just that: a narrative literary text, with Jezebel simply a literary character. To probe the writer's (or writers') damning portrayal of this female character and her literary connection with the goddess Asherah, a female representation of the divine, I will need the tools of both literary and ideological criticism. For this text is the product of an educated male elite, who, it can be assumed, had an interest in maintaining and perpetuating both the gender and the cultic constructions that drive the plotlines of their script. I will need to read this textual Jezebel with suspicion, for what is written about her will have been written for a particular purpose from a particular perspective. Yet texts are porous. They leak their ideologies. In Terry Eagleton's words, literature "is the most revealing mode of experiential access to ideology that we possess. It is in literature, above all, that we observe in a peculiarly complex, coherent, intensive and immediate fashion the workings of ideology."[7] It is not only a matter of observing. Texts are risky: readers need to be careful. As Patrocinio Schweickart observed, writing already in the 1980s, "literature acts on the world by acting on its readers."[8] Questions pile up: how will this text act upon me? Will I recognize what I am seeing? There is, of course, a further complication: my probing will not and cannot be objective. That is not possible.

Rather, I will be reading this text from within the worldview I inhabit. This is true of all readers, whether we are conscious of it or not. What drives me is the awareness that this textual Jezebel narrative will have had, and continues to have, an impact on the lives of its readers. The probing and rereading will be a matter of *cui bono*.

Jezebel is introduced in the context of her marriage to King Ahab, and, in the way of the books of Kings, Israelite kings do not get good press. Ahab is immediately Othered. He, the son of Omri, "did evil in the sight of YHWH more than all who were before him" (1 Kgs 16:30). Marriage to Jezebel provides further fuel for the accusation. The text is indeed "sardonic," as Cameron Howard describes it: "And as if it had been a light thing for him to walk in the sins of Jeroboam ... he took as his wife Jezebel" (v. 31).[9] But whose daughter is she? Ethbaal's! Further Otherness! For that name, *with Baal*, anticipates what now follows: Ahab *went and served* Baal and *worshipped* him. I note the cultic weighting of those verbs. It gets worse: he erects an altar to Baal *in the house of Baal, which he built in Samaria*. Jezebel's name, too, is part of this damning Otherness, a likely distortion of one of Baal's titles (*zabul*), or even a pun on a word for dung (*zebel*).[10] Coming to 1 Kings by way of 2 Samuel 2–4, assuming both are from the Deuteronomistic school (although that in itself is a contested issue), I am aware of the attitude to Baalist names, for there the names of the royal sons, Eshbaal and Meribbaal, were changed to the "shaming" Ishbosheth and Mephibosheth.[11] How does one explain those Saulist names? Is it, as Mark Smith suggests, that "in Saul's family, either *ba'al* was a title for Yahweh, or Baal was acceptable in royal, Yahwistic circles, or both?"[12] While these remain open questions, there is at least a hint here of a past inclusion. The accusation of supposed apostasy does not stop here, however. Ahab also set up an *asherah* pole, and that leads immediately into the damning statement that he provoked Yhwh, the God of Israel, more severely than all the previous kings of Israel. The implication is clear: it is his wife, Jezebel, who is responsible. It is she who causes him to sin so heinously, by worshipping Other gods. The *asherah* pole brings the Othering gender issue into focus. It is not only the representation of Jezebel that I need to probe but the matter of the feminine representation of the divine. To quote Linda Tuhiwai Smith, "representation is important as a concept because it gives the impression of 'the truth.'"[13] The words impression and truth are key.

What is clear is that the representation of Jezebel works on several levels. Not only is she a woman, but ethnically Sidonian, and not only Sidonian but the daughter of the Sidonian king. Thus she is non-Israelite; she is Other to Israel. Reading through 1 Kings, I have already been alerted in 11:1–18 to what happens when kings take foreign wives. Married, Jezebel becomes the Israelite queen, which in a Judahite text means she is doubly Other. Take all of this, along with the Baalist and Asherah connections, and Jezebel is a danger on more than one level. While, as Homi Bhabha writes, "to exist is to be called into being in relation to an otherness, its look or locus,"[14] such a piling up of Otherness, of gender, status, ethnicity, and religious allegiance, would seem to bear the marks of an acute ideological program. I need to sharpen my probe.

Am I already implying that feminist biblical criticism is solely a literary matter? Do I need to consider these Judean scribes? Cheryl Exum, writing of feminist biblical criticism, notes that "recent research can best be described as located on a continuum between historical and literary analysis."[15] So do I need to turn aside to consider the text's historical context? Ahab's name as King of Israel is well attested, but not Jezebel's.[16] But, and this is a significant but, this is a text written much later in Judah, well after the northern kingdom had fallen. In the aftermath Judah inherited many of Israel's traditions, recording aspects of life, particularly of the cult, that did not conform to the "pan-Israelite ideology" now developed in the south. I need to be aware that what I am reading is a text written by a much later scribe, and "as such," to quote Israel Finkelstein, "it transmits Judahite ideas regarding territory, kingship, temple, and cult," with the male god Yhwh held supreme.[17] Memories of a powerful Israel, more powerful and prosperous in Ahab's time than Judah, in all likelihood exacerbated the animosity. Academic diachronic studies paint a complex picture of the textual processes behind these texts, although conclusions vary in certain details, depending on particular arguments.[18]

I hesitate and consider the complexity. I can imagine those later scribes in Judah, Babylon, or even Yehud scratching their heads and planning their countermoves. They have a possible answer to this seemingly heretical Israelite material close at hand: the Elijah narratives, also inherited from northern Israel. What better material for providing a high-profile Yahwistic antagonist than these early Israelite legends of Elijah, with their "man of god," who will speak the Word of the one and only male God Yhwh![19] But can they be turned and twisted around to serve the purpose? The answer is yes! As Phyllis Trible declared in her 1994 Presidential Address, "if the Society of Biblical Literature gave awards for excellence in polarized thinking, the Deuteronomistic theologians would capture first prize."[20] For example, regarding that Phoenician marriage, Phoenicia was a thriving neighbor, so, as a political alliance, the marriage was a shrewd move, ensuring stability and good trade relations. Marriages cementing such relationships were simply part of life in a multi-kingdom world, with royal wives pawns in the system. Yet in this polarizing text? As Carey Walsh writes, in the eyes of the Deuteronomistic scribes this was "enraging idiocy on Ahab's part."[21] This is a text about sin, with the holy YHWH-is-my-God prophet Elijah and the sinful Asherah-worshipping Jezebel as major antagonists. They are the "quintessential opposites," as Trible reads them, each carrying their religious allegiance in their name.[22] They are like the competing forces in so many contemporary computer or electronic games, ancient Judahite style.

Recognizing that the writer is not merely transmitting what has been received from the northern kingdom, but rearranging and even twisting it ideologically, highlights in turn further methodological issues. For how am I to understand Elijah, challenging and killing the prophets of Baal in one section, yet fleeing for his life from Jezebel in another? What sort of character is this? Literary criticism typically tends to study texts in their final form, intent on seeing how they read as "whole cloth" with their own literary integrity. Yet I need to keep in mind, following Tchavdar Hadjiev and others, that "what we have before us is … an ancient composition created … out of various pre-existing traditions in order to address the religious questions facing Judeans living in exilic and post-exilic times."[23] I can expect such complications as the ideological polarities are heightened.

I have been warned. Not only has this later Judah's narrative an ideological "tendency to blacken and delegitimize the northern kingdom and its kings," but also its queen![24] In particular, Jezebel, Ahab's queen, with her worrying Baal/Asherah allegiance. The fact that most queens are never included in introductions to kings in these texts sends an immediate message: watch this one. She is in textual danger.[25] I hesitate, considering this Baal/Asherah allegiance that so provokes YHWH's man of god Elijah. Jezebel, Ahab, and Elijah may be the human protagonists in this conflicted text, but I find myself agreeing with Neil Glover that Elijah's enemies are "darker, more shadowy entities than the oaths of Jezebel," and more deadly.[26] I am already suspecting that the human characters are merely the pawns in the plot, and that the pitting of YHWH against Baal/Asherah lies at its core, that it is indeed primarily a matter of the "true" representation of the divine. I need to consider again that pertinent historical question: were Baal and Asherah, in fact, Other divine representations? Were they regarded as an abomination in Judah, but accepted in Israel? And was Asherah closely aligned with Baal, or is this yet another defamatory scribal move? The eighth-century inscription at Kuntillet ʿAjrud, which may have been a "royal Israelite trade station," refers to YHWH *of Samaria and His Asherah,* so pairing her with YHWH, not Baal.[27] And, if "the mention of YHWH of Samaria probably allud[es] to a temple of YHWH in the capital of the northern kingdom," as some are suggesting, this would seem to indicate Asherah was acceptable as part of Israel's Yahwistic representation of the divine, albeit a feminine representation.[28] Would the command in Deuteronomy 16:21

not to plant any tree as an *asherah* beside an altar to Yнwн make any sense unless this had, in fact, been happening? But, of course, for the later Judahite scribes, and their refashioned puppet Elijah, there can be no feminine or Other representation of the divine.

I return to the text to read 1 Kings 18. That this is set in a time of drought and famine, already prophesied by Elijah in Chapter 17, is a clear sign of Yнwн's displeasure. So enter Elijah, Yнwн's prophet—this time with a divine Word of hope (vv. 1–2). An authorial word, however, inserts an ominous aside (v. 4): Jezebel has been killing Yнwн's prophets. Horrors! Those who have escaped owe their survival solely to the undercover Yahwistic administrator, Obadiah (vv. 3–4, 13), who now is terrified by Elijah's order that he announce the prophet's arrival to Ahab. So the "troubling" meeting of Ahab and Elijah results in Elijah's call for a meeting of all Israel, which is to include not only the 450 prophets of Baal but the 400 prophets of Asherah, who eat at Jezebel's table (v. 19). I note the word *nabi'* is used for both. While the definite article is applied, it would seem that *ha'asherah* is none other than the goddess herself. Is adding the definite article a further deliberate ideological ploy, attempting to turn the goddess into an inanimate object?[29] While this may be a way of writing out Asherah's divine consort status, the text seems equally keen to show just how closely she is aligned with the human queen consort, Jezebel. Horrors again! And the number of these dreaded prophetic followers! I feel the scribe's abhorrence. He is doing all he can with only his pen as his weapon. Elijah goes on to kill the prophets of Baal (v. 40), one prophet defeating the many. I note too that Asherah's prophets have now fallen out of the text. Elijah's killing is, of course, not a problem, unlike Jezebel's killing of Yнwн's prophets reported back in verse 4. On the contrary, this is a sign of his Yahwistic zeal and commitment. Of course! This fact is indeed confirmed by the heavy rain that now falls, the Baalist prophets having failed miserably in the preceding fiery competition. All is well, or is it? Not for Elijah, for Jezebel must be brought out again for further denigration in Chapter 19, threatening to kill him in turn. What can he do but flee! It seems the Masoretes had some trouble here, pointing the verb as "he saw" (1 Kgs 19:3, NKJV), although the Septuagint, Syriac, and Vulgate manuscripts all read "he was afraid." A prophet of Yнwн in fearful flight from a woman, a murderer of prophets and devotee of the goddess! And Jezebel? As Alan Hauser writes, she "singlehandedly … dramatically alters the course of events. Elijah … is transformed by (her) into a whimpering defeatist … Jezebel serves once again … as a powerful agent of death."[30] Am I surprised? The scribe has piled up the case against Jezebel, choosing what to use and how to use the early Elijah legends. If Elijah looks wimpish where earlier he was in full command, that does not matter.

But this is not the end: as Howard reminds me, "the replacement of Ahab with Jezebel as Elijah's most terrible enemy looks forward to the story of Naboth's vineyard (21:1–29)" where Jezebel again usurps Ahab's place.[31] As an episode it seems self-contained, a tale that may have been told down the years, and then seamed into place in the longer Jezebel narrative. Interestingly, there is no Asherah connection. This is not a matter of gods and acceptable devotion, but of royal injustice with Jezebel the perpetrator of the murderous deed that gains the victim's land. This is its narrative strength: Jezebel's evil is omnipresent; she is evil through and through. There is no need to mention Asherah. Her influence is assumed and deadly. It is all part of the literary construction of the stereotype, that feature of Othering with its "concept of 'fixity' " that, as Bhabha explains, "vacillates between what is always 'in place', always already known, and something that must be anxiously repeated."[32] Jezebel must continuously be seen as the evil Other: Other in rank and ethnicity, Other in gender, Other in religious faith. And yet, something seems to be amiss in the seaming, for when Elijah later enters the story in verse 17, it is Ahab who is to be accused of having killed and taken possession of the vineyard. Not Jezebel!

I have been writing *about* Jezebel, in the accepted academic tradition of critical appraisal. I am now moving to "creative imagination," as encouraged by Elisabeth Schüssler Fiorenza, as part of her "dance of interpretation." It is a methodological shift within her feminist hermeneutic, in which each part brings the drama of the text into ever-clearer focus.[33] So I am now giving Jezebel her own voice, a little different from that allotted by the scribes. Thus Jezebel:

Have you read this story? Because that's what it is—just a story. Imagine it: my husband, the great Israelite king Ahab, going into a sulk, lying down and refusing to eat, just because a subject refuses to hand over his vineyard! And Naboth, a mere subject claiming, on such moral high ground, that this was land gifted by Yʜwʜ as a divine inheritance! How could you believe it? No. It's the work of some poor scribe, ordered to pour out this stuff. I, of course, am the evil wife. But I'm clever and I can write! So here I am, dealing with the Naboth problem all by correspondence, writing deadly letters in my deathly trickery. Can you believe it? But that's how the text has it: letters sent—a false accusation made—and that disposes of Naboth. I know the system and I manipulate it, all done with a script. But it's cleverly ironic: Ahab wants to grow vegetables but it's he who gets to be eaten, according to Elijah, supposedly speaking for Yʜwʜ (21:19). But did you notice the slip? The scribe has Yʜwʜ accusing Ahab: "have you killed and also taken possession?" Not me! But I'm not forgotten for long. There's an ominous tag, "also concerning Jezebel" (21:23). I'm to be eaten too, for in all the evil Ahab did he was "urged on by his wife, Jezebel" (21:25). This scribe makes mistake after mistake: my husband was killed in battle and died in Ramoth-gilead, not Naboth's Jezreel (21:19). It's a grisly pen, with dogs licking Ahab's blood, while prostitutes wash themselves—supposedly, in it (22:38). It's positively dog-obsessed. Turn to 2 Kings 9, and now it's a young prophet declaring dogs are going to eat me (2 Kgs 9:10). But again Ahab is Naboth's killer (2 Kgs 9:26). This is a nasty chapter, Jehu killing my son, Jehoram, and throwing his body onto that same disputed vineyard plot. All very clever. Great storytellers, these scribes! Did you notice Jehu's charge against me? Virtually calling me a whore and a witch, and suggesting that I'm the sole obstacle to peace (2 Kgs 9:22)! Really?! If it's my Asherah devotion that's behind that, then I suggest he's cribbing from Hosea. Did you read my challenge to Jehu, venomously addressing him as a

Zimri, "murderer of your master" (2 Kgs 9:31)? I do like that! But there's no truth here. What this scribe has written is just lies, lies, lies, and more lies!

I leave the imagined talking Jezebel here, but the story continues, for the scribe has a further move to make. There is to be no happy ending for such an evil Other. No one is to be left in any doubt as to the winner in these ideological contests. So in 2 Kings 9 Jezebel is set, having painted her eyes and coiffed her hair, as the "woman at the window" (v. 30), a pose that strikingly mirrors a motif found on ivory plaques of the ninth or eighth century. Are these goddesses? Possibly Egyptian Hathor, renowned for her carefully styled "Hathor wig," who, scholars suggest, had Asherah connections. So is this the shattering of Hathor/Asherah?[34] Is it, as I wrote some years ago, "not only the tipping out of an earthly human queen but also the degrading and bringing down to earth of a queen who embodies the sacred, an embodiment soon to be consumed in a parody of sacred feasting by the dogs?"[35] And those chilling final words, supposedly endorsed by "the man of god": "so no one can say, This is Jezebel" (2 Kgs 9:37). Complete eradication. But has the goddess been eradicated? Not quite yet! 2 Kings 13:6 notes an Asherah image remaining in Samaria under Jehu's son, Jehoahaz, while Chapter 17 declares that the Assyrian conquest of Israel was precisely due to the people's secretive worship of Other gods, including Asherah devotion "on every high hill and under every green tree" (v. 10). It seems the feminine representation of the divine lives on for a while, too useful as the ideological expression of an Othering aberration to be discarded too soon.

These characters have been ciphers in a highly political Deuteronomistic text. Jezebel has been fused with Asherah, the feminine representation of the divine, and together they have been annihilated, in contrast to Elijah, the prophet and spokesperson for Yhwh, the male one and only God. Yet Elijah's ascent to heaven in 2 Kings 2:11 also seems to breach the human/divine barrier. Is this porous and does that not matter if the human is a male Yahwistic prophet? What is unquestionable is the fusing of the theological with the earthly (political), with Jezebel and Ahab also ciphers for a northern Israel that the much later Deuteronomistic text is determined to denigrate. Readers are to be left in no doubt about the "truth" of its Judahite orthodoxy. So, in this rewriting of the past, the scribe has set Jezebel as the arch-apostate, poised at the intersection of race, gender, and class: Otherness at every turn.

I find this Othering disturbing on many counts, particularly in terms of cultural memory. As Gayle Greene wrote some years ago, "memory is our means of connecting past and present and constructing a self and versions of experience we can live with."[36] This rewritten version of northern Israel's history was an important document for its readers and audience, working out who they were as the people of Yhwh, and what that meant for the lives they were now living. For the rewriters of Kings, the later Israel's historical memory had to be reshaped. Exclusive devotion to Yhwh had to be absolute, with no stray female representations of the divine in sight. Jezebel was to symbolize the negative, providing a "memory" of a sinful past not to be repeated. Her association with Asherah was the path to be avoided at all cost if one was to self-identify as Israelite in Babylon or Yehud. *Cui bono*? Certainly not for real, flesh and blood women. As Walsh recognizes, these Jezebel texts were to become part of later Israel's "collective memory," heard and read with "a sense of *Schadenfreude*, a gloating" that "forged unity in the remembering community. Since no one in the community was likely to be as despicable as Jezebel all could feel included." It added to the message that "foreign spouses brought abominations to Yehud (Ezra 9:1) … The ideological message in her cultural memory would be clear to the Persian period community: better to divorce foreigners than risk religious contamination."[37] There are to be no feminine abominations as representations of the divine in this later Israel!

My response has been to use a feminist critical analysis as "an interventionist instrument which refuses to take the dominant reading as an uncomplicated representation of the past and introduces an alternative reading," which is R. S. Sugirtharajah's description of postcolonialism.[38] Israel, of course, was not colonized by southern Judah; that was Assyria's later act, although the taking of Naboth's vineyard does fit the category of land grab, with the term "take possession" recalling the language of conquest texts such as Deuteronomy 15:4. Here, however, conquest happens through the grabbing power of an apostate monarchy. It is the dominant Jezebel/Asherah reading that is my primary concern, and so I have attempted this alternative reading. Yet I am loath to put away my feminist probing tools, for there are always more questions to be asked. Was there an Asherah sequel? Texts are not confined to scrolls. The inscriptions at Kuntillet 'Ajrud and Khirbet el-Qom would seem to indicate that Asherah, now consort of YHWH, was still bestowing gifts years after Jezebel, Ahab, and Elijah had vanished from the earth, and the small passage in Jeremiah 44 has the Queen of Heaven, who may or may not be Asherah, still regarded as powerfully beneficent. While the women declare they will continue to make offerings to her, the writer strongly decries this, so the passage here too may be another literary ploy, penned by a scribe also in the Deuteronomistic tradition. So the question remains: did those of this orthodoxy succeed in ridding the world of Asherah and the goddess tradition? Was there to be no representation of the feminine divine in Jewish spirituality? While the Kabbalah would suggest a diversion to another byway, it seems that they did succeed in eradicating her, and with her, any overt feminine representation of the divine, from the mainstream. It may be, as Judith Hadley and others suggest, that she became textualized as a literary trope, becoming the female figure of biblical Wisdom as "a literary compensation" for her eradication, so she could be seen "with seemingly divine attributes but very much 'under the thumb' of Yahweh."[39] Nor does the Christian New Testament have a place for such a feminine representation of the divine, for there Wisdom is textually absorbed into the figure of the male Christ.[40]

I have been reading this biblical text from my own postcolonial context. This, in turn, has led me to read letters and journals, as well as historians' accounts, of some of the Protestant Evangelical missionaries who came to New Zealand in the early nineteenth century. While the literary genres differ, I am finding some striking and disturbing links. For these missionaries were also attempting to impose their own orthodoxy upon a people whose spirituality included *atua wahine* (female "gods").

In reading 1 and 2 Kings I have been immersed in one cultural/religious clash. Now I am taken into another. Living in the present world, I am well aware that virulent strategies to combat supposedly religious aberrations are not confined to the past of ancient Israel/Yehud. My interest here is in how these early missionaries reacted when faced with a different culture, different spirituality, and different cosmology. And how did they see themselves? While most were British, they did not come as colonizers. Some even contested the very notion of colonization. Dandeson Coates, the London-based Church Missionary Society (CMS) secretary, for example, made a submission in 1838 to the Select Committee of the House of Lords Appointed to Inquire into the Present State of the Islands of New Zealand, declaring that "to acquire Sovereignty in that Country would be a Violation of the Fundamental Principles of international Law."[41] Yet these missionaries were essentially part of a colonizing world, and, as Melanie Kampen writes, "imperialism's most overlooked mechanism is its universal/absolute claim to Truth and its accompanying power/drive to convert that which is other-than-itself to itself."[42] Historians' views are nuanced. For Ranginui Walker, the missionaries came as "the advance party of cultural invasion,"[43] while Tony Ballantyne suggests they "functioned as kind of cultural irritant."[44] Even if they did not regard themselves as colonizers per se, as people coming specifically to evangelize, they were, in a sense, intent on colonizing the mind. So I am now adding postcolonial criticism to my analytical arsenal. As the quote above from Sugirtharajah indicates, this is not so much a move from feminist to postcolonialist analysis, but simply a matter of merging the two and widening the focus. My interest here is in how this particular cultural/religious clash, set in the context of colonialist ideology and power, impacted on the matter of the feminine representation of the divine. As before, it is a matter of orthodoxy, which is writ large in this missionary enterprise.

I am mindful of Homi Bhabha's statement that "the objective of colonial discourse is to construe the colonized as a population of degenerate types on the basis of racial origin in order to justify conquest and to establish systems of administration and instruction."[45] This might seem an ill fit with a missionary project, yet traces of it appear as early as 1807, when Samuel Marsden, honored as the founding Protestant Evangelical missionary to New Zealand, presented the London-based CMS secretary with the case for mission. As he wrote in his journal, "I stated my views on the degraded state of the New Zealanders for want of moral and religious instruction." It appears even more clearly in William Yate's account written after seven years with the CMS:

> When first discovered by Europeans, the New Zealanders were indeed a savage and a barbarous people; and, till within a very few years, there has apparently been little or no difference in their national character. The intercourse which they have latterly held with civilized man, and their knowledge of the blessings which are to be derived from the acceptance of the Gospel, have, in some measure, changed the character of all the inhabitants of these islands on the eastern coast, and north of the Thames. The great body, however, of even these natives still retain a large portion, if not all, of their original manners; and are,

in many instances, still addicted to the superstitions and observances of their forefathers.[46]

I had not expected such a fit with Bhabha's colonial discourse description. As Judith Binney comments, "the gospel and 'civilization' were … inextricably linked."[47] A report from that same Select Committee to which Dandeson Coates made his submission makes this very clear: "What the savage wants is to have before his eyes the example of a civilized and Christian community."[48] The word "wants" leaps from the page. Thomas Kendall, writing in 1818, is equally clear about what the mission wants: "Nothing can secure them permanently to our interests, but a participation with us in the blessings of the Gospel."[49] Although he is concerned about "the Native Heart with its blind attachment to its barbarous customs," he was one who did make an effort to understand something of the indigenous spirituality. Yet, in 1823, he is writing like a Deuteronomist, albeit quoting Isaiah: "I have taken hold of the dirty cart ropes and dirty cart wheels of their abominations; have been shewn [*sic*], as it were, the secret lurking place of Satan, which I trust through mercy I shall yet be enabled to expose."[50] Marsden's comments on Kendall's interest are sharp: "By prying into the obscene customs and notions of the natives with a vitiated curiosity, his own mind has become so polluted that it will be very difficult for him to purify his ideas so far as to render what he writes acceptable to the public eye, and to make himself, at the same time, understood."[51] It is, again, the Othering of what is neither understood nor able to be fitted within a strictly held orthodoxy. I imagine the Deuteronomists nodding in sympathy. They might have had more difficulty in appreciating Binney's comment "that the social criteria he believed absolute were merely the product of the society that had formulated them," and that this, in turn, meant that he "remained trapped in the web of his own social, theological, and intellectual limitations."[52]

Once again, the feminine representation of the divine is part of an Othering. It lies within these claims of superstitions and abominations as the missionaries met a spirituality and cosmology very different from their own. If northern Israel incorporated more than one representation of the divine into its Yahwistic cult, so too the Maori term *atua* covered, as it still does, *atua wahine* (female "gods") as well as *atua tane* (male "gods"), both in the plural. Female representation of the divine was already here. Papatuanuku, the great earth mother whose separation from Rangi, the sky father, brought the world into being, was honored and understood, as she still is, as the one in whom "the creative generative principle resides." Aroha Yates-Smith, whom I am quoting, explains: "The concept of whakaahuru … of warming and cherishing another is inherited from Papatuanuku, her nature being to extend her aroha (love) to others."[53] This was a challenge indeed to people who considered Maori "governed by the Prince of Darkness."[54]

How even find a word for god/God when *atua* not only covered "gods" of both genders, but deified ancestors and various "spirits"? Kendall's solution, in his work of translation *A Korao no New Zealand* was to use Atua Nue (*atua nui*), the "great God," implying there were others of lesser significance.[55] How then enforce an orthodoxy, when this required no less a task than attempting to remake the indigenous cosmology?[56] William Yate's journal entry noting "the belief in a spirit land to which all souls went after death" hints at this. "I think if we can dive to the bottom of this we shall have some good ground to break up & work upon."[57] While he does not mention her, it was the great goddess Hine-nui-te-po who ruled over the realm of death. Did he even know about her? The difficulties were almost insuperable. Maori rarely shared their understanding of the sacred with the missionaries. Even the very term *tapu* (sacred) did not equal the missionary understanding, which, to quote Tony Ballantyne, led "many missionaries to doubt that Maori actually possessed any systematic body of beliefs and practices that could be designated as a 'religion.'" It was simply "an assemblage of superstitions and folk beliefs."[58] How else describe a belief system that included such powerful *atua wahine* as Papatuanuku and Hine-nui-te-po, "their roles complementing those of their well-known male counterparts and providing balance within the pantheon."[59]

In one of his letters, Kendall sounds again like the Deuteronomists, referring to Maori religion being drawn "from the study of nature" and therefore "frequently obtained from very impure sources."[60] I imagine Jezebel nodding. If Asherah was associated with trees, which would seem to be the case, she too had "nature" connections, and was certainly considered an "impure source" of spirituality.[61] What to do with images too powerful, too threatening for an opposing orthodoxy? All signs of her, all those pillars set up on the high places and under leafy trees, must be cut down, must be broken, must be burned.[62] So, too, quickly, quickly, deal with the offensive "erotic, sinful, and evil" Maori carvings of figures with their genitalia in full view, sacred symbols of fertility and procreation. Emasculate them! An act that, as Ranginui Walker writes, "was like a thrust to the jugular by the cultural invader."[63]

But what can be done to an earth figure like Papatuanuku? One who is the land itself, loved and honored because "the bounty that sprang from her breast nurtured and sustained her children"?[64] Find another solution. Again there is that linking with the past of the biblical text. Textualize her, and all the other *atua wahine*, alongside their male counterparts. They could not be considered divine or part of the acceptable theology, but they could be written about as mythical or legendary beings. So Richard Taylor can write, without reproach, in a chapter headed "Mythology":

> There were two grand orders of gods: the first and most ancient were the gods of the night, as night preceded light, and then followed the gods of the light. Of the former the chief was Hine-nui-te-po, great mother night, the grand parent of the rest. Of the latter, Rangi and Papa, or Heaven and Earth, were the parents.[65]

And the German missionary Johann Wohlers can write sensitively, even poetically, in a chapter headed "On the Mythology of the Maoris," "although Rangi (the God of Heaven) and Papatuanuku were separated, their mutual love still continued. He wept tears of love on to her in the shape of dew drops, and sighs of love rose from her bosom up to him in the mists of the woody mountains."[66] It gives him license to record "legends" of these *atua wahine*. So he writes of Maui's attempt "to enter the womb of Hine-nui-te-po, that is Hades, where the living water—the life-giving stream—was situated. Hine-nui-te-po draws all into her womb, but permits none to return."[67] The Wesleyan missionary James Buller, also in a chapter headed "Legends," has Maui, the great ancestor, ask, "What was Hine like? He was told that her eyes shone like the sun; her teeth were as sharp as pounamu [greenstone]; her body was like that of a man; the pupils of her eyes were jasper; her hair resembled seaweed; and her mouth was an image of that of a large fish."[68] The textualizing ploy worked. "Legends" were "loosened from landscape and tribe to become 'New Zealand' legends, retold in Victorian styles, and even turned into 'fairy tales' for Pakeha children."[69] This is how I, and most non-Maori in New Zealand, came to know something of these *atua* traditions. We heard them as stories, nothing more. We, as children, were not aware that Paptuanuku was a living force in Maori spirituality. While I became aware that "after the birth of a child the whenua (placenta) is returned to the whenua (land)," I did not understand that by this earthing "the child's mana tangata, or personal dignity … [was] sustained throughout life until, in death, the body is returned to Paptuanuku."[70] I, and most Pakeha of my generation, are inheritors of a similar Christian orthodoxy.

Texts are powerful tools, their effects varied and considerable. The Protestant Evangelical missionaries not only brought the Bible with its already eradicated and absorbed representation of the feminine divine; they brought a textual culture. While there were plusses in this, such as Maori becoming a written language, there were also minuses in that "paradoxically," as Binney notes, "they preached doctrines which were destructive of the old culture."[71] Destructive of the *atua wahine*: as Yates-Smith notes, "the Christian influence on Maori spirituality virtually rendered the feminine invisible in the old religion."[72] And that "old culture" with its "old religion" was oral. This meant that ethnographers, mostly male and non-Maori, who were keen to gather material from this "old culture," had to rely on what they were told by Maori, usually male, who censored what they told. The ethnographers, in turn, censored and edited out anything that seemed to them at all fantastic or offensive. Jane Simpson recognizes the strategy when she writes that "texts enabled Europeans who came across a non-literate culture to textualize the people in that culture in what might be termed 'intellectual colonization.'"[73]

What then happened to the feminine representation of the divine? I turn again to the work of Yates-Smith, whose thesis researches the feminine in Maori spirituality. She notes how

> references made to Maori goddesses in books written about Maori life and customs, and, in particular, religion and mythology, were fragmentary and skimpy. The roles of the female entities were generally downplayed, marginalised, or, in many instances, completely omitted … The impression gained was that Maori goddesses, if they existed at all, held insignificant positions.[74]

This had consequences within Maori society: "the loss of knowledge about goddesses and the complementary role played with male gods within the Maori pantheon had a detrimental effect on the social values in Maori society and the status of women."[75] I hesitate and wonder about women's lives in Yehud. Was this also the case there? Consequences are not limited to the past, as Yates-Smith notes: "the impact of nearly two centuries of British colonization on Maori society has resulted in the loss of oral access to traditional spiritual lore."[76] Yet not all was lost. Papatuanuku still has a place in the traditions of the oral culture that survive: on the *marae*, formal speeches and *waiata* continue to honor Rangi and Papa—Sky Father and Earth Mother.[77] There, to quote another writer, "all who hear the words are reminded that we are not separate; we are one through them and they influence us still."[78] Yet the losses from the past do remain a present reality. Vapi Kupenga, Rina Rata, and Tuki Nepe write of the need "to nurture and preserve Paptuanuku," in terms of "reclaiming women's autonomy," while Yates-Smith calls for the full power of the feminine to be recognized "to establish the balance needed in these modern times."[79]

Why does this issue bother me? Why do I haul out my critical tools and engage with these texts? I have also been reading Gerald O'Collins and David Braithwaite's paper "Tradition as Collective Memory: A Theological Task to Be Tackled," which reminded me, in turn, of Ricoeur's work on collective memory, of how the memory of what has been lost can remain as "a haunting" of a "past that does not pass."[80] Am I haunted? There is no sense of a feminine representation of the divine in the services I attend as a member of the Christian church in Aotearoa, New Zealand. Papatuanuku, the earth that nourishes us, on which we live, and in which we bury our dead, may still be a significant representation of the divine in the indigenous culture of this land, but I, as a Pakeha, rarely hear of her. Is it too easy to criticize and blame those in the past who worked hard to make sure this would be the case? Ballantyne concludes his study of the early missionaries, observing that they "were ambivalent figures positioned between cultures, translating between worlds."[81] Does this apply also to the Deuteronomists? There is such sadness in looking and reading back through these feminist postcolonial lenses.

What has been the plus in adding postcolonial criticism to the feminist? Jeremy Punt writes of postcolonial theory's "concern for the contemporary politics of identity, regarding the categories and institutions, the knowledges and the power plays by means of which social dynamics and people are structured and regulated."[82] This, I agree, is key, not only for postcolonial criticism but equally for feminism. It is the effect of polarizing ideologies, together with textual (mis) representation, upon people's sense of identity that I have been keen to explore through this double reading. It is the textual and interpretive processes and their long-term effects that interest me. So too, Tat-Siong Benny Liew writes of postcolonial criticism that it "seeks to confront and contest not only just past devices and dynamics of domination but also their legacies."[83] As is evident in this essay, this is equally true of the feminist quest. I am not suggesting in this essay that the Deuteronomistic writer(s) of 1 and 2 Kings are to be blamed for the missionary reactions to the indigenous beliefs of the people they came to evangelize. The connection, if one can call it that at all, is certainly not causal. What such a double reading has highlighted is the way in which both attempts to assert an orthodoxy depended in large measure on denigrating the Other and the Other's spirituality. My contrapuntal move, in terms of adding a reading from the past of my own postcolonial context to that of the Jezebel narrative, has brought this into sharper focus. It also serves as a warning that this issue is not to be left enclosed in the world of biblical academic study, allowing us to close the book, re-shelve it, and carry on with our lives unaffected. Jezebel and Elijah are long dead, if they ever existed, and so are the Deuteronomists with their polarizing campaigns. However, the issues surrounding orthodoxies and Otherness in contemporary contexts like my own are very much alive. It is the feminist critical analysis, with its sharp gender focus, that has highlighted the matter of the representation of the feminine divine, revealing a worrying gender issue at the heart of these programs. What has become apparent is that it takes the combined lenses of feminist and postcolonial readings to bring such matters into the open to consider them afresh.

Finally, I wish to add a further issue. How are those of us who are feminist academics to present our work? To what extent do we follow the traditional academic style, writing in the third person, supposedly disinterested and objective? Can a particular literary form negate the value of the analysis? As I stated in the introduction, not only have I chosen to use the personal "I" throughout this essay, with an occasional whimsy, but I have added an, admittedly small, fictional touch in giving Jezebel a voice to emphasize the point I want to make. A crucial question is: who are we writing for? Sugirtharajah writes of scholars' use of "an insider writing style that involves complicated phrases and syntax" that excludes the outsider.[84] This, of course, raises the matter of publishers' and reviewers' expectations and requirements. Those of us who attempt, even gently, to modify our style soon find out which to approach. These are not new questions. Alicia Ostriker already wrote back in 1993 of not wanting "to separate what I do as a scholar and critic from what I do as a poet," and more recently Julie Kelso has combined both in her Irigaray-inspired reading of Chronicles.[85] Few of us, however, are following in their footsteps, and so the question remains: how are feminist scholars to write? I sense Jezebel, urging us not to be afraid of both reading and writing Otherwise.

Notes

1. Simone de Beauvoir, "*On ne naît pas femme: on le devient,*" in *le deuxième sexe* (1949), trans. H. M. Parshley as *The Second Sex* (New York: Vintage Books, 1973), 301.
2. See Judith Butler's works, *Gender Trouble: Feminism and the Subversion of Identity* (New York: Routledge, 1990), and *Bodies that Matter: On the Discursive Limits of "Sex"* (New York: Routledge, 1993).
3. Esther Fuchs, *Sexual Politics in the Biblical Narrative: Reading the Hebrew Bible as a Woman*, LHBOTS 310 (Sheffield: Sheffield Academic, 2000), 19.
4. Esther Fuchs, "Biblical Feminisms: Knowledge, Theory and Politics in the Study of Women in the Hebrew Bible," *BibInt* 16 (2008): 205–26 (222).
5. Stephen D. Moore, "A Modest Manifesto for New Testament Literary Criticism: How to Interface with a Literary Studies Field that Is Post-Literary, Post-Theoretical, and Post-Methodological," *BibInt* 15 (2007): 1–25 (23).

6. J. Cheryl Exum, "Developing Strategies of Feminist Criticism/Developing Strategies for Commentating the Song of Songs," in *Auguries: The Jubilee Volume of the Sheffield Department of Biblical Studies*, ed. David J. A. Clines and Stephen D. Moore (Sheffield: Sheffield Academic, 1998), 206–49 (207).
7. Terry Eagleton, *Criticism and Ideology: A Study in Marxist Literary Theory* (London: New Left Books, 1976), 101.
8. Patrocinio P. Schweickart, "Reading Ourselves: Towards a Feminist Theory of Reading," in *Gender and Reading: Essays on Readers, Texts, and Contexts*, ed. Elizabeth A. Flynn and P. P. Schweickart (Baltimore: Johns Hopkins University Press, 1986), 31–62 (39).
9. Cameron B. R. Howard, "1 and 2 Kings," in *The Women's Bible Commentary: Revised and Updated*, ed. Carol A. Newsom et al. (Louisville, KY: Westminster John Knox Press, 2012), 164–83 (172).
10. As attested in Arabic and Akkadian. See John Gray, *I & II Kings*, second edition (Philadelphia: Westminster, 1970), 368.
11. Compare 1 Chronicles 8:33, 34; 9:39, 40 with 2 Samuel 2:10, 12; 3:7; 4:1, 4, 5, 8; 9:10–13.
12. Mark S. Smith, *The Early History of God: Yahweh and the Other Deities in Ancient Israel* (San Francisco: Harper & Row, 1990), 14. In later chapters Jezebel and Ahab's children bear the Yʜᴡʜ-honoring names Ahaziah, Jehoram, and Athaliah, which Lester L. Grabbe attributes to Ahab, seeing him as a Yahwist, adding that "it would not have been unusual at this time if he also honoured other gods," Lester L. Grabbe, "Reflections on the Discussion," in *Ahab Agonistes: The Rise and Fall of the Omri Dynasty*, ed. Lester L. Grabbe, LHBOTS 421 (London: T&T Clark, 2007), 331–41 (338).
13. Linda Tuhiwai Smith, *Decolonizing Methodologies: Research and Indigenous Peoples*, Second Edition (New York: Zed Books, 2012), 37.
14. Homi K. Bhabha, *The Location of Culture* (London: Routledge, 1994), 44.
15. Exum, "Developing Strategies of Feminist Criticism," 209.
16. His name is found on Shalmaneser III's Kurkh monolith inscription. Carey Walsh notes that while the name Jezebel appears on a seal, there is "no real consensus about whether or not this is Queen Jezebel," Carey Walsh, "Why Remember Jezebel?," in *Remembering Biblical Figures in the Late Persian and Early Hellenistic Periods: Social Memory and Imagination*, ed. Diana Vikander Edelman and Ehud Ben Zvi (Oxford: Oxford University Press, 2013), 311–31 (312 n. 3).
17. Israel Finkelstein, *The Forgotten Kingdom: The Archaeology and History of Northern Israel*, ANEM 5 (Atlanta: SBL, 2013); Finkelstein, *The Forgotten Kingdom*, 157, notes that "the author incorporated the northern … traditions but subjected them to his main ideological goals."
18. See Dagmar Pruin, "What Is in a Text?—Searching for Jezebel," in *Ahab Agonistes*, ed. Lester L. Grabbe, 208–35 (213), who considers chapters 17–19 post-Deuteronomistic additions.
19. See Howard, "1 and 2 Kings," 172.
20. Published as Phyllis Trible, "Exegesis for Storytellers and Other Strangers," *JBL* 114 (1995): 3–19. The quote comes from p. 3.
21. Walsh, "Why Remember Jezebel?," 311.
22. Trible, "Exegesis for Storytellers and Other Strangers," 3.
23. Tchavdar S. Hadjiev, "Elijah's Alleged Megalomania: Reading Strategies for Composite Texts, with 1 Kings 19 as an Example," *JSOT* 39 (2015): 433–49 (439–40).

24. Finkelstein, *The Forgotten Kingdom*, 65.

25. Patricia Dutcher-Walls, *Jezebel: Portraits of a Queen*, Interfaces (Collegeville, MI: Liturgical Press, 2004), 128, suggests it is likely that Ahab had other wives as well, so that mentioning only Jezebel "already spotlights her as the power behind the throne."

26. Neil Glover, "Elijah versus the Narrative of Elijah: The Contest between the Prophet and the Word," *JSOT* 30 (2006): 449–62 (451).

27. Another reference to Yʜwʜ and his Asherah was found near Khirbet el-Qôm, variously dated either ca. 750 BCE or nearer the end of the eighth century.

28. See Finkelstein, *The Forgotten Kingdom*, 137–8, with reference to the work of other scholars in the field, particularly Tallay Ornan. So, too, Judith M. Hadley, "From Goddess to Literary Construct: The Transformation of Asherah Into Hokmah," in *A Feminist Companion to Reading the Bible: Approaches, Methods and Strategies*, ed. Athalya Brenner and Carole Fontaine (Sheffield: Sheffield Academic, 1997), 360–99 (384–5). Pruin, "What Is in a Text?," 224–5, notes Susanne Otto's opposing view in *Jehu, Elia und Elisa. Die Erzählung von der Jehu-Revolution und die Komposition der Elia-Elisa-Erzählungen*, BWA(N)T 152 (Stuttgart: Kohlhammer, 2001).

29. See Hadley, "From Goddess to Literary Construct," 383, "The idea that a cultic object can bear the same name as the deity it represents would not be a foreign concept to the people of the ancient Near East." See also Diana Edelman, "Huldah the Prophet— Of Yahweh or Asherah?," in *A Feminist Companion to Samuel and Kings*, ed. Athalya Brenner (Sheffield: Sheffield Academic, 1994), 231–50 (244), who refers to this as "deliberate tampering with the grammatical construction." The editor of the BHS suggests that the mention of the four hundred prophets of Asherah should be deleted from the text, although no textual evidence is given for such a deletion.

30. Alan J. Hauser, "Yahweh Versus Death – The Real Struggle in 1 Kings 17–19," in *From Carmel to Horeb: Elijah in Crisis*, ed. A. J. Hauser and Russell Gregory, JSOTSup 85 (Sheffield: Almond Press 1990), 9–89 (60).

31. Howard, "1 and 2 Kings," 173.

32. Bhabha, *Location of Culture*, 66.

33. Elisabeth Schüssler Fiorenza, *But She Said: Feminist Practices of Biblical Interpretation* (Boston: Beacon Press, 1992), 72–5.

34. I note that Lesley Hazleton, *Jezebel: The Untold Story of the Bible's Harlot Queen* (New York: Doubleday, 2007), 184, reads it this way, although she assumes the goddess is Astarte.

35. Judith E. McKinlay, "Negotiating the Frame for Viewing the Death of Jezebel," *BibInt* 10 (2002): 305–23 (316), later included as chapter 5 in *Reframing Her: Biblical Women in Postcolonial Focus*, BMW 1 (Sheffield: Sheffield Phoenix), 2004.

36. Gayle Greene, "Feminist Fiction and the Uses of Memory," *Signs: Journal of Women in Culture and Society* 16 (1991): 290–321 (293).

37. Walsh, "Why Remember Jezebel?," 314, 325–6.

38. R. S. Sugirtharajah, *The Bible and Empire: Postcolonial Explorations* (Cambridge: Cambridge University Press, 2005), 3.

39. Hadley, "From Goddess to Literary Construct," 396, 398.

40. See Celia Deutsch, "Jesus as Wisdom: A Feminist Reading of Matthew's Wisdom Christology," in *A Feminist Companion to Matthew*, ed. Amy-Jill Levine (Sheffield: Sheffield Academic, 2001), 88–113, and Diana Jacobson, "Jesus as Wisdom in the New Testament," *WW* Supplement Series 3 (1997): 72–93.

41. Quoted in Tony Ballantyne, *Entanglements of Empire: Missionaries, Māori, and the Question of the Body* (Auckland: University of Auckland Press, 2014), 242.
42. Melanie Kampen, *Unsettling Theology: Decolonizing Western Interpretations of Original Sin* (MThS diss., University of Waterloo, Ontario, Canada, 2014), 127. Available at: https://uwspace.uwaterloo.ca/bitstream/handle/10012/8368/Kampen_Melanie.pdf?sequence=1, accessed June 21, 2015.
43. Ranginui Walker, *Ka Whawhai Tonu Matou: Struggle Without End* (Auckland: Penguin Books, 1990), 85.
44. Ballantyne, *Entanglements of Empire*, 253.
45. Bhabha, *Location of Culture*, 70.
46. William Yate, *An Account of New Zealand; and of the Formation and Progress of the Church Missionary Society's Mission in the Northern Island*, Second Edition (London: Seeley and Burnside, 1835), 81. Available at: http://www.enzb.auckland.ac.nz, accessed August 3, 2015.
47. Judith Binney, *The Legacy of Guilt: A Life of Thomas Kendall* (Auckland: Published for the University of Auckland by the Oxford University Press, 1968), 8, quoting from Marsden's journal.
48. Quoted in Hilary M. Carey, *God's Empire: Religion and Colonialism in the British World, c. 1801–1908* (Cambridge: Cambridge University Press, 2011), 315.
49. Thomas Kendall, "Letter to Josiah Pratt, 16 December 1818," republished in *The Missionary Register* 1820. Hocken Library, University of Otago, MS 56/117, included in *Anthology of New Zealand Literature*, ed. Jane Stafford and Mark Williams (Auckland: The Auckland University Press, 2012), 27–9.
50. Letter to Thomas Hassall, quoted by Binney, *Legacy of Guilt*, 76. The quote is from Isaiah 5:18.
51. J. Elder, ed., "Chapter Five, Marsden's Fourth New Zealand Journal," in *The Letters and Journals of Samuel Marsden* (1932), 347. Available at: http://www.enzb.auckland.ac.nz, accessed July 28, 2015.
52. Binney, *Legacy of Guilt*, 78.
53. G. R. Aroha Yates-Smith, *Hine! e Hine!: Rediscovering the Feminine in Maori Spirituality* (PhD diss., University of Waikato, Hamilton, 1998), 154.
54. Henry Williams, "Journal 16 February, 1828," in *The Early Journals of Henry Williams 1826–40*, ed. Laurence M. Rogers, 103, quoted by Bronwyn Elsmore, *Like Them That Dream: The Maori and the Old Testament*, Second Edition (Auckland: Libro International, 2011), 20. The phrase appears again and again in many of the missionary writings.
55. Tony Ballantyne, *Webs of Empire: Locating New Zealand's Colonial Past* (Wellington: Bridget Williams Books, 2012), 148, who notes that "he also produced Maori sentences which simply incorporated 'Jehovah' and 'Lord' as the name of the 'Atua Nue.'" As Binney, *Legacy of Guilt*, 156, comments, "It was a brave thing to do—to take the phrases of the great God whom he knew and to apply them to the great God of the Maori world whom he thought he had found." The book, subtitled *or, the New Zealander's First Book*, was published in 1815.
56. Ballantyne, *Entanglements of Empire*, 174.
57. Judith Binney, "Christianity and the Maoris to 1840: A Comment," *New Zealand Journal of History* 3 (1969): 143–65 (152), quoting from an entry in Yate's journal, dated May 23, 1828.
58. Ballantyne, *Entanglements of Empire*, 190.

59. Yates-Smith, *Hine! e Hine!*, 1.
60. Quoted by Binney, *Legacy of Guilt,* 126. See Walker, *Ka Whawhai Tonu Matou,* 13, "The personification of natural phenomena in the Maori pantheon is fundamental to the holistic world-view of the Maori."
61. See the recent discussion by Sung Jin Park, "The Cultic Identity of Asherah in Deuteronomistic Ideology of Israel," *ZAW* 123 (2011): 553–64.
62. Deuteronomy 12:2; 1 Kings 14:23.
63. Walker, *Ka Whawhai Tonu Matou,* 86–7.
64. Walker, *Ka Whawhai Tonu Matou,* 13.
65. Richard Taylor, *Te Ika a Maui, or New Zealand and Its Inhabitants* (London: Wertheim and Macintosh, 1855), 15–16. Available at: http://www.enzb.auckland.ac.nz, accessed April 3, 2015.
66. Chapter XI, "On the Mythology of the Maoris," in *Memories of the Life of J. F. H. Wohlers,* trans. J. Houghton (1895), 131. Available at: http://www.enzb.auckland.ac.nz, accessed April 30, 2015.
67. Wohlers, "On the Mythology of the Maoris," 31.
68. James Buller, *Forty Years in New Zealand* (London: Hodder & Stoughton, 1878), 189–90. Available at: http://www.enzb.auckland.ac.nz, accessed April 30, 2016.
69. Peter Gibbons, "Cultural Colonization and National Identity," *New Zealand Journal of History* 36 (2002): 5–17 (13).
70. Vapi Kupenga, Rina Rata, and Tuki Nepe, "Whāia te Iti Kahurangi: Māori Women Reclaiming Autonomy," in *Te Ao Mārama. Regaining Aotearoa: Māori Writers Speak Out,* Volume 2, ed. Witi Ihimaera (Auckland: Reed Books, 1993), 304–9 (304).
71. Binney, *Legacy of Guilt,* 185.
72. Yates-Smith, *Hine! e Hine!*, 4.
73. Jane Simpson, "Io as Supreme Being: Intellectual Colonization of the Māori?," *History of Religions* 37 (1997): 50–85 (56).
74. Yates-Smith, *Hine! e Hine!*, 114, 117.
75. Yates-Smith, *Hine! e Hine!*, 221.
76. Yates-Smith, *Hine! e Hine!*, 1.
77. The *marae* is the meeting place where formal ceremonies are performed, as well as where social gatherings are held. *Waiata* are traditional songs.
78. Philip Cody, *Seeds on the Word: Ngā Kākano o te Kupu.* (Wellington: Steele Roberts, 2004), 71.
79. Kupenga, Rata, and Nepe, "Whāia te Iti Kahurangi," 308; Yates-Smith, *Hine! e Hine!*, 283.
80. Gerald O'Collins, S. J. and David Braithwaite, S. J., "Tradition as Collective Memory: A Theological Task to Be Tackled," *TS* 76 (2015): 29–42 (40).
81. Ballantyne, *Entanglements of Empire,* 359.
82. Jeremy Punt, "Intersections in Queer Theory and Postcolonial Theory and Hermeneutical Spin-Offs," *The Bible and Critical Theory* 4, no. 2 (2008): 2, who applies this equally to queer theory.
83. Tat-Siong Benny Liew, "Echoes of a Subaltern's Contribution and Exclusion," in *Mark & Method: New Approaches in Biblical Studies,* ed. Janice Capel Anderson and Stephen D. Moore, Second Edition (Minneapolis: Fortress Press, 2008), 211–31 (219).
84. R. S. Sugirtharajah in D. N. Premnath, "Margins and Mainstream: An Interview with R. S. Sugirtharajah," in *Border Crossings: Cross-Cultural Hermeneutics,* ed. D. N. Premnath (Maryknoll, NY: Orbis Books, 2007), 153–65 (157).

85. Alicia Suskin Ostriker, *Feminist Revision and the Bible: The Unwritten Volume* (Oxford: Blackwell, 1993), 30; Julie Kelso, *O Mother, Where Art Thou? An Irigarayan Reading of the Book of Chronicles* (London: Equinox, 2007). See Samuel Tongue, *Between Biblical Criticism and Poetic Rewriting: Interpretative Struggles over Genesis 32:22–32*, BibInt 129 (Leiden: Brill, 2014).

Chapter 6

THE "FOREIGN" WOMEN IN EZRA-NEHEMIAH: INTERSECTIONAL PERSPECTIVES ON ETHNICITY

Christl M. Maier

As a biblical scholar trained in Germany, my approach to biblical texts is first of all historical-critical; that is, I aim to interpret the text in its sociohistorical context. My feminist interests lead me to read with a critical eye to reveal the ideology of the biblical text, its hidden agenda or bias. Within the feminist paradigm, the perspective on gender has broadened to what is now called the intersection of gender, class, ethnicity, and religion. While teaching in the United States from 2003 to 2006, I encountered postcolonial studies as an instrument to identify colonialist ideas and practices as well as multiple reactions to imperialism by subjugated people. The latter facilitated my understanding of postexilic Israel as a community struggling with Persian imperialism.

In this essay, I read texts that argue against intermarriage with "foreign"[1] women in Ezra-Nehemiah in terms of an intersectional lens, that is, analyzing ethnicity, gender, and religion as intersecting categories. To this aim, I first explain what I mean by intersectional analysis as well as feminist and postcolonial perspectives, then offer my interpretation of Nehemiah 13 and Ezra 9–10, and lastly come back to hermeneutical reflections at the intersection of historical-critical, feminist, and postcolonial perspectives.

Reflections on My Approach

The term intersection was coined in 1989 by the US attorney Kimberlé Crenshaw with regard to the lawsuit of five black female workers against General Motors.[2] Their complaint against their layoff was rejected because the court could detect neither sexism (GM employed white women) nor racism (GM employed black men) in the firm's policy. The jury also thought that multiple instances of discrimination could not be added up to create a "super claim." In her case study, Crenshaw demonstrated how discriminatory practices based on race and gender intersect and reinforce each other. While the term has been coined by Crenshaw, the idea of multiple discrimination and the interrelatedness of race, class, and gender had been discussed before, especially in black feminism and critical race theory.[3] In the 1980s, many feminist scholars addressed this classical triad in reaction to the critique by black women that feminist claims were focused on white, middle-class women as well as to the critique by minority women regarding hegemonic positions in feminist discourse. In this context, Patricia Hill Collins's definition of intersectionality seems appropriate: "As opposed to examining gender, race, class, and nation, as separate systems of oppression, intersectionality explores how these systems mutually construct one another."[4] Within this seemingly balanced analysis of multiple discrimination, the feminist advantage, in my view, is retained by a "hermeneutics of suspicion," which "does not take the kyriocentric text and its claim to divine authority at face value, but rather investigates it as to its ideological functions in the interest of domination."[5] Such a perspective aims at dismantling and deconstructing any discrimination of women, although the category of gender may not always be foregrounded. As a feminist undertaking, intersectional analysis is critical toward hegemonic structures and ideologies.

The intersection of ethnicity and religion is discussed in studies that seek to characterize what ethnos means in ancient sources. Most of these studies refer to the Greek term *ethnos*, defined as a group of people who are related not only by kinship but also by common language, specific manners, and shared religious rituals and sites.[6] In many groups, religious practices and the veneration of a specific deity were crucial to their self-identification. Without explicitly including religion, the sociologist Anthony Smith arrives at a similar definition: "We may define the '*ethnie*' or ethnic community as a social group whose members share a sense of common origins, claim a common and distinctive history and destiny, possess one or more distinctive characteristics, and feel a sense of collective uniqueness and solidarity."[7] In his book *The Beginnings of Jewishness*, Shaye Cohen argues that ethnicity is a cultural construct established by drawing boundaries between one group and another.[8] By analyzing ancient Jewish sources he finds that Jewish identity was elusive and uncertain, and before the second century BC, the most common definition of *Ioudaios* was related to a sense of common descent and geography—the Judeans living in or originating from Judea.[9] In the century following the Hasmonean rebellion, however, religious and political ties became salient, the boundaries became permeable, and Judaism developed into an ethno-religion. Worshipping the God of Jerusalem and observing the ancestral laws of the Judeans were more important than genealogy.[10] As Denise Buell demonstrates in her analysis of early Christian texts, any definition of *ethnos* contains both fixed and fluid elements and is thus a permeable concept of a group's self-perception.[11] She even argues that kinship and descent are not always fixed elements of ethnicity but can be redrawn discursively or ritually.[12] It is in the framework of these studies of ethnicity in antiquity that I place my intersectional analysis.[13]

Before I use this interpretive tool, I briefly expound what, in my view, a postcolonial perspective may add to dismantle hegemonic structures and ideologies. Postcolonial theory has been involved in analyzing the power structures, oppressive attitudes, and effects of imperialist regimes. According to Edward Said, "imperialism is the practice, the theory, and the attitudes of a dominating metropolitan center ruling a distant territory. Colonialism, which is almost always a consequence of imperialism, is the implantation of settlements on distant territory."[14] While the Persian Empire did not build colonies in Palestine, its policy of domination and economic exploitation constitutes sufficient grounds on which to designate it an imperialist regime. Some insights of the postcolonial theorist Homi Bhabha are helpful in assessing the context of biblical texts of the Persian and Hellenistic periods. A central tenet of postcolonial approaches is that an imperialist regime seeks to impose its attitudes, values, and habits upon the colonized, that is, the subjugated people. It establishes structures of control that simultaneously teach the colonized to resemble the society of its oppressor, but never to fully replicate it, since replication would threaten colonial authority.[15] Bhabha names the complex mix of attraction and repulsion that characterizes the relationship between the colonizer and the colonized "ambivalence."[16] The attempt of the colonized to adjust to colonial society he calls "mimicry," yet he points out that the colonized will be "almost the same, *but not quite.*"[17] Such mimicry is mostly performed by groups and persons that collaborate with the regime as administrative personnel or as groups that are exempted from tax or given specific privilege. With regard to the colonized, Bhabha observes an ambivalence in their attempt to "narrate" their nation, that is, to establish their narrative of community-building in a situation of colonial command.[18] Their response to colonial rule is characterized by "hybridity," which Bhabha defines positively as an "in-between space," in which new transcultural forms and other sites of meaning are created.[19] Therefore, the narratives of subjugated groups are influenced by imperialist rule and thought; they often mirror an ambivalent attitude toward the ruling regime or show ambivalences in the self-description of their group. Yet, they also create new, hybrid forms of discourse that challenge the authority of the colonizer. These ideas of Bhabha are relevant for my assessment of the biblical texts in their sociohistorical context in the final part of this essay.

In the following section, I analyze the arguments offered in Ezra-Nehemiah against intermarriage with "foreign" women in terms of a perspective that is sensitive to the intersection of gender, ethnicity, and religion. In a first step, I analyze the plot and terminology of a given passage as well as the arguments with regard to these women, asking why they are called "foreign," what exactly is found missing or disreputable in them, and how the ones who argue against intermarriage characterize themselves. As will be evident, the definition of "foreign" women in Ezra-Nehemiah is closely associated with religious practice and social issues, which for the purpose of this essay involves a focus on ethnicity.

Intermarriage in Nehemiah 13

The biblical writing titled Ezra-Nehemiah narrates the rebuilding of Jerusalem and the Judean community after the exile and the return of Golah groups from

Babylonia. The story focuses on the activities of two men, namely, the scribe Ezra and the Judean governor Nehemiah, who present themselves as authorized by the Persian king (Ezra 7:1–6; Neh 2:1–9). Until the fifteenth century CE, the texts were passed down as a unit in the Hebrew tradition, whereas today they are treated as two "books," which nevertheless overlap in topic and protagonists.[20] According to the story, Ezra arrives in the seventh year of the Persian king Artaxerxes (Ezra 7:8) and inaugurates the Torah as divine law in the Persian province Yehud. Nehemiah's rebuilding of Jerusalem's wall and the resettlement of the city are dated to the twentieth year of Artaxerxes (Neh 2:1). The two men do not really interact with each other, and there are only two notes (Neh 8:9; 12:36) that supply the name of the other protagonist. Since there were four Persian kings named Artaxerxes, historians correlate Nehemiah's mission with Artaxerxes I and the year 445 BCE based on a letter found in Elephantine, while Ezra's mission is mostly dated to the rule of Artaxerxes II and thus to 398 BCE.[21] Since Nehemiah deals with the topic of foreign women rather briefly and is often dated earlier, I begin with this text.

Nehemiah's Provisions against Intermarriage (Neh 13:23–31)

The passage Nehemiah 13:23–31 is part of the so-called Nehemiah memoir, a self-account addressed to God, in which Nehemiah talks about the measures he took for rebuilding Jerusalem's city wall, resettling the city, and organizing the temple service. The governor reports that he castigated Judeans who had married "foreign" women and evicted a member of the high priest's family who had married a daughter of Sanballat, the governor of Samaria. Since Nehemiah introduces these actions rather casually and lists them among his efforts to prohibit trade on the Sabbath, to arrange the duties of priests and Levites, and to organize offerings of wood and first fruits, his dealing with the intermarriage issue appears randomly and framed by issues of Jerusalem's temple cult.

The incriminated men had married Ashdodite, Ammonite, and Moabite women.[22] Nehemiah also notes that "a good number of their children spoke the language of Ashdod and the language of those various peoples, and did not care (נכר *hiphil*)[23] to speak Judean (יהודית)" (Neh 13:24). The issue is obviously the different ethnic origin of the women and the fact that their children speak the language of their mothers. Yet these ethnic groups are close neighbors to the Judeans. The Philistine city of Ashdod, in Persian times the administrative center of the province of Ashdod, is situated west of Judah. Ammon and Moab are Judah's neighbors beyond the Jordan River in the northeast and east. It is unclear, however, what sort of language Ashdodite exactly is. It may be the non-Semitic Philistine language, or Nabatean, or Aramaic, which is close to Judean, that is, Hebrew.[24] The differences between the vernacular languages of these neighboring groups may have been quite small.[25] In arguing against intermarriage, Nehemiah refers to the religious tradition by connecting two texts (Neh 13:25–26). First, he alludes to the prohibition of intermarriage (Deut 7:3), assuming that his addressees would know its sanction, namely extinction from the land. Then he refers to King Solomon's foreign wives who caused him to sin (1 Kgs 11:3–8). Both traditions throw a negative light on marriage with other ethnic groups, which explains Nehemiah's conclusion that marrying "foreign" women (נכריות נשים) is a great evil and an unfaithful act against "our God" (Neh 13:27). The term נכריות (feminine plural, cf. the masculine singular נכרי) refers to persons outside the group, thus strangers. While this term often characterizes persons who are foreign, that is, belonging to a different nation, it also may mean "strangers" or "estranged" as Leah and Rachel call themselves vis-à-vis their father (Gen 31:15), or Job vis-à-vis his family (Job 19:15). Therefore, the term has to be specified by its given context. In the case of the Ashdodite, Ammonite, and Moabite women in Nehemiah 13:23, they are indeed ethnically different from Judeans. The daughter of Sanballat the Horonite (Neh 13:28), who as governor of the province of Samaria opposed Nehemiah's efforts to rebuild Jerusalem's city wall (Neh 2:10, 19; 4 passim), however, is not necessarily foreign. The clan name *Horonite* may refer either to the upper or lower Beth-Horon, two settlements close to Jerusalem (Josh 16:3, 5), which belong to Yehud, or to the Moabite Horonaim (Isa 15:5; Jer 48:3). In light of this unclear origin, naming Sanballat, whose Babylonian name *Sîn-uballiṭ* means "Sin (the moon god) gives life," *the Horonite* may be a rhetorical move to characterize him as non-Judean.[26]

Nehemiah's sanctions against the men who had intermarried seem emotional and violent at the same time, and he distinguishes between the priest and lay persons. The latter are censured, cursed, flogged, their hair torn out, and adjured by God (Neh 13:25)—actions that amount to public shaming. The priestly son, however, receives a harsher treatment. He is expelled, apparently from his service in the temple because he has "polluted the priesthood" (Neh 13:29). Nehemiah summarizes both sanctions in the statement, "I cleansed them from everything foreign," and adds that he rearranged the duties of priests and Levites (Neh 13:30). Thus, his actions against intermarriage seem to be targeted especially at the independence and "unspoiled" pedigree of the priesthood.

Reading Nehemiah 13:13–24 Intersectionally

Nehemiah's account offers not much help in assessing the interrelations between gender, ethnicity, and religion. Neither the women nor their husbands mentioned in the Nehemiah memoir have a voice; thus their self-understanding is not revealed to the reader. Although the men are publicly humiliated, Nehemiah does not demand that they divorce their wives. Whereas the Ashdodite, Moabite, and Ammonite women belong to a different ethnos, this is unclear with regard to Sanballat's daughter. Why are marriages of Judean women with "foreign" men not mentioned at all? The reason for the text's focus on "foreign" women lies in the structure of the society at that time, its patrilineal inheritance, and patrilocal custom. Land property was passed on to sons who stayed with their family of origin.[27] Women, however, were required to leave their family and live in the hometown of their husband's kin; they would not inherit land and, in the case of exogamous marriage, would not count any longer as Judeans. Since marriages often establish political ties, especially among leading families, it is highly probable that in the Persian period, the leading families of the rather small provinces would intermarry to increase their property and influence. A good example is Sanballat's daughter, who married a descendant of the high priest of Jerusalem. In terms of this perspective, Nehemiah's eviction of her husband looks like a political action against Nehemiah's personal opponent Sanballat (cf. Neh 4).

Nothing is said in the text concerning whether these women's religion was any different from the veneration of Yнwн, the Israelite deity. Yet, one argument can be drawn indirectly from Nehemiah's reasoning with the religious tradition of his audience. His allusion to the prohibition of marriage with the people native to the land in Deuteronomy 7 implies that these groups worshipped other deities. According to Deuteronomy 7:4–5, these peoples' gods, altars, and cult images are the main reason for the prohibition of intermarriage. Also in the narrative about Solomon's foreign wives, the king's sin is portrayed as abandonment of Yнwн and veneration of the deities of his wives' ethnic groups—the Phoenician goddess Ashtoreth, the Ammonite god Milcom, the Moabite Chemosh, and the Ammonite Molech are explicitly listed (1 Kgs 11:5–8). Thus, "foreign" wives are associated with a different religious practice related to their ethnic origin. Against this background, be it a cliché or an actual practice, Nehemiah's point about the language of the children becomes more intelligible. To master the language of a specific ethnic group also includes knowledge and dissemination of its religious tradition. This is highly important for Judah, because in Persian and Hellenistic times, Aramaic gradually replaced Hebrew as a spoken language, as attested by documents and everyday correspondence.[28] The Torah, the Mosaic Law, however, was still read in Hebrew, as is the custom to this day in Jewish synagogues. Nehemiah 8 narrates Ezra's public reading of the Torah and its explanation by several men who are Levites (Neh 8:7–8). This explanation may not only include the teaching of the Torah, but may also refer to a practice that was later codified in the Targum, namely, the ad hoc translation from Hebrew to Aramaic.[29] Now, if the children born of "foreign" women did not understand Hebrew any more, their religious education would be impeded.

Similarly, Nehemiah's expulsion of Sanballat's son-in-law makes more sense when the contemporary religious contest between Jerusalem and Samaria is taken into consideration. Excavations on Mount Gerizim, which continues to be the Samaritans' holy place, revealed a building from the fifth century BCE that is interpreted as a temple of Yнwн due to some of the ceramics, coins, and inscriptions (among them one with the tetragrammaton) found at this site.[30] Therefore, the marriage of a woman from Samaria to a descendant of Jerusalem's high priest would yield legitimate priests for the service of Yнwн. From a Judean point of view, however, a rival temple and priesthood outside of Jerusalem would be outrageous.

In sum, in Nehemiah's actions against Judean men who married women of other ethnic groups, one may discern an effort toward, or at least the idea of, establishing Judah as an ethnically, religiously, and politically autonomous entity.

While leading families in Yehud may seek to gain influence through intermarriage with elite groups of the neighboring provinces, Nehemiah plays the religious card that opts for a general staying away "from everything foreign" (Neh 13:30). That Nehemiah's position is not shared by everybody may be gleaned from the fact that there is no word of divorce. Obviously, Nehemiah has the power to dismiss a son of the high priest's family from the temple service, but not to forcibly divorce the incriminated marriages.

The Crisis Regarding Intermarriage in the Time of Ezra

Ezra 9–10 narrates an episode of Ezra's mission in Jerusalem, the dispute over intermarriage, of which some returnees from the Golah are accused. Being the narrator of the event, Ezra is first outraged, then prays to God, fasts, and finally addresses the problem by appointing groups of officials, elders, and judges to adjudicate intermarriage cases locally.

A closer look at the two chapters reveals that there are different positions about intermarriage, some of which are legitimized by references to the Torah. With regard to terminology, style, genre, and ideological position, my analysis is indebted to Yonina Dor's study. She distinguishes two narrative accounts (Ezra 10:7–44; 10:2–6) from Ezra's prayer in 9:6–15, which is framed by Ezra 9:1–5 and 10:1, the latter verse linking the prayer to Chapter 10. Dor plausibly argues that the two stories reflect an actual debate, whereas the prayer deals with the issue in a general way by explicitly citing the Torah.[31] I analyze these passages in their current sequence to carve out the dramatic presentation of the plot as well as its tensions.

Introduction to the Situation (Ezra 9:1–5; 10:1)

Ezra 9:1–5 introduces the situation of crisis with a general verdict on the whole community and an allusion to the Torah. Ezra reports:

> After these things had been done, the officials approached me and said, "The people of Israel and the priests and the Levites have not separated [בדל *niphal*] themselves from the peoples of the lands [עמי הארצות] with their abominations, from the Canaanites, the Hittites, the Perizzites, the Jebusites, the Ammonites, the Moabites, the Egyptians, and the Amorites. For they have taken some of their daughters as wives for themselves and for their sons. Thus the holy seed [זרע הקדש] has mixed itself with the peoples of the lands, and in this faithlessness the officials and leaders have led the way." (Ezra 9:1-2)

According to the officials' report, the whole community has breached Deuteronomy 7's divine prohibition of intermarriage by marrying daughters of other ethnic groups. This list of peoples, however, is unique since it combines several traditions. From the well-known Deuteronomistic list of seven foreign nations (Deut 7:1; cf.

Exod 3:8, 17; Josh 3:10, et al.), Ezra 9:1 refers to five ethnic groups (Canaanites, Hittites, Perizzites, Jebusites, and Amorites).[32] The two neighbors of Judah, the Ammonites and Moabites, are the ones who according to Deuteronomy 23:4 (23:3 NRSV) are not allowed to join Yʜᴡʜ's community, although intermarriage is not forbidden. The Egyptians do not appear in any such list, but may be identified with the offspring of those Judeans who fled to Egypt after Jerusalem's destruction (cf. Jer 41:16–18).[33] Therefore, the author combines peoples from an earlier tradition (as reflected in Deuteronomy 7), who no longer exist, with some groups that are contemporaneous to the author of Ezra-Nehemiah. The argument that marriage with these "peoples of the land" would intersperse the holy seed combines the motif of Abraham's seed (Gen 12:7; 21:12; cf. Isa 41:8) with the idea of the holy people (Deut 7:6; 14:2, 21).[34] The term *holy seed* (זרע הקדש) is used only here and in Isaiah 6:13, where it represents a tenth of Israel who remained in the land during exile and is compared to the stump of a felled tree.[35] The verb *to separate* (בדל *niphal* and *hiphil*) is a key word in Leviticus that advocates the separation between holy and profane, pure and impure.

In sum, Ezra 9:1–2 formulates a separatist position that relates Israelite ethnicity to divine election and purity, thus arguing that those Judeans who observe strict boundaries to all other groups are the legitimate heirs of Abraham.[36] Intermarriage is only a consequence of deficient separation. Obviously, ethnicity is here defined primarily by a religious idea, divine election, and exclusive relation to Yʜᴡʜ. Yet, Israel's holiness is not an essence or status, but contingent on religious behavior,[37] namely, separation from the other peoples' religious practices, here disparagingly called "abominations." Positively stated, Israel's holiness depends on exclusive worship of Yʜᴡʜ and strict in-group relations. Compared to Nehemiah 13, the threat of losing one's identity is deepened and expanded since any out-group relation carries the hazard of assimilation. As Katherine Southwood says it well, "priestly, genealogical, and ethnic endogamy are transferred onto the entire community."[38]

To this massive insult Ezra reacts with grand gestures: he mourns by tearing his garment, pulling hair from his head and beard, and sitting appalled until the time of the evening offering (Ezra 9:3–4). Then, he utters a penitential prayer in the name of the people (Ezra 9:6–15). It is noteworthy that two different groups are mentioned: in Ezra 9:4, "all who trembled [כל חרד] at the words of the God of Israel, because of the faithlessness of the returned exiles [Golah, הגולה]" gather around the mourning Ezra. Sharing his shock and mourning, this group approves of Ezra's reaction. The term החרדים (*hā-ḥărēdîm*), those who "tremble" in Isaiah 66:2, 5, refers to people who are God-fearing and fervently pious.[39] While Ezra is praying at the time of the evening offering, "a very large assembly [קהל] of Israelites gathered around him, men, women, and children" (Ezra 10:1). This assembly is often mentioned in Ezra-Nehemiah as the body who is informed and sometimes decides upon matters of public interest (Ezra 10:12, 14; Neh 5:13; 8:2). Thus, the persons involved slowly increase. First there are the presumably male officials and Ezra, who are then joined by the *ḥărēdîm*, and finally by a large assembly of mixed gender.

Ezra's Prayer Acknowledges the Guilt (Ezra 9:6–15)

Ezra's prayer does not use the specific terminology for intermarriage employed in Ezra 9 or 10, but rather Deuteronomistic language and thought.[40] The guilt of Israel's ancestors led into captivity and exile, but God left a "remnant" that is allowed to rebuild Jerusalem and its temple, although as slaves and due to the mercy of the Persian rulers. The prayer characterizes the return of the Golah as renewed inhabitation of the land that was defiled by the peoples of the lands (הארצות עמי), but is now Israel's heritage, granted by God. The allusion to the prohibition of intermarriage (Deut 7:3) and to the commandment never to seek the peace or prosperity of the land's inhabitants (Deut 23:7) is presented as God's orders. Therefore, Ezra's prayer corresponds to a halachic Midrash to Deuteronomy 7:3.[41]

The land is designated "unclean" due to the pollutions of the peoples of the land by a term that refers to female impurity (ארץ נדה, v. 11).[42] The "impure" land contrasts with the "holy seed" in Ezra 9:2, and the call to separate from the peoples of the land implies that the land then will be purified. Because the land is further characterized as a divine gift to those who just entered it (Ezra 9:11), that is, the returnees from Babylonia, the prayer excludes all Judeans who were not exiled and counts them among the discriminated "peoples of the lands." Thus, the prayer excludes not only ethnically different groups but also a group that is Judean by descent.[43] By naming the intermarriage a breach of divine commandments (Ezra 9:14), the prayer acknowledges the guilt and its possible consequence, namely, the extinction from the land, without even asking for God's mercy. In sum, Ezra 9 provides the exclusionist lens that influences the reader's perception of the following narrative.

An Oath as Solution (Ezra 10:2–6)

Suddenly a certain Shecaniah, son of Jehiel, of Elamite descent, stands up and utters a collective confession of guilt. He proposes to make a covenant with God by promising "to bring out" or "to lead out" (יצא hiphil) the women and their children "according to the counsel of my lord and of those who tremble at the commandment of our God" (Ezra 10:3). Finally, he urges Ezra to be brave and take action (Ezra 10:4). After this speech, Ezra has the leaders of the priests, of the Levites, and of the people[44] swear this oath and then withdraws to the chamber of a son of the high priest in the temple to fast and mourn (Ezra 10:5–6).

This episode introduces some gaps and tensions into the context that point at different authors: given the allusion to the god-fearing followers of Ezra (cf. Ezra 10:3 with 9:4), Shecaniah seems to side with their separatist position. Jehiel's name, however, appears in the list of those who intermarried (Ezra 10:26) so that Shecaniah— at least on the level of the story—is a son of such an incriminated marriage and therefore would be affected by the measures that he proposes.[45] A second tension is created by the verb יצא hiphil (to bring out), which is frequently used in the Exodus formula (Exod 6:6, 27; 20:2; Deut 4:20; 5:6, etc.). In Ezra 10:3, however, the context implies a negative connotation—hence the common translation "to expel, to send away, to dismiss" (RSV, NRSV, NAB, JPS). Since in Chapter 9 Ezra is determined to solve the problem, Shecaniah's encouragement in Ezra 10:4 seems unnecessary. And finally, it remains unclear why Ezra fasts after the issue has been decided. If, according to Ezra 10:5, only the officials responsible for the different groups take this oath, the following passage narrates Ezra's effort to implement this decision. If one reads from Ezra 10:1, which has the people's assembly being present at the oath, the following is yet another attempt at solving the issue.

Generating a List as Solution (Ezra 10:7–44)

Ezra 10:7–44 does not mention the oath and narrates the debate about intermarriage in yet another terminology. First, "all the sons of the Golah" (v. 7) are called to assemble at Jerusalem and threatened with exclusion from the community should they not appear. So "all the men of Judah and Benjamin" gathered (v. 9). This double reference presumes that there are only returned exiles living in Judah and Benjamin, that is, in the territory of Yehud. As in Ezra's prayer, Judeans who were not exiled are implicitly excluded from the community. Ezra, introduced as priest (Ezra 10:10, 16; cf. Neh 8:2), accuses the men who have "settled" (יֹשֵׁ *hiphil*)[46] "foreign" women of acting unfaithfully (מעל, v. 10); he demands that they separate (בדל *niphal*) from the peoples of the land and the women (v. 11). The assembly fully agrees, asking that local judicatory bodies be appointed to identify the offenders in each town. Four men who oppose this procedure are named; their opposition does not succeed (v. 15). The appointed groups work for three months and finally provide a list of 110 names of men who had married "foreign" women, among them priests, Levites, temple singers, gatekeepers, and lay persons (vv. 18–43). The list is appended to the story. Only men of the high priest's family (cf. Ezra 2:36; 3:2) are said to pledge that they would "bring out" (יצא *hiphil*) their wives and dedicate a ram as guilt offering (v. 19).[47]

In most English Bibles, the last sentence in Ezra 10:44 reads, "all these had married foreign women, and they sent them away with their children" (RSV, NRSV, NAB, NJB). The Masoretic Text, however, does not state any separation but offers the rather cryptic line, "All these had taken foreign women, among them some women, with whom they had set children."[48] The difference is based on a text-critical decision. Although the Masoretic Text is supported by the Old Greek and Syriac translations as well as the Vulgate, the Greek parallel in 1 Esdras 9:36 is often preferred.[49] This version, however, differs in several aspects and in this verse is an adaptation to the context.[50] Thus, in the original Hebrew text, the plot in Ezra 9–10 remains open-ended, and only some priests pledge to send away their wives (Ezra 10:18–19). In sum, Ezra's effort to implement a rigorist endogamous marriage practice in Yehud was not successful.[51]

Reading Ezra 9–10 Intersectionally

The question of ethnic origin is again at the heart of the narrated debate, yet the texts do not specify exactly which women belong to the "peoples of the land" (Ezra 10:2, 11).

In the Hebrew Bible, the singular expression עם הארץ (people of the land) initially referred to the rural population. Due to the social differentiation of Judah's society in later preexilic times, this term included, in fact, only the land-owning rich of the rural towns, often called *landed gentry*.[52] In this sense, עם הארץ is also used in Ezra 4:4 for a group of Judeans who oppose the rebuilding of the temple. In Ezra-Nehemiah and Chronicles, there are similar expressions, which in their current context all carry a negative connotation: עמי הארץ are other ethnic groups living in Yehud, from which the audience is to be separated (Ezra 10:2, 11). The double plural עמי הארצות (peoples of the lands) is used in Nehemiah 10:29; Ezra 3:3; 9:1, 11; and 2 Chronicles 32:13 together with key words such as separation, veneration of other deities, and defilement of the land. Thus, in Ezra-Nehemiah and Chronicles, these peoples no longer comprise the land-owning leading families, but the terms serve as excluding ethnic markers to segregate groups.

As discussed later in this essay, the texts' ideologies not only exclude groups that are actually of different ethnic origin, such as the neighboring Moabites and Ammonites (Ezra 9:1), but also Judeans who in exilic times fled to Egypt—and are now called "Egyptians" (Ezra 9:1)—or stayed in the land of Judah and now implicitly belong to the "peoples of the land" (Ezra 10:7, 9). In contrast, those who oppose intermarriage self-identify as sons of the Golah (Ezra 10:16)—among them Ezra, the envoy of the Persian king. Within this group the text distinguishes a particular pious subgroup of *ḥārēdîm*, "those who tremble at God's word" (9:4; 10:3). This group has a separatist position and defines ethnicity as strongly linked to Israelite religious tradition, especially its divine election. They follow, like Ezra's prayer, the exilic Deuteronomistic line of thought that the exile is God's punishment for their trespassing of his commandments. In line of this thinking, the repatriated sons of the Golah are God's remnant who will again inherit the land. The cited biblical passages propagate the exclusive worship of Yhwh and strict separation from all groups deemed "foreign." As in Nehemiah 13, ethnicity is primarily defined by religious practice. In contrast to Nehemiah's account, however, one can detect competing identity claims in Ezra 9–10 as well as in a dispute about political influence in Yehud.

Reading these texts with a hermeneutics of suspicion, one may see that both the separatist and the particularistic perspectives on ethnicity draw clear boundaries both outside and inside the community—probably because they did not exist in reality. In contrast to this literary witness to ethnic separation within Judah, historical studies about Persian-period Yehud argue that the province had a mixed population with groups of different ethnic origin.[53] In the middle of the fifth century BCE, after almost fifty years of Babylonian and about eighty years of Persian hegemony, these different groups certainly did not live in separation but were bonded by marriage, which in the case of the leading families was based on political considerations. The even more extreme position of in-group separation, that is, a separation of repatriated Golah members from Judeans whose ancestors were not exiled, is historically even more implausible. It is therefore an ideology based on religious claims that serves the building of an identity, in which case ethnicity and religion are closely linked. Before

I try to explore possible reasons for this ideology, I analyze the intersection of ethnicity and gender.

Considering the category of gender, in Ezra 9–10 the hierarchy is obvious.[54] It is the "foreign" women who are deemed to be the problem (Ezra 10 passim), the daughters of the "peoples of the lands" (Ezra 9:2), although the cited religious tradition speaks of women and men as potential marriage partners (Ezra 9:14; cf. Deut 7:3). Moreover, the people who speak and act are all men. Women as part of the audience are mentioned only once in Ezra 10:1—a verse that frames Ezra's prayer and links it to the following episode in what is probably a late insertion. Due to this link, women of the Judean community seem to be present at the oath ceremony and conceivably in accordance with the expulsion of the "foreign" women. Yet, neither these women nor the women excluded as "foreigners" speak, and therefore their views play no role. The discrimination against the "foreign" women is threefold: they are deemed to be outsiders with regard to gender, ethnicity, and religion and therefore denied the status of wives of the returnees from the Golah. The unusual terminology of "settling them" (Ezra 10:10), "bringing them out" (Ezra 10:3, 19), and "setting children" (Ezra 10:44) probably serves to diminish their marital status. Despite the differing language in Ezra 9 and 10 with regard to ideology, all the positions presented in Ezra 9–10 discriminate against "foreign" women.

The extreme separatist position in Ezra 9:1–5, 6–15 presents a dualistic gender construction by contrasting the masculine holy seed with the feminine polluted land. The group around Ezra, named *ḥārēdîm*, radicalizes the priestly concept and stigmatizes the "peoples of the lands" as the feminine Other. The female menstruating body serves to construe the impure, and thus women even signify the stranger within the community.[55]

As for the men affected by the accusations and the measures proposed, most of them have no voice either. There are only four men who oppose the commonly accepted procedure (Ezra 10:15). Shecaniah, supposedly a son of intermarriage, even serves as a protagonist of the separatist view and advocates in favor of expelling the women and their children (Ezra 10:2). Yet, there is an interesting distinction among the men between priests and laypersons. It is the priests, especially those from the high priest's family, whose repentance is in focus and whose guilt offering is mentioned (Ezra 10:19). In Ezra 10:5, the Levites as lower clergy seem to stand between both groups. Yet, with regard to the solution, the Levites are not treated differently from the laypeople.

Reading the Story from Different Perspectives

My intersectional analysis of Nehemiah 13:23–31 and Ezra 9–10, based on a synchronic reading of the texts, yielded several ideological positions and different arguments against marriage with "foreign" women. I would like to underline three results: first, the tensions and gaps within Ezra 9–10 as well as the different terminology hint at different authors. Although there are some similarities with regard to the reasoning, the passage of Nehemiah's memoir has to be attributed to yet another author. Second, in all passages, the argumentation foregrounds a specific view on the issue and other views are not mentioned, with one exception in Ezra 10:15. Thus, the passages do not offer a debate with pro and contra arguments, but three powerful voices of Nehemiah, Ezra, and Shecaniah. Third, the intersection of gender, ethnicity, and religion is at play in all of the texts cited above. Although ethnicity is related to descent, it is closely linked to religion and specifically to religious practice (cf. Neh 13:23–27; Ezra 9:1–2, 6–15). While most of the passages share the bias against "foreign" women who are said to turn their husbands away from Yhwh and the Judean practice of religion, Ezra 9:1–2 foregrounds a complete separation from the neighboring groups. In addition, Nehemiah 13:24 advances the Hebrew language argument and implies that Hebrew is crucial to religious education.

In terms of a hermeneutics of suspicion, the ideology of these texts may be easily deconstructed—and my analysis has already presented some arguments—by pointing to the tensions and gaps as well as to a diachronic development and by contrasting the sociohistorical context in Persian-period Yehud. Thus, a historical-critical perspective reveals that although these positions against intermarriage are hegemonic in their literary context, historically they were at the margin.

From a feminist perspective, I tried to deconstruct the texts' ideology by revealing the threefold discrimination against "foreign" women, in which their gender is basic to the issue of marriage but indissolubly linked with aspects of ethnicity and religion. In retrospect, the postmodern distinction between ethnicity and religion seems rather problematic in terms of the analysis of these ancient texts, since ethnicity is a cultural construct based on common descent and religious practice, as well as common history and customs. While I would argue that any discrimination is to be revealed and resisted, be it only in thought or in practice, the evaluation of its power and outreach hinges on the question of how plausible it was in historical terms. If my analysis so far has revealed how and through which arguments the texts' authors tried to stop intermarriage, the question of why they did so is still open. While no one can say for sure what the Judeans in the time of Nehemiah and Ezra actually thought and did, I would argue that the texts would not have been passed down if the positions were not plausible for ancient readers. For postmodern readers, however, including myself, the arguments against intermarriage are unconvincing and discriminatory, and thus the texts do not offer guidance for similar situations today.

From a postcolonial perspective, however, both the particularistic and the separatist ideology appear more reasonable if one studies the power relations and dependencies of people subjected to imperialist regimes. The thesis that the opposition to intermarriage was initiated by the Persians has been proposed already in historical studies. For instance, Kenneth Hoglund argues that the Persian policy aimed at establishing regions with a population defined in ethnic terms throughout the empire, which would cultivate land that could be controlled and taxed.[56] The Golah community served as an economically viable example, and its concern for ethnic and religious purity also sustained its claim to land. Lisbeth

Fried supports this view when she argues that Nehemiah and Ezra were Persian officials who tried to implement a Persian agenda, but the Judeans considered them to be representatives of the occupying power.[57] Daniel Smith-Christopher argues that the Babylonian exiles developed and maintained a particular religious and social identity out of necessity, and after their return to Judah, Ezra and his group held a minority position that advocated endogamous marriage relations against the common practice of intermarriage.[58]

A postcolonial perspective, especially Bhabha's analysis of the relation between colonizer and colonized, brings to this discourse a heightened awareness of the political pressures and a blurring of the reasons for adaptation. What Bhabha defined as *mimicry*, the attempt to be like the colonizers, may also be applied to the repatriates, the sons of the Golah. Because they could return due to Persian policy, they may be loyal to the new hegemonic power. A hint of this is the benevolent portrayal of the Persian kings in Ezra's prayer (Ezra 9:9). Since Ezra-Nehemiah in its entirety portrays the collaboration between Persian authorities and the sons of the Golah as effective and successful—although challenged by several other groups—the authors can be characterized as collaborators of the imperialist policy. This is not to denounce them, but to understand their in-between space, their hybrid situation, better.

To discuss this perspective further, more texts from Ezra-Nehemiah need to be analyzed. With regard to Nehemiah 13 and Ezra 9–10, it is important for me that these—from my feminist viewpoint—utterly unconvincing and discriminatory arguments against intermarriage are the product of a sociopolitical situation that I have never experienced and can hardly imagine. The postcolonial lens thus challenges my feminist indignation and my inclination to dismiss the texts as misogynist and racist. From a postcolonial perspective these texts are part of how the Judeans "narrated their nation," a story that evidently is ambivalent and oscillating between collaboration with and resistance to the imperialist Persian Empire.

Notes

1. I use quotation marks throughout to note that foreignness is a social construct often used to exclude people.
2. Kimberlé W. Crenshaw, "Demarginalizing the Intersection of Race and Sex: A Black Feminist Critique of Antidiscrimination Doctrine, Feminist Theory, and Antiracist Politics," *University of Chicago Legal Forum* (1989): 139–67.
3. See, e.g., the statement of the Combahee River Collective issued in 1977, available at http://historyisaweapon.com/defcon1/combrivercoll.html, accessed January 27, 2015; bell hooks, *Ain't I a Woman? Black Women and Feminism* (Boston: South End Press, 1981).
4. Patricia Hill Collins, "It's All in the Family: Intersections of Gender, Race, and Nation," *Hypatia* 13/3 (1998): 62–82 (63).
5. Elisabeth Schüssler Fiorenza, *Wisdom Ways: Introducing Feminist Biblical Interpretation* (Maryknoll, NY: Orbis Books, 2001), 175. Schüssler Fiorenza has

substituted the common word *androcentric* by *kyriocentric*, which means "centered on the *kyrios*," i.e., the master or lord (211).

6. At least this is the definition of Hellenic identity by the Greek historian Herodotus (*Hist.* 8,144,2) and has become the proof text for defining ethnicity in Greek antiquity; cf. Katerina Zacharia, "Herodotus' Four Markers of Greek Identity," in *Hellenisms: Culture, Identity, and Ethnicity from Antiquity to Modernity*, ed. Katerina Zacharia (Aldershot: Ashgate, 2008), 21–36.

7. Anthony D. Smith, *The Ethnic Revival in the Modern World* (Cambridge: Cambridge University Press, 1981), 66.

8. Shaye J. D. Cohen, *The Beginnings of Jewishness: Boundaries, Varieties, Uncertainties* (Berkeley: University of California Press, 1999), 5–7.

9. Cohen, *Beginnings of Jewishness*, 104–5.

10. Cohen, *Beginnings of Jewishness*, 109–39.

11. Denise Kimber Buell, *Why This New Race: Ethnic Reasoning in Early Christianity* (New York: Columbia University Press, 2005), 6–10.

12. Buell, *Why This New Race*, 9; similarly Cohen, *Beginnings of Jewishness*, 7.

13. This is not to say that the discourse on ethnic boundaries is novel. See, e.g., the discussion in Tamara Cohn Eskenazi and Eleanore P. Judd, "Marriage to a Stranger in Ezra 9–10," in *Second Temple Studies 2: Temple and Community in the Persian Period*, ed. Tamara Cohn Eskenazi and Kent H. Richards, JSOTSup 175 (Sheffield: JSOT Press, 1994), 266–85 (272–75); Willa M. Johnson, *The Holy Seed Has Been Defiled: The Interethnic Marriage Dilemma in Ezra 9–10* (Sheffield: Sheffield Phoenix, 2011), 20–1.

14. Edward W. Said, *Culture and Imperialism* (London: Chatto & Windsor, 1993), 8; similarly Fernando F. Segovia, "Mapping the Postcolonial Optic in Biblical Criticism: Meaning and Scope," in *Postcolonial Biblical Criticism: Interdisciplinary Intersections*, ed. Stephen D. Moore and Fernando F. Segovia (New York: T&T Clark, 2005), 23–78 (40).

15. See Homi K. Bhabha, *The Location of Culture* (London: Routledge, 1994), 122–5.

16. Bhabha, *Location of Culture*, 121–31, 153–6.

17. Bhabha, *Location of Culture*, 123 (italics in original).

18. Homi K. Bhabha, ed., *Nation and Narration* (London: Routledge, 1990), 1–7; the introduction written by Bhabha is titled "Narrating the Nation." His essay "DissemiNation: Time, Narrative, and the Margins of the Modern Nation," 291–322, appears as Chapter 8 in his book *Location of Culture*, 199–244.

19. Bhabha, *Nation and Narration*, 4.

20. The Old Greek had one book; the Greek tradition began to distinguish two books from the third century CE onward, first attested in Origen's writings. The Old Greek also includes several writings associated with the name of Ezra. The Vulgate (fourth century CE) also has two books. Cf. John J. Collins, *Introduction to the Hebrew Bible* (Minneapolis: Fortress, 2004), 427–8.

21. For an overview of the different proposals and arguments see H. G. M. Williamson, *Ezra, Nehemiah*, WBC 16 (Nashville: Nelson, 1985), xxxix–xliv; for the dating followed here see Lisbeth S. Fried, *Ezra: A Commentary* (Sheffield: Sheffield Phoenix, 2015), 198–9, 304–5, 395.

22. Some scholars regard "Ammonite and Moabite" in Nehemiah 13:23 as a gloss, since the terms have no copula and the next verse names only the Ashdodite language. The glossator may have explained the single reference to Ashdodite by the well-known neighbors of Judah. Cf. Williamson, *Ezra, Nehemiah*, 397.

23. Following the translation of Ingo Kottsieper, "'And They Did Not Care to Speak Yehudit:' On Linguistic Change in Judah during the Late Persian Era," in *Judah and the Judeans in the Fourth Century B. C. E.*, ed. Oded Lipschits, Gary N. Knoppers, and Rainer Albertz (Winona Lake, IN: Eisenbrauns, 2007), 95–124 (100).

24. Cf. Kottsieper, "Speak Yehudit," 100–1. 2 Kings 18:26, 28; 2 Chronicles 32:18; and Isaiah 36:11, 13 distinguish Judean/Hebrew from Aramaic. Cf. also Williamson, *Ezra, Nehemiah*, 398.

25. Cf. Johannes Thon, "Sprache und Identitätskonstruktion: Das literarische Interesse von Neh 13, 23–27 und die Funktion dieses Textes im wissenschaftlichen Diskurs," *ZAW* 121 (2009): 557–76 (574).

26. Cf. Williamson, *Ezra, Nehemiah*, 182–3. Kessler also doubts that Sanballat and his daughter worshipped a god different from Yʜᴡʜ. Cf. Rainer Kessler, "Die interkulturellen Ehen im perserzeitlichen Juda," in *Moderne Religionsgeschichte im Gespräch: Interreligiös—interkulturell—interdisziplinär. Festschrift Christoph Elsas*, ed. Adelheid Herrmann-Pfandt (Berlin: EB-Verlag, 2010), 276–94 (283).

27. Cf. Sara Japhet, "The Expulsion of the Foreign Women (Ezra 9–10): The Legal Basis, Precedents, and Consequences for the Definition of Jewish Identity," in *"Sieben Augen auf einem Stein" (Sach 3,9): Studien zur Literatur des Zweiten Tempels. Festschrift Ina Willi-Plein*, ed. Friedhelm Hartenstein and Michael Pietsch (Neukirchen-Vluyn: Neukirchener Verlag, 2007), 141–61 (150). Only if there are no sons may daughters inherit, and only under the condition that they marry within their patrilineal kinship group; cf. the postexilic additions in Numbers 27 and 36.

28. This is the mainstream view. For a critical evaluation, see Thon, "Sprache," 557–61.

29. For this interpretation, see Jacob M. Myers, *Ezra. Nehemiah*, AB 14 (Garden City, NY: Doubleday, 1965), 154. This is also the rabbinic interpretation in b. Meg. 3a; for other interpretations cf. Joseph Blenkinsopp, *Ezra-Nehemiah: A Commentary*, OTL (London: SCM, 1988), 288.

30. See Yitzhak Magen, "The Dating of the First Phase of the Samaritan Temple on Mount Gerizim in Light of the Archaeological Evidence," in *Judah and the Judeans in the Fourth Century B. C. E.*, ed. Oded Lipschits, Gary N. Knoppers, and Rainer Albertz (Winona Lake, IN: Eisenbrauns, 2007), 157–93 (166–83).

31. See Yonina Dor, "The Composition of the Episode of the Foreign Women in Ezra IX–X," *VT* 53 (2003): 26–47. She offers a source and redaction-critical assessment. Even if one reads the text synchronically, the differences are perceptible and her observations valid.

32. Fried, *Ezra*, 363, points to a change in the meaning of *Amorites*. In Assyrian texts, the name refers to all the Western people in the Levant; in Persian-period Babylonian texts, the term refers to North Arabia. The different meanings may explain the fact that *Amorites* closes the list and is linked to the author's contemporaries, not to the peoples cited from Deuteronomy 7, who disappeared.

33. Williamson, *Ezra, Nehemiah*, 131, proposes that the reference to the Egyptians takes up Leviticus 18:3: "You shall not do as they do in the land of Egypt, where you lived, and you shall not do as they do in the land of Canaan, to which I am bringing you."

34. Cf. Williamson, *Ezra, Nehemiah*, 132.

35. Cf. Fried, *Ezra*, 365–6.

36. Cf. Katherine Southwood, "The Holy Seed: The Significance of Endogamous Boundaries and Their Transgression in Ezra 9–10," in *Judah and the Judeans in the Achaemenid Period: Negotiating Identity in an International Context*, ed. Oded

Lipschits, Gary N. Knoppers, and Manfred Oeming (Winona Lake, IN: Eisenbrauns, 2001), 189–224 (199–200).

37. Cf. Fried, *Ezra*, 365.

38. Southwood, "Holy Seed," 201.

39. In modern Israel, *ḥārēdîm* is a term for ultra-orthodox Jewish movements, which flourished under the British Mandate, especially its political pressure to create a Jewish religious authority, the Chief Rabbinate. Cf. Eskenazi and Judd, "Marriage to a Stranger," 279–85, who hint at similarities to the situation under Ezra, assuming colonial pressure and Jewish reaction. Blenkinsopp, *Ezra-Nehemiah*, 178–9, regards the *ḥārēdîm* as "a prophetic-eschatological group which espoused a rigorist interpretation of the law and which was out of favor with the religious leadership in the province."

40. According to Dor, "Composition," 30, the author deliberately chose this terminology to establish a new interpretation of intermarriage. She takes the prayer as an originally independent piece of work (44). Following Williamson, *Ezra, Nehemiah*, 128, I would argue that due to the contents of verses 8–9, 11–14, the prayer has been formulated with regard to its current context.

41. Following Dor, "Composition," 47.

42. Cf. Leviticus 12:5; 15:19; in Ezekiel 18:6 נדה refers to a menstruating woman. Ezra 9:11 alludes to Leviticus 18:24–30, a passage that describes the land's pollution as a consequence of sexual transgressions. The term נדה, however, is taken from Ezekiel 18:6. Cf. Harold C. Washington, "Israel's Holy Seed and the Foreign Women of Ezra-Nehemiah: A Kristevan Reading," *BibInt* 11 (2003): 427–37 (434–5).

43. So with Tamara Cohn Eskenazi, "The Missions of Ezra and Nehemiah," in *Judah and the Judeans in the Persian Period*, ed. Oded Lipschits and Manfred Oeming (Winona Lake, IN: Eisenbrauns, 2006), 509–29 (518). As Rom-Shiloni plausibly demonstrates, the rhetoric of exclusion that favors the repatriates over against those who remained in Judah is characteristic of Ezra-Nehemiah not only with regard to intermarriage. Cf. Dalit Rom-Shiloni, *Exclusive Inclusivity: Identity Conflicts Between the Exiles and the People Who Remained (6th–5th Centuries BCE)*, LHBOTS 543 (New York: Bloomsbury T&T Clark, 2013), 33–47.

44. The Hebrew text talks about officials set over the different groups. With regard to the assembly mentioned in Ezra 10:1, however, most translations and commentators assume that the entire people took this oath. Cf. Fried, *Ezra*, 394–5, who follows Dor in arguing that 10:1 was inserted later to connect Ezra's prayer (9:6–15) to the narrative. This would mean that in this scene (10:2–6) Ezra is surrounded by only a few Persian officials.

45. Fried, *Ezra*, 393–4, argues that Shecaniah has a Judean name and patronym, but came from Elam, a central province of Achaemenid Iran, and thus was probably a Persian official. Acknowledging that Jehiel appears in the list of men who had intermarried, she surmises that Jehiel had two wives and Shecaniah may have tried to remove his "foreign" stepmother and her children from his family. The fact that 1 Esdras 8:92 (see note 49) notes Shecaniah's pedigree as Israelite, not Elamite, demonstrates that the tension between Shecaniah's descent and his position against intermarriage was perceived early on.

46. The terminology ישׁב hiphil, literally "to cause to dwell" (Ezra 10:2, 10, 14, 17–18; Neh 13:23, 27), is highly unusual. Kessler, "Die interkulturellen Ehen," 284–5, argues that the semantics of the verb in this context mirrors the idea and perhaps practice of land property and inheritance. According to Japhet, "Expulsion," 153, the verb is used to

characterize these marriages as irregular. In contrast, Eskenazi, "Missions," 520–2, argues that the terminology indicates that the Judean men try to integrate their wives into the community by allotting land property to them.

47. Cf. Fried, *Ezra*, 409–10, who argues that this guilt offering implies an admission of guilt. The traditional custom in the case of divorce would be to repay the wife's father the full amount of the marriage contract plus one-fifth of it.

48. The use of the verb שׂים (to put, set) in the sense of *to beget* is unique. According to Japhet, "Expulsion," 153, the author invented the term to minimize the status of these children of mixed marriages.

49. 1 Esdras is a Greek translation of 2 Chronicles 35–36; Ezra 1–10; and Nehemiah 8:1–13, with some differences and additions; cf. Collins, *Introduction*, 428. Blenkinsopp, *Ezra-Nehemiah*, 200, favors the emendation of Ezra 10:44 according to 1 Esdras 9:36, yet finds it also possible that the author of 1 Esdras imposed his own meaning.

50. Cf. Williamson, *Ezra, Nehemiah*, 145; Fried, *Ezra*, 409, 412.

51. Similarly Blenkinsopp, *Ezra-Nehemiah*, 200–1.

52. Cf. Rainer Kessler, *The Social History of Israel: An Introduction*, trans. Linda M. Maloney (Minneapolis: Fortress, 2008), 98–100.

53. Cf. Daniel Smith-Christopher, "The Mixed Marriage Crisis in Ezra 9–10 and Nehemiah 13: A Study of the Sociology of the Post-Exilic Judean Community," in *Second Temple Studies 2: Temple and Community in the Persian Period*, ed. Tamara Cohn Eskenazi and Kent H. Richards, JSOTSup 175 (Sheffield: JSOT Press, 1994), 243–65 (269–70); Rainer Albertz, *Israel in Exile: The History and Literature of the Sixth Century B. C. E.*, trans. David Green, Studies in Biblical Literature 3 (Atlanta: SBL Press, 2003), 137–8; Kessler, *Social History*, 155–6.

54. For a similar feminist critique see Christiane Karrer-Grube, "Ezra and Nehemiah: The Return of the Others," in *Feminist Biblical Interpretation: A Compendium of Critical Commentary on the Books of the Bible and Related Literature*, ed. Luise Schottroff and Marie-Theres Wacker (Grand Rapids, MI: Eerdmans, 2012), 192–206.

55. Following Washington, "Holy Seed," 431; similarly Karrer-Grube, "Ezra and Nehemiah," 205.

56. Kenneth G. Hoglund, *Achaemenid Imperial Administration in Syria-Palestine and the Missions of Ezra and Nehemiah*, SBLDS 125 (Atlanta: Scholars Press, 1992), 231–40; cf. also Karrer-Grube, "Ezra and Nehemiah," 202.

57. Cf. Fried, *Ezra*, 17.

58. Cf. Smith-Christopher, "Mixed Marriage Crisis," 255–65.

PART III
INTERROGATING POWER

Chapter 7

THE VIOLENCE OF POWER AND THE POWER OF VIOLENCE: HYBRID, CONTEXTUAL PERSPECTIVES ON THE BOOK OF ESTHER

Marie-Theres Wacker

Toward a Hybrid, Contextual Theoretical Framework of Feminist Biblical Studies

Reflecting on my theoretical—methodological and hermeneutical—framework when reading the Bible puts me on a journey through nearly four decades of my life. I started as a rather classical historical-critical scholar in Old Testament from the University of Tübingen and its faculty of Catholic Theology, although the subject of my doctoral thesis did not touch upon one of the classical fields of research, but on the so-called intertestamental literature: I wrote on the Ethiopic book of Enoch, which, in fact, is not a book but a composition of very different pieces and whose linguistic tradition—fragments in Aramaic and Greek, a whole book in Ge'ez—blurs clear distinctions between text, source, and redaction criticism.[1] During the time of my doctoral studies, in the late 1970s, I spent one academic year at the École Biblique et Archéologique, the French Biblical School in Jerusalem, a year that confronted me with fantastic and at the same time challenging experiences. I lived in the Arab (former Jordanian) district of the city, in a politically complex situation between Palestine and Israel, at a wonderful place within a community of professors and students from five continents, myself being the only person from Germany—hence a multicultural diversity bringing us sometimes to the opaque aspects of difference.

When I in 1981 obtained my first academic position as a research and teaching assistant at a German university, my students urged me to take note of a new development: feminist theology. Quickly I found myself interested. Mary Daly's book *Beyond God the Father*, just translated into German,[2] opened my eyes, and I realized how deeply Christianity and its symbols were permeated with patriarchal power.[3] Methodologically, I decided to continue working along two lines in my further pursuit of biblical studies: one line had to be historical, on the religious history of ancient Israel, the reconstruction of its religion in different segments of its society, and the search for ancient women's spaces and practices.[4] In terms of this line of inquiry, I am aware of the hermeneutical circle of working on ancient texts with methods developed in modern times, and I am ready to reflect on the presuppositions of historical reconstructions in general, especially concerning silent, silenced, or distorted agents. I am also ready to renounce giving very precise dates in favor of at least an approximate narrowing down of the possible era of origin, but I feel I have to stick to that type of work as it links me with women's lives in cultures different from mine, and also with my own cultural and religious roots, nourishing roots and also poisoned roots, traditions that influence me whether I wish it or not and that have to be brought to consciousness within myself.

The second line of inquiry that I pursued, especially with regard to narrative biblical texts, is connected to a shift in my reading focus. Instead of primarily trying to identify different layers of a text to understand its historical evolution (source or redaction criticism), I moved on rather to reading the text as it stands now and to including methods of literary criticism, structural analysis, and narratology,[5] subsequently including intertextuality and reception history. These methods allowed for readily relating biblical texts to contemporary themes or problems, which constitutes the regular way feminist rereadings of the Bible were done and continue to be done. But again I did not want to renounce an in-depth understanding of a biblical text in its historical context. The text as it stands now comes from a world very different from mine, and I want to—I *have* to—listen to these distant voices before I can go on reading the text as a texture in explicit dialogue with problems in our own context. One reason for this is that I want to relate to these voices from the past, respecting the specific struggles hidden in the texts; another reason is that going back to the world behind the texts is one possible way to prevent fundamentalist, literal understanding, as one has to respect the difference between the first readers' understanding and that of oneself. But there is also a third reason that shapes this line of inquiry that pertains to a deep desire to learn more about the ideologies that ancient texts transmit.

In this regard, before I discovered the notion and the concepts of gender, I experienced a double controversy, which marked the 1980s in Germany. One controversy concerned racism in feminist theory and theology, pertaining to color blindness and exoticism, as one of the German feminist theologians of the day, Christine Schaumberger, puts it.[6] Women are different in their skin colors, a difference indicating a number of other differences according to contexts, and a feminism of the "White Lady," as Elisabeth Schüssler Fiorenza labeled it,[7] should not claim to speak in the name of all women. As I did some work with refugees from Eritrea at that time, I learned much about racism in my country, of well-meaning, stupid, and also aggressive forms, and I felt I had to know more about that community and their gender relations before being able to support these women, men, and children in their struggle to root themselves in their new context. I discovered that many of them were Roman Catholics, this forming between us a bridge of common experiences and values.

The other controversy starting in 1986 was centered on anti-Judaism in Christian feminist theology. I had some experience with Jewish studies during my time in Tübingen and knew about Christian anti-Judaism and modern anti-Semitism; however, I was surprised and sometimes shocked by the ignorance of some Christian feminist theologians in Germany who fell into the traps of such stereotypes or thought patterns.[8] I tried to learn more about Jewish feminist theology, and I began to develop a better sense for similarities to as well as differences from Christian feminism. There is not only the problem of the White Lady, but also the problem of Christian women silencing women of other religions! In the context of the commemoration of fifty years of the Reichspogromnacht/Kristallnacht pogroms (November 9–10, 1938) in Germany I carried out, together with my husband, a research project on the history of the Jewish community in the small town in which we were living at that time—one of the many Jewish communities erased in the Third Reich. We published our findings in a book,[9] which gave rise to much public dispute regarding our perceived arrogance as late-born youngsters, but also regarding our boldness in showing the everyday collaboration of all those citizens of that town, most of them Catholics, in the process of discrimination, persecution, and elimination of their Jewish neighbors, men, women, and children.

A deeper understanding of what the concept of gender comprises came through my collaboration with the practical theologian Stefanie Rieger-Goertz. Together we organized, in spring 2005, the first colloquium in a German-speaking country on masculinity studies in theology[10] including a wonderful tandem presentation about lesbian and gay theology—in the largest classroom of our Roman Catholic faculty at Münster. My contribution was on *ādām*, the first man according to Genesis 2, the first male, and the instability of his maleness.[11] Since then I have used gender perspectives to include masculinity studies and to sharpen Simone de Beauvoir's notion that we are not born women but made into them. My most recent attempt at an explicitly gendered approach is a study on the so-called Cycle of Elijah in 1 and 2 Kings. In this contribution, I also work with a queer perspective to understand the strange image of Elijah the hairy man in 2 Kings 1:8–9.[12] Queer studies help me to interrogate the matrix of a simple duality of sexes as well as the matrix of heteronormativity and to explore transgressions of the boundaries between the human and the animal.

Stephanie Feder, an expert on African biblical studies who also turned my attention to South African biblical studies on the book of Esther,[13] helped me to discover postcolonial theory. Together we studied some of the classics by which we found affirmed and theoretically underpinned the importance of decentering perspectives and deconstructing meanings, and which provided us with new analytic or descriptive categories, such as orientalism in literature, but also in sciences and politics (Edward Said);[14] the effects of colonialism on colonized people of color who take over white masks (Frantz Fanon);[15] the constraints of nationalism and the need to perceive, think, and construct a third space accepting hybridity (Homi Bhabha, who builds on both Said and Fanon);[16] and the multifaceted and not strictly class-related concept of (female) subalterns who cannot speak, or better, whose voices pass unheard within existing economic or cultural structures (Gayatri Chakravorty Spivak).[17] Musa Dube's fine book

Postcolonial Feminist Interpretation of the Bible[18] and her Rahab prism of analysis greatly helped us to apply postcolonial theory to biblical studies. For me it was rather a painful experience to embrace that prism and to understand—in the sense of perceiving and accepting as correct—that the Exodus-to-Joshua narrative of the Hebrew Bible reveals structures of colonialism. I tried to find out more about concepts of land in the Hebrew Bible[19] and the reception of such concepts in contemporary Christian-Palestinian and Jewish-Israeli approaches,[20] as I felt that such *receptions* influence our *perceptions* of what is at stake in the biblical texts. Postcolonial biblical studies involve the critical study of the reception or appropriation of biblical concepts, so that these two recent trends in biblical studies intersect. However, postcolonial studies want to go beyond a mere critical standpoint and toward new, hybrid perspectives and spaces, and perhaps hybridity is indeed a concept that does justice to complexity, to the increasing complexity of situations, needs, and challenges people have to face—even when one has to be aware that such a concept can be co-opted to stabilize old forms of hegemony and establish new ones.[21]

In this regard, allow me to add an observation about international scholarship: it seems to become more and more difficult to follow developments in biblical research going on around the world. Language barriers—but even more, economic limitations—prevent easy exchange. Efforts to listen to voices outside the mainstream are necessary, together with the acknowledgment of our own inevitable limitations.

The Challenges of a Biblical Book

The text I suggest as an example to show how my theoretical framework informs my interpretive practice is the book of Esther.[22] I chose Esther about fifteen years ago as a text I wanted to explore more deeply, for many reasons. It is one of two writings in the Hebrew Bible with its heroine in the title of the book, which of course makes it interesting for feminist readings. Its heroine, Esther, is in close interaction with three male figures: her cousin Mordecai; her husband, the Persian king; and the figure of the antagonist, Haman, the king's counselor. A gendered perspective seems promising, then—all the more so since two other women characters complete the image: Vashti, Esther's predecessor as Persian queen, and Seresh, Haman's wife. And there is even a third gender emerging at the stage, the eunuchs at the court of the king. Today most biblical scholars agree that the book of Esther is a fictional book with typecasted characters, and that it is a book from Hellenistic times, using the Persian court as background for a reflection on Jewish identity under Hellenistic rulers, an identity, by the way, without reference to a land of Israel where Jews should live. The book is hence a voice from and for Jewish diaspora.

Esther is moreover a book that stands in rich intertextual relationship to the rest of the Jewish Bible, especially with regard to its wisdom traditions. Furthermore, it is a book with a complex reception history already in Jewish antiquity, as besides the Hebrew version there is the version of the Septuagint and a Second Greek Text, considered today as another Jewish variant of the story;[23] there is an early commentary on the book in the Talmud's tractate Megillah, and there are two extant Targumic versions. They all show that, in its Jewish contexts, the story of Esther was not considered a fixed and intangible text but a fluid entity to tell, retell, and comment upon. The book of Esther, for Catholics, constitutes a canonical text different from the one in the Jewish Bible or in Bibles from churches after the Reformation. In modern Roman Catholic Bible translations, the six so-called additions of the Septuagint are usually inserted into the text taken from the Hebrew Bible. The book is hence presented as a *mixtum compositum* of the Hebrew and the Greek text, translated into a contemporary Western European language, a hybrid text.

At the same time, the book of Esther has quite a problematic reception history in Christian contexts. The first complete commentary appeared rather late, in the early Middle Ages only, when Rhabanus Maurus read the book as an allegory with Queen Esther standing for the church and Queen Vashti for the synagogue. Since Martin Luther and his turn to the literal meaning of the text, the book was found to be too Jewish, not "promoting Christ" as he would say, and in modern times Christian commentators took offense at an alleged Jewish particularism speaking through its text. The question of why, how, or in what way the book can be of interest for Christian readers is not trivial, then.

Finally, Esther is a book whose story, namely, the genocide of the Jewish people planned and set in motion by state authority (although under premodern conditions), cannot, for German contemporary readers, be heard without the specific background of our history: the Holocaust planned, set in motion, and realized by the German state and by the collaboration of many ordinary people. Against this background of genocide for reasons of racist anti-Semitism, the fact that in the Hebrew book of Esther God is not mentioned, and the motives given to annihilate the Jews are not religious, gained much significance. In my context, then, it seems obvious that I have to connect gendered readings of the book of Esther to an analysis of the dimensions of power and violence as detectable in the text of that book and in its early receptions. Building on my former publications,[24] I have proceeded in three steps (I–III in the following sections). To grasp the book's narrated (and probably historical) setting better, and also the challenge of multiple possible receptions today by readers under different political circumstances, it becomes meaningful, if not indispensable, to include aspects of postcolonial studies in my analyses.

Structures of Power and Violence I—Image of the Persian Empire

In a first step, I want to bring to the fore the violence of power by which the Persian Empire is held together in the narrated world.[25] The king's political and economic power stretches over a gigantic area, from India to Ethiopia (Esth 1:1). The first chapter shows how the king exercises his power toward his rebellious and insubordinate wife, Queen Vashti, which results in the promulgation of a law affirming the subordination of women, children, and slaves to the patriarch of every house in the empire (1:22). The second chapter regards the extension of the king's power into every household of the kingdom, by "[gathering] all the beautiful young virgins to the harem in the citadel of Susa," as the king's servants suggest (2:3). The Persian king is presented as lord of times and lord of the bodies, as Sarojini Nadar has pointed out,[26] as each of these young women is prepared during twelve months, one whole year, to meet the king for one night. One could add the king's lordship over the bodies of eunuchs, boys or men transformed into no-males by genital mutilation. This king creates a specific gender system with one male, himself, at its top, hence claiming hegemony. The king is subsequently surrounded by a body of male representatives of different ethnic origin (cf. Esth 1:3), thus integrating ethnic difference into the gendered structure—the other males dependent on him with restricted power over women, children, and slaves, as well as no-males who for their part participate in the king's power as his servants.

It is within these structures of gendered violating power that Esther enters the stage (cf. Esth 2:7). Esther herself is a vulnerable person, an orphan but under protection of her cousin Mordecai, a woman of great beauty, which is her risk and her chance. The way Mordecai is introduced (2:5–6) does not give him much political power, which is quite different from the Septuagint version, in which Mordecai is called a great man at the king's court from the outset of the story. Both Mordecai and Esther belong to a specific ethnic group, the Jews, within an empire, the Persian Empire. The book of Esther reflects the situation of people not so much colonized in their country of origin but colonized as displaced persons. Under these precarious conditions of absolute or even absolutistic power, the Jewish woman and the Jewish man tried to make their way. The book of Esther seems to be structured around these two characters: a man and a woman, who together represent their people. A feminist focus on Esther only would not allow one to see this complexity; the book invites a gendered reading. However, a mere gendered reading, on the other hand, misses the intersection of gender and ethnicity.

Once Esther is taken into the king's harem, she seems to collaborate with the system. Vashti, on the other hand, resists and refuses collaboration. This is why, in early feminist commentaries, all sympathies were with Vashti as a model of resistance, resistance interpreted as directed against patriarchy. But things seem to be more complex. Later in the story, Esther will also be insubordinate and risk her life when going to the king who did not call her to come (Esth 5:1–8)—an inverted correspondence to the character of Vashti, who did not go to the king in spite of having been called (Esth 1:12). Esther's insubordination has become necessary because her cousin chose rebellion or resistance against the king's order and provoked Haman's desire to annihilate all the Jews, Mordecai's people. Mordecai, in his own way, performs anew Vashti's refusal of a royal order that, in her case, provoked a decree of submission for all women. The Hebrew book of Esther seems to negotiate the scope of actions for Jews under the conditions of an empire; it does so by showing the agency of a singular Jewish man and woman. Read in the context of Jewish scriptures, Mordecai and Esther together rewrite the life of Joseph, Jacob's son, in Egypt, in the context of the book of Esther.

Moreover, both Mordecai and Esther remember in their actions a non-Jewish woman, Vashti. Madipoane Masenya, in her efforts to reclaim Vashti for African South African female readers,[27] believes that "the Jewish narrator attempts to erase her [Vashti] from our memories,"[28] and asks if the figure of Vashti might have gotten a better narrative treatment if she had been construed as part of the Jewish people.[29] If seen the way I suggest, Mordecai and Esther's actions continue Vashti's presence rather than erase her memory, and moreover place her on the side of the biblical Joseph. Nevertheless, it is true that no textual voice is given to Vashti, and her reasons for not obeying a royal order remain unexplained. Vashti, in a way, is comparable to the Rani of Sirmur, a female ruler (1815–1827) in the northeastern part of British India, whose reasons to ask for suttee/sati at a time in which she was supposed to function as guardian of the minor king, her son, remained unsaid or at least untransmitted. For Gayatri Chakravorty Spivak, the Rani of Sirmur serves as an example of a subaltern who cannot speak.[30] The literary figure of Vashti remains incomplete: a question mark for critical readers.

Two lengthy descriptions in these first two chapters, the only ones in the book, attract attention. They expand on the splendor and luxury in the king's garden opened for the public (1:2–8) and on the inner space of the king's harem (2:8–9, 12–14). In their style they represent, in terms of Edward Said, an "orientalizing gaze" on the Eastern world as seen by Hellenistic authors. It is true that Jewish readers familiar with their Scriptures would connect these descriptions with the Deuteronomic prescriptions for a king according to God's will (cf. Deut 17:17: a king has to be moderate in his riches and moderate in the number of his wives). Such readers would understand that these descriptions add to the Persian king's character as problematic. Jewish readers, further, familiar with Greek-Hellenistic discourse on virtue, would find philosophical confirmation for such a negative judgment of the king not practicing temperance. Conveying this message by using "orientalizing" stereotypes borrowed from the global culture, then, might be a stylistic means of Jewish-Hellenistic authors to further denigrate the figure of the Persian king. On the other hand it remains true, as Sarojini Nadar underlines, that the passage Esther 2:1–18 silently ignores the violent aspects of what is happening with the young women during the night with the king.[31] On a superficial level, readers might have delighted in peeping through the keyhole of the harem's door.[32] But were critical readers or listeners in Hellenistic-Roman times able to fill the lacunae differently? Given the fact that the book of Judith, in many regards similar to the (Greek) book of Esther, is quite sensitive to sexual violence, one may admit that Hellenistic Judaism must have been a culture in which such sensitivity could be found. Indeed, the Septuagint version of the book of Esther seems to grapple with the problem. Esther 2:7 LXX mentions Mordecai's intention to enter into marriage with his cousin Esther, thus underlining the violent separation of a couple, when Esther is brought to the king's harem. In 2:13 LXX the *lectio difficilior* of the manuscript tradition has Esther taking with her not an object (2:13 MT) but a person of her choice during the night with the king. The king's falling in love with

Esther (2:17 LXX) might sound romantic but also might remind critical Jewish readers of Dinah, Jacob's daughter. In this story told in Genesis 34:2–4, Shechem, the king's son who falls in love with Dinah and wants to marry her, first is said to have raped her (Gen 34:2). In contrast to the book of Judith, though, Greek Esther does not explicitly side with a women's perspective. Nor does the Hebrew book of Esther, as Itumeleng Mosala has already argued convincingly.[33]

Structures of Power and Violence II—Genocide

Second, it is important to focus on Haman and his planned genocide. When Haman explains to the king that a certain nation has to be eliminated to stabilize the empire (Esth 3:8–9), the king immediately agrees, genocide obviously being for him an acceptable political strategy. By handing over his signet ring to Haman, the king transfers his power to his counselor, thus making possible the planned genocide of men, women, and children as legalized by the state. In the world of the text it is clear that this monarch is ruthless when his power is concerned, and that he has no specific interest in the life of his subordinates. Therefore, Queen Esther cannot just go to the king and ask for the lives of the Jewish people. She tries to avert the imminent danger by taking advantage of the king's attention. She does this by virtue of her being an attractive woman who finds herself under the king's control as his wife. Moreover, Esther uses the king's preference for luxurious festivities. During a banquet, she describes Haman's attack as directed toward her person together with her people so that her husband finds his possession threatened by Haman (7:3–6). Ironically, Haman confirms the king's suspicion when he is found stretched out on Esther's couch (7:8). In postcolonial terms, what Esther performs is a sort of mimicry, playing the game of the emperor, to save the lives of her people.

Linked to this is the fight between the two males Mordecai and Haman.[34] Mordecai refuses to bow down before Haman knowing that he transgresses a commandment of the king. The Hebrew text does not give any explicit reason except that it refers to Mordecai's explanation of being a Jew. Many Jewish and Christian commentaries see the biblical antagonism of Israel/Saul and Amalek/Agag (Exod 17; 1 Sam 15) coming back to the stage in Mordecai the Benjaminite and Haman the Agagite. This is certainly one possibility well rooted in the text. Besides this, I would like to highlight another perspective: at any rate, the gesture of bowing down and prostration expresses submission, recognizing a hierarchy of bottom and top. Mordecai will not bow down, not even when he faces the king (cf. 8:1–2). For readers in Hellenistic times, it must have been clear without explication that Mordecai is painted as the prototype of resistance against self-divinization of any human being. For Jewish readers this resistance would signify fidelity to their one and only God; for non-Jewish Hellenistic readers it was rather an expression of human dignity.

One should note that in light of the fact that the book of Esther is without direct reference to God, both readings might well be possible. Haman's hatred of

Mordecai, then, is hatred for a man who does not submit to him, and Haman's hatred of the Jews is hatred for a whole people who, like Mordecai, will not submit. Against this background it appears significant that Esther, when going to see the king without being called to him, does *not* bow down. Instead, she stands upright in the inner court; she is perceived by the king as standing upright, and she approaches him to touch his scepter (5:1–2). Esther remains, so to say, on an equal footing with the king, and her gesture can be seen as Esther acting as a Jew without identifying her as such. In that moment she acts in a hybrid way, melting her appearance as queen and her Jewishness into one. On the other hand, she prostrates herself when she asks for the reversal of Haman's counter-edict (8:3). Here, her prostration seems to be her last resort as she has to rely wholly on the king's mercy. Ironically, Haman tries to save his life by bowing down (or falling down) before Esther the queen, by humiliating himself, but the king perceives this gesture as expression of Haman's attempt to gain royal power.

Haman, in the Hebrew book of Esther, is the prototype of a person in power ready to use his power for lethal violence. The proposal he presents to the king is suggestive: there is a people with their own laws, dispersed all over the empire; moreover they do not obey the king's laws. To eliminate these people would fill up the king's treasuries (3:8–9). For contemporary German readers, Haman's proposal to the king is reminiscent of the myth of the global Jewish conspiracy effective in Western and Eastern Europe since the late nineteenth century. It moreover reminds one of Nazi Germany robbing its Jewish citizens before allowing them to leave the country and even before their deportation into the death camps. In an anachronistic way and referring to his speech before the king, one could label Haman an anti-Semite. For German readers, it consequently seems inevitable to admit that German politics during the Third Reich was Hamanic. State officials at that time could point to Martin Luther's invectives in his writing *On the Jews and Their Lies* (1543), according to which this leader of the Reformation suggested that the Jews' houses were to be burned, their fortunes confiscated, and that they be drafted into forced labor, or expelled.

In Germany, there is indeed a long history of specifically Christian contempt, even hostility toward Judaism and Jews that, together with accepted forms of secular anti-Semitism, certainly prevented many faithful Christians during the Third Reich from developing deeper moral scruples against the ongoing disfranchisement of the Jewish population. One of the well-known German Old Testament scholars active in Jewish-Christian dialogue since the 1970s, the Catholic Erich Zenger, suggested to Christian readers to accept the book of Esther as examining their conscience, individually and in their faith communities, regarding anti-Judaism and anti-Semitism.[35]

In the context of the origin of the (Hebrew) book of Esther, Haman could be conceived of as a dangerous but finally ridiculous figure. He falls into the pit he dug for others. In the Septuagint version, Haman even forgot to seal his decree of annihilation, so that it did not come into force at all (Esth 3:10–13 and 14–15 LXX; cf. 8:8–10 LXX). The historian Erich Gruen points out that for Hellenistic Jewish readers the portion of humor inherent in the Hebrew book of Esther is considerable.[36] Commentators tend to neglect this aspect of the narrative and assume or reconstruct a situation of imminent threat or persecution as the historical frame of the book of Esther without being able to determine a specific point of reference. Another, perhaps even better possibility is to read the book without such a presupposition and rather think of Jewish everyday experiences of being rejected as different or of being confronted with latent or open mistrust. Against such a background, the book of Esther might be understood as a story of a Jewish community in a non-Jewish environment, condensing such experiences through a plot of lethal threat and a happy ending into wisdom language: of death and life, to encourage one another and to affirm to one another that they are in control of the situation.

Structures of Power and Violence III—Massacre

A third aspect is the power of violence exercised by the Jews as described in Chapter 9. It is true that the counter-edict that Esther and Mordecai are allowed to write and to seal with the king's ring (8:11) is not the simple reversal of Haman's edict commanding the elimination of the Jewish people, men, women, and children (3:13). Esther's and Mordecai's edict focuses on self-defense against a military attack, and the syntax leaves serious doubt about whether the Jews are allowed to kill women and children along with the attacking men.[37] Chapter 9, however, does not fit into that logic of restricted violence.[38] The swords in the hands of the Jewish fighters cause a massacre without direct need of self-defense (cf. in particular 9:5). Esther demands a second day of fighting (9:13), which is not in correspondence to the one day of annihilation ordered by Haman, thus breaking the pattern of reversal as indicated by the metanarrative comment in Esther 9:1.

Esther 9 in particular has earned the book of Esther harsh criticism as an expression of mere thirst for revenge, in Christian as well as in modern liberal Jewish commentaries. It is interesting, then, that already the Septuagint version of that chapter seems to have felt the need to work on this problem. In the Septuagint, the most offensive verse (9:5) is simply skipped and not translated, and the number of persons killed is considerably reduced. As a whole, the Septuagint version places much importance on insisting that cultural and religious differences of the Jews are no threat for the dominant order. The Septuagint version tries, as I read it, to trace the king as a modest, righteous, and rational ruler who is eager to eliminate criminals from his empire. The problem is his trust in Haman, who succeeds in persuading the king that the Jewish ethnos is a people of criminals and parasites. Haman is the representative of Judeophobia,[39] already a reality in the ancient world, and the Greek book of Esther is a document written to show that such Judeophobia is a result of malign perception of cultural differences. This version of the Esther story tries to define a space and a place for the Jewish people under conditions of an empire. It does not challenge the structures of that empire, but believes in its moral foundations as largely compatible with Jewish moral and theological presuppositions (cf. Addition E in the LXX). There are limits, however, to this compatibility: if a human, be it even a counselor or an emperor, claims veneration by prostration like a god, a Jewish man has to refuse, as Mordecai does (Addition C, 1–10)[40]—and as Esther does: when going to see the king she would not bow down, but faint! And a mixed marriage between a Jewish woman and a non-Jew is something to avoid, as Esther presupposes in her prayer (Addition C, 12–30). She describes her own situation as a kind of permanent mask as wife of the Persian king, but at the same time she has interior distance toward her non-Jewish husband.

The Hebrew version, on the other hand, is not interested in mixed marriage or circumcision, but in submission versus refusal only, and in the resulting mortal threat. It puts all emphasis on the reversal of the situation after the counter-edict was sent out. It can be read as a book of rejoicing about having been able to escape a desperate situation, as a book of suppressed people who imagine being for once on the bright side, being victorious. This is how South African scholar Gerrie Snyman describes the reception of this text by some of his students who were asked to prepare a sermon on Esther 9: they were ready to read apartheid structures and the upheaval against them into the text and side as black people with the Jews as the former victims who had to fight against their oppressors.[41] Snyman writes how he himself was shocked by the fact that he as an Afrikaner white male is put on the side of the Persians, the enemies who were to be killed. Perhaps this shock is analogous to the hermeneutical process Erich Zenger suggests for German Christian readers.

However, the book of Esther can also be read as in itself offering resistance against a mere justification of counter-violence. If we take into account the fictitious character of the book, it can be read as a counterfactual story, a counter-history. Later in Jewish history the feast of Purim to which the book is attached was enriched by carnivalesque customs. If we follow the analyses of Mikhail Bakhtin,[42] carnival is a space and a time for subalterns to express their fears, hopes, and aggressions and to show their power—a limited space and time granted by the rulers, as the rulers are always uncertain about the stability of these limits.

Jewish interpreters of the book, such as biblical scholar Stan Goldman and Israeli film producer Amos Gitai, have emphasized the many reversals and ironies in the book. They ask whether Chapter 9 could not be seen as a text showing what happens when those who are downtrodden come to power, when the oppressed take on the masks of their oppressors. Amos Gitai's film *Esther* (1984)[43] places the reading of Haman's annihilation edict against the Jewish people in a scenic context evoking the suffering of the Palestinian people during the Naqba, but also later in the territories occupied by Israel. Moreover, he shows, at the end of his film, in a kind of visualized reversal, Mordecai in the garments of Haman, while the text of Esther 9:1–18 is read aloud by a speaker's voice: the Jews have taken over the masks of their enemies, and these masks become part of their identity and transform them deeply. But as a further, hybrid reversal, in a kind of epilogue, Gitai has the actors of his film appearing and "Mordecai" revealing himself as Muhammad Bakri, a Palestinian from

Nazareth. "We both hate Mordecai," he says, pointing to Gitai, "and that is why we made this film."

While Gitai's film on the book of Esther concerns a dynamic in Israel/Palestine, Stan Goldman, on the other hand, reads the book as a message for Jews who live outside Israel and want to live in diaspora.[44] For Goldman, the book, with its continuing reversals and ironies, stimulates a continuing self-critical reflection on Jewish identity between adaption to the non-Jewish context and belonging to the Jewish community.

Let me conclude with one last glance at the figure of Esther in Chapter 9. She asks for a second day of fighting in Susa. And the king, overwhelmed by the reports of successful Jewish fighters outside the city, grants it to her. For a moment Esther seems to appear in the colors of the Assyrian goddess Ishtar, the goddess of love and war, to whom she probably owes her name.[45] For a moment she is part of the excess of bloodshed. How can feminist theologians deal with that? I think the Jewish feminist rabbi Elisa Klapheck and the Christian theologian Marianne Heimbach-Steins, who developed independently from each other,[46] bring in a good perspective: both point to the development of Esther as a character—from a young woman, beautiful, charming, and silent, to a woman who speaks up and risks her life; from a morally quasi-innocent being to someone who becomes a moral person, who dares to take decisions, who takes on responsibility, and who is involved and entangled in violence and runs the risk of becoming guilty. The ironic, subversive style of the narrative would then be a self-critical stimulus that women, too, badly need.

Notes

1. Marie-Theres Wacker, *Weltordnung und Gericht. Studien zu 1 Henoch 22*, FB 45 (Würzburg: Echter-Verlag, 1982; 2nd ed. 1985).
2. Mary Daly, *Beyond God the Father: Toward a Philosophy of Women's Liberation* (Boston: Beacon, 1973); translated into German by Marianne Reppekus, *Jenseits von Gottvater Sohn & Co. Aufbruch zu einer Philosophie der Frauenbefreiung* (München: Frauenoffensive, 1980).
3. My first publication after the doctoral thesis was an overview of the current state of discussion in feminist theology—the first one in a German-language theological handbook; see Marie-Theres Wacker, "Feministische Theologie," in *Neues Handbuch Theologischer Grundbegriffe*, Volume 1, ed. Peter Eicher (München: Kösel-Verlag, 1984), 353–60; reworked for the Second Edition (1991), 45–51.
4. In this intellectual journey, I found myself closely aligned with the work of Phyllis Bird. See her essays collected later in Phyllis A. Bird, *Missing Persons and Mistaken Identities: Women and Gender in Ancient Israel*, OBT (Minneapolis: Fortress, 1997). My own investigation was rather centered on questions of goddess veneration and emerging monotheism in ancient Israel; cf. Marie-Theres Wacker, *Von Göttinnen, Göttern und dem einzigen Gott* (Münster: LIT, 2005); essays between 1986 and 2001; and also Marie-Theres Wacker, "Traces of the Goddess in the Book of Hosea", in *The Latter Prophets. A Feminist Companion to the Bible*, ed. Athalya Brenner, First Series (Sheffield: Sheffield Academic, 1995), 219–41.

5. I was deeply impressed by Mieke Bal, *Femmes imaginaires. L'Ancien testament au risque d'une narratologie critique*, Collection ES/Écrire les Femmes 1 (Utrecht: HES Publishers, 1986). The rewritten English version has a less theoretical discussion, *Lethal Love: Feminist Literary Readings of Biblical Love Stories*, ISBL (Bloomington: Indiana University Press, 1987). Another author who impressed me strongly was J. Cheryl Exum, *Fragmented Women: Feminist (Sub)Versions of Biblical Narratives*, JSOTSup 163 (Sheffield: JSOT, 1993).

6. Christine Schaumberger, "Verschieden und vereint. Frauen der Dritten und Frauen der Ersten Welt," *Schlangenbrut: Zeitschrift für feministisch und religiös interessierte Frauen* 3 (1983): 40–2.

7. Cf., e.g., Elisabeth Schüssler Fiorenza, "Transforming the Legacy of the Woman's Bible," in *Searching the Scriptures Vol. 1: A Feminist Introduction*, ed. Elisabeth Schüssler Fiorenza (New York: Crossroad, 1993), 1–24; also Elisabeth Schüssler Fiorenza, *Sharing Her Word: Feminist Biblical Interpretation in Context* (Boston: Beacon, 1998), 36–40.

8. One of my early statements in this controversy was published in German, French, and English; see Marie-Theres Wacker, "Feministische Theologie und Antijudaismus. Diskussionsstand und Problemlage in der BRD," *Kirche und Israel* 5 (1990): 168–76; "Theologie Féministe et Anti-judaïsme. Mise à Jour et Évaluation de la Situation en R.F.A.," *Recherches féministes* 3 (1990): 155–65; "Feminist Theology and Anti-Judaism: The Status of the Discussion and the Context of the Problem in the FRG," *JFSR* 7 (1991): 109–17. For an overview of my commitment to Jewish-Christian dialogue in general and Jewish-Christian feminist exchanges in particular, cf. Marie-Theres Wacker, "Von der Wurzel getragen. Feministische Exegese und jüdisch-christliches Gespräch in biographischer Brechung," in *Der jüdisch-christliche Dialog veränderte die Theologie. Ein Paradigmenwechsel aus ExpertInnensicht*, ed. Edith Petschnigg and Irmtraud Fischer (Vienna: Böhlau, 2016), 97–111.

9. Bernd Wacker and Marie-Theres Wacker, ... *verfolgt, verjagt, deportiert. Juden in Salzkotten 1933–1942. Eine Dokumentation aus Anlaß des 50. Jahrestages der "Reichskristallnacht"* (Salzkotten: Private Publication, 1988); and the Enlarged Edition, Bernd Wacker and Marie-Theres Wacker, *Ausgelöscht. Erinnerung an die jüdische Gemeinde Salzkotten* (Salzkotten: Judentum in Salzkotten, 2002).

10. Cf. Marie-Theres Wacker and Stefanie Rieger-Goertz, eds., *Mannsbilder. Kritische Männerforschung und Theologische Frauenforschung im Gespräch*, Theologische Frauenforschung in Europa 21 (Münster: LIT, 2006).

11. Cf. Marie-Theres Wacker, "Wann ist der Mann ein Mann? Oder: Geschlechterdisput vom Paradies her," in *Mannsbilder. Kritische Männerforschung und Theologische Frauenforschung im Gespräch*, ed. Marie-Theres Wacker and Stefanie Rieger-Goertz, Theologische Frauenforschung in Europa 21 (Münster: LIT, 2006), 93–114.

12. "Homme sauvage et femmes étrangères. Le cycle d'Élie (1 Rois 17–2 R 2) selon les perspectives 'Genre'/Gender (I–II)," *Lectio Difficilior* 2 (2014). Parts III–IV on postcolonial approaches and on monotheism in the Cycle of Elijah are in preparation; cf. http://www.lectio.unibe.ch/14_2/wacker_marie_theres_homme_sauvage_et_femmes_etrangeres.html, accessed January 27, 2016.

13. Stephanie Feder, "Esther Goes to Africa: Rezeptionen des Esterbuches in Südafrika," in *Esters unbekannte seiten. Theologische perspektiven auf ein vergessenes biblisches buch*, ed. Stephanie Feder and Aurica Nutt, Festschrift Marie-Theres Wacker (Ostfildern: Grünewald-Verlag, 2012), 41–55.

14. Edward W. Said, *Orientalism* (New York: Pantheon, 1978).

15. Frantz Fanon, *Peau noir, masques blancs* (Paris: Edition de Seuil, 1952), translated by Charles Lam Markmann as *Black Skin, White Masks* (New York: Grove Press, 1967); Frantz Fanon, *Les damnés de la terre* (Paris: Maspéro, 1961), translated by Constance Farrington as *The Wretched of the Earth* (New York: Grove Weidenfeld, 1963).

16. Homi K. Bhabha, *The Location of Culture*, with a new preface by the author (London: Routledge, 2006); Homi K. Bhabha, "DissemiNation: Time, Narrative, and the Margins of Modern Nation," in *Nation and Narration*, ed. Homi K. Bhabha (London: Routledge, 1990), 291–322; Jonathan Rutherford, "The Third Space. Interview with Homi Bhabha," in *Identity, Community, Culture, Difference*, ed. Jonathan Rutherford (London: Lawrence & Wishart, 1990), 207–21; see also Homi K. Bhabha, *Über kulturelle Hybridität. Tradition und Übersetzung*, trans. Katharina Menke, ed. Anna Babka and Gerald Posselt (Berlin: Turia & Kant, 2012). This volume, which was based on a conference in Vienna, also included a round-table conversation with Homi Bhabha.

17. Gayatri Chakravorty Spivak, "Can the Subaltern Speak?," in *Marxism and the Interpretation of Culture*, ed. Cary Nelson and Lawrence Grossberg (Urbana: University of Illinois Press, 1988), 271–313; Gayatri Chakravorty Spivak, *A Critique of Postcolonial Reason: Toward the History of the Vanishing Present* (Cambridge: Harvard University Press, 1999). Cf. especially chapter 3 on "History," 198–311.

18. Musa W. Dube, *Postcolonial Feminist Interpretation of the Bible* (St. Louis: Chalice, 2000).

19. Extremely illuminating in this regard is the work of Norman C. Habel, *The Land Is Mine: Six Biblical Land Ideologies*, OBT (Minneapolis: Fortress, 1995).

20. One outcome is the issue on *Land Conflicts, Land Utopias*, ed. Marie-Theres Wacker and Elaine M. Wainwright, Concilium 2007/2 (London: SCM, 2007), in which we included Mitri Raheb from Bethlehem as a Palestinian voice. Another outcome is my article on Ben-Gurion's reading of the book of Joshua; cf. Marie-Theres Wacker, "Feldherr und Löwensohn. Das Buch Josua—angeeignet durch David Ben-Gurion," in *The Book of Joshua*, BETL 250, ed. Ed Noort (Leuven: Peeters, 2012), 609–47. My aim was to get an idea of Ben-Gurion's thinking against the background of the world political situation of his time, especially around the year 1948—the year of the proclamation of the State of Israel and the year of the Naqba/"Calamity," as the Palestinians call the expulsion of several hundreds of thousands of Arab people from their territories.

21. See, e.g., Kien Nghi Ha, "Crossing the Border? Hybridity as Late-Capitalistic Logic of Cultural Translation and National Modernisation," *Transversal Texts* 11/2006, available at: http://eipcp.net/transversal/1206/ha/en, accessed January 27, 2016.

22. Two commentaries I find particularly illuminating are Adele Berlin, *Esther: The Traditional Hebrew Text with the New JPS Translation*, JPS Bible Commentary (Philadelphia: JPS, 2001); and Linda M. Day, *Esther*, AOTC (Nashville: Abingdon, 2005). Cf. the extensive bibliography by Edith Lubetski and Meir Lubetski, *The Book of Esther: A Classified Bibliography* (Sheffield: Sheffield Phoenix, 2008). A great source for a compared narratological approach to Esther MT and LXX, but without interest in feminist or gender perspectives, is Cathérine Vialle, *Une analyse comparée d'Esther TM et LXX: Regard sur deux récits d'une même histoire*, BETL 233 (Leuven: Peeters, 2012). Beate Ego has announced her new commentary on Esther for the year 2016, BKAT (Neukirchen-Vluyn: Neukirchener). The deadline of submission for my manuscript did not allow me to refer to it.

23. I am happy to have had the opportunity to work with Kristin de Troyer on a German translation and a short commentary on the two Greek texts of Esther for the German "LXX.de." Cf. Kristin de Troyer and Marie-Theres Wacker, "Esther (Das Buch Ester)," in *Septuaginta Deutsch. Das griechische Alte Testament in deutscher Übersetzung*, ed. Martin Karrer and Wolfgang Kraus (Stuttgart: Deutsche Bibelgesellschaft, 2009), 593–618; Kristin de Troyer and Marie-Theres Wacker, "Das Buch Ester," in *Septuaginta Deutsch. Erläuterungen und Kommentare Vol. I: Genesis bis Makkabäer*, ed. Martin Karrer and Wolfgang Kraus (Stuttgart: Deutsche Bibelgesellschaft, 2011), 1,253–96. See also my contributions on EstLXX, Marie-Theres Wacker, "Mit Toratreue und Todesmut dem einen Gott anhangen. Zum Esther-Bild der Septuaginta," in *Dem Tod nicht glauben. Sozialgeschichte der Bibel*, ed. Frank Crüsemann et al., Festschrift Luise Schottroff (Gütersloh: Gütersloher Verlagshaus, 2004), 312–32; Marie-Theres Wacker, "'Three Faces of a Story:' Septuagintagriechisches und pseudolukianisches Estherbuch als Refigurationen der Esther-Erzählung," in *La Septante en Allemagne et en France/Septuaginta Deutsch und Bible d'Alexandrie*, ed. Wolfgang Kraus and Olivier Munich, OBO 238 (Fribourg: Universitätsverlag, 2009), 64–89; Marie-Theres Wacker, "Innensichten und Außensichten des Judentums im septuagintagriechischen Estherbuch (EstLxx)," in *Gesellschaft und Religion in der spätbiblischen und deuterokanonischen Literatur*, ed. Friedrich V. Reiterer, Renate Egger-Wenzel, and Thomas R. Eißner, DCLS 20 (Berlin: De Gruyter, 2014), 55–92.

24. Marie-Theres Wacker, *Ester: Jüdin, Königin, Retterin* (Stuttgart: Katholisches Bibelwerk, 2006); Marie-Theres Wacker, "Tödliche Gewalt des Judenhasses—mit tödlicher Gewalt gegen Judenhass? Hermeneutische Überlegungen zu Est 9," in *Das Manna fällt auch heute noch. Beiträge zur Geschichte und Theologie des Alten, Ersten Testaments*, ed. Frank-Lothar Hossfeld and Ludger Schwienhorst-Schönberg, Festschrift Erich Zenger, Herders Biblische Studien 44 (Freiburg: Herder, 2004), 609–37; Marie-Theres Wacker, "Widerstand—Rache—verkehrte Welt Oder: Vom Umgang mit Gewalt im Esterbuch," in *Ester*, ed. Klara Butting, Gerard Minnaard, and Marie-Theres Wacker, Die Bibel erzählt … (Wittingen: Erev Rav, 2005), 35–44; Marie-Theres Wacker, " … ein großes Blutbad'. Ester 8–9 und die Frage nach Gewalt im Esterbuch," *Bibel Heute* 167 (2006): 14–16.

25. I owe this insight to Klara Butting's chapter on the book of Esther in *Die Buchstaben werden sich noch wundern. Innerbiblische Kritik als Wegweisung feministischer Hermeneutik* (Berlin: Alektor-Verlag, 1994), 49–86; see also Klara Butting, "Esther: About Resistance Against Anti-Judaism and Racism," in *Feminist Biblical Interpretation: A Compendium of Critical Commentary on the Books of the Bible and Related Literature*, ed. Luise Schottroff and Marie-Theres Wacker, trans. Martin Rumscheidt et al. (Grand Rapids, MI: Eerdmans, 2012), 207–20.

26. Sarojini Nadar, "'Texts of Terror' Disguised as the 'Word of God': The Case of Esther 2:1–18 and the Conspiracy of Rape in the Bible," *Journal of Constructive Theology* 10 (2004): 59–79; republished as " 'Texts of Terror': The Conspiracy of Rape in the Bible, Church, and Society: The Case of Esther 2:1–18," in *African Women, Religion, and Health: Essays in Honour of Mercy Amba Oduyoye*, ed. Isabel Apawo Phiri and Sarojini Nadar (Maryknoll, NY: Orbis, 2006), 77–95. Cf. also Sarojini Nadar, "The Politics of Reconciliation: Re-inscribing the Wounded Body Through a Feminist Body Hermeneutic," *Concilium: International Journal of Theology* (2013): 35–41.

27. Cf. Madipoane Masenya (ngwana' Mphahlele), "Their Hermeneutics Was Strange! Ours Is a Necessity! Reading Vashti in Esther 1 as African Women in South Africa," in *Her Master's Tools? Feminist and Postcolonial Engagements of Historical-Critical*

Discourse, ed. Caroline van der Stichele and Todd Penner, GPBS 9 (Atlanta: SBL, 2005), 179–94; Madipoane Masenya (ngwana' Mphahlele), "'A Small Herb Increases Itself (Makes Impact) by a Strong Odour': Re-imaginig Vashti in an African-South African Context," *OTE* 16 (2003): 332–42. For her specific *bosadi* perspective of reading, cf. also Madipoane Masenya (ngwana' Mphahlele), "Esther and Northern Sotho Stories: An African-South African Woman's Commentary," in *Other Ways of Reading: African Women and the Bible*, ed. Musa W. Dube, GPBS 2/2 (Atlanta: SBL, 2001), 27–49.

28. Masenya, "Small Herb," 334.
29. Masenya, "Small Herb," 339.
30. Spivak, *Critique of Postcolonial Reason*, 209–46.
31. See my note 26 and also Sarojini Nadar, "Gender, Power, Sexuality and Suffering Bodies in the Book of Esther: Reading the Characters of Esther and Vashti for the Purpose of Social Transformation," *OTE* 15 (2002): 113–30.
32. See Marie-Theres Wacker, "Ester im Bild," in *Ester*, ed. Klara Butting, Gerard Minnard, and Marie-Theres Wacker, *Die Bibel erzählt …* (Wittingen: Erev Rav, 2005), 78–87 (86–7).
33. Itumeleng J. Mosala, "The Implications of the Text of Esther for African Women's Struggle for Liberation in South Africa," *Semeia* 59 (1992): 129–37.
34. Both characters act out their maleness against a female figure, a line of argumentation that is beyond the scope of this essay. On Haman's wife Seresh, cf. Marie-Theres Wacker, "Seresch," in *Lieblingsfrauen der Bibel und der Welt. Ausgewählt für Luise Metzler zum 60. Geburtstag*, ed. Christina Duncker and Katrin Keita (Norderstedt: BoD, 2009), 140–51.
35. Erich Zenger, "Das Buch Ester," in *Einleitung in das Alte Testament*, ed. Christian Frevel, Eighth Edition (Stuttgart: Kohlhammer, 2012), 376–86 (386).
36. Erich S. Gruen, *Diaspora: Jews amidst Greeks and Romans* (Cambridge: Harvard University Press, 2002), 137–48. In his effort to retell the story of the book in a humorous way, Gruen does not escape, for his part, an orientalizing gaze, proving that the text strongly suggests it.
37. See Rainer Kessler, "Die Juden als Kindes- und Frauenmörder? Zu Est 8,11," in *Die Hebräische Bibel und ihre zweifache Nachgeschichte*, ed. Erhard Blum, Christian Macholz, and Ekkehard W. Stegemann, Festschrift Rolf Rendtorff (Neukirchen-Vluyn: Neukirchener, 1990), 337–45. Kessler suggests that, grammatically, the phrase *along with women and children* can well be part of the grammatical subject—those threatened (= the Jews themselves)—instead of the object—those who are allowed to be killed (= the adversaries).
38. Tricia Miller, in her two books on Esther, tries to show that Jewish defense in the face of planned genocide is the red thread in the Esther story. See Tricia Miller, *Three Versions of Esther: Their Relationship to Anti-Semitic and Feminist Critique of the Story*, CBET (Leuven: Peeters, 2014); Tricia Miller, *Jews and Anti-Judaism in Esther and the Church* (Cambridge, UK: James Clarke, 2015). Miller's books are very illuminating in that she shows the broad anti-Jewish and even anti-Semitic reception the Esther story found through the centuries. I agree that Christians need to examine their conscience. I feel, though, that the line she draws between anti-Semitism/anti-Judaism and critical rereadings of the Book/s of Esther is too clear-cut, leaving no room for divergent readings—also from Jewish perspectives—or negotiations on the violent aspects within the story, quite apart from the actual situation between Israel and Palestine.

39. An expression I take from Peter Schäfer, *Judeophobia: Attitudes toward the Jews in the Ancient World* (Cambridge: Harvard University Press, 1998). On Haman's Judeophobia, cf. Marie-Theres Wacker, "Innensichten," 68–76.

40. Mordecai, in his prayer, reflects on his reason for not bowing down: he would have bowed down for the sake of Israel (add. C:5–7)—conceivably a rehabilitation of Esther's prostration later in the narrative (cf. 8:3–4).

41. Gerrie Snyman, "'Ilahle Elinothuthu'? The Lay Reader and/or the Critical Reader—Some Remarks on Africanisation," *Religion & Theology* 6 (1999): 140–67; Gerrie Snyman, "Narrative Rationality, Morality and Readers' Identification," *OTE* 15 (2002): 179–99; Gerrie Snyman, "Identification and the Discourse of Fundamentalism: Reflections on a Reading of the Book of Esther," in *Rhetorical Criticism and the Bible*, ed. Stanley E. Porter and Dennis L. Stamps, JSOTSup 195 (Sheffield: Sheffield Academic, 2002), 160–208; Gerrie Snyman, "Race in South Africa: A Hidden Transcript Turned Public? The Problem of Identifying with Esther/Mordecai or Haman in the Book of Esther," *Scriptura* 84 (2003): 438–52.

42. This is how Kenneth Craig suggests one read the book of Esther: Kenneth M. Craig, *Reading Esther: A Case for the Literary Carnivalesque* (Louisville, KY: Westminster John Knox, 1995).

43. Cf. Marie-Theres Wacker, "Das biblische Estherbuch zwischen Palästina und Israel. Zum Film 'Esther' von Amos Gitai (1985) und seiner Kontextualisierung," in *Religion und Gewalt im Bibelfilm*, ed. Reinhold Zwick, Film und Theologie 20 (Marburg: Schüren, 2013), 39–59.

44. Stan Goldman, "Narrative and Ethical Ironies in Esther," *JSOT* 47 (1990): 15–31.

45. Ludger Hiepel, "Ester das ist auch Ištar. Eine Lesebrille für die hybride Esterfiguration vor dem Hintergrund der altorientalischen Kriegs- und Liebesgöttin," *BN* 163 (2014): 53–71.

46. Elisa Klapheck, "Ester und Amalek. Ein jüdisch-feministisches Selbstverständnis nach der Shoah," in *Von Gott reden im Land der Täter. Theologische Stimmen der dritten Generation seit der Shoa*, ed. Katharina von Kellenbach, Björn Krondorfer, and Norbert Reck (Darmstadt: Wiss. Buchgesellschaft, 2001), 242–55; Marianne Heimbach-Steins, "Subjekt werden—Handlungsmacht gewinnen. Eine Glosse zu Est 4,13–14," in *Esters unbekannte Seiten. Theologische Perspektiven auf ein vergessenes biblisches Buch*, ed. Stephanie Feder and Aurica Nutt, Festschrift Marie-Theres Wacker (Ostfildern: Grünewald-Verlag, 2012), 189–92.

Chapter 8

"IS THERE A MAN HERE?": THE IRON FIST IN THE VELVET GLOVE IN JUDGES 4

Charlene van der Walt

During a recent road trip, I caught the tail end of a radio competition in which listeners had to call in and play a yes/no game with the radio station's host. The name of this game was poignantly deceptive in the sense that the aim of the game was precisely to *not* use the words yes or no when answering the questions, which were set up to lead contestants into just that trap. It was remarkable to hear how quickly contestants stepped into the host's carefully set snare by answering with a simple yes or no before even knowing it. It was also refreshing to hear contestants carefully choosing their words and laboring at formulating an answer beyond the simple one-syllable conversation killer.

This radio game reminded me again of the active, creative, and reflective praxis that ethical reflection and moral development imply. When really engaging the question "what might be a good way to live?" it seems that, similar to the game, a simple yes/no or right/wrong approach will not suffice—life, relationships, and circumstances become messy, complex, and muddled. When considering a good life from the perspective of a believing community, it seems that hard-and-fast rules deduced from biblical laws will seldom encourage creative moral development of identity and community. Wolfgang Huber, in his inaugural lecture as honorary professor at Stellenbosch University, remarks in this regard:

> Theological ethics does not yet reach its own core as long as it uses the biblical traditions mainly as a collection of rules that simply has to be applied to the problems of our days. The procedure is not plausible because the moral rules of the biblical tradition are obviously rooted in their own times and cannot be applied to our present without critical reflection on their historical context and background.[1]

In an attempt to find a creative alternative to the previously mentioned rules approach regarding the formation of morality, I turn to the genre of narrative.[2]

Stanley Hauerwas points to the potential alternative space for modern ethical reflection when remarking:

> Christians do not have a "morality" per se, but rather our morality is embedded in the stories that require constant retellings. Telling a story, particularly stories like those Christians tell of God's dealings with them, is a frightening business since in the tellings one frequently has the story retold in a manner that is surprising and challenging to the teller.[3]

According to Hauerwas, it is in the telling and retelling of the stories of faith that we learn who we are as a faith community, but also what is expected of us and how to live an ethical life. Denise Ackermann continues along the same lines when stating:

> Telling stories is intrinsic to claiming one's identity and in the process finding impulses for hope ... Narrative has a further function. Apart from claiming identity and naming the evil, narrative has a sense-making function. The very act of telling the story is an act of making sense of an often incomprehensible situation, of a suffering and chaotic world in which people wrestle with understanding and in so doing seek relief.[4]

The overarching question of this essay is thus an ethical one: "how do we live a good life?" But importantly, this question is embedded into the frightening complexity of life. In the process of ethical reflection this essay strives to read together two narratives from very different times and places: one situated within the biblical tradition and the other from the contemporary South African landscape. In Judges 4 we meet the promised deliverer of Israel in the unexpected figure of Jael. In a narrative that challenges traditional binary gender constructions, Jael emerges as the ironic answer to Sisera's hypothetical question "is there a man here?" Similarly, we find embedded within an equally complex social landscape of South Africa in the struggle against apartheid, the figure of Winnie Madikizela-Mandela in Justin Chadwick's biographical motion picture *Mandela: Long Walk to Freedom*.[5] Within this film, Winnie's trajectory is traced from the seemingly innocent girl who meets Nelson Mandela to the militant counter-icon to Mandela's call for peace and reconciliation during the transformation process to establish a democratic South Africa.

The ultimate aim of this creative intertextual reading is not to come to a final or correct analysis of the intent of the individual narratives, but rather to allow these narratives to dynamically inform the creative process of meaning-making.[6] The aim is thus not to extract some sort of ethical essence from the narrative or to set up an exercise in ethical judgment of particular characters, proposing that some are worth emulating while others should best be avoided. Rather, while facilitating a creative act of dynamic interaction between the two stories in question, I propose that the messy, complex, painful, and often muddled world depicted in narratives through the act of reading and interpretation becomes a reflective surface for ethical reflection by contemporary readers.[7] In deducing ethical pointers from biblical narratives I take my cue from the work of Jacqueline Lapsley, who states:

> For the most part I want to move away from asking which characters are worth emulating or not, and which text is "good" or "bad" … As a rule, the kind of ethical reflection I propose here asks the reader to allow herself to be drawn into a complex moral world evoked by the narrative. In the narrative worlds of the Old Testament easy moral judgments are elusive and most often miss the mark. The kind of ethics I envision has more to do with how the reader *enters into the story*—it is *narrative* ethics—and less to do with the reader standing outside the story making ethical judgments about character.[8]

It is important to note that Lapsley's understanding of narrative ethics is rooted in the emotional response of the reader to the text and the reader's capacity to empathize with the characters in the story. A narrative ethics does not, however, deny injustice or smooth over wrongdoing. Rather, it creates a reader with empathy and moral imagination. Martha Nussbaum writes with reference to Andrea Dworkin's novel *Mercy*, in which the main character who had been a rape victim responds to her violation by killing homeless men: "If you really open your imagination and heart to admit the life story of someone else, it becomes far more difficult to finish that person off with a karate kick. In short, the text constructs a reader who, while judging justly, remains capable of love."[9]

In the first part of this essay, I facilitate a creative dialogue between the stories of Jael and Winnie in an attempt to draw the reader into the complex moral world of the narratives presented. In the encounter of these two female characters as presented to the reader by the biblical writer and the film director, the reader gets the opportunity to encounter the Other. As Lapsley remarks: "Reading becomes an ethical activity because I engage an *Other* … who poses a fundamental challenge to my identity and self-understanding, who questions the nature of my relationships with others and with the world."[10]

In the final part of this essay, I reflect on the challenge that the combined reflective surface of the two narratives poses to contemporary readers—the "so what?" question of the analysis. After sitting in front of the mirror that is the combined stories of Winnie and Jael, I would like, for a moment, to consider again the question of how to live a good life. How do these narratives challenge us, how do they comfort us, how do they warn us, and, fundamentally, how do they invoke in us the longing for a good life—not only for ourselves, but also for a life together?

Jael in Judges 4

Imbedded within the narrative landscape of the book of Judges we find the story of Deborah and Jael.[11] The often-observed pattern of apostasy/punishment/cry for help and deliverance is simultaneously upheld and slightly adapted in the exposition of the narrative.[12] Because of Israel's wrongdoing, Deborah and Jael are being oppressed by the Canaanites introduced to the reader in the figures of King Jabin and Sisera, the leader of the oppressing army. The traditional formula of the Israelite cry for help sets the stage for the narrative to begin. As Katharine Sakenfeld argues:

> Often when the Israelites cry out to God the text reports immediately that God heard their cry and undertook a response … But here the divine response is reported less directly. The narrator does turn immediately to introduce an Israelite leader, Deborah, but it is not self-evident that she is to be the deliverer; indeed, the identity of the deliverer is made obscure to heighten the narrative tension.[13]

Deborah is introduced as a woman, a prophet, and a judge leading Israel, and the one who summons a reluctant man named Barak to engage in battle with the enemy forces led by General Sisera.[14] As Yairah Amit aptly remarks, "The first scene of the narrative proper does not answer the question of the savior's identity. On the contrary it produces a complication and underscores the lack of unequivocal solution."[15] The possibility of Barak being the savior is seriously undermined when he states that he would not be willing to go into battle if Deborah (a woman) does not accompany him and is consequently completely ruled out when Deborah states that the honor for the victory will be placed in the hands of a woman.[16]

In a classic, comic-strip "meanwhile, elsewhere" scenario, Heber the Kenite in verse 11 is introduced to the reader in a noticeably strange interjection. Heber the Kenite, who is related to the Israelites but living in isolation removed from his own people as well as the Israelites and the Canaanites, is indeed the outcast par excellence.[17] Verse 12 skips back to the main action of the plot as Barak, accompanied by Deborah, moves into battle and is met by the enemy forces in the person of Sisera. As was prophesied, Israel soon gets the upper hand in the battle, and Sisera is forced to get down from his chariot and flee on foot.

Bringing into focus the reason for the earlier interjection regarding Heber the Kenite, the point of view is shifted to that of Sisera. Johanna Bos, picking up on the shift in point of view, remarks:

> The audience sees Sisera running for his life, to a tent. The phrasing implies that he sees "the wife of Heber the Kenite whose house is at peace with Yabin, the king of Hazor." Sisera seems to be fleeing towards safe shelter. At the very least, Sisera sees someone who can aid him, with supplies at hand, who can serve as a lookout. He sees falsely, for he is looking in the direction of her clan and not of Jael herself.[18]

Jackson points out that it is ironic that "Jael assures Sisera that he should 'have no fear'" given the fact that "(1) this is a woman making assurances about having no fear to an army general, and (2), contrary to her assurances, he should, in fact, feel much fear—of her, the very one comforting him."[19] Irony continues when Sisera instructs Jael, in what I consider to be one of the pivotal moments of the narrative, to answer no when asked if there "is a man here." Blinded by androcentric enemy identification he fears faceless men while mistaking the fair face he encounters at the tent as a friend rather than a femme fatale. Jael, the "wife of Heber" as she is again described, is indeed not all she appears to be. In a sensually described scene in which maternal and sexual imagery abound,[20] Jael tricks Sisera into a deceptive caring and hospitable space, and when he is most vulnerable she kills him in brutal and violent fashion.[21] Again Jael, on this occasion named without any reference to Heber her husband, perhaps attesting to the fact that her loyalties have now become clear, comes out to meet a man, in this case Barak, and she continues to show him "the man that he is looking for." The death of Sisera seems to be the tipping point for the fate of Israel on this occasion as King Jabin is destroyed by the men of Israel.

Against this overview of the plot I would like to pick up on three important strands in the story that might enhance a creative and dynamic ethical engagement. First, it is important to note that Jael's assassination of Sisera is embedded in a complex social reality. Israel, a fragile community in flux, is engaged in war with a stronger enemy, however hyperbolic the depiction of the enemy might be. Fewell and Gunn comment on the position of women in the battle chiefly described as a masculine event, when stating:

> In patriarchal society women are, of course, among the people to be controlled, no matter who wins. If their own men win, they will at least be secure, though belittled. If the enemy men are victorious, the women will be raped, killed, taken as slaves (cf., e.g., Gen 34:27–29). In time of war, women's fates are sealed by men. Violence determines control.[22]

Niditch continues along the same lines when arguing that women in the battles among men "frequently serve as prizes of war and as valuable items of exchange."[23] The inevitable vulnerable position of women in war is probably brought into the sharpest focus at the end of the poetic account of the story in Judges 5 when we are privy to the inner thoughts of Sisera's mother as she ponders why her son has not yet returned from his victorious conquest with "a (womb) girl or two" for every man (v. 30). As Sakenfeld argues, "The poem and its singers are well aware that rape is part of the traditional aftermath of victory."[24] When Jael, who is vulnerable in this context not only because she is a woman but also because she is the wife of an outsider, meets Sisera, the odds are indeed not in her favor. As Bos comments on Sisera's identity in light of his mother's previously mentioned reflection: "It is a warrior/rapist whom Yael invites to 'turn' to her, to whom she offers refreshment; it is the spoiler of women whom she spoils."[25] It is therefore not surprising that Jael has been appropriated as a story of "rejection of rape, or a protest against rape, especially rape of women victims of war."[26]

Second, and continuing from the previously mentioned strand, it is almost impossible to ignore the "gender trouble"[27] being stirred up in the narrative. To grasp something of the gender queer[28] representation in the narrative, it is important to note that the default within dominant patriarchal discourse is that men are mainly defined within a binary relationship to women. Men are essentially everything that is opposite to women. Within this binary construction men also become everything that is superior to women.

In terms of a queer reading of the text, narrative strategies are employed to interrogate the boundaries and categories that structure traditional binary discourses on sexuality and gender within a patriarchal frame. Jackson remarks on the gender-bending that takes place in Judges 4–5 when two men (Barak and Sisera) and two women (Deborah and Jael) are represented in a text in a way that reverses the "expected gender roles, and humour is created when both men and women behave in ways unorthodox for their gender in their context."[29] We thus find women in positions of leadership and military conquest where we would usually expect men, and we find a man asking for assistance and hesitating before entering into battle. We find a woman coming out of the domestic space to meet a man (a dangerous one at that) in public to seduce him, trick him into a false sense of safety, and kill him in a fatal act of penetration.[30]

Gale Yee, in a seminal article on Judges 4, engages the anomaly of Deborah and Jael's representation within the patriarchal norm by exploring the dynamics of the metaphor of the warrior woman. She convincingly argues that in the hands of the male author, the warriors Deborah and Jael become "metaphorical strategies of entitlement, functioning primarily as agents of male shame."[31] Her argument is constructed by highlighting the shaming practices within the narrative:

> In a descending cycle of male characters, Barak is shamed by Deborah in his refusal to go into battle without her. Sisera is shamed by Jael in the desertion of his battalion and his cowardly retreat to a woman's tent. Barak is shamed by Jael, when he confronts his impotence in the form of Sisera's body, killed by the hands of a woman, and not by his own. *This shaming by a woman is only effective if war is defined solely as a male activity.* Rather than a story about female military power, Judges 4 becomes a reflection on what it means "to be or not to be a man."[32]

Sisera's hypothetical question "is there a man here?" is thus not only ironic when the danger comes from the unlikely figure of a woman, but also becomes more complicated when considering the speculated intention of the male author.[33]

Finally, and following from the two previously mentioned strands, Deborah and Jael, the vulnerable, liminal female characters constructed by the male author as shaming agents, employ violence as their selected strategy of resistance in a situation of dehumanization. Juliana Claassens alludes to this when arguing: "In situations of extreme duress these two women emerged as liberators of their people, both of them resorting to violence in order to save the Israelites."[34] One may argue that these women had few other options in the context of war. In particular, one could understand Jael's decision to use violence given the widespread rape culture that exists especially in the context of war, which is powerfully reflected in the mother of Sisera's assertion in Judges 5. Jael, finding herself in a vulnerable position—not only because she is a woman but also because she is a stranger—thus employs violence as her strategy of resistance. An anti-rape reading of the text would thus argue that Jael kills Sisera to avoid rape.[35]

Winnie in Mandela: Long Walk to Freedom

If engaging Jael is a daunting task, it does not even begin to reflect the reality of the contemporary figure of Winnie Madikizela-Mandela. As I now turn to Winnie Mandela, I limit my discussion of this larger-than-life figure to the 2013 portrayal of Winnie by Naomie Harris in Justin Chadwick's biographical motion picture *Mandela: Long Walk to Freedom*. The film is an adaptation of Nelson Mandela's nearly 700-page biography by the same name.[36] The approach applied by Chadwick in trying to tell an epic story with much detail in two-and-a-half hours has led to less than favorable reviews.[37] Xan Brooks consequently poignantly describes it as "a conservative film about a radical man, a movie so bowed down by the weight of responsibility that it occasionally trudges when you wish it would dance."[38]

The charismatic Idris Elba portrays Nelson Mandela to critical acclaim. Scott Foundas alludes to his brilliance:

> What holds the movie together … is Elba, who doesn't look as much like the real Mandela as other actors who've played the role … but who does share his looming 6-foot frame and proves an uncanny mimic of his vocal inflections, speech patterns and accent. What's more, Elba catches the spirit of Mandela in the way no other actor quite has.[39]

As would inevitably be the temptation, the film does overwhelmingly succumb to the "hero's complex" in the depiction of Nelson Mandela, treating him as a hallowed figure and viewing his life through the lens of his sacrifice, consequently elevating him to the status of a martyr.[40] The film, however, does well in exploring the more human dimensions (albeit half-heartedly)[41] of the man who became an icon when Chadwick "shows him cheating on his first wife, neglecting his infant son and smoking like a chimney."[42] Even though the film is primarily about Nelson Mandela (to the point of severe critique),[43] for the purpose of this essay, I would like to focus my attention on the film's depiction of Winnie Mandela, who by no means is a simple character to capture. The film's blurb says it well: "The leader you knew. The woman you didn't." And the film indeed shows a "Winnie Madikizela-Mandela to whom moviegoers have not been introduced previously."[44]

Winnie steps into the life of Nelson Mandela soon after the exit of his first wife. Evelyn Mase was driven away due to her husband's lack of attention—mainly because of his involvement in the struggle, but also as a result of his womanizing.[45] Initially "Winnie is portrayed as a naïvely sweet love interest of Mandela."[46] Critics have, however, undermined this interpretation:

> In truth, Winnie was not saccharin-sweet when she met Nelson but determined and independent (she was by then the first black medical social

worker in South Africa, she'd run away from her family to avoid traditional marriage, she'd turned down a US scholarship to remain active in the ANC etc.). Neither did she simply fight her "husband's" struggle (she fought *her* struggle, which was also black South Africa's struggle and the women's struggle). And she did not turn into a bitter woman (but rather a wronged one). Yet in the movie she is depicted in these ways to juxtapose to her ex-husband's messianic portrayal.[47]

After a whirlwind courtship and marriage, little became of a life together as the demands of the political landscape drew Nelson into the armed struggle and the subsequent treason trial (1963), resulting in a sentence to lifelong detention. Harris beautifully brings across a sense of Winnie's resolve and sense of purpose during this time. As one reviewer writes: "She is staunchly behind her husband's radical activism even at great personal cost, but also hints at the ideological divide to come during the long years of Nelson's incarceration."[48]

Harris makes tangible something of the hardening that takes place within Winnie Mandela when she is subjected to numerous raids, violence, and police brutality in the absence of the now incarcerated Nelson. The film highlights some of the tactics employed by the apartheid government's security police when she comments on the fact that they often come "to pay her a little visit" right before the girls return from school, taking her away and leaving them to return to an empty house. The tipping point in the film in terms of Winnie's character formation is the painful depiction of her 16-month period in solitary confinement. Harris does well to embody the rage and hatred instilled during this time of violation and dehumanization. She returns in an iconic scene to a jubilant crowd chanting her name and waving banners with the slogan "home at last." Her transformation is evident when she states: "I say to my jailors … thank you. I say to the government … thank you. You have helped me grow up. I was very young when I married Nelson. I am not young anymore. I am not afraid anymore."

One of the strongest motives developed during the second half of the film is the contrasting reality of life for Mandela on Robben Island and the one developing for Winnie during the anti-apartheid struggle—a division emphasized by often setting up camera shots that show Mandela and Winnie on different sides of barriers, glass panels, and walls. Alyssa Rosenberg comments:

> The most interesting idea advanced in *Mandela* is that while Mandela's long imprisonment on Robben Island and on the mainland stole almost three decades of his life from him, his incarceration not only made him a powerful symbol, but protected him from what he might have become. Robben Island is absolutely presented as unpleasant … but while inside, Mandela studies, grows tomatoes and deepens his bond with his co-defendants … Life on the outside for Winnie, by contrast, comes across as even more grinding and humiliating.[49]

For Nelson, being removed from the anti-apartheid struggle means being denied the opportunity to contribute to the country's future, but it also protects him from being involved in the worst of it. Winnie, by contrast, experiences some of the worst excesses of the struggle, and breaks under the unbearable cruelty and strain.[50]

The film does not flinch in the portrayal of Winnie's increasing radicalization but nonetheless tries to offer some context for it. Her growing militant demeanor and her punishment of traitors and informers within her own community are in ways every bit as horrifying as the regime she professes to fight. In the span of the film, Winnie thus becomes the counterpoint for Mandela's journey from principled revolutionary to pragmatic yet still principled negotiator and conciliator. The almost lifelong physical separation between Nelson and Winnie goes some way to explain the emotional and ideological separation that reaches its climax when an older and more moderate Mandela, more forgiving and politically triumphant, communicates his displeasure with Winnie's staunchly radical tactics.

The film does not dwell on the atrocities and murders committed by the Mandela United Football Club,[51] a gang of anarchical youths who acted as Madikizela-Mandela's bodyguards in the 1980s, yet as Will Gore notes in an interview with the lead actress, "neither Harris nor [the film] shies away from the dark side of this divisive woman."[52] Harris admits that she was terrified to take on the role and is quoted saying:

> I thought: What? This woman is like seven different women in one. Everyone had such different ideas about who Winnie was. One biography painted her as a demon, another as a saint and I thought how can you create a cohesive character from all that? ... She's so hugely complex, this mixture of tremendous warmth and compassion as well as anger and rage ... She's a warrior as well as a nurturer.[53]

Harris, in her comments and character portrayal, picks up on something of the "un-neat" nature of Winnie Mandela: "She is a troublemaker," a villain, a caring mother, "a political icon, a woman who makes heavy sacrifices for the struggle, a symbol of resistance, a femme fatale," and she cannot simply be pinned down into an all-encompassing definition.[54]

Chadwick's representation of Winnie Mandela is but one attempt at creating a space for engagement, reflection, critique, and encounter on her life, and he chooses to portray her in many ways as a counter-figure to Mandela. In his novel, *The Cry of Winnie Mandela*, Njabulo Ndebele does something similar when he places the following words in the mouth of his fictive Winnie Mandela:

> There is one thing I will not do. It is my only defense of the future. I will not be an instrument for validating the politics of reconciliation. For me, reconciliation demands my annihilation. No. *You*, all of you have to reconcile not with me, but with the meaning of me. For my meaning is the endless human search for the right thing to do. I am your pleasure and your pain, your beauty and your ugliness. Your solution and your mistake. Your hell and your heaven. I am your squatter camp shack and your million rand mansion. I am all of you who maim

and rape. I am all of you who give love and succour. I am your pride and your shame. Your honour and your humiliation. The journey to your future goes through the dot of loving me, despite myself, on the world map that lays out journeys toward all kinds of human fulfilment.[55]

In conclusion of this section, I would again like to briefly allude to the three strands that run through the narrative, as was earlier identified in the Jael narrative in Judges 4. First, as was the case with Jael, Winnie Mandela's narrative is imbedded in a complex social reality.[56] South Africa under the apartheid regime implied a social organization that rests on the systematic dehumanization of the counter-group, the so-classified non-whites. The struggle against this regime was violent, dangerous, and complex to negotiate in the light of the constant threat of betrayal, death, and dehumanization. Second, as was alluded to in the discussion of the film, the gendered nature of the resistance narrative cannot be denied. To the hypothetical question "is there a man here?" the enemies of Winnie Mandela knew the answer. They successfully removed Nelson from his home, place, and, consequently, the political landscape, leaving Winnie compromised and vulnerable, exposing the Achilles' heel of her role as single mother and fragile "mother of the nation." As is the case with Jael and Deborah, Winnie, however, finds a way to challenge traditional gender expectations, roles, and norms. Third, and maybe even more tangible in this narrative due to its proximity, Winnie employs violence as her strategy of resistance: brutal, unflinching, life-denying violence. In Antjie Krog's *Country of My Skull*, the Methodist bishop Peter Storey is quoted when he reflects on the essence of the Stompie Seipei case and on Winnie Mandela's violent involvement:

> The primary cancer will always be and has always been Apartheid. But secondary infections have touched many of Apartheid's opponents and eroded their knowledge of good and evil. And one of the tragedies of life is it's possible to become that which we hate most—a ruthless abuse of power and a latitude that allows our deeds to resemble the abuses we fought against.[57]

In Front of the Collective Reflective Surface

After considering the narratives of Deborah, Jael, and Winnie, I would like to conclude by returning to the overarching question of this essay, namely: "how do we live a good life?" When ethically engaging the reflective surface and allowing the narratives to speak to me and perhaps even to touch my heart, I embark on a deeply personal, but also fundamentally collective journey. In this quest, I am confronted with two pertinent challenges in the pursuit of a good life. These challenges are of course my own, and would theoretically differ for different readers/viewers due to their situatedness and relation to the narratives. However, in engaging my own particular questions, I hope to perhaps start a collective, creative, and imaginative conversation on these texts in our context.

First, when being confronted with the complex social landscape that serves as backdrop for the stories of Winnie, Jael, and Deborah, I am again sensitized to the complex social landscape that serves as the background of my life and of our lives collectively. As I am engaging contexts of war, rape, violence, and discrimination in these narratives, I am once again being made aware of the situations of injustice in my own context. In taking up the challenge of Martha Nussbaum to read ethically and cultivate the capacity for imagination, I do not only view complex social landscapes as something that exist outside of me, but I also have to engage my own complicity in situations of discrimination, hatred, violence, and injustice.[58] The reflective surface created by the stories of Jael and Winnie forces me to ask questions about my own positions of privilege and my own involvement and collusion in structures and constructions that deny others' lives, well-being, and the opportunity to flourish.

Second, and perhaps even more pertinent, I read in the narratives of Jael and Winnie of women who, in their acts of resistance, painfully and complexly become that against which they fight so hard. Jael, in her resistance of rape, kills a man; Winnie, in her resistance of the dehumanization of apartheid, perpetuates violence that looks remarkably like that which she opposes with the essence of her being. If we are courageous enough to look into the mirror held up by the reflective surface of the text, we have to ask ourselves serious questions regarding our own acts of resistance and the strategies we employ when confronting discrimination and dehumanization. When confronted by the various manifestations of violence—sometimes as clear as meta-structures or constructions in systematic constellations represented by terms such as racism, sexism, xenophobia, and homophobia, and sometimes as subtle as coercing or leaving, shutting down, and punishing, defending, withholding, justifying, controlling, judging, meddling, and giving unsolicited advice—we have to ask critical questions as to the creativity, the imagination, and the life-affirming quality of our response when we push back. When engaging what Alanis Morissette calls in her song "Underneath" "the wars in our bedrooms, the cliques in our sandboxes, and the dictatorships on our own block,"[59] we have to ask ourselves whether our resistance makes life possible for not only ourselves, but also for those who travel this fragile journey of life with us. How does my resistance against violence and dehumanization not succumb to the allure of a subtly violent response, but instead open up the fragile possibility of compassion, care, and community—essential elements for the vulnerability of life together?

Notes

1. Wolfgang Huber, "Why Ethics?," Inaugural Lecture as Honorary Professor of Stellenbosch University, February 19, 2015.
2. When ethically engaging the reflective surface and allowing the narratives to speak to me, to touch my heart, I take pointers from Wayne Booth's thought on the development of a narrative ethics described in his book *The Company We Keep: An Ethics of Fiction* (Berkeley: University of California Press, 1988), 3–20. Booth identifies four important guiding principles in the process of developing a narrative ethics.

Ethics for Booth is a very broad term that can be discussed in relation to the question "how should one live?" He is interested not so much in the aftermath of reading as in the process of reflection while reading. He encourages readers to move away from simple character or situational judgment, to move away from the "cheap and easy," and to rather sit with the complexities. Martha Nussbaum engages Booth's work in an essay, "Reading for Life," in her book *Love's Knowledge: Essays on Philosophy and Literature* (Oxford: Oxford University Press, 1990).

3. Stanley Hauerwas, "Christians in the Hands of Flaccid Secularists: Theology and 'Moral Inquiry' in the Modern University," in *Ethical Perspectives* 4 (1997): 32–47 (32).

4. Denise Ackermann, *Tamar's Cry: Re-reading an Ancient Text in the Midst of an HIV/AIDS Pandemic* (Johannesburg: Ecumenical Foundation of Southern Africa, 2001), 18–19.

5. Justin Chadwick, director, *Mandela: Long Walk to Freedom* (2013), starring Idris Elba and Naomie Harris.

6. Cf. Ackermann, *Tamar's Cry*, 18–19.

7. Jim Fodor argues that this act of reading is unavoidably bodily and communal in character when he states: "Reading is never simply a cognitive decoding of written signs, a logical assessment of linguistic content, or following an argument; it is also—and perhaps even primarily—a means of forming and disciplining the emotions and affections, offering an orientation, schooling dispositions, re-ordering desires," "Reading the Scriptures: Rehearsing Identity, Practicing Character," in *The Blackwell Companion to Christian Ethics*, ed. Stanley Hauerwas and Samuel Wells (Oxford: Blackwell, 2004), 154.

8. Jacqueline E. Lapsley, *Whispering the Word: Hearing Women's Stories in the Old Testament* (Louisville, KY: Westminster John Knox, 2005), 11. Italics in original.

9. Martha C. Nussbaum, *Sex and Social Justice* (Oxford: Oxford University Press, 1999), 183.

10. Lapsley, *Whispering the Word*, 12.

11. The complex narrative landscape of the book of Judges is well described by Eric S. Christianson: "Judges threatens the stability of Israel's covenantal relationship and exposits the contingency of access to the promised land. The cycle of judges stories in particular destabilizes the reader's ability to come to a positive assessment of Israel's relationship to the land because of the fundamental ambiguity of its stories: narrative gaps, lack of narratorial judgment and conflicting testimony all mean that we cannot know whether the 'judges experiment' was ultimately good," "The Big Sleep: Strategic Ambiguity in Judges 4–5 and in Classic *Film Noir*," *BibInt* 15 (2007): 519–48 (524–5).

12. J. Cheryl Exum, "The Centre Cannot Hold: Thematic and Textual Instabilities in Judges," *CBQ* 52 (1990): 410–31 (411–12). Exum not only describes a subtle variation to the traditional Deuteronomistic framework but also alludes to the dissolution of the framework when stating: "It is not, as often observed, a pattern of apostasy/punishment/ repentance/deliverance but rather one of apostasy/punishment/cry for help/deliverance (or as Robert Polzin puts it, punishment/mercy). Although we are led to expect a consistent and regular pattern, what happens is that the framework itself breaks down. Rather than attributing the lack of consistency in the framework pattern to careless redaction, I take it as a sign of further dissolution. The political and moral instability depicted in Judges is reflected in the textual instability. The framework deconstructs itself, so to speak, and the cycle of apostasy and deliverance becomes increasingly murky."

13. Katharine D. Sakenfeld, "Deborah, Jael, and Sisera's Mother: Reading the Scriptures in Cross-Cultural Context," in *Women, Gender, and Christian Community*, ed. Jane D. Douglass and James F. Kay. (Louisville, KY: Westminster John Knox, 1997), 13–22 (14).

14. Melissa A. Jackson alludes to the wordplay that is employed to introduce Deborah. In addition to noting Deborah's being described as a woman, prophet, and judge, Jackson also refers to the phrase traditionally translated as *wife of Lappidoth*. When rather translating *wife of* as *woman of*, it "yields possibilities such as 'women of torches', 'women of flames/fire', and 'fiery/spirited woman'," *Comedy and Feminist Interpretation of the Hebrew Bible: A Subversive Collaboration*, Oxford Theological Monographs (Oxford: Oxford University Press, 2012), 101.
15. Yairah Amit, "Judges 4: Its Contents and Form," *JSOT* 39 (1987): 89–111 (93).
16. Deryn Guest does not take Barak to be an equal or partner to Deborah, but rather an inferior contrast when she describes him as "a comic slowcoach … a thoroughly wet fish," *When Deborah Met Jael: Lesbian Feminist Hermeneutics* (London: SCM Press, 2005), 153.
17. Ellen van Wolde, "Yaʿel in Judges 4," *ZAW* 107 (1995): 240–6 (245).
18. Johanna W. H. Bos, "Out of the Shadows, Genesis 38; Judges 4, 17–22; Ruth 3," *Semeia* 42 (1988): 37–67 (56).
19. Jackson, *Comedy and Feminist Interpretation of the Hebrew Bible*, 104.
20. Christianson describes the sexual connotations with reference to Sisera's murder as follows: "In Judges the ch. 5 account especially eroticizes the slow murder … Judges 4 does not lack for hints about Jael's sexual strategies either. Jael, clearly aware of what she will do, is offering a false sense of security," "The Big Sleep," 535.
21. Jael depends on Sisera's misconception of her loyalties and therefore initially acts exactly as he would expect. As Bos argues: "Her coming out to meet Sisera in v. 18 and her words and actions through v. 20 are set against the background of her family or clan alliance. She speaks and acts as the wife/servant. She hides Sisera in her tent; she gives him the liquid which she has at hand and makes a move to stand at the tent opening to peak out," "Out of the Shadows," 55. In doing this she tricks Sisera into believing that her loyalties lie with him, when indeed they are securely elsewhere. Danna N. Fewell and David M. Gunn continue: "Sisera understands the world as patriarchy: if Heber is a Canaanite ally then so must his wife be. Jael further confirms his patriarchal understanding by portraying herself as sympathetic and as subservient to him personally: 'Turn aside, my lord, turn aside to me. Do not fear,' " "Controlling Perspectives: Women, Men, and the Authority of Violence in Judges 4 & 5," *JAAR* 58 (1990): 389–411 (392). Susan Niditch continues in the same vein when referring to the poetic description of events: "Double meanings of violent death and sexuality emerge in every line. He is at her feet in a pose of defeat and humiliation; he kneels between her legs in sexual pose. He falls and lies, a dead warrior assassinated by a warrior better than he … ," "Eroticism and Death in the Tale of Jael," in *Women in the Hebrew Bible: A Reader*, ed. Alice Bach (New York: Routledge, 1999), 305–16 (310–11).
22. Fewell and Gunn, "Controlling Perspectives," 403.
23. Susan Niditch, *Judges: A Commentary* (Louisville, KY: Westminster John Knox, 2008), 5.
24. Sakenfeld, "Deborah, Jael, and Sisera's Mother," 21.
25. Bos, "Out of the Shadows," 56.
26. Sakenfeld, "Deborah, Jael, and Sisera's Mother," 19. Sakenfeld continues: "Both in psychological theory and in our common knowledge of behavior of armies, sex and violence are closely intertwined. A number of scholars, both women and men, have recently suggested that these dimensions are at work in the story of Jael."
27. The allusion is to Judith Butler's seminal work, *Gender Trouble: Feminism and the Subversion of Identity* (New York: Routledge, 2011).

28. Queer theory is a critical discipline that develops and builds on the work of the French philosopher Michel Foucault and aims to unmask and undermine the heteronormative myth. It questions the normativity of heterosexuality by showing the inherent plurality, ambivalence, and fluidity of sexual constructions. Queer theory functions from the margins and has as its aim the destabilization of everything that is deemed normal about sexuality and the celebration of diversity. Queer theory strives to question the normal and to trouble the generally accepted. "While queer studies have become well-known for interrogating the boundaries and categories that structure discourses of sexuality and gender (e.g., the binary distinction between 'heterosexual' and 'homosexual', 'straight' and 'gay', 'male' and 'female', etc.) queer analysis today increasingly brings a critical lens to bear on the intersection of sexual dynamics with other dynamics such as race, class, nation, and culture." Cf. Teresa J. Hornsby and Ken Stone, "Already Queer: A Preface," in *Bible Trouble: Queer Reading at the Boundaries of Biblical Scholarship*, ed. Teresa J. Hornsby and Ken Stone (Atlanta: SBL, 2011), ix–xiv (ix).

29. Jackson, *Comedy and Feminist Interpretation of the Hebrew Bible,* 106.

30. Considering Jael's role in the construction of gender confusion in the narrative, especially in the description of her deception and deviant pleasure in exotic, revitalized, and sexual violence, Christianson describes Jael as a femme fatale constructed as "a symptom of male anxieties about women, a creature who threatens to castrate and devour her male victim," "The Big Sleep," 532.

31. Gale A. Yee, "By the Hand of a Woman: The Metaphor of Woman Warrior in Judges 4," *Semeia* 61 (1993): 93–134 (117).

32. Yee, "By the Hand of a Woman," 115. Italics in original.

33. Harold Washington argues in this regard: "Imbrications of violence and gender in the Hebrew Bible are more than just reflections of the social conditions of biblical antiquity. In this literature, gender becomes a crucial articulator of the experience of violence, and thus gendered discourse becomes a means of *producing* relations of violence and domination, authenticating a violent male prerogative that remains culturally potent into the present," Harold C. Washington, "Violence and the Construction of Gender in the Hebrew Bible: A New Historicist Approach 1," *BibInt* 5 (1997): 324–63 (331). Italics in original.

34. L. Juliana M. Claassens, *Mourner, Mother, Midwife: Reimagining God's Delivering Presence in the Old Testament* (Louisville, KY: Westminster John Knox, 2012), 4.

35. Susan Niditch alludes to this line of interpretation: "The Jael tale read by modern women provides an alternate symbolism. One is not suggesting that women become men-slayers in some simple-minded reading, but rather that the tale is rich in images of directed action, self-assertion, and consciousness on the part of the underdog. The archetype expressing on many levels male anxieties can thus become a powerfully charged model for all marginals, in particular women," "Eroticism and Death in the Tale of Jael," 313.

36. The film's royal premiere in London on December 5, 2013, also marks the day on which Nelson Mandela quietly died in his home in Johannesburg. Some account for the critical reception of the film because of its situatedness among a myriad of documentaries. Wamuwi Mbao writes that "the mourning period saw the television and radio networks being flooded with documentaries about the life and the time of a man who had, in the true winter of a life whose autumn had been uncharacteristically long, banished from public view to be replaced by images and ideas. There was no small amount of memorialisation even before Nelson Mandela died, but the name that had for so many years stood for ideas of freedom and reconciliation, also began attracting images and ideas that weren't so appealing," "Not Our Long Walk to

Freedom," *Slip* (January 9, 2014), available at: http://slipnet.co.za/view/reviews/not-our-long-walk-to-freedom/, accessed January 15, 2015. As David Gritten continues, "with Mandela's recent death, the blanket media coverage of the mourning period and subsequent lengthy tributes to him, might the public's appetite for such a film now be dimmed?," David Gritten, "Mandela: Long Walk to Freedom, Review," *The Telegraph* (January 2, 2014), available at: http://www.telegraph.co.uk/culture/film/filmreviews/10323655/Mandela-Long-Walk-To-Freedom-review.html, accessed January 15, 2015.

37. Mbao's final judgment is even more negative: "Overall the film's greatest flaw is that it doesn't feel authentically South African. It's hard to be enthusiastic about a film that feels like a cross between a beer advert and Gladiator. It's a problem summed up at the end of the film, when the credits roll and the end music is supplied by Bono/U2. This feels like a shallow waltz through the life of Mandela, glibly polished for the attention of an international audience. It reduces Mandela even as it tries to show us what a complex man he was. Perhaps it's that the movie is so showy where subtlety would have done more, and too blasé when explicit links should have been drawn, that it leaves the watcher alienated. Long Walk to Freedom, as it is adapted here, is not our story," "Not Our Long Walk to Freedom."

38. Xan Brooks, "Mandela: Long Walk to Freedom—Review," *The Guardian* (January 5, 2014), available at: http://www.theguardian.com/film/2014/jan/05/mandela-long-walk-to-freedom-review, accessed January 15, 2015.

39. Scott Foundas, "Toronto Film Review: 'Mandela: Long Walk to Freedom,'" *Variety* (September 8, 2013), available at: http://variety.com/2013/film/reviews/mandela-long-walk-to-freedom-review-toronto-1200604107/, accessed January 15, 2015.

40. Simon Abrams, in a critical review, notes: "In a key scene … a judge tells Mandela that he's being sentenced to life imprisonment so that he can't become a martyr. Mandela says he's willing to die for his cause, and the judge replies, 'I will not give you that satisfaction.' The makers of 'Mandela: Long walk to Freedom' did what that judge refused to, though for very different reasons: they let their admiration for Mandela's suffering define their drama." Simon Abrams, "Mandela: Long Walk to Freedom," *Rogerebert* (November 29, 2013), available at: http://www.rogerebert.com/reviews/mandela-long-walk-to-freedom-2013, accessed January 15, 2015.

41. Mbao questions the depiction of Mandela's vices when arguing: "The film is at pains, or wants us to believe it is at pains, to show us that 'Mandela was no saint,' a clichéd idea that finds expression in odd ways: while Mandela is single-handedly revolutionising the ANC … we also see him as a wife-beater and casual philanderer. There is no depth to these depictions and they feel like they were inserted slap-dash into the hero-narrative because they have to be there, rather than because they add anything." "Not Our Long Walk to Freedom."

42. Brooks, "Mandela: Long Walk to Freedom—Review."

43. Mbao points out that in contrast to Nelson Mandela's own conviction that his story of resistance is a communal one, it is somewhat odd how the film depicts the main leaders of the ANC: "Walter Sisulu, Ahmed Kathrada and Oliver Tambo become voiceless supplicants, appealing to the broad-shouldered boxer to help deliver the people from oppression," "Not Our Long Walk to Freedom."

44. "Winnie Mandela's Derivative Portrayal in a Long Walk to Freedom," *MSAfropolitan* (January 13, 2014), available at: http://www.msafropolitan.com/2014/01/winnie-mandelas-long-walk-to-freedom.html, accessed January 15, 2015.

45. Alyssa Rosenberg remarks in this regard: "*Mandela* is unsparing in its portrait of Mandela's marriage to his first wife, Evelyn. Though in their courtship, he's flirtatious

and fun, he's quick to abandon her for the movement, to mock Evelyn's belief in religion, to cheat on her, and even to physically abuse her during an argument. 'You care about all the children of South Africa except your own,' she tells him bitterly, leaving Nelson during his first stint in prison," " 'Mandela: Long Walk to Freedom' Is an Unsentimental but Flawed Portrait of Nelson Mandela," *Think Progress* (December 23, 2013), available at: http://thinkprogress.org/alyssa/2013/12/23/3097611/mandela-long-walk-freedom/, accessed January 15, 2015.

46. "Winnie Mandela's Derivative Portrayal in a Long Walk to Freedom."

47. "Winnie Mandela's Derivative Portrayal in a Long Walk to Freedom."

48. David Rooney, "Mandela: Long Walk to Freedom." Toronto Review (9 August 2013) Available at: http://www.hollywoodreporter.com/review/mandela-long-walk-freedom-toronto-624015, accessed May 2, 2017.

49. Rosenberg, " 'Mandela: Long Walk to Freedom.' "

50. Nelson Mandela himself comments on this reality when stating: "But just as I am convinced that my wife's life while I was in prison was more difficult than mine, my own return was also more difficult for her than it was for me. She married a man who soon left her; the man became a myth; and then the myth returned home and proved to be just a man after all," *Long Walk to Freedom* (London: Abacus, 1995), 109.

51. The film has received critique in this regard: "Although the movie goes some way in depicting the under-examined civil violence that tore through South-Africa between 1985 and 1994, it takes on a decidedly sentimental tone, and here again the pace speeds up, as if to prevent watering down the chronological thread," Mbao, "Not Our Long Walk to Freedom."

52. Will Gore, "Interview with Naomie Harris," January 4, 2014 in *The Spectator*, available at: https://www.spectator.co.uk/2014/01/interview-with-naomie-harris/, accessed June 23, 2017.

53. Julia Llewellyn Smith, "Star Tells of Daunting Task of Portraying Former Mrs Mandela," *Dispatch Live* (January 7, 2014), available at: http://www.dispatchlive.co.za/leisure/winnie-delighted-with-harris/, accessed January 15, 2015.

54. "Winnie Mandela's Derivative Portrayal in a Long Walk to Freedom."

55. Njabulo S. Ndebele, *The Cry of Winnie Mandela: A Novel* (Cape Town: David Philip, 2003), 182–3.

56. Anné Mariè du Preez Bezdrob describes this context as follows: "In situations where an entire society is victimised and traumatised, virtually every member of the community becomes a potential perpetrator of violence. By the mid-1980s, South Africa's black population had suffered three decades of gradually escalating government-sponsored victimisation and violence at the hands of the police … townships had been turned into war zones, where security forces committed acts of brutality with impunity and total disregard for human life or acceptable norms of behaviour," *Winnie Mandela: A Life* (Cape Town: Zebra Press, 2005), 218.

57. Peter Storey, quoted in Antjie Krog, *Country of My Skull: Guilt, Sorrow, and the Limits of Forgiveness in the New South Africa* (New York: Broadway Books, 2007), 248.

58. Nussbaum, *Sex and Social Justice*, 183.

59. The reference is to "Underneath" by Alanis Morissette from her 2008 album *Flavors of Entanglement*.

Chapter 9

MIRIAM AND MOSES'S CUSHITE WIFE: SISTERHOOD IN JEOPARDY?

Funlola Olojede

A Feminist Framework from the Margins

One reason feminist readers of the Bible fault and oppose dominant traditional exegesis is not so much that it is carried out predominantly by men but because of the androcentric bias of the interpretations. Male exegetes usually analyze and retell biblical stories as if women hardly exist. The explanation for such oversight is that the biblical text itself minoritizes women and their roles, or that the tendency to sideline women is only a reflection of the reality in the society to which the interpreter belongs. My position is that without doubt women's stories not only need to be told, and be told by women, but also be told in a sensitive or relational way that takes into account other characters in such stories. Women's stories should not be told in isolation as if others hardly exist, but in relation to women, to children, to men, and to other members of the society at large—especially those in the margin and the vulnerable. My interpretation of the text is especially sensitive to female characters and issues that are hidden in liminal spaces of Scripture, perhaps due in part to my social location and experiences in a racially mixed South Africa as an immigrant from West Africa where the communities are inherently homogeneous in terms of race and mixed marriages are a rarity. And given one's liminal status as an outsider or foreigner in the present context, one cannot but be sensitive also to issues that relate to hybridity, intersectionality, and marginality—not only in social relations but also in academic circles. It is my contention that power dynamics among women—in particular destructive or negative dynamics that can influence or even threaten feminist discourse in Old Testament studies—have been underexplored.

Miriam, the Sister-in-Law?

In this essay, I wish to examine the story in which Miriam and Aaron complain against Moses in Numbers 12:1–16 in the light of attitudes of family members to mixed marriages in South Africa. The story is used to illustrate the power dynamics among participants in feminist discourse and the way this relates to the context of mixed marriage that informs the present reading of the text.

In the story, God is said to overhear the complaint of Moses's two siblings. He then summons Miriam and Aaron to the Tent of the Meeting, where he expresses his displeasure over their utterance and pronounces punishment on Miriam, who seems to spearhead the confrontation. A number of critics have noted that in Numbers 12 the complaint against Moses is twofold, that is, about his mixed marriage and his claim of possessing unique authority.[1]

To me, however, it seems that the complaint is actually only that Moses arrogates unique authority to himself while the underlying basis for complaining is the disapproval of his mixed marriage. Therefore, God reacts only to the complaint or utterance and does not address the motive behind it. Accordingly, exegetes tend to focus only on the complaint and not the basis of it, which is Moses's importation of a Cushite wife into the *bêt āb* (household).

As a sister, Miriam has been upheld as an exemplary figure and a true Israelite heroine. But the question is, is Miriam an exemplary sister-in-law? What is her attitude toward this Cushite sister-in-law, and what could be the implications for sisterhood, or the idea of female solidarity that is observable in the book of Exodus or other parts of the Old Testament? Feminist critics have observed that the book of Genesis contains stories of rivalry among its women—for example, between Sarah and Hagar or between Rachel and Leah. On the other hand, the book of Exodus, in which Miriam features quite visibly, is endorsed as one in which women act cooperatively to achieve common goals. For instance, women cross ethnic lines and form an alliance to defy Pharaoh's order.[2] It is noteworthy that the same Miriam who in Exodus collaborates with other women to save Moses and to celebrate Israel's deliverance at the Red Sea is now pitted against another woman in Numbers 12.

Many questions concerning this chapter have been raised, most of which remain unanswered, such as the issue of the identity of Moses's wife or the reason why Miriam alone is singled out for punishment. Is the Cushite woman the same person as Zipporah, the daughter of Jethro, the Midianite priest? If the answer is affirmative, what is the reason for identifying her as Cushite in this text rather than Midianite? Phyllis Trible, who concludes that we can only speculate about the matter, asks another salient question: "Whoever the woman is, is the attack racist, suggesting opposition to black Cushite skin?"[3] One thing is clear—Moses has married a non-Israelite, a foreigner. He is in a mixed marriage. Before we probe this question further, it might help to consider what constitutes a mixed or exogamous marriage both in the Old Testament world and in the present location of the author—South Africa.

The issue of mixed marriage[4] or foreign wives is not foreign to the Old Testament; there is ample evidence of the practice of mixed marriage in the ancient world. As we shall see later in this chapter, to curb its spread or its effects, laws abound in the biblical text against exogamy. Interestingly, in South Africa (as in some other places such as the United States), various legislations were issued in the past to prohibit and criminalize interracial intimate relationships. In what follows, the issue of mixed marriage will be examined first in the Old Testament in particular in the light of the attitude of Miriam toward Moses's Cushite wife, and then in the South African context.

Mixed Marriage in the Old Testament

On the institutional level, the Torah contains legislation that prohibits exogamous marriages (Deut 7:1–3, 16; Exod 34:16; cf. Mal 2:11). In Numbers 25:1–14, we read of an outcry against Israelite men who engaged in intimate relations with Moabite women. In that particular episode, Phineas, Aaron's son, made a public example of Zimri and his Midianite girlfriend Cozbi, who were both children of leaders in their countries, by impaling them. However, the classic anti-miscegenation edict is found in the book of Ezra-Nehemiah (Ezra 9:11–12; Neh 13:25–27). During the Second Temple period, Yehud had become a breeding ground for mixed marriages, and Ezra and Nehemiah were compelled to evoke the Mosaic Law to outlaw mixed marriages. Interestingly, while the Deuteronomic law prohibited marriage to foreigners by both Israelite male and female, Ezra seems to be fixated on getting rid of the foreign wives without mentioning foreign husbands.[5] Ezra is not content with preventing interracial marriage; existing mixed marriages (that involved foreign wives) have to be dissolved as well.

On the private level, the initial reaction of Samson's parents to his proposal to marry outside his group is met with disapproval (Judg 14:1–3). Rebekah complains to Isaac that she is weary of her life because of the daughters of Heth whom Esau had taken as wives (Gen 27:46). Abraham implores his servant to swear by God that he would not take a wife for Isaac from among the Canaanite maidens but would go back to Mesopotamia to find a bride from among his own people (Gen 24:1–9). Dinah's brothers Simeon and Levi would rather resort to killing than allow their sister to marry Shechem the Hivite (Gen 34), even though their father does not oppose the union as long as Shechem complies with Israel's religious obligations.[6] These cases suggest that interethnic marriages were as problematic as interracial marriages in the Old Testament world, and on the family level, family members, especially parents and siblings, were prone to disapprove of mixed marriages.

Nonetheless, in spite of all the negative attitudes toward mixed marriages and the legislations that prohibited them, the prevalence of mixed marriages is noticeable throughout the Old Testament. Kings and other people in positions of authority married foreign wives—Joseph married an Egyptian woman, Asenath (Gen 41:50); Solomon married many foreign women (1 Kgs 11:1–2); and Ahasuerus, a non-Israelite king, married Esther (Esth 2:17). Commoners also intermarried with foreigners, as evident in Mahlon and Chilion's marriage to the Moabite women Orpah and Ruth (Ruth 1:2–4). In some of these cases, there appears to be little if any disapproval on the part of society or the biblical narrator/writer. Even though the biblical text contains laws against intermarriage, there are ample cases of the reality of intermarriage among the people that show that, historically, society's stance toward intermarriage was somewhat ambivalent. For instance, Moses married Zipporah, a Midianite, but ironically, the same Moses called for the destruction of Midian at Baal of Peor (Num 25) because the Israelite men had begun to philander with Midianite girls.[7] This contradiction has been attributed to the existence of ideological conflicts and opposing practices in society. Claudia Camp affirms that the real issue is that the male reaction in Numbers 25 is borne out of fear that men were unable to control their women's sexuality.[8] In the exilic-postexilic period, however, it seems that all boundaries were already broken as people freely crossed ethnic and racial lines in marriage. In light of the previously mentioned precedents, it seems that Miriam and Aaron's complaint against Moses because of his Cushite wife is not that peculiar. But who is Miriam? A brief consideration of Miriam's persona could help us to understand her reaction to Moses and by implication to his wife.

Miriam in Relationship

In biblical interpretation, the character of Miriam is upheld as a true Israelite heroine in various readings based on her roles as a prophetess, women's leader, public figure, and religious and worship leader. She is seen as a woman of influence and power.[9] No mother could ask for a better daughter and oldest child—she is portrayed as obedient, thoughtful, smart, articulate, and able to take initiative. Miriam's first appearance in Scripture, however, is as a sister—the older sister to the infant Moses who had just been thrown "in the river" by his own mother (Exod 2:4). We are introduced to a protective and caring big sister who with her ingenuity and intuitive action connives with Pharaoh's daughter to save Moses's life. Without a doubt, there is a special bond between these two siblings. Miriam probably sang to Moses as a child and taught him how to sing as he grew, such that in the aftermath of the crossing of the Red Sea in Exodus 15, they both sing—first the protégé, then the mentor. It is not surprising that when Miriam gets into trouble with YHWH who releases his wrath upon her, Moses cries to God to save his sister from the skin affliction that is meted out as punishment for her sin (Num 12:13).

Again, as a sister, Miriam also seems to share a bond with her other brother Aaron, as her conspiracy with him against Moses suggests. Although the text does not explicitly admit to any emotional attachment between Aaron and his sister, his passionate appeal to Moses to do something to save Miriam shows he could not bear to see her flesh rot away (Num 12:11). Before the Numbers 12 episode, these "Three Musketeers" appeared to be a close-knit bunch, but now their friendship is being threatened by Moses's marriage to the Cushite.[10]

As a woman and a leader, Miriam enjoys the support of her fellow women and of the entire congregation of Israel. From the narrative portrayal in Exodus, it seems that Miriam is able to network freely and effectively with other women. For instance, at the Nile, she engages Pharaoh's daughter in conversation and connects her with a wet nurse (her own mother) who would nurse baby Moses

(Exod 2:5–9). It is quite likely that Miriam also networked with other women, both Israelite and Egyptian alike, in the course of the sojourn in Egypt. In this regard, Carol Meyers has argued that the fact that the Israelite women could freely borrow jewelry and clothes from their Egyptian counterparts suggests that there must have existed some form of neighborhood networks and solidarity between the two groups (Exod 3:21; 12:35–36).[11]

Moreover, on the other side of the Red Sea, Miriam leads the women in singing and dancing (Exod 15:20–21).[12] The high regard that the people had for Miriam is most evident from the Numbers 12 episode in which the people refused to continue on their journey until the quarantined Miriam was restored to them (v. 15). Finally, it is significant that the whole congregation in Numbers 20:1 would later witness her death and burial.

Without the Numbers 12 account, perhaps one could conclude, based on other textual references to Miriam that cast her in a positive light, that there is not a single mean bone in her body. Numbers 12 reveals, however, that there is a dark side to this reputable character after all. This same Miriam is now at odds with Moses over his marriage to a Cushite woman! It is clear that she harbors deep resentment against her brother because of his mixed marriage to the Cushite. And she acts on this resentment in Numbers 12:1: "Miriam and Aaron spoke against Moses because of the Cushite woman whom he had married (for he had indeed married a Cushite woman)."

Pinpointing the identity of Moses's unnamed Cushite wife, who is mentioned only in this verse, is problematic. Some exegetes assume that she is the same woman as Zipporah, the daughter of Jethro, whom Moses had married while living in Gershom (Exod 2:16–22); hence, they try to build some alliances between the Midianites and the Cushites. On the other hand, most interpreters suggest that the Cushite woman, a black woman, is a new wife Moses took after his marriage to Zipporah.[13] At any rate, she is a foreign wife, of a foreign nationality, which means Moses has entered into a mixed marriage. And from Numbers 12 it is clear that Miriam—and Aaron—do not approve of this arrangement. If we accept that the Cushite wife is a different woman from Zipporah, then Miriam's grudge against Moses's mixed marriage could be interpreted rightly (or wrongly) as having racial or even xenophobic undertones.

Here we see Miriam, an upstanding member of the society, a great daughter, sister, leader, and elder, now in her twilight years succumbing to racist expectations and attitudes. It seems that as a sister-in-law Miriam is quite capable of tolerating the ethnically different Zipporah. She must have thought that after all, even Father Abraham himself married a Midianite, Keturah (Gen 25:1). But a Cushite sister-in-law? That seems too close for comfort. Miriam and Aaron must have wondered: "Why would Moses marry a foreigner?" But why should Moses *not* marry a foreigner? Moses was born a Hebrew, raised an Egyptian, exiled into Midian. Surely, his hybrid position could have helped him to be accommodative of racial and ethnic differences.

It is remarkable that opposition to Moses's mixed marriage does not emanate from outside but from within his own household and family. Hurt beyond words,

Moses could not respond to the accusation by Miriam and Aaron. Therefore, YHWH rises to his defense. Interestingly, God does not seem to have a problem with Moses's marriage to a Cushite, for not only does God not side with Miriam and Aaron, He actually punishes Miriam. Ironically, the one who abhors another's skin color is punished with a skin disease.[14] In this regard, Mukti Barton remarks that "Miriam would like to see her sister-in-law put outside the camp of the Israelites and she herself is put outside the camp."[15] And yet one cannot help but notice that Miriam is judged while Aaron is left unscathed. Indeed, many feminist interpreters have attributed to patriarchal prejudice the fact that only Miriam is punished while Aaron gets away scot-free.[16]

It is disappointing to note that Miriam's reputation as a solid networker, bridge builder, women's leader, and mouthpiece crumbles in the face of racial intolerance. It appears that Miriam's idea of sisterhood does not accommodate race or the Other. She chooses loyalty to her own ethnic group rather than to sisterhood, without recognizing that allegiance to sisterhood does not diminish in any way her commitment and responsibility to her people. How does Moses's Cushite wife then feel, seeing that she is not even worthy enough to appear on the scene or elsewhere in the text? She lurks in the shadows, confined to a liminal space in which she remains unseen, unheard, excluded, and scorned even by a fellow sister. Zierler writes of this hidden figure:

> In the biblical text … the Cushite woman is a geographical or topological sign rather than a fully empowered human agent or subject. She is spoken about and never spoken to, and she herself never speaks. As the poem observes, Moses says nothing about the Cushite woman, nor does the Cushite woman speak about herself; and Numbers 12, after verse 1, says nothing more about her. More road sign than signifier, she is not even given a proper name. Does she even have a mouth?[17]

Mixed Marriage in South Africa—a Brief Sociohistorical Overview

In general, mixed marriages, whether interracial or interethnic, are cross-cultural in essence and involve the idea of crossing boundaries by the parties concerned. Rebecca Sherman and Melissa Steyn confirm that "cross-cultural relationships have necessarily involved transgression of boundaries separating groups in power hierarchy."[18] Sherman and Steyn trace the history of interracial relationships in South Africa back to the early European settlement period and show that growing anxiety over miscegenation that was fueled by anti-miscegenation rhetoric by the church (specifically the Dutch Reformed Church) was noticeable in the pre-apartheid era, that is, in the early 1900s.[19] In South Africa, the idea of mixed marriage cannot be separated from the issue of race or racism, and the discourse on mixed marriage hence profoundly intersects with the discourse on race. Claire Jaynes asserts that "opposition to interracial intimate relationships may be indicative of underlying racism."[20] In fact, such relationships are seen not as the dissolution of racial boundaries but an indication that such boundaries remain.[21]

Historically, opposition to mixed marriage in South Africa was also rooted in racial considerations. Jonathan Hyslop recounts that there was a growing proletarianization of Afrikaner women in the 1920s and 1930s. White women had become predominant in the manufacturing workforce in the Johannesburg area with their percentage rising to 73 percent of the total workforce by 1935. Their newfound socioeconomic independence began to threaten the patriarchal order of the white society and the patriarchal authority of the Afrikaner man. In this regard, therefore, gender relations could explain the reasons behind the calls for anti-miscegenation. The deteriorating economic situation in the early 1930s presented a crisis in gender relations, and Hyslop describes it aptly: "Daughters who had left their families in rural areas were not only free of parental control but were also playing a major role in supporting their families … It was this crisis in gender relations within the Afrikaner family which fueled the appeal to racist sentiment of the Malan Nationalists[22] in the 'mixed marriage' campaign."[23]

Politicians began to portray urban working-class white women, who were also perceived to be sexually out of control, as being sexually threatened by black men, and they called for the denunciation of interracial intimacy to "protect" white women from black men. Hyslop sees this call for racial purity in terms of sexual relations as a means of reestablishing gender hierarchy and "reasserting their patriarchal control." Consequently, the Immorality Act (No. 5 of 1927) was enacted to prohibit sexual interactions between white men and African women but not between Whites, Coloureds, and Indians. This was followed by the Prohibition of Mixed Marriage Act (No. 55 of 1949) as well as several other related acts and amendments.[24] Hyslop concludes that the discourse on mixed marriage was a political tool that was used to manipulate the white working class. This means that there were ideological factors behind the resentment of interracial relationships and the subsequent prohibition of mixed marriages in the pre-apartheid era. The ruling class used these measures to preserve male interest and hegemony. In other words, the underlying motivation for these acts was power and control. The white ruling-class members sought to retain control over their women. The anti-miscegenation acts eventually paved the way for the apartheid legislation in 1948.[25]

Anti-miscegenation sentiments were, however, not limited to the South African context. For example, Hyslop draws a parallel between developments in the South Africa of the 1930s and racist populism in the southern part of the United States during the same period. In the United States, anti-miscegenation laws were enacted that forbade interracial marriage in North Carolina as early as 1741. No doubt, opposition to marriage across racial boundaries could well stem from some form of racial supremacy and imbalance.[26] While one of the parties in an interracial relationship usually comes from a dominant, powerful group, the other invariably has roots in a subordinate group. Accordingly, opposition to mixed marriage across racial lines intersects with issues of power and hierarchy. In time, the various anti-miscegenation acts in South Africa became weakened especially with the growing international outcry against the apartheid policy and system. By 1985, the Prohibition of Mixed Marriage Act and the Immorality Act were repealed and interracial intimate relationships were decriminalized.[27] The way was open once again for interracial marriage.

But interracial or mixed marriage is a complex phenomenon because ultimately it is controlled on various levels of societal life such as ideological, political, socioeconomic, religious, and institutional. Even though the cultural and spatiotemporal milieu in which mixed marriages took place in the ancient world differs markedly from the manifestation of mixed marriages in, for example, the South African context, the current discourse on interracial marriage could be helpful in illuminating the related phenomenon in the Old Testament, and vice versa. After all, substantively, a mixed marriage is nothing but a mixed marriage, irrespective of the context.

Of particular interest for this essay is the social reaction to mixed marriage as well as the effect this reaction has on the relationship. Reactions to mixed marriage occur mostly on two levels—the public level (societal and institutional) and the private level (family and friends). As Sherman and Steyn point out, "social reactions to interracial relationships, ranging from violence to acceptance, also vary with the context."[28] It should be noted, however, that perceptions of and attitudes toward mixed marriage differ significantly in post-apartheid South Africa from the time of apartheid. Because mixed marriage under the apartheid regime was perceived as a disruption of the racial and power hierarchy, it was stiffly opposed.[29] The previous discussion shows that on the institutional level, mixed marriage was outlawed altogether. However, in post-apartheid South Africa, reactions and attitudes toward mixed marriage are diverse. Some mixed-race couples are found to experience various forms of "abuse from families, friends and community members of all race groups."[30]

In a contemporary study of the experiences, perceptions, and challenges of interracial couples (white and black), Emily Mojapelo-Batka employs psychological tools to probe the various social reactions to interracial couples in South Africa. Mojapelo-Batka's findings range from acceptance to outward rejection and ostracism of the mixed couples she interviewed. Overall, her respondents experienced more negative reactions from the white communities and families than from their black counterparts.[31] Another interesting finding is that the nature of the reactions also varies along opposing gender lines, with females reacting negatively toward the men from their in-group who are engaged in interracial relationships, and vice versa. For example, a black man tends to react negatively toward a couple when the woman is black and the man is white, and a white man tends to react negatively when the woman is white and the man is black. The converse is also true. The negative reaction stems from the perception that the member of their race in the interracial relationship is disloyal to the in-group.[32]

On the private level, while a few of the respondents experienced some level of support from their families and friends, others encountered disapproval, rejection, and hurt. Most of the respondents attributed the negative reactions that they experienced to the harmful effects of the previous apartheid policies, which had generated much distrust, hatred, and suspicion across racial lines.[33] Although it is evident from Mojapelo-Batka's study that several other variables, including social class, level of education, and age, also influence people's attitudes and reactions toward interracial intimacy and marriage, race is a central factor. It is remarkable that, like the phenomenon of mixed marriage itself, these attitudes and reactions to mixed marriage are not new, as is evident from the narrative portrayal of mixed marriage in the Old Testament.

It seems that the same hurt and rejection that Moses's wife experienced is being experienced by many of her sisters in interracial marriages in South Africa today. Even though the anti-miscegenation policies that represent the material boundaries have long since been removed, the invisible but perceptible barriers remain secure. Reminiscent of the South African respondents in Mojapelo-Batka's study regarding their detractors, Miriam also seems to react to Moses's mixed marriage negatively as a way of enforcing loyalty to her in-group. And whereas mixed marriages indicate that boundaries are being crossed, the negative attitudes and reactions to such marriages remind us that such boundaries continue to be strengthened. As long as complex and hybrid identities remain on the increase in a world in which globalization, multiculturalism, internationalization of businesses, integration and liberalization of economies, and migration prevail, mixed marriages are inevitable. Since mixed marriage is a reality that cannot be wished away, especially in a multiracial and multicultural context such as that of South Africa, social harmony would be enhanced if members of the society would consciously work on ways to improve their attitudes toward mixed couples.

Feminist Biblical Criticism and Sisterhood—a Way Forward

Various strands of feminist hermeneutics have emerged in the last half century, including feminist, womanist, postcolonial feminist, black/African feminist, and Asian feminist criticism, to mention a few. At times, some of these frameworks come together to form various alliances:—their proponents organize a conference, publish a collection of essays, support a worthy feminist cause, or simply enjoy the bond of sisterhood. Besides variations in their subgroups and disciplines, differences in nationality, ethnicity, and race are also common. In some cases, these alliances and the intersection of various feminist discourses could be compared metaphorically to a mixed marriage of sorts in the sense that the "partners" have divergent backgrounds. But in such a mixed marriage, whose voice is the dominant one? Does Miriam epitomize the dominant feminist voice, while the voice of Moses's Cushite wife who remains in the shadows continues to be repressed? In terms of opportunities for publications, employment, and other academic privileges, does Miriam still frown at Moses's Ethiopian wife?

Remarkably, it is women who sometimes oppress other women.[34] Here we are not faced with male power but with female power. In her seminal essay, "Bringing Miriam out of the Shadows," Phyllis Trible asks a poignant question: "Why does the narrator set woman against woman?"[35] If I were to respond to this matriarch of feminist criticism, I would ask in return: does the narrator indeed set woman against woman, or is it that in reality women sometimes do set themselves against one another? In the bid to maintain racial or other group alliances, women do at times set themselves against other women at the expense of sisterhood and female solidarity. Again, is Miriam really still in the shadows, or is it not Moses's black wife who should be brought out of the shadows? For Barton, the Cushite should indeed be brought out of the shadows.[36] No doubt, South Africa as a nation has a long way to go in the area of race relations and improving attitudes toward mixed marriage. But mixed marriage is here to stay. As we press forward in upholding the dignity of women and of humanity, perhaps we should consider reassessing the structures and frameworks that we employ and not inadvertently succumb to forces of discrimination and intolerance as Miriam has done. Perhaps in the spirit of Numbers 12, those of us who are committed to defending the ideals that promote human dignity, equity, and a safe space for all should ask: what is the way forward? Should Moses divorce his Cushite wife? This is rather unlikely if mixed marriage is indeed inevitable in a multicultural and multiracial context as argued previously in this essay. Should the Ethiopian then change her skin? Evidently, this is not feasible. Or perhaps Miriam should rather change her ways?

Notes

1. According to Katharine Doob Sakenfeld, "The complaint made against Moses is twofold: that he has married a Cushite, and that he claims an exclusive authority as God's spokesperson," *Numbers: Journeying with God*, ITC (Grand Rapids, MI: Eerdmans, 1995), 79. Cf. also Philip J. Budd, *Numbers*, WBC 5 (Waco, TX: Word, 1984), 133; Mary Douglas, *In the Wilderness: The Doctrine of Defilement in the Book of Numbers*, JSOTSup 158 (Sheffield: JSOT Press, 1993), 196.

2. Irmtraud Fischer, *Women Who Wrestled with God: Biblical Stories of Israel's Beginnings* (Collegeville, MN: Liturgical Press, 2005), 122. J. Cheryl Exum notes that "Exodus 1–2 showed the cooperation between women across ethnic boundaries," "Second Thoughts about Secondary Characters: Women in Exodus 1.8–2.10," in *A Feminist Companion to Exodus and Deuteronomy*, ed. Athalya Brenner, FCB 6 (Sheffield: Sheffield Academic, 1994), 85, 82.

3. Phyllis Trible, "Bringing Miriam out of the Shadows," in *A Feminist Companion to Exodus and Deuteronomy*, ed. Athalya Brenner, FCB 6 (Sheffield: Sheffield Academic, 1994), 175.

4. The term mixed marriage could imply interethnic or cross-cultural marriage besides interracial or multiracial marriage, and in this essay it is used loosely and interchangeably with interracial marriage and interracial intimate relations. For a good analysis of the terminology associated with mixed marriage, cf. Christian Frevel, "Introduction: The Discourse on Intermarriage in the Hebrew Bible," in *Mixed Marriages: Intermarriage and Group Identity in the Second Temple Period*, ed. Christian Frevel, LHBOTS 547 (New York: T&T Clark, 2011), 3–7.

5. Mary Douglas, "Responding to Ezra: The Priests and the Foreign Wives," *BibInt* 10 (2002): 1–22 (8, 10). Frevel argues that the "mixed marriage issue is without doubt a gender issue in several respects … It is mostly foreign women, not men, who are said to be dangerous (Num 25:2; 1 Kgs 11:3, 33; Ezra 9:2, etc.)," "Introduction," 11. Cf. also

Claudia V. Camp, "Feminist and Gender-Critical Perspectives on the Biblical Ideology of Intermarriage," in *Mixed Marriages: Intermarriage and Group Identity in the Second Temple Period*, ed. Christian Frevel, LHBOTS 547 (New York: T&T Clark, 2011), 303–15 (304).

6. A list of Hebrew Bible passages related to mixed marriages is provided by Frevel, "Introduction," 14. Benedict J. Conczorowski argues that negative attitudes toward mixed marriage unavoidably devalue that marriage and the out-group to which the foreign spouse belongs; "All the Same as Ezra? Conceptual Differences between the Texts on Intermarriage in Genesis, Deuteronomy 7 and Ezra," in *Mixed Marriages: Intermarriage and Group Identity in the Second Temple Period*, ed. Christian Frevel, LHBOTS 547 (New York: T&T Clark, 2011), 89–108 (92, 94).

7. Despite the negative reactions to mixed marriage at different stages of Israelite history, the point remains that foreign wives such as Tamar, Asenath, Zipporah, and Moses's Cushite wife as well as Rahab and Ruth "were essential to the formation, preservation, and deliverance of Israel," Karen S. Winslow, "Mixed Marriage in Torah Narratives," in *Mixed Marriages: Intermarriage and Group Identity in the Second Temple Period*, ed. Christian Frevel, LHBOTS 547 (New York: T&T Clark, 2011), 132–49 (132, 144). On contradictions between Moses's stance toward the Midianites and his marriage to a Midianite, cf. Yonina Dor, "From the Well in Midian to the Baal of Peor: Different Attitudes to Marriage of Israelites to Midianite Women," in *Mixed Marriages: Intermarriage and Group Identity in the Second Temple Period*, ed. Christian Frevel, LHBOTS 547 (New York: T&T Clark, 2011), 150–69 (150-5).

8. Camp, "Feminist and Gender-Critical Perspectives," 307; Winslow, "Mixed Marriage," 147.

9. On Miriam's influence and power, see Sakenfeld, *Numbers: Journeying with God*, 83, who points out that Miriam had developed a following among the women. Moshe Reiss confirms that Miriam's mention in the Prophets (alongside Moses and Aaron) shows her as "a striking personality in her own right, the first woman in the Tanakh who appears not in the role of someone's wife or mother but as an active figure in the affairs of the emerging nation of Israel," Moshe Reiss, "Miriam Rediscovered," *JBQ* 38 (2010): 183–90 (189).

10. The three siblings are mentioned together in several passages of the Old Testament (cf. Exod 15:1, 20; Num 12:1–15; 26:59; 1 Chr 6:3; Mic 6:4).

11. Carol Meyers, *Exodus*, The New Cambridge Bible Commentary (Cambridge: Cambridge University Press, 2005), 277.

12. Meyers points out that Miriam engaged simultaneously in three interconnected and performative acts associated with women—dance, drum-playing, and song. Carol Meyers, "Miriam the Musician," in *A Feminist Companion to Exodus and Deuteronomy*, ed. Athalya Brenner (Sheffield: Sheffield Academic Press, 1994), 207–30 (208).

13. There is a general notion that from late antiquity through the medieval period, most Midrashic interpretations regard the Cushite wife as Zipporah. Barton argues that the woman in question is Zipporah and that Zipporah is black; Mukti Barton, "The Skin of Miriam Became as White as Snow: The Bible, Western Feminism and Colour Politics," *Feminist Theology: The Journal of the Britain and Ireland School of Feminist Theology* 27 (2001): 68–80 (69–72); David S. Sperling, "Miriam, Aaron and Moses: Sibling Rivalry," *HUCA* 70 (2000): 39–55 (45). For further discussion on the identity of the Cushite wife, see Sakenfeld, *Numbers: Journeying with God*, 80; Reiss, "Miriam Rediscovered," 186; Dor, "From the Well in Midian," 166–7; Katharine Doob

Sakenfeld, "Numbers," in *Women's Bible Commentary*, Third Edition: Revised and Updated, ed. Carol A. Newsom et al. (Louisville, KY: Westminster John Knox Press, 2012), 79–87 (83).

14. Douglas, *In the Wilderness*, 198; Sakenfeld, *Numbers: Journeying with God*, 80; Reiss, "Miriam Rediscovered," 187.
15. Barton, "The Skin of Miriam," 74.
16. Barton, "The Skin of Miriam," 74.
17. Wendy Zierler, "'On Account of the Cushite Woman that Moses Took': Race and Gender in Modern Hebrew Poems about Numbers 12," *Nashim: A Journal of Jewish Women's Studies and Gender Issues* 19 (2010): 34–61 (54).
18. Rebecca Sherman and Melissa Steyn, "E-race-ing the Line: South African Interrelationships Yesterday and Today," in *The Prize and the Price: Shaping Sexualities in South Africa*, ed. Melissa Steyn and Mikki van Zyl (Cape Town: HSRC Press, 2009), 55–81 (55–6).
19. Sherman and Steyn, "E-race-ing the Line," 56–62.
20. Claire Jaynes, "The Influence of *The Family* on Interracial Intimate Relationships in Post-apartheid South Africa," *South African Journal of Psychology* 40 (2010): 396–413 (399).
21. Jaynes, "The Influence of *The Family*," 410.
22. The National Party came to power for the first time in 1924 under Prime Minister Hertzog. In 1933, the United Party took over as the governing party. In 1935, D. F. Malan became the leader of a newly formed "Purified" National Party that served as the opposition before it became the ruling party in 1948.
23. Jonathan Hyslop, *The Representation of White Working Class Women in the Construction of a Reactionary Populist Movement: "Purified" Afrikaner Nationalist Agitation for Legislation against "Mixed" Marriages, 1934–1939* (Johannesburg: African Studies Institute, University of the Witwatersrand, 1993), 4, 8–11.
24. Hyslop, *The Representation of White Working Class Women*, 4, 6. Cf. also Sherman and Steyn, "E-race-ing the Line," 63–5; Megan Du Toit and Michael Quayle, "Multiracial Families and Contact Theory in South Africa: Does Direct and Extended Contact Facilitated by Multiracial Families Predict Reduced Prejudice?," *South African Journal of Psychology* 41 (2011): 540–51 (543).
25. Hyslop, *The Representation of White Working Class Women*, 26. This view that South Africa's anti-miscegenation acts had ideological and political undertones resonates with Claudia Camp's argument earlier in the essay that the men's reaction to Zimri and Cozbi in Numbers 25 was borne out of fear that they had no control over their women's sexuality.
26. Hyslop, *The Representation of White Working Class Women*, 6–8. George Yancey and Richard Lewis Jr. also point out that "the harassment of interracial families reflected the overt racism in the United States. This racism emphasized the supposed superiority of Europeans and European Americans over other racial groups. Because of this perceived superiority, interracial sexuality with 'inferior' races was seen as defiling the purity and superiority of the majority group," *Interracial Families: Current Concepts and Controversies* (New York: Routledge, 2009), 3.
27. Sherman and Steyn, "E-race-ing the Line," 67.
28. Sherman and Steyn, "E-race-ing the Line," 69.

29. Du Toit and Quayle maintain that under the apartheid regime, "mixed marriages and interracial relations were viewed as social parasites that required extermination," "Multiracial Families," 543.

30. Sherman and Steyn, "E-race-ing the Line," 543.

31. Emily Mapula Mojapelo-Batka, "Interracial Couples within the South African Context: Experiences, Perceptions and Challenges" (PhD dissertation, University of South Africa, 2008); Jaynes, "The Influence of *The Family*," 410, 170. Mojapelo-Batka further remarks that "most participants indicated that white people expressed reactions like shock, surprise, frustration, anger, distance, racism, pretence, bad remarks, and a level of obsession with racial boundaries. Black people, on the other hand, expressed reactions such as appreciation, respect, envy or anger for choosing a person from the out-group, and mistrust of the motives of the white partner. The negative reaction of the white people could be interpreted as a perceived threat to their superiority in terms of their social status. The positive reactions from the black people could be seen as a sense of pride for having broken through the higher level of the social hierarchy. There were also negative reactions by the black people, which could be seen as an expression of a sense of loss of a partner from the in-group as well as the mistrust of the motives of the partner from the out-group," 186–7.

32. Mojapelo-Batka, "Interracial Couples," 187.

33. Mojapelo-Batka, "Interracial Couples," 140–1, 187.

34. Salvador Armando Macule and Sarojini Nadar, "Women Oppressing Women: The Cultivation of *Esprit de Corps* in Xirilo (Women's Association) of the UCCSA in Mozambique," *The Ecumenical Review* 64 (2012): 357–65 (357–8).

35. Trible, "Bringing Miriam Out of the Shadows," 175.

36. I came across Barton's article "The Skin of Miriam" after completing the original draft of this essay. Incidentally, she also picks up on Trible's question and holds that the Cushite should be brought out of the shadows.

PART IV
EMBRACING AMBIGUITY

Chapter 10

IS THIS NAOMI? A FEMINIST READING OF THE AMBIGUITY OF NAOMI IN THE BOOK OF RUTH

Carolyn J. Sharp

In August 2014, we moved from a house in Middletown, Connecticut, a city of 55,000, to a small 1924 cottage in the village of Old Saybrook on the coast. Our cottage sits at the edge of a marsh that lies to the northeast; a five-minute walk toward the southwest brings us to the glittering waters of Long Island Sound, a vast tidal estuary of the Atlantic Ocean. In early evenings we take long walks along the Sound, and we never fail to marvel at the stunning changeability of the sunsets. One day, the sun is small and golden, dropping swiftly through a tapestry of magenta and blue shadows. The next evening, the sun is a huge orange ball hanging motionless in a purple sky. Another time, the sun's muted light strains through a pearly gray veil of fog. The sunset glows luminous and peaceful over the marsh, with tall grasses outlined crisply in the foreground, the water serene like glass. The same sunset is strikingly different on the ocean side: vibrant colors crash into white-capped waves rolling in from a distant horizon. Sunset in Old Saybrook is never predictable. Changeable beauty meets shifting perspectives in a way that draws us into wonderment.

The guild of biblical studies, too, finds itself in a liminal moment of shifting perspectives. An older form of uninterrogated historical positivism that had dominated Western scholarship is in decline. The sun is beginning to set on forms of biblical scholarship that assume the adequacy of an "objective," androcentric, white, Western interpretive gaze and the marginalization of the female, or one of its corollaries, an essentialist romanticizing of women's bodies and agency. Tracing a slow descent are interpretive approaches that refuse to theorize the interpreter as shaped by powerful *a priori* understandings of text, language, and history. As the sun of naïve historical empiricism continues its inexorable decline, the changing light is beginning to reveal methodological horizons astonishing in their sweep and breathtaking in a new interplay of light, color, and shadow. Feminist scholars working in this liminal moment can explore a rich variety of approaches to the biblical text, many characterized by a rigorous interdisciplinarity, all marked by attentiveness to power relations across intersections of race, gender, sexuality, class, and other dimensions of subjectivity, bodiedness, and communal identity.

In this essay, I will outline methodological convictions that undergird my engagement of the Hebrew Scriptures as works of literary art, as politicized sociocultural productions, and as a sacred polyphony that witnesses to the Holy. I read as a literary critic, I read as a feminist ideological critic, and I read as an Episcopal priest who prays and preaches with these texts. For me, it goes without saying that Israel's official literatures were generated by male scribal elites in processes characterized by pervasive androcentrism. Women may have been involved in oral storytelling, at least in domestic settings if not necessarily in the public sphere; there were some female scribes in the ancient Near East.[1] But in a society in which priests and the vast majority of prophets, scribes, and political leaders were male, the occasional woman's participation as such would not have radically reshaped the androcentric worldview that infuses Israel's founding myths, historiographies, and liturgical poetry. The centrality of female characters in a handful of biblical plots does not change my mind on this. I do not join those who speculate that Judges, Ruth, or Esther may have been written from what has been called a woman's perspective. The Hebrew Bible brims with contestations and subversions of power, to be sure. But I see no evidence that specifically misogynistic and androcentric norms were interrogated with any regularity within the scribal circles that produced the Hebrew Bible. Nevertheless, the texts and traditions of the Hebrew Bible constitute a rich resource for feminist ideology critique, deconstructive explorations, and other transgressive modes of engagement.[2] First, then, some comments on feminist method.

Feminist Methodological Considerations

By way of prolegomenon, I observe that my preferred way of working with texts and theorists is as a *bricoleuse*. I pursue idiosyncratic trails as they unfold, constructing my interpretations using ideas as "found objects" in intellectual and cultural history. I search for fragments that are catalytic for my hermeneutical, theological, and ethical engagement of the Hebrew Scriptures. I am uninterested in the systematizing of thinkers' ideas, because I consider the ostensible "discovery" of coherence in a body of intellectual work, first, to be produced by the desires of the interpreter, and second, to be replicating the kind of master narrative in Western scholarship that inevitably suppresses contradiction and dissent. I find it intellectually stimulating and ethically important to work with ideas of others through the bricolage of quotation and local engagement. I am intentional about declining to summarize others' oeuvres and thereby to "master" or commodify their work, giving it a potentially false center or supplying a putative governing structure that might smooth out productive tensions or mask aporia. Bringing insights from a variety of sources into a pastiche of connections and entangled wisdoms is, for me, a feminist way of working.

I have articulated elsewhere[3] three goals of my feminist hermeneutics: to honor all subjects, to interrogate relations of power, and to reform community. As a feminist, I decline to collude in distorted representations of the bodies, voices, and imaginations of female, non-normative male, genderqueer, and other subjects marginalized in patriarchy. I seek clarity regarding the formations and effects of relations of power, aiming to interrogate and destabilize those relations that produce harmful effects. Finally, I am committed to the feminist revisioning of community, especially through pedagogical strategies that foreground learner empowerment and challenge the status quo, through seeking to embody a spirit of generosity in hierarchical contexts such as Yale, and through writing and preaching for social justice.

In feminist interpretation of the Hebrew Scriptures, my focus is not on figures to emulate but, rather, on cultural processes of contestation and deconstruction. In this work, I am intent on using my heteronormative cisgender privilege in alliance with queer and genderqueer readers and their communities. Queer advocacy is central to my feminism. I am profoundly dissatisfied with articulations of feminism that focus only on "women," as if that identifier were a simple biological fact or natural given across cultures, bodies, and gender performances, though I do recognize the continuing virulent oppression of those in bodies construed by dominant cultures as feminine or feminized. I bring two feminist strategies to my interpretive work in the academy and my political work in communities, including communities of teaching and learning. First, I embrace dissensus[4] as vital for authentic dialogue in groups, honoring spirited and irreducible disagreement as a way of welcoming the Other. I invite alternate viewpoints in my pedagogy, and I avoid tactics of dismissal or shaming when I explore the vulnerabilities of a particular hermeneutical position in my scholarship. Second, I explore ambiguity in biblical texts as a potentially subversive resource with which to dismantle oppressive structures and ideological distortions. The Hebrew Scriptures offer many marvelous examples of ellipsis, ironic misdirection, unexpected juxtaposition, and freighted silence. All these modes underscore the fragility and infinite possibilities of language understood as both the spoken and the unspoken. Ambiguity invites the response of voices, perspectives, and truths that cannot be mastered by the utterances of official rhetoric, whether that be the master narrative of the Deuteronomistic History, the canons of ecclesial interpretation, or the dominant norms of the Society of Biblical Literature.

So in embrace of dissensus and with high hopes for a productive reading of the ambiguity of Naomi, I confess: my feminist hermeneutics will not laud Naomi as a courageous heroine for contemporary women to emulate. I will not celebrate the solidarity of Naomi and Ruth as two women collaborating to survive. I will not honor the resilience of their sisterhood or hymn the beauty of their queer love. Make no mistake: I value courage, solidarity, collaboration, resilience, sisterhood, and queer love! Other feminist work on Ruth has brought out powerful positive values. Noteworthy in this regard is the excellent Ruth commentary of Katharine Doob Sakenfeld, who argues that Naomi and Ruth together build community as "a microcosm of the peaceable kingdom envisioned by the prophetic tradition ... [a] community in which the marginalized person has dared to insist upon full participation ... a community in which joy is the dominant note."[5] So beautiful! I wish I could read Ruth that way. But as an ideological critic concerned to identify and resist the androcentrism pervasive in official Israelite literature, I must allow that my focus is elsewhere when I consider Ruth and Naomi. Here I am grateful for the astute observation of Juliana Claassens in her article "Resisting Dehumanization: Ruth, Tamar, and the Quest for Human Dignity." Claassens writes, "The ways in which the female characters respond to the forces that seek to diminish their worth, albeit fraught with ambiguity, may create a space for moral reflection."[6] I see the dynamics between Naomi and Ruth as creating a space in which contemporary feminist interpreters can honor all subjects struggling against commodification of their bodies and labor, can interrogate distorted relations of power, and can reconfigure community as a place of resistance against the exploitative predations of imperialism.

Diaspora Changes the Indigene: Naomi as Ambiguous

Key to my reading of Ruth is the text's representation of Naomi as ambiguous. Scholarly analysis of the book of Ruth has yielded a wide spectrum of feminist views of the purpose of the book and contestatory views of the merits of its characters.[7] Phyllis Trible has outlined opposing views of Naomi as manipulative or altruistic, a disempowered "cipher for male values" or an impressive exemplar of proto-feminist initiative.[8] Relevant here is the important comparative work of Madipoane Masenya, who reads Ruth in light of economic and social household relations in tribal households in South Africa. Masenya's insights about the exploitation of foreign brides in these tribal contexts lend support to a negative construal of Naomi's character.[9] Ruth's working from morning until night may be read in light of Masenya's observation that

> hard work [is] expected of a *ngwetši* in the new household. It is disturbing that even the female folk in this new and strange setting (the mother-in-law and her daughters) tend to leave everything to the foreigner-*ngwetši* ... She becomes a virtual slave in her new household.[10]

As to whether Naomi should be interpreted as strategizing in loving solidarity with Ruth or instead manipulating and exploiting her, the reader might consider Masenya's comment about unbalanced power relations in the tribal setting:

> The oppression of a younger, subordinate woman by an elder woman becomes easy to understand when one remembers that the elder herself has been in a subordinate position within her own household for a long time. Once she gets an opportunity to enforce her superior status on someone below her, she may use it to her full advantage.[11]

Trible suggests that "disparate judgments attest to Naomi's commanding, if ambiguous, presence" in the story.[12] There are other protagonists in artful biblical novellas of the postexilic period who are commanding but ambiguous;

I find it profitable to frame the characterization of Naomi in light of two of those narratives: the stories of Joseph and Esther.[13] We can discern in the book of Ruth a powerful anxiety animating the postexilic Judean imagination about ways in which diaspora changes the Judean indigene. This anxiety is evident also in the postexilic Joseph novella and the book of Esther. Those three literary articulations of this anxiety rely on subtle ironies of characterization and plot to underscore ways in which the experience of diaspora has deformed the character of powerful Judeans, perhaps for short-term good but ultimately to the grave harm of the postexilic Judean social body. In the cases of all three protagonists—and I do maintain that Naomi is the protagonist of the book of Ruth—profound literary ironies are at play in the depiction of each protagonist's elevation from a situation of near-fatal threat to a position of significant social power.

Joseph is promoted by the Egyptian court to a position second only to that of Pharaoh himself. Joseph saves his family and the Egyptians from famine, yet also becomes so wholly assimilated to Egyptian identity (Egyptian dress, Egyptian family, Egyptian name; Gen 41:39–45) that he is literally unrecognizable to his brothers. A shrewd economic strategist, Joseph enslaves the Egyptians[14] during a time of famine, while Israel settles in Egypt and flourishes (Gen 47:13–27) to a degree that eventually alarms the Egyptian hierarchy (Exod 1:7–13). The very flourishing enabled by Joseph's political leadership finally leaves his people enslaved once again and facing extermination under a new pharaoh who fears their strength.

Esther is elevated to the position of queen in the Persian court, yet her thoroughgoing assimilation implicitly comprises the boundaries of the Jewish social body. She makes herself sexually available to a boorish Persian king and guards no boundaries regarding *kashrut* or other halakhic observance, in marked contrast to the faithful hero Daniel in his diaspora setting. In response to the genocidal plot of Haman, Esther shows herself more zealous for the obliteration of Persians everywhere than the case for self-defense can reasonably sustain. There are ferocious arguments about this in the history of interpretation; it is my conviction that the narrator is not in favor of what Esther becomes. Esther is excessive, becoming more Persian than the Persians themselves, generating an authoritative new festival—Purim—not ordained by God on Sinai, one that amounts to a carnivalesque remembrance of hyperbolic slaughter. The pressure to assimilate—entirely justifiable in light of the danger of obliteration—brings with it new risks that can gravely compromise Jewish identity in diaspora.

In the cases of Joseph and Esther, it is a minority position within scholarship that the protagonist is only ostensibly to be admired and that the narratorial perspective underscores the harm done to the Hebrew people by the protagonists' actions over the long historical view. But that is indeed my position: these postexilic stories warn of the complications and compromises attendant upon Jews' survival in situations of threat. Diaspora changes the indigene, and not for the better. In Naomi's case, the deprivation and loss she endured in Moab have changed her in ways that the narrative takes exquisite care to describe: she is metaphorically and perhaps literally unrecognizable to the women of Bethlehem when she returns

(Ruth 1:19: "Is this Naomi?," they ask), and she renames herself as "Mara," an embittered distortion of who she once had been. The consequences of her actions in Bethlehem will yield David: glorious monarch to some, but ruthless manipulator and cruel despot to others.

The book of Ruth bridges the theologically anarchic time of the judges and the establishment of the monarchy, the latter going against the express warning of the prophet Samuel that instituting a human ruler would be tantamount to sedition against God-as-king. Theological concerns are powerful in this liminal moment in Israel's historiographical metanarrative, so we may inquire into the theologies expressed by characters in the book of Ruth. How does the Judean protagonist Naomi speak of God in her local context?

Naomi the Theologian

In the book of Ruth, there is a single narratorial comment about the LORD: the LORD is said to have granted pregnancy to Ruth (4:13). God is spoken of by the characters otherwise—by Ruth in her declaration of fidelity to Israel's God, by Boaz in optative phrases that invite blessing upon those around him, and by Naomi. Literary critics know well not to confuse the narratorial perspective with the perspective of a character in a narrative as if they were one and the same. Thus we should not take remarks about God from within characters' perspectives as if they represented the position of the narrator or the author of the story. How, then, might the feminist interpreter construe Naomi's agency as theologian?

Her husband, named Elimelech—"My God is King"—has died. The symbolism of the personal names in the book of Ruth is considered important by many scholars and is flagged overtly, with a touch of irony, by the narrative's use of *peloni 'almoni*, "So-and-So," as the designation of the nearer kinsman who chooses not to redeem, someone who is merely instrumental in the plot and whose name does not matter.[15] So: Elimelech, God-as-ruler, is dead, absent from the story, in keeping with the narrative setting of the story in the morally degenerate time of the judges. Naomi declares that the LORD has caused the devastating loss she has experienced. She renames herself from "Pleasant" to "Bitter," resignifying her own identity rather than faithfully lamenting, petitioning God for mercy, or striving with God to vindicate her integrity. Naomi may have experienced calamity of Joban proportions, but she is no Job.[16]

Naomi mentions God only once more. When Ruth reports that she gleaned for Boaz, Naomi exclaims, "Blessed by the LORD be he, whose *hesed* has not forsaken the living or the dead!" (2:20). Her exclamation is usually read as praise of the LORD's *hesed*, but *hesed* in this story is otherwise constitutive of *human* actions. As many have recognized, the Hebrew can be translated with Boaz as the referent. Ruth and Naomi are pointedly looking for assistance from human quarters, not divine, in every other respect in this plot.[17] Thus Naomi's faith is ambiguous at best, something notable—and troubling to rabbinic commentators—in Esther as well.

Naomi and Ruth: The Economy of Exploitation

Christl Maier writes, "Feminist discourse on domination has long revolved around the (male) exploitation, inferiorization, exclusion, and control of women's bodies."[18] I would add that male-identified women, too, can be fully complicit in such systems of exploitation, whether knowingly or unknowingly, for their own gain or as a matter of survival. Naomi declines to have Ruth and Orpah accompany her. As a widow who chose to live in enemy territory for more than a decade, she is already at risk for social opprobrium, crushing poverty, and violent rejection. Bringing a Moabite with her would increase the economic strain on Naomi and harm Naomi's chances of reintegration into the Bethlehem community. When Naomi "says no more to Ruth" after her thrice-repeated command for Ruth to depart goes ignored, it is reasonable to infer that, far from being touched by Ruth's "devotion," Naomi may be enraged by her daughter-in-law's disobedience. Her silence about Ruth when they meet the women of Bethlehem indicates that she does not rejoice in the presence of Ruth with her.

Naomi then allows this Moabite woman, for whom she has *not* vouched to the Bethlehem community, to go out unattended and work uninvited in a random field. That Naomi is releasing Ruth to possible sexual assault or worse is clear: the narrative overtly flags the potential threat of assault when Boaz moves to protect Ruth from his male workers ("Keep close to my young women … I have ordered my male workers not to molest you," 2:9). Naomi sends Ruth into a second dangerous situation when she instructs her to go late at night and unattended to the threshing floor (a type of location known as a site of prostitution, Hos 9:1). Ruth is to make a frank sexual overture to the drunken Boaz (the euphemistic nature of "uncover his feet" is widely recognized) and see what he tells her to do. Naomi does not want Ruth with her, chooses not to introduce her to the women of Bethlehem, and sends her into dangerous situations twice without any kind of warning.[19] When Ruth finally has a baby, Naomi appropriates the child. The most plausible explanation for Naomi's actions is that she is callously exploiting Ruth for economic gain, exposing Ruth to the very real possibility of violence with no warning or preparation to commodify Ruth's body as a source of field labor, a sexual lure to ensnare patriarchal support, and a producer of children.

The Genesis intertexts cited in Ruth 4 underline the unspoken manipulation and antagonism underlying the women's relationship. The people of Bethlehem pray that Ruth will be made "like Rachel and Leah, who together built up the house of Israel"—indeed, through a fierce childbearing competition that mocked the notion of sisterhood. The Bethlehemites also pray that Boaz's line may be "like the house of Perez, whom Tamar bore to Judah"—indeed, after Tamar's sexual entrapment of him in the guise of a prostitute yielded a pregnancy that caused her to come within moments of being burned alive. Some feminists see Naomi as having changed over the course of the story. They read her strategizing positively, as a sign of her resilience and initiative. Trible offers, "From being the receiver of calamity, Naomi has become the agent of change and challenge."[20] Agent of manipulation, perhaps, but change? Naomi has not been accorded the narratological terrain to demonstrate a change of heart or a transformation of personality. Her motivations are never depicted; neither Ruth nor Naomi speaks in the last chapter of the book. When Naomi takes Ruth's child, there is no shared naming of the child. He is named by the women of the neighborhood, yet another displacement that may signal the lack of relational connection between Ruth and Naomi. Fidelity? I see only manipulation, commodification, and erasure.

Ideological Consequences

The ambiguity of Naomi is of powerful consequence for the literary purposes of this story, especially given that the narrative links a time of moral chaos with the emergence of the monarchy. I honor the multivalence of this brilliant text and welcome a polyphony of divergent interpretations. But I cannot myself promote a reading of Ruth that depicts a faithful Moabite ancestor whose *ḥesed* serves to glorify David. Moab is despised early and late in Israelite tradition. Ruth forces her way into the Bethlehem community. She is manipulated into acting in a sexually aggressive manner so as to infiltrate this community more deeply, and in no time she has secured Judean economic holdings. The ostensibly idyllic book of Ruth is best read in conjunction with those biblical traditions that critique David as a conniving schemer and immoral manipulator, a "careerist and survivor" who was "calculating, ruthless, and cold," as Jacob Wright notes.[21] David was a king who did not go out to battle as kings should; instead he willfully appropriated Bathsheba and had her husband, the loyal soldier Uriah, killed.[22] David was a mercenary leading brutal raids on local groups. David was a soldier whose long-standing alliance with the Philistines may have contributed obliquely to the deaths of Saul and Jonathan,[23] a monarch whose bloody grip on power required the assassinations of almost all in the house of Saul and many in his own family as well. This is the king in whose genealogy stands Ruth the Moabite, with Naomi the ambiguous Judean in the shadows behind her.

The postexilic book of Ruth offers a sophisticated warning about the ways in which diaspora changes the indigene. Those who suffer the deprivations and risks of exile may return unrecognizable, desperation having deformed them into manipulators who commodify the labor of others for their own survival, destroying the integrity of the Judean body politic in the process. The Davidic kingship highlighted at the end of Ruth stands as an emblem, retrojected into the distant past, of these unsavory mercenary tactics. Consider again the warning of the prophet Samuel about the exploitative practices of kings:

> These will be the ways of the king who will reign over you: ... He will appoint ... some to plow his ground and to reap his harvest ... He will take the best of your fields and vineyards and olive orchards and give them to his courtiers ... He will take one-tenth of your flocks, and you shall be his slaves. (1 Sam 8:11–17)

The machinations of Ruth and Naomi foreshadow David's own corruption, which is a significant theme in the biblical material about David. Monarchical exploitation is carefully traced further by the Deuteronomistic narrator(s) as the Davidic line continues to unfold. The conspicuous consumption of the Solomonic palace is noted in a literary context that extolls the king's power, wisdom, and ability to secure peace for his people (1 Kgs 4:20–34), but the warning of Samuel surely would have echoed in the ears of an astute audience considering the descriptions of the lavish provisions for the monarchy. As to Samuel's warning about enslavement, Solomon's forced-labor practices clearly subjugated Israelites (see 1 Kgs 5:13–18; the anxiety of 1 Kgs 9:15–22 to deflect the concern about corvée involving Israelites serves only to highlight the problem). Rehoboam, too, is portrayed as a ruthless exploiter of his people (1 Kgs 12:1–19). It is this dimension of monarchy that, I argue, is most relevant for understanding the characterization of Ruth and Naomi as preparation for what David will represent.

My feminist reading of Naomi has interrogated the power relations in this story in a way that seeks to honor the subjectivity of all those under repressive regimes—political or cultural, ancient or contemporary—who struggle with oppression and economic injustice. I am convinced that the book of Ruth is no idyll and that Naomi is best understood as a disturbing figure. Deep darkness lies just beyond the light cast by the surface signifying of the book of Ruth. Contemporary Serbian-American poet Charles Simic captures well the interplay between sanitized official narrative and sinister reality in his poem "The Lights Are on Everywhere":[24]

> The Emperor must not be told night is coming.
> His armies are chasing shadows,
> Arresting whip-poor-wills and hermit thrushes
> And setting towns and villages on fire.
>
> In the capital, they go around confiscating
> Clocks and watches, burning heretics
> And painting the sunrise above the rooftops
> So we can wish each other good morning.
>
> The rooster brought in chains is crowing,
> The flowers in the garden have been forced to stay open,
> And still yet dark stains spread over the palace floors
> Which no amount of scrubbing will wipe away.

"No amount of scrubbing" can remove the "dark stains" that spread through the stories of the Israelite monarchy, from David's bloody rise to power and brutal suppression of dissent to the bloodshed for which Manasseh is excoriated (2 Kgs 24:3–4). The narratology of Ruth trades on subtleties of characterization and freighted silences to present an "official" portrayal of the lineage of the monarchy meant to be understood as (un)masking the violence and commodification that have riven the Judean body politic.

Loss, poverty, and exploitation harm communities in disastrous ways. Vividly depicting that truth was an urgent mandate not only for the ancient prophets but also, I have argued, for the brilliant book of Ruth. It remains an urgent feminist mandate to uncover practices of exploitation, especially the exploitation of those whose marginalized social status may diminish their capacity for resistance. In the end, those who read Naomi and Ruth as models of resilience and strategic thinking may not persuade those of us who read Naomi and Ruth as cautionary figures. Thus a lively dissensus may characterize our ongoing feminist engagements of the book of Ruth—something to be celebrated as the struggle continues.

Notes

1. On women scribes in ancient Mesopotamia, see A. Leo Oppenheim, *Ancient Mesopotamia: Portrait of a Dead Civilization*, rev. ed. completed by Erica Reiner (Chicago: University of Chicago Press, 1977), 47, 386; Karen Rhea Nemet-Nejat, *Daily Life in Ancient Mesopotamia* (Westport, CT: Greenwood, 1998), 56, 150–1; Jean Bottéro, *Everyday Life in Ancient Mesopotamia*, trans. Antonia Nevill (Baltimore: Johns Hopkins University Press, 2001; orig. *Initiation à l'Orient ancien*, Paris: Editions du Seuil, 1992), 117.

2. Reading as a feminist intellectual, I understand "transgressive" as a positive term connoting courageous refusal to yield to dysfunctional and poorly thought-through social norms. Reading as a Christian, I affirm the term "transgressive" as connoting a faithfulness to the Gospel of Jesus Christ that requires resistance to distorted and oppressive human ideation.

3. Carolyn J. Sharp, "'Are You for Us, or for Our Adversaries?': A Feminist and Postcolonial Interrogation of Joshua 2–12 for the Contemporary Church," *Int* 66 (2012): 141–52; and "Feminist Queries for Ruth and Joshua: Complex Characterization, Gapping, and the Possibility of Dissent," *SJOT* 28 (2014): 229–52.

4. As regards inner-biblical contestations, the theological work of Walter Brueggemann has been important for my formation as a biblical scholar. See, among many relevant works by Brueggemann, his *Texts Under Negotiation: The Bible and Postmodern Imagination* (Minneapolis: Fortress, 1993) and *Theology of the Old Testament: Testimony, Dispute, Advocacy* (Minneapolis: Fortress, 1997). A feminist theory of dissensus has been proposed by Ewa Płonowska Ziarek in her *An Ethics of Dissensus: Postmodernity, Feminism, and the Politics of Radical Democracy* (Stanford, CA: Stanford University Press, 2001). Ziarek defines dissensus as "the irreducible dimension of antagonism and power in discourse, embodiment, and democratic politics" (1), the honoring of which can yield "transformative praxis motivated by the obligation for the Other" (2). Ziarek seeks to avoid fruitless struggles in the "politics of difference without ethics," on the one hand, and the pressure toward consensus embodied in any "grand theory of normative justice that transcends conflict" (4), on the other. Her goal is to realize "an anarchic responsibility ... based on the affirmation of the irreducible alterity and the asymmetry of the Other" (8).

5. See Katharine Doob Sakenfeld, *Ruth*, IBC (Louisville, KY: John Knox, 1999), 10. Also relevant is Sakenfeld's chapter 2, "Ruth and Naomi: Economic Survival and Family Values," in *Just Wives? Stories of Power and Survival in the Old Testament and*

Today (Louisville, KY: Westminster John Knox, 2003), 27–47. Another commentary in the positive feminist trajectory of interpretation is that of Kirsten Nielsen, *Ruth: A Commentary* , Old Testament Library (Louisville, KY: Westminster John Knox, 1997). Jacqueline E. Lapsley holds that restored community is the focus of characters' relationships in Ruth: "Naomi's turmoil is an unraveling of the threads of her family and communal life, and the task of each of the characters (including Naomi herself) is to pick up the threads of that life and weave them back into a restored life in community," *Whispering the Word: Hearing Women's Stories in the Old Testament* (Louisville, KY: Westminster John Knox, 2005), 103.

6. L. Juliana M. Claassens, "Resisting Dehumanization: Ruth, Tamar, and the Quest for Human Dignity," *CBQ* 74 (2012): 659–74 (661).

7. See Phyllis Trible's comment in "Ruth" in *Women in Scripture: A Dictionary of Named and Unnamed Women in the Hebrew Bible, the Apocryphal/Deuterocanonical Books, and the New Testament*, ed. Carol Meyers (Grand Rapids, MI: Eerdmans, 2000), 146–7: "Feminist assessments of Naomi diverge widely, depending often upon the cultural, social, ideological, and experiential biases of readers ... One perspective faults her for ... being compliant, self-effacing, and a mere pawn of Naomi. Another praises her for faithfulness, for making radical moves, for risking dangerous acts, and for being a devoted partner of Naomi. Still another sees her used to espouse the patriarchal values of marriage and progeny, and then discarded. The counter view sees her challenging patriarchy even while trapped within it" (147).

8. Trible, "Naomi," *Women in Scripture: A Dictionary of Named and Unnamed Women in the Hebrew Bible, the Apocryphal/Deuterocanonical Books, and the New Testament*, ed. Carol Meyers (Grand Rapids, MI: Eerdmans, 2000), 130–1 (131).

9. Madipoane J. Masenya, "*Ngwetši* (Bride): The Naomi-Ruth Story from an African-South African Woman's Perspective," *JFSR* 14 (1998): 81–90.

10. Masenya, "*Ngwetši*," 86.

11. Masenya, "*Ngwetši*," 87.

12. Trible, "Naomi," 131.

13. I have worked out analyses of Joseph and Esther in significant detail elsewhere. See Sharp, "'Am I in the Place of God?': Joseph the Pretender" and "The Ending of Esther and Narratological Excess," in Carolyn J. Sharp, *Irony and Meaning in the Hebrew Bible*, ISBL (Bloomington: Indiana University Press, 1985), 54–61 and 65–81 respectively.

14. I emend לערים אתו העביר to לעבדים אתו העביד in Genesis 47:21 with ancient versions, translations such as the NRSV, and many commentators. Among those retaining the original consonantal text are the NJPS and Reina Valera 1995 translations, which render the relevant clause as "And he removed the population town by town" and "Y al pueblo lo hizo pasar a las ciudades" respectively.

15. Eskenazi and Frymer-Kensky say that this formulation is "used when a name (of a person or place) is immaterial to the narrative (see 1 Sam 21:3). Here, however, the term is intentionally and conspicuously used to avoid naming the character. The purpose for the anonymity of the man remains a mystery. As scholars note, it is not likely that Boaz does not know the man's name. If the name were insignificant to the author, the designation could simply have been eliminated. Some Rabbinic sages, as well as modern scholars ... suggest that not naming implies measure-for-measure justice: the one who refuses to 'preserve the name' of a kin ... deserves to have his own name vanish"; Tamara Cohn Eskenazi and Tikva Frymer-Kensky, *Ruth*, JPS Bible Commentary (Philadelphia: Jewish Publication Society, 2011), 71. In my view, the

absence of the name may instead, or also, be serving to point up the importance of the appellations of the named characters.

16. Lapsley compares Naomi to Job (see *Whispering the Word*, 94–104), noting key differences, among them the failure of characters in the book of Ruth to address God directly and the healing of Naomi occurring not through the medium of rhetoric and debate but through the *ḥesed* of other people. The analogy between Naomi and Job is suggestive indeed, but I would argue that it may be ironizing Naomi's standing as claimant, the comparison implicating her in an attenuated piety, a striking lack of moral righteousness, and a failure to engage with the Almighty that are all the more obvious when held up against the example of the flawless Job.

17. Commentators have long noticed that where Boaz says to Ruth, "May the LORD reward you" (2:12), Ruth counters with redirection back to his own potential largesse, "May I continue to find favor in *your* sight, my lord" (2:13). Naomi too may be praising this man as her savior. Eskenazi and Frymer-Kensky opt for God as referent of *ḥasdô* in 2:20, but they remark, "The author may nevertheless intend an ambiguity. Perhaps we are being led to see that, for Naomi, the role of God and the role of a powerful man like Boaz are interchangeable"; *Ruth*, 43. Tod Linafelt (*Ruth*, Berit Olam [Collegeville, MN: Liturgical, 1999]) offers, "The author has worked hard to establish a confusion, or at least an overlap, between the LORD and Boaz in the story, and will go on to make problematic the separation of divine and human activity" (42). I agree but would argue that the problematic blurring is to be attributed to *the characters' (distorted) view* and not the position of the narrator; it is not intended as a good thing but, rather, is representative of the characters' flawed perspectives in the time of the judges.

18. Christl M. Maier, *Daughter Zion, Mother Zion: Gender, Space, and the Sacred in Ancient Israel* (Minneapolis: Fortress, 2008), 23.

19. Judith E. McKinlay: "Can one trust a woman who has shown such ambivalence to her daughter-in-law, who both incites her to resistance and yet exposes her to danger and the charge of cultural dishonor? Is it not a case now of daughter beware, and daughter be on guard against the power-wielding Israelite woman? … What has happened to that idyllic tale of love and devotion that I have treasured for so long? … I need to hear Ruth in more than one key," *Reframing Her: Biblical Women in Postcolonial Focus*, BMW 1 (Sheffield: Sheffield Phoenix, 2004), 54–5.

20. Trible, "Naomi," 131.

21. Jacob L. Wright, *David, King of Israel, and Caleb in Biblical Memory* (New York: Cambridge University Press, 2014), 2.

22. 2 Samuel 11, with the scathing indictment of David by the prophet Nathan following in 2 Samuel 12:1–15a.

23. See 1 Samuel 27:1–28:2 and 1 Samuel 29, in which the king of the Philistines reassures David that he trusts his loyalty (to the Philistine army, against Israel!) with the words, "I know that you are as blameless in my sight as an angel of God" (1 Sam 29:9). One of David's skills as commander was to have his army designees (especially Joab) perform the assassinations necessary to secure David's hold on power; David could then seem distraught publicly to preserve his reputation. For more on the complex subtleties of negative characterization of David in the books of Samuel, see Baruch Halpern, *David's Secret Demons: Messiah, Murderer, Traitor, King*, The Bible in Its World (Grand Rapids, MI: Eerdmans, 2001). The ideological critic may read as calculated political moves David's instances of hyperbolic public mourning at Saul's and Jonathan's having been killed by Philistines on

the battlefield (see 1 Sam 31–2 Sam 1), at the fatal illness of his first child with Bathsheba due to divine wrath about David's horrendous ethical breaches in that situation (2 Sam 12:15b–23), and at the execution of his insurrectionist son Absalom (2 Sam 15–19).

24. "The Lights Are on Everywhere," from Charles Simic, *That Little Something: Poems* (Boston: Mariner, 2009). Copyright © 1990 by Charles Simic. Reprinted by permission of Houghton Mifflin Harcourt Publishing Company. All rights reserved.

Chapter 11

STUCK BETWEEN THE WAITING ROOM AND THE RECONFIGURED LEVIRATE ENTITY?: READING RUTH IN MARRIAGE-OBSESSED AFRICAN CHRISTIAN CONTEXTS

Madipoane Masenya (ngwan'a Mphahlele)

Malebogo Kgalemang uses the concept of the waiting room to denote the space where young unmarried Pentecostal Christian women find themselves before marriage. This waiting room is not an easy place because the license "to practice sex and to procreate comes via the institution of marriage," and marriage is very significant, sanctioned by the community, and attached to a culture of honor. Through "the politics of respectability" marriage bestows honor on the married woman and "pits single women against married women" by loss of honor for the single woman. "On the other hand, the waiting period sets the rubric for the single woman, as it ultimately comes to define whether the single woman can easily endure a single life to an advanced age, or they can wait for marriage."[1]

South Africa as Social Location

In the context in which I live and work, citizens have been singing and continue to sing praises to democracy, at least for the past twenty-three years. However, many a previously disadvantaged person continues to live in poverty. A new class of elitist black individuals is emerging, while a new class of poor people of Caucasian descent, a definite rarity in South Africa's apartheid past, is also noticeable. Although some will choose to designate it otherwise, South Africa can be described as a distinctly African context. The challenge though is that due to the systems of colonialism and apartheid, most of what constituted the identity of indigenous African people, including the different types of marriages, came to be vilified. The Christian religion has also been used toward the vilification of many aspects of African cultures. Although with the dawn of democracy South Africa became a secular state, Christianity as a major religion continues to enjoy some status[2] in the lives of many believers in South Africa. Within the constituency of my preoccupation, that is, Pentecostal Christianity, the Christian Bible continues to enjoy considerable authority as an authoritative text. Hence the Bible and certain understandings of the Bible have profound material consequences for people's lives, including their sexual lives. Indeed, women's spirituality is believed to have an impact on their lives as a whole. My choice of the present topic has been precisely motivated by this fact, that is, the perceived power of the Word to nurture and form people's lives, particularly single African Christian women's lives. The growing phenomenon of single women in African South African Pentecostal churches is also notable on the broader African continent as well as elsewhere in the world.[3]

Although the face of the South African Parliament appears to be politically correct in terms of its affirmation of women, on the ground and particularly within the African church in South Africa patriarchy continues to reign supreme. In the faith communities that I engage in this essay, marriage, and in particular heterosexual marriage, basically remains the norm.[4] On account of the changed and/or changing globalized face of South Africa, the impact of urbanization and industrialization, the rigid, solid, prescribed requirements surrounding typical African marriage arrangements seem to be eroding slowly but surely (not necessarily in the subconscious minds of African people). With the African renaissance having become the buzzword today, though, some African men (e.g., Nguni royalties such as King G. Zwelithini, and people such as President Jacob Zuma, among others) are taking full advantage of the moment to choose polygyny, one legitimate marriage type in Africa. The democratic South African constitution also gives room for the practice of customary marriage.

Considering the gradual erosion of some of the African customs (read: marriage types) today,[5] it is important to note that within Pentecostal settings heterosexual monogamous marriage continues to be celebrated as the only legitimate form of marriage.[6] In the previously mentioned ecclesiastical settings the fundamentalist Bible readings appear to perpetuate not only patriarchy but also apparent Western imperialistic readings. Is it any wonder that in such settings some readings of a book such as Ruth in the Hebrew Bible tend to reveal such a Western outlook? A Western, individualistic, African-unfriendly outlook, however, is not only appealing to present-day Westernized and individualized African minds. Gender-sensitive biblical scholars claim that a Western, individualistic outlook is found to be liberating and affirming toward many a subordinated African woman.

A crucial question, however, with which this present essay grapples is: what if that which is claimed to be a legitimate, biblical, and liberating reading is not affirming to many a single woman within African Pentecostal churches? Or put in other words, what if that which might be viewed as dated (read: traditional African), unbiblical, and illegitimate could in fact be found by some to be affirming? What if that which runs against the grain of the interpretive status quo might be found to be both affirming and empowering by those directly affected (read: African Christian single women)? For the faithful female adherents of Christianity, in particular Pentecostal Christianity, sexual pleasure has to occur only within monogamous marriage.[7] The taboos linked to widowhood, divorce, and single life,[8] in addition to the disproportionately high ratio between males and females in the Pentecostal church, result not only in the perpetual growth of the number of single women in the churches but also, more importantly for the present investigation, in sexual starvation on the part of committed, self-controlled single women—many of whom do not have the "guts" (or do they?) to argue with Yolanda Jordan as she poignantly reflects in her *Ebony* article, "Single, Saved—and Having Sex":

> My mind was telling me one thing, my body another. I was grown [and] longing to be touched. I am not perfect; I struggle with sin. I strive to live a righteous life. Just because I have the Bible on my nightstand and condoms in the drawer doesn't mean I love God any less or that he doesn't love me.[9]

Moreover, Malebogo Kgalemang, referred to at the beginning of this essay, also warns that the waiting room is not easy to occupy. For she writes: "The walls of the waiting room are bound to crack, especially in the desire for companionship, and the quest for child bearing."[10]

The main question that this essay seeks to address is as follows: given a context in which a specific biblical hermeneutic and its construction of a particular kind of marriage do not seem to provide sufficient solutions to many single African South African Pentecostal Christian women's concerns, could a rereading of the form of marriage entered into by Ruth in the Hebrew Bible, a form akin to the levirate form of marriage in many African contexts, offer any helpful insights to a single woman's dilemma? In this regard, it is important to consider what it is that has motivated me to choose the book of Ruth as a text of my preoccupation.

Why the Book of Ruth?

My preoccupation with the single African South African Pentecostal Christian woman's dilemma and in particular my choice of the book of Ruth go back to a session within a theology seminar hosted by the University of Pretoria, South Africa, more than two decades ago. A UNISA colleague, Professor Christina Landman, then was arguing for time-share marriages, which rightly can be described as a kind of polygyny. For the convenience of both man and woman, Landman proposed that a man could marry more than one woman. Such an arrangement would also benefit a career woman who may not always feel the pressure of a monogamous marriage as she for example is traveling abroad without her husband.

I was invited to give a response to Landman's paper. The title of my paper was revealing: "Polygyny or a Nobody? A Response." As a member of royalty,[11] I was/am conversant with the challenges linked to polygyny. I therefore had no sympathy whatsoever with Landman's arguments, which I simply dubbed as androcentric and thus an invitation to gender-identified scholars to become bedfellows with patriarchy. Those who have listened to my arguments in this particular response and those who have read my previous published works on the book of Ruth will be able to detect a noticeable shift (or one could even say a contradiction?)

in my approach to the book of Ruth in this current essay. This shift will reveal not only the reality of multivalent voices in our reading of the Bible but also my commitment to engage the various struggles encountered by African Christian women in South Africa. My hope is that the present reading may open up a helpful debate regarding the affirmation of the bodies of single African Christian women, not only as spiritual but also as sexual. The reader might also be assisted in glimpsing some of the challenges faced by many single women who seem to remain permanently "in the waiting room."[12]

Given my particular social location in South Africa—one marked by its broken political past—which can be described as patriarchal and rampant with poverty, a context that is both African and Christian and more importantly one in which the Christian Scriptures still play an important role in shaping lives, particularly women's lives, I am drawn to the book of Ruth in the Hebrew Bible. Some African women scholars have documented apparent resemblances between the Israelite and African worldviews displayed by this book.[13] Such perceived similarities make the book of Ruth, whether for better or for worse, familiar if not popular in many African contexts. The "levirate" marriage into which Ruth, a poor Moabite widow, manages to secure survival for herself and Naomi can be cited as a case in point. In the following section I will present the narrative of one African woman's reflection through a *bosadi* (womanhood-redefined) rereading of Ruth's marriage to Boaz within the context of marriage-obsessed African Pentecostal Christianity. A brief word about the *bosadi* approach is in order at this stage.

The Bosadi *(Womanhood-Redefined) Approach to Biblical Texts*

The Northern Sotho/Sepedi word *mosadi* (woman) is found not only in the Sepedi/Northern Sotho language. Though in different forms, the word also occurs in other South African indigenous languages such as *wansati* (Xitsonga); *umfazi* (isiZulu); *musadzi* (Tshivenda); and *mosadi* (Setswana and Sesotho).[14] The coinage of a globally unfamiliar term, *bosadi*, was intentional. Why? To deliberately make an African South African women's context the main hermeneutical focus in my interaction with the Bible. By employing a familiar word, "a male-construct,"[15] the intention was to give priority to my own context by responding to questions asked first and foremost within this specific context.[16]

The main hermeneutical focus of the *bosadi* biblical hermeneutic is the unique experiences of an African South African woman, with a commitment to her liberation. It is thus an African gender-sensitive hermeneutic. African women, facing multiple life-denying forces such as sexism in the broader South African society that was exacerbated by the legacies of colonialism and apartheid, sexism in the African culture, post-apartheid racism, classism, HIV and AIDS, as well as xenophobia among others, are made the main hermeneutical focus. Using the *bosadi* approach, I have reread numerous texts from the Hebrew Bible, including the book of Ruth. Informed by a different agenda, I now turn again to my reading of the book of Ruth using the *bosadi* approach.

Reading from a Contemporary African Context

The narrative of Ruth in the Hebrew Bible allows present-day African (South African) readers to be exposed to the familiar realities in our African past and present. The following sociocultural dimensions of contemporary African life may be illuminating for the interpretation of the book of Ruth. First, a holistic outlook on life: in Africa, the social, political, economic, physical, and spiritual spheres are all believed to be integrated into the whole. Second, the challenges faced by single women, including the struggle for survival, especially by non-literate widows. Third, the apparent feminized character of poverty: in Africa in general, and South Africa in particular, the majority of people who are at the lowest rung of the socioeconomic ladder are women. Fourth, ethnocentrism: the divide-and-rule strategy adopted by the apartheid regime has left a legacy of ethnocentrism among Africans in South Africa. There is thus a tendency for each indigenous ethnic group to promote its own identity rather than the identity of the South African rainbow nation as such. Fifth, patriarchy: a system of male domination in which the male still basically remains the norm in both the public and the private spheres. Sixth, the African spirit of *botho/Ubuntu/ḥesed* in which the communality of African people is displayed, thus "I am because you are," because it is believed that a human being is a human being because of other human beings. Seventh, the prominence of the family mentality: African cultures set great store by family. Thus a daughter-in-law like Ruth will not only belong to her own nuclear family, but she will belong to the nuclear and extended families, and even the clan to which her husband belongs. Within such contexts, it is therefore no surprise that an androcentric notion of "community" may be privileged over the needs of single women. Eighth, heterosexual marriage is extremely important to African people. Irrespective of the different forms of marriage found in African cultures, the heterosexual union seems to remain the norm.

Reimagining and Reconstructing Levirate Marriage in the Book of Ruth

The form of marriage that seems to bring a few of the preceding themes together is that of levirate marriage and/or widow inheritance. Through the patriarchal institution of widow inheritance the notions of family, communality, *botho/ḥesed*, and the desire for (male) progeny are advanced. In the Northern Sotho language, for example, the expression "go kgobelwa" literally means "to be allocated somebody" and would be used to describe levirate marriage or widow inheritance. In a family-oriented culture that invested greatly in the birth of sons and also in the spirit of kindness to marginalized women such as widows, a widow would be allocated to the younger brother of her deceased husband. Just like in the biblical setting of the *bêt 'āb*, the house of the father, the main head of the household would not necessarily have been the deceased brother, or the *levir*, but their father (cf. Elimelech in the case of Chilion and Mahlon). The levirate arrangement would mean neither the relocation of the widow to the compound of the "new" husband, nor the relocation of the *levir* to the compound of his deceased brother. What are emphasized within such an arrangement are the levirate/marital *duties* that the *levir* is/was expected to perform in his brother's household. Such duties also include the *levir's* taking care of the widow's sexual needs. The proverb *Lebitla la mosadi ke bogadi* ("a (married) woman's grave belongs to her husband's home village") captures this fact.[17] Children born within such a union would be regarded as children of the deceased (cf. also Ruth 4:5, 10). Viewed from a *bosadi* perspective, such an observation may persuade present-day readers of this practice both in our African contexts and within the context of the production of the book of Ruth to reason that the male community members continue to call the shots even from their graves. However, in the context of cultures in which the dead are not believed to die[18] (cf. the words of Naomi in the narrative in Ruth 1:8 and 2:20), would it be far-fetched to argue that there is a blurred line between the dead and the living? The younger brother was usually the preferred *levir* candidate, possibly to enable a smooth relationship between the man and his wife, and would also traditionally have been younger than his brother's widow. This scenario would be enhanced by the fact that the majority of older men tend to be fascinated by relationships with younger women rather than with their counterparts or even older women. If the siblings had no brothers, an arrangement almost akin to what happens to Ruth (cf. Ruth 3:11–12 and 4:6) would be set in place. In fact, what happens in the book of Ruth was not typical if judged by the standards of levirate marriage as it occurred within Israelite law (cf. Deut 25:5–10). In the latter, just like in the African setting, a male sibling of the deceased was the one who was directly involved. In addition, the notion of the *go'el* did not form part of the typical levirate marriage arrangement in biblical Israel. The term *go'el*, Sakenfeld argues,

> is a legal one, but it is highly charged socially because it focuses on the preservation of family and community. And yet there is a glaring gap between the appearance of the word *go'el* associated with rights or responsibilities pertaining to marriage. The regulation having to do with rights and responsibilities in cases where a man is to marry his brother's widow to perpetuate the family line is the law of levirate marriage ... but the levirate provisions contain no reference to the *go'el*. Only in the Book of Ruth do the two spheres of marriage among kin and land redemption among kin come together.[19]

Although the institution as it is displayed in the book of Ruth has levirate undertones, it appears to be a reenvisioned, reconstructed one. Why? Apart from the inclusion of the functions of the *go'el* in the equation as already noted, it involves a relative who was not a blood brother to the deceased. Although the idea of a visit to the threshing floor came from Naomi (Ruth 3:1), the proposition for the marriage was initiated by the widow herself (Ruth 3:9)—something that was also not typical. What is also intriguing for the present investigation is that the form of levirate marriage presented by the narrator in Ruth was seemingly entered into voluntarily by all the parties involved. The fact that the *go'el* who was a closer relative refused to get involved buttresses this observation. In addition, though the marriage proposition was initiated by a Moabite woman, Boaz's attraction to Ruth was already revealed at the threshing floor (Ruth 3:11–13). Despite this information, though, the gist of the levirate arrangement as presented in the book of Ruth would make sense within an African (traditional) setting.

In my view, the African levirate arrangement shares commonalities with a polygynous marriage because more than one woman gets attached to one man in a legitimate marital relationship. Viewed through a gender-sensitive Western lens, such an arrangement may be viewed as perpetuating patriarchy and thus disempowering to the women involved. Why? The following reasons, among others, may be cited: the fact that two women share one man; the likelihood that the first wife's consent was not sought; the challenges of hostilities and jealousies among the women involved—a situation thus created in which women become enemies of each other—as well as the humiliating rituals around widow cleansing in various African cultures.[20] The importance of these arguments cannot be disputed. If viewed from a different perspective, however—a perspective in which the institution of levirate marriage is reimagined and reconstructed; one in which the welfare of *all*, particularly the more marginalized woman (i.e., the widow), would be taken into account—could such a new entity be embraced as affirming to all? Within the reenvisioned levirate arrangement, *all* the parties involved— the families, the two women, and the *levir*—would consent to the arrangement in the first place. From a gender-conscious perspective, it is usually assumed that institutions such as polygyny and levirate marriage of necessity almost always benefit the male individuals. Reality, however, does not seem to always point in the latter direction. According to Mercy Oduyoye, some of the women who formed part of the survey conducted in Nigeria that measured whether women were pro- or anti-polygyny "stated that it [polygyny] was not the best solution, not even for men; they added that if the men wanted to have their way on polygyny, they could go ahead but they must be willing to face the consequences."[21] If an institution such as the levirate was that easy for men, and if the desires for more women (and thus for more sex) and more male power were the main driving factors, why did the rightful *go'el* in the case of Ruth decline the precious offer? If it was all that easy even in the case of the kind Boaz, why did Naomi, an elderly, experienced woman, have to devise such a risky strategy for her daughter-in-law? It would appear that for the reenvisioned, reconstructed levirate marriage to work, all the parties have to agree.

What is also notable—though not as conspicuous as elsewhere in the narratives whose content highlights male characters in the Hebrew Bible—is the hand of Yhwh believed to be working behind the scenes, also concerning the issue of marriage. When Naomi exhorts her daughters-in-law to go back to their mothers' households to seek security, she prays that Yhwh would provide them with security through marriage (Ruth 1:9). When Naomi introduces Boaz to Ruth as the *go'el*, she pronounces blessings on Boaz, also announcing that he is one of the closer relatives (Ruth 2:20). In Ruth 3:1, Naomi becomes the agent of God in seeking the security for Ruth (Ruth 3:1). No longer is she requesting that the Lord grants security for her daughter-in-law as she did in Ruth 1:9. In Ruth 3:1–4,

Naomi serves as a human agent toward the facilitation of the marriage for her daughter-in-law. After the marriage proposition by Ruth (Ruth 3:9), Boaz invokes the blessing of YHWH upon Ruth, reminding her that her *botho (ḥesed)* this time surpassed the previous one (Ruth 3:10). Even the promise to fulfill the levirate duties is couched in religious language: "If he is not willing to act as next-of-kin for you, then, as the LORD lives, I will act as next-of-kin for you" (Ruth 3:13). Also, in the last chapter (Ruth 4), after Boaz had announced his new position as the *goʾel* in Mahlon's family (Ruth 4:9–10), the witnesses pronounced their wishes and/or requests for the blessing of progeny upon the widow of Mahlon so that she, like the matriarchs Rachel and Leah, would be able to build the house of Israel (Ruth 4:11–12). Highlighting the apparent involvement of the deity in the endorsement of the kind of marriage that takes center stage in the book of Ruth (one that is hardly conventional in our day) might prove interesting particularly within those marriage-obsessed fundamentalist contexts in which only one marriage option is affirmed.

For the purposes of the present investigation, we may ask whether (coital) sex has a place in the book of Ruth. At face value, we may immediately answer this question positively since one of the conspicuous themes displayed by the book of Ruth is that of marriage, in whatever way marriage is understood. The following possibilities are noteworthy: it could be marriage in the form of the ordinary heterosexual monogamous marriage between Naomi and Elimelech (Ruth 1:1–2); or it could be some form of abduction[22] as in the case of Ruth and Mahlon and Orpah and Chilion (Ruth 1:4). Could it be a reconstructed levirate marriage as in the case of Ruth and Boaz (Ruth 4:10)? Such an understanding will be guided by the understanding that sex belongs in marriage. That is a legitimate form of marriage depending on specific constituencies' definitions of such an institution. Indications of the possibilities of forced sex or sexual molestation are notable in the warnings to Ruth to stay in the field of Boaz and in the company of women (cf. Ruth 2:8). The word translated as molest as used in this context carries the sense of sexual molestation. The object of molestation is always a woman who is likely to be abused by a male subject.[23] Women scholars, among others, have engaged in the theme of the possibility of a sexual encounter between Ruth and Boaz at the threshing floor. Although the tone of the language, the actions of the characters, and the threshing floor atmosphere may all be used toward the argument that there was indeed coital sex between the "dating" couple, the text is not clear in that regard. In my view, only one explicit text pointing to coital sex appears in the last chapter of the book. Sex indeed happens after the levirate marriage: "So Boaz took Ruth, and she became his wife; and he went in unto her, and Jehovah gave her conception, and she bare a son" (ASV). Sex happens in marriage, but in an unconventional form of marriage, that is, a reenvisioned, reconstructed levirate form of marriage. The covert nature of the subject of sex (unless perhaps if it is violent as in the case of rape) is typical in the Hebrew Scriptures. The Song of Songs is the only book in the Hebrew Bible in which sex and the sexuality of human beings are celebrated. Perhaps Carolyn Pressler is right when she states that marriage in the Old Testament was "less a matter of individuals than of households," and more about economics than about emotions.[24]

What needs to be mentioned about the other point of noncompatibility between the levirate marriage in Ruth and that in African contexts is that Boaz is presented as a loner, with no extended family, no nuclear family, but a rich, elderly, kind man. One of the participants, a widow, who was part of the Bible study group whose session I conducted on the book of Ruth, remarked: "1) Some of the widows today do not have people like Boaz among their relatives; 2) Some of the widows have children whereas Ruth did not have children; 3) The book presents a single difficult story; what if today's widows do not have Naomi's wisdom?" Another one, a divorcée for more than a decade at the time, responded as follows: "The book of Ruth does not speak to me because it presents the story of a woman who started out single. But the story culminates with her prayers being answered through a man: marriage, love, child, and provision."[25]

Unlike the women from the survey, which was conducted on polygyny and according to which a small majority supported the notion of polygyny, in my church context only 20 percent of the single women, including widows in the Bible study group I conducted, agreed that the levirate form of marriage could serve as one of the means to address some of the challenges experienced by single women in Pentecostal churches. In a nutshell, the majority of the single women provided reasons why the levirate form of marriage should *not* be recommended as a solution for the challenges, including sexual starvation, experienced by many if not all of them.[26]

Conclusion

Our rereading of the book of Ruth in this essay has revealed that a reenvisioned levirate union in which *all the parties* consent to the union can be possible—a possibility that, if embraced, could contribute somewhat to the plight of single African Christian women. The words of Mercy Oduyoye come to mind here:

> It is not whether a marriage is polygynous or monogamous that defines the status of women; rather it is the dependence and domination mentalities of the women and men sharing marriage that need transformation. Above all, I feel that the real challenge will come about when women can say—with or without husbands, with or without children—that the most important fact is that women are human and will find fullness in reaching for goals that we set for ourselves.[27]

However, if the survey from the Bible study group in the preceding paragraph is something to go by, the responses to which in my view have been informed mainly by a specific type of hermeneutic about what an ideal form of marriage should be, little or no hope can be entertained regarding the waiting room saga—an undesirable situation for many committed, self-controlled single women in our churches. It therefore first and foremost calls for a commitment, especially on the part of those who have been vested with the authority to interpret the sacred texts as well as the many women interpreters who occupy our pews on Sundays, to have the desire to accommodate other possible forms of heterosexual marriage.

Perhaps from the words of Phiri, a spark of hope could be cherished in this regard. She gives the reader a clue that levirate arrangements still happen elsewhere on the continent:

> Most African societies practice levirate marriage or widow inheritance, and most African churches accommodate such marriages by approving the union of a single kinsman-redeemer with a widow. Yet such arrangements seldom work out in practice as most men want to marry virgins even though they themselves may not be virgins. In the HIV/AIDS era, a levirate marriage can be a death trap for a woman.[28]

The results of the Lagos survey[29] on the small majority of professional women (both young and old) who for various reasons supported polygyny (not necessarily as an ideal), as well as the new form of polygamy by young educated women described by Nasimiyu-Wasike,[30] which is also a new form of polygyny typical in the Democratic Republic of the Congo (DRC) in recent years, might perhaps be pointing to the possibility of light at the end of the proverbial tunnel regarding the reenvisioning, reconstruction, and reformation of some of the (traditional) African marriage forms. It is hoped that such transformed institutions might assist the church and the academy alike to move, even if only an inch, toward addressing the concerns of those single women who still choose marriage as an option.

Notes

1. Malebogo Kgalemang, "Sex and the Single Pentecostal Christian in Botswana," *JTSA* 149 (2014): 90–110 (104–5). Kgalemang adopted the idea of a *waiting room* from Julia Duin's "No One Wants to Talk about It: Why Are Evangelical Singles Sleeping Around?," available at: http://www.djchuang.com/sex/singles/bpsingles.htm, accessed January 15, 2015.
2. Madipoane Masenya (ngwan'a Mphahlele), "Biblical Studies in South(ern) Africa: An Overview," in *Handbook of Theological Education in Africa*, ed. Isabel I. Phiri and Dietrich Werner (Pietermaritzburg: Cluster Publications, 2013), 454–65.
3. See the elevation of monogamy and the negative view toward the traditional African culture, including the distaste for the leviratic form of marriage, Madipoane Masenya (ngwan'a Mphahlele), "Engaging with the Book of Ruth as Single African Christian Women: One African Christian Woman's Reflection," *Verbum et Ecclesia* 34 (2013): doi:10.4102/ve.v34i1.771; see also Madipoane Masenya (ngwan'a Mphahlele), "'For Better or for Worse?': The (Christian) Bible and Africana Women," *OTE* 22 (2009):126–50.

4. In fact whether we care to acknowledge it or not, the apparent normativity of (heterosexual) marriage does not appear to be an African concern only. It seems to be a persistent desire in the lives of women across all cultures. My recent encounters in my reading of the book *There Is a Bitch in the House*, which includes stories mainly by American women of Caucasian descent, has confirmed this observation. Despite the problematic encounters that some of the women have had with men in previous relationships, they still reveal a desire to get married, should such an opportunity open up, Cathi Hanauer, *There Is a Bitch in the House: 26 Women Tell the Truth about Sex, Solitude, Work, Motherhood, and Marriage*. (New York: HarperCollins, 2002).

5. Anne Nasimiyu-Wasike, "Polygamy: A Feminist Critique," in *The Will to Arise: Women, Tradition, and the Church in Africa*, ed. Mercy A. Oduyoye and Musimbi R. A. Kanyoro (Maryknoll, NY: Orbis, 2006), 101–18; Mercy A. Oduyoye, *Daughters of Anowa: African Women and Patriarchy* (Maryknoll, NY: Orbis, 1995); Judith M. Bahemuka, "Social Changes in Women's Attitudes toward Marriage in East Africa," in *The Will to Arise: Women, Tradition, and the Church in Africa*, ed. Mercy A. Oduyoye and Musimbi R. A. Kanyoro (Maryknoll, NY: Orbis, 2006), 119–34.

6. Eunice Kamaara observes such tensions between African and Christian values on family and marriage within the East African setting when she argues: "Christian communities embody the same family values … Yet tensions exist regarding reproduction; polygamy is anti-Christian and celibacy is anti-African. Consequently, many profess Christian values but practice traditional African values," Eunice Kamaara, "Family in Eastern Africa," in *The Cambridge Dictionary of Christianity*, ed. Daniel Patte (Cambridge: Cambridge University Press, 2010), 410. In more or less the same vein, but with a focus on African Independent Churches (AIC), Philomena Mwaura reveals the tensions notable in the AIC "to balance cultural values, Christian ideals, and modernity," citing specifically the tension between monogamy, a Christian ideal, and polygamy, Philomena N. Mwaura, "Family in African Instituted Churches," in *The Cambridge Dictionary of Christianity*, ed. Daniel Patte (Cambridge: Cambridge University Press, 2010), 410.

7. See an elaborate discussion of the major impact of the Pauline injunction "to flee immorality" as one of the key pillars upon which Pentecostal understanding of immorality is based, Kgalemang, "Sex and the Single Pentecostal Christian in Botswana," 98–102.

8. In the view of Anne Nasimiyu-Wasike, unmarried or childless women were considered incomplete in African cultures, "Polygamy: A Feminist Critique," in *The Will to Arise: Women, Tradition and the Church in Africa*, ed. Mercy A. Oduyoye and Musimbi R. A. Kanyoro (Maryknoll, NY: Orbis, 2006), 101–8 (106). In the same vein, John S. Mbiti views non-marriage and the lack of children in African cultures as tantamount to being excluded from the community. He argues: "To die without getting married and without children, is to be completely cut off from the human community … to become an outcast and to lose all links with mankind [sic]. Everybody therefore must get married and bear children: that is the greatest hope of the individual for himself [sic] and of the community for the individual," *African Religions and Philosophy* (Oxford: Heinemann, 1989), 31. Note should also be taken of the observation that male children were the more preferred ones. The institution of levirate marriage was precisely put in place to rectify the reality of the absence of a male child in case a man died without a potential heir.

9. Yolanda Jordan, "Single, Saved—and Having Sex," *Ebony* 2 (May 2012).

10. Kgalemang, "Sex and the Single Pentecostal Christian in Botswana," 105.

11. At some point, Kgoši Matime Mphahlele, my paternal grandfather, was a *kgoši* (traditional leader) of the Mphahlele clan.

12. Kgalemang, "Sex and the Single Pentecostal Christian in Botswana," 103–10.

13. See in particular Musimbi R. A. Kanyoro, *Introducing Feminist Cultural Hermeneutics: An African Perspective* (Sheffield: Sheffield Academic, 2002); Madipoane Masenya, "Ngwetši (Bride): The Naomi-Ruth Story from an African-South African Woman's Perspective," *JFSR* 14 (1998): 81–90; Masenya (ngwan'a Mphahlele), "Engaging with the Book of Ruth as Single African Christian Women"; and Isabel A. Phiri, "Ruth," in *Africa Bible Commentary*, ed. Tokunboh Adeyemo (Nairobi: World Alive Publishers, 2006), 319–24.

14. Madipoane Masenya (ngwana' Mphahlele), *How Worthy Is the Woman of Worth? Rereading Proverbs 31:10–13 in African-South Africa*, Bible and Theology in Africa 4 (New York: Peter Lang, 2004), 122.

15. See Tinyiko S. Maluleke, "African Ruths, Ruthless Africas: Reflections of an African Mordecai," in *Other Ways of Reading: African Women and the Bible*, ed. Musa W. Dube (Atlanta: SBL, 2001), 237–51 (243–4). Although Maluleke is correct in arguing that the *bosadi* concept is a male construct, I find this to be an unfortunate criticism given the patriarchal history that has shaped the languages of the world. I am not aware of any words used to designate women, for example, *woman, feminine*, and *female*, that were originally coined by women. In light of such a history, I have employed this male-constructed terminology and redefined it to affirm those who have not only been named but those whose roles have been defined and prescribed by outsiders to their gender; see Masenya (ngwana' Mphahlele), *How Worthy Is the Woman of Worth?*, 122–58.

16. See Teresa Okure, "Invitation to African Women's Hermeneutical Concerns," *AJBS* 19 (2003): 71–95 (74).

17. The tenor of this reveals that once a husband dies, a widow is expected neither to return to her father's household nor to make an independent decision to remarry. As marriage is communal in African contexts (cf. also the book of Ruth), the widow will naturally expect her husband's family to take care of *all* her needs after his death. A levirate marriage usually becomes the widow's option, Madipoane Masenya, "Is Ruth the 'Ēšet Ḥayil for Real? An Exploration of Womanhood from African Proverbs to the Threshing Floor (Ruth 3:1–13)," *Studia Historiae Ecclesiasticae* 36 Supplement (2010): 253–72 (259).

18. Refer to John Mbiti's notion of the living dead, John S. Mbiti, *African Religions and Philosophy*, second edition (Oxford: Heinemann, 1989), first published in 1969.

19. Katharine Doob Sakenfeld, *Ruth*, IBC (Louisville, KY: John Knox, 1999), 59.

20. Oduyoye, *Daughters of Anowa*, 133; Peter K. Kareem, "A Critical Examination of Naomi's and Ruth's Use of Feminine Insight and Wisdom for Survival as a Tool for Solving Widowhood Socio-Economic Problems in Africa," in *Biblical Studies and Feminism in the African Context: In Honour of the Late Dr. Dorcas Olubanke Akintunde*, ed. Olabiyi A. Adewale (Ibadan: National Association for Biblical Studies 3 (NABIS Western Zone), 2012), 229–47 (234).

21. Oduyoye, *Daughters of Anowa*, 129.

22. See Wilda Gafney, who argues on the basis of the similarities in the verb used in the present case, that is, the marriages of Orpah and Ruth to Chilion and Mahlon (Ruth 1:4), as well as in Judges 21:21 in the narrative of the abduction of the young women of Shiloh. If Gafney's argument holds water, she brings to light the violence that occurred at the initial encounter between Naomi's sons and her would-be

daughters-in-law—a very sad story indeed! Wilda C. Gafney, "Ruth," in *The Peoples' Bible: New Revised Standard Version with the Apocrypha*, ed. Curtis P. De Young et al. (Minneapolis: Fortress, 2009), 398–403.

23. Madipoane Masenya (ngwana' Mphahlele). "What Differences Do African Contexts Make for English Bible Translations?," *OTE* 14 (2001): 281–96.

24. Carolyn Pressler, "The 'Biblical View' of Marriage," in *Engaging the Bible in a Gendered World: An Introduction to Feminist Biblical Interpretation in Honor of Katharine Doob Sakenfeld*, ed. Linda Day and Carolyn Pressler (Louisville, KY: Westminster John Knox Press, 2006), 200–11 (204).

25. Listening to single women's narratives, Participants 1–4 and A-E Mankweng, IAG Church Sovenga, Limpopo Province, South Africa, April 28, 2012.

26. Oduyoye, *Daughters of Anowa*, 129.

27. Oduyoye, *Daughters of Anowa*, 130–1; cf. also pages 128–9 of the survey from the Bible study group regarding the pros and cons of a polygynous marriage; the small margins between the pros and cons reveal the debatable nature of polygyny. In the end, a small majority accepts it due to the recognition of its usefulness.

28. Phiri, "Ruth," 323–4.

29. Lagos Survey, *Sunday Times*, Lagos (February 24, 1985).

30. Nasimiyu-Wasike, however, is not optimistic about the new invention as she reasons, "It is rather the arrangement between the young woman and the man of her choice. She can have a number of men as she pleases and can drop them if she does not like them. Although the young woman is rejecting the African woman's traditional roles, she in turn is ending up in new forms of enslavement and exploitation." The economic and social changes and pressures contribute, in her view, to this form of polygamy, Nasimiyu-Wasike, "Polygamy," 113.

Chapter 12

DAUGHTERS, PRIESTS, AND PATRILINEAGE: A FEMINIST AND
GENDER-CRITICAL INTERPRETATION OF THE END OF THE
BOOK OF NUMBERS

Claudia V. Camp

Opening Reflections: A Retrospective

I got hooked by the Hebrew Bible in 1974, in a required introductory course of my first year in a M.Div. program. I was never planning on a career in ministry; the M.Div. was intended simply as a first step toward a Ph.D. program, but in what? New Testament, I'd thought, which I already knew something about, but one had to learn a bit about the Old Testament to do that; so there I was, and I never left. The academic study of the Hebrew Bible drew me into a world of stories and storytelling, the altered consciousness of ritual, the agony of theodicy, and the passion of social justice. I fell in love. The historical-critical method itself, for all its faults, directed my attention not to a search for the one right answer to "the meaning" of a text, but to the people and communities who produced it. My question was not "what does it really mean?" but "why did they say that?" Not "what is the authority of the Bible?" but "why do we have a Bible at all?" These questions were at the time historically naïve and ideologically uninformed; paradoxically, they are at the heart of the feminist, ideologically oriented discourse analysis that marks my later work. Though my underlying question now is: why do we *keep* a Bible, and should we stop reading it? I'm no longer in love.

Two important things happened in biblical scholarship in the late 1970s that allowed me to do what I now do. One was the methodological explosion that opened the iron fist of historical criticism; the other was the feminism that was beginning to eddy around at the edges of the field (though for me at the time it seemed like a tidal wave). Historical critics regarded the then-new sociological criticism as a red herring—an epithet I heard one famous historical scholar use to another as they departed a session on Norman Gottwald's *Tribes of Yahweh*.[1] But the new biblical social scientists often had equally little time for the new biblical literary critics, and vice versa. (I was advised by my publisher, himself a well-known literary critic, to omit the sociohistorical section from my dissertation when I sought to publish it as a monograph, though he later saw the error of his ways!) But I wanted to do it all, and fortunately I had an advisor, Roland Murphy, with a sufficiently open mind to give me free rein. Perhaps it took a Carmelite monk to have that open a mind in the late 1970s, but, though no feminist himself, Roland placed no obstacles before me as I journeyed down that new road. And, though Roland was my advisor, even more credit for mentorship must go to Carol Meyers, also a committee member, who paved the way for me, intellectually and professionally, as a woman attempting feminist work in biblical studies.[2]

Wisdom and the Feminine in the Book of Proverbs[3] asked the question: what is *she*, this elevated female figure of Woman Wisdom, doing *here*, in the middle of a patriarchal canon? The answer, it seemed to me, had to be both literary and sociohistorical. But mine was also an answer of the heart, a reformist feminist heart that wanted to think both that the Woman Wisdom figure had benefited women in the past and that she could still do so today. Feminist criticism, though, pressed ever more critical questions. Even if Woman Wisdom had valorized women on some level, how much more did ancient appeal to this figure benefit the men who constructed it? On the other hand, why could a feminist interpreter not escape the tyranny of the past, appropriating Woman Wisdom in a new and empowering way for women of today? But, again, a more subversive feminist voice returned with its challenge: didn't my use of the text for a liberating empowerment of women also, in the same move, reinscribe textual authority for oppressive purposes?

It took a few more years for the Strange Woman to take center stage in my work. It happened by accident, but the impact was irreversible. Cheryl Exum asked me to write an article for a *Semeia* volume on women as tricksters.[4] Through the backdoor of structuralist anthropological analysis of the trickster,[5] I came to see Woman Wisdom and the Strange Woman as two sides of a coin, not simply the madonna-whore coin of the patriarchal realm, but also the magician's shiny quarter on which heads could be tails and tails heads, a coin flipped at the liminal, culture-creating, *and* culture-destroying margin where the trickster lives. I thus backed myself into deconstruction at the same time, with the realization that, no matter what its author's intent, a text could provide the means for its own counter-reading. The Strange Woman was not only the creation of patriarchy; precisely in her alliance with Woman Wisdom she was also the means to its ideological undoing, just as the patriarchs feared she would be!

In *Wise, Strange, and Holy: The Strange Woman and the Making of the Bible*,[6] I carried this sense of the deep and subversive interconnection between female-embodied wisdom and strangeness in the Hebrew Bible to the stories of Samson and Solomon. I argued that the ancient scribes used gender ideology to embed an anti-authoritarian ambiguity into the literary work they were creating, one that would later be available for deployment against a future they could not even envision, when their work would be accorded the status of God's word. Here as elsewhere in the Hebrew Bible—and I regard this as an important and often underexplored avenue of feminist criticism—gender rhetoric is deployed for ideological purposes beyond those of gender construction and control. Gender is not a separate matter, either in biblical interpretation or in understanding the world around us.[7]

But there was another girl hanging around on my deconstructive playground, whom I also wanted to meet. I called her the Estranged Woman, the Israelite woman who was pushed out, as opposed to the one identified as an outsider by definition. She appears in biblical narrative as Dinah, and as Miriam. She is the sister of priests, Levi and Aaron, and I realized that the binary in which she is constructed is not the inherently unstable opposition of wisdom and strangeness but a more rigid and deadly one: strangeness and holiness. In her case too, though, gender ideology is the conceptual vehicle; it does not operate simply for its own sake. Rather, it is deployed in the interest of a particular formation of community identity that will result in the control of a particular group of men; in the case of Numbers, the Aaronite priests. And, yet again, the material vehicle is textual. This strange woman, too, is part and parcel of the making of the Bible.

Gender ideology is, then, at the heart of the biblical canon, diverse as its various component parts may appear. The ideology is always the same: men and women are different, and difference is dangerous. Sometimes, as in the stories of Samson and Solomon, that danger is textually engaged in a way that deconstructs its generative difference with humor, ambiguity, and a challenge to authority. Other times, as in Numbers, those in authority attempt to eliminate difference altogether, by textually eliminating the Other. But this strategy foregrounds another dimension of the text's gender ideology, namely, its need to construct manhood, a structurally impossible effort without Woman as a counterpoint. The culture that attempts such impossible unisexual reproduction should destroy itself, consume itself, and there is plenty of internal annihilation at work in Numbers. Only one thing can save it, and that is turning its consuming force outward to feed on *other* Others, "real" foreigners like the Moabite Cozbi and the Midianite wives, though these remain, for the producers of Numbers, embodied as women, the original Other. Numbers is a book of the wilderness, yet its ending looks forward, again by means of female characters, to Israel's life in the land to which they are coming. A land full of Others. This essay considers that transitional moment, in which the Others-within take center stage, as if the Others-without did not, would not, exist.

Gender in Numbers

The world of the book of Numbers is a constructed world, one built on a foundation of gender ideology. It begins with an idealized utopia of well-counted warrior men, well-arranged, tribe-by-tribe (except for the Levites), around *the* Man whose tabernacle sits in the middle of the camp (chs. 1–2). The men of the tribes, however—regularly referred to in Numbers as *zar*, strange—have to be protected from the dangerous holiness of YHWH, a goal accomplished in part by divine acceptance of the Levites as a substitute for the sacrifice of the first born (3:5–13, 40–45), and then by the Levites' own special numbering, assignment of sacred duties involving the tabernacle, and arrangement around the sanctuary by ancestral house. The houses of the Levites are set between the sanctuary and the placement of the other tribes (chs. 3–4). As I have argued elsewhere, Numbers consistently presents the Levites as a line between the holy, with its true, Aaronite priests, and the "strange," non-priestly Israelites.[8] When we look through the lens of gender criticism, we become attuned not just to the distinctions constructed between men and women, but also to those between men and other men, and to how manliness is constructed in both ways.[9]

Beginning in Chapter 5, however, reality (or at least a version thereof!) sets in, with all its impurity, rebellion, and, of course, women. There is the wife suspected of adultery (ch. 5); the sister, first rebellious (ch. 12), then dead (ch. 20); the all-too-appealing foreign (Cushite, Moabite, and Midianite) women, sometimes accepted (ch. 12) and sometimes rejected and killed (ch. 25); then also the foreign (Midianite) women taken in war, to be killed or not depending on their sexual status (ch. 31). And finally, there are the daughters, whose vows (along with those of wives) must be overseen (ch. 30) and whose land claims must be adjudicated (chs. 27 and 36). I contend that these stories or instructions relating to women are not told to inform us about women's lives, nor even simply to establish male authority over women, though they certainly do the latter. More importantly, they define by contrast what it means to be a man, in particular, an *Israelite* man, and, above all, a *priestly* man. I have made this case in several publications on the suspected adulteress (the so-called Sotah), on Miriam, and on the foreign women, arguing that the problem of the (wished for but impossible) identity of the true priests, the Aaronites, distinct and separate from all other Israelites, is refracted in various ways through the role of the liminal Levites (of priestly lineage but not true priests), as well as through the stories of Miriam as sister (also of priestly lineage yet not a priest), and the other female characters whose sexuality is narratively at issue.[10]

Here my focus is on the brotherless daughters of Zelophehad, who appear toward and at the end of Numbers (chs. 27; 36), in fact bookending the final section of the book, following the second census of Chapter 26. The daughters are first named— Mahlah, Noah, Hoglah, Milcah, and Tirzah—as part of the Manassite genealogy in Numbers 26:33. In Chapter 27, they insist to Moses and Eleazar and the other leaders that they should inherit from their dead father so that his name should not be lost. Moses consults YHWH, who agrees with the women. The question is reopened in Chapter 36, however, the book's final chapter, in which the heads of the fathers' houses complain that land inherited by daughters will be taken into the inheritance of their husbands' tribes if they remarry outside. Moses responds with a new word from YHWH, restricting inheriting daughters to marriage within their father's tribe. There is a follow-up account in Joshua 17:3–6, after the conquest, when the daughters confront Joshua to assert their claim, but my main focus here is on Numbers. Why does the book end as it does, with these women, and how does the portrayal of the daughters relate to those of the other women in the book, and thus to its larger agenda of identity construction?

I will begin with a consideration of feminist work on this material,[11] but then turn to other sorts of matters raised by (mostly male) interpreters. These other concerns may not be as removed from matters of gender as they might appear.

Feminist (or, at Least, Gender-Oriented) Interpretations

Since the time of the rabbis, both male and female interpreters have attended to the gender dynamics of these chapters.[12] In the interest of space, however, I will move directly to modern, mostly explicitly feminist, interpretation. It is not hard to see the mixed blessing here as far as women are concerned. On the one hand, the possibility of women inheriting is recognized, and the five bold daughters of Zelophehad are named no less than three different times in the account. On the other hand, their right to inherit is limited by the presence of even one brother, and their marital choices are restricted in the interests of the patrilineage even if they do inherit. Feminist scholars have, however, disagreed on the implications of the gendered issues of power and authority in evidence here.

Beginning already with the contributors to the 1898 *Woman's Bible*, some focus on the downside. Elizabeth Cady Stanton and Phebe A. Hanaford both condemn the injustice shown to the daughters, with barely a comment even on their remarkable initiative (Stanton does describe them as "noble").[13] Michelle Ellis Taylor[14] and Jione Havea[15] also focus mainly on the patriarchal pall cast by Chapter 36—"strength in a woman is allowed only in service of patriarchy"[16]—setting this discrimination alongside the exclusion of foreigners. Other negative judgments include the fact that even though daughters can inherit, the marriage restriction means that it is only for a lifetime, with no right to bequeath their property to whom they choose;[17] the five women never act or speak as independent individuals, nor is their mother ever named;[18] the point of the story is not to be a comfort to women, but a comfort to sonless men who feared the loss of their name—in other words, it deals with a problem of patriarchy, which remains intact despite their valor;[19] the daughters do not even appear at all in Chapter 36;[20] because the women married sons of their father's brothers, they effectively did not inherit, since these men would have ultimately received the land anyway;[21] Chapter 36 is an oppressive response based on men's fear of women's power.[22] Dora Mbuwayesango's imperial-critical analysis extends the latter point to connect the Israelite women in the occupation stories with the Canaanite women as well: "Whether imperial or colonized, women [in these stories] are viewed as sources of possible danger to the equilibrium of the patriarchal society."[23]

Many feminist interpreters find here, though, a glass half-full, if also half-empty. Most cite textual evidence like the daughters' boldness and agency in coming before the male leaders, the righteousness of their cause (both as a matter of their concern for their father's name and as affirmed by YHWH's judgment), and the threefold repetition of their names (with no mention of their eventual husbands' names). The daughters become "the first rightful female landowners in the biblical text"[24] and they are "the first persons that challenge divine law and succeed in bending it in their favor," creating a ruling that will serve other women as well.[25] For contemporary women of faith, such characterizations can make the daughters "a positive model of sisterhood,"[26] a "source of hope,"[27] and a reason for celebration in their independence and the text's concern for their well-being.[28] Such readings, however, make a deliberate choice to read for liberation, focusing on the apparent good news of Moses's first ruling (ch. 27) while keeping its less woman-friendly emendation in Chapter 36 in the shadows.[29]

There are three interpretations that find a positive value in the two-part story as a whole. Two of these, by Dean Ulrich and John Litke, are not sufficiently gender-critical to qualify as feminist readings, but they do enlarge the scope of the inquiry and introduce a new theme worth further consideration, namely, a focus on community membership, or what I would call identity.[30] The third, by Tamara Eskenazi,[31] warrants more consideration.

Virtually alone among current feminist interpreters, Eskenazi characterizes the story of the daughters of Zelophehad (including the coda in Josh 17:3–6) as an egalitarian break from much of the biblical material. Eskenazi appropriates but also develops some of the positive textual features mentioned earlier. She casts the daughters as disenfranchised people who "successfully confront an unjust system and propose a more equitable law,"[32] by means of a skillful navigation that does not disrupt the social order. Since preserving a man's name—that is, his property and legacy—is a "venerable obligation in the Bible," the women cleverly work around this by framing their request "in the shared language of communal, especially male, concern."[33] Eskenazi argues further that Chapter 36 is "less constricting than it might seem." Her strategy in this case, as opposed to what I have called liberationist readings, which simply ignore the downsides of the text, is to make her case precisely from its wealth of detail, properly understood, as it were. To take a couple of examples: she argues that the text's "attempt to secure the greater good of protecting tribal ownership of the land, rather than a gender-specific goal, stands as the basis for restricting the marriage choices of the sisters." That is, "the issue of who inherits land is not depicted as an objection to women's owning land but rather as a concern for preserving tribal ownership of allotted land."[34] Further, she notes the daughters' freedom to decide on their own marriage partners, though within their father's tribe, rather than being subject to male guardianship.[35]

While I can affirm Eskenazi's admiration for the daughters' negotiating savvy, her feminist analysis does not address the larger patriarchal structure. The Bible often presents women who uphold the social order in a positive light, even when they behave in otherwise questionable ways (Tamar in Gen 38 and Ruth, e.g.). But placing the value of tribal ownership over the sisters' freedom to choose their husbands from any tribe is, contra Eskenazi, very much a gender-specific goal: its purpose is to maintain the patrilineage, as is the women's argument for preserving their father's name in the first place. The real issue here is not about marital choice in any case, but about who controls the land inheritance. The daughters do seem to have retained possession during their lifetimes, but they also appear to have been one-generation placeholders who could not pass the inheritance on in their own names, even on behalf of their father.[36] Further, daughters' inheritance right still starts only where sons' ends; men are still privileged, and women's right to inherit is limited to a few. Whether or not such regulations were actually enforced, they represent a gender ideology within the Bible that desires restrictions on women's ownership. The feminist glass remains, in my view, rather less than half full.

More hermeneutically subtle are the postcolonial analyses of Judith McKinlay[37] and Juliana Claassens.[38] As she does always so artfully, McKinlay speaks in her own voice to address the gendered push and pull of the text. She recognizes, on the one hand, the ethical obligation of her own political positioning, "embedded and complicit … in the politics of a postcolonial society."[39] On this ground, McKinlay *makes her choice* for a reading that privileges the losses of the Canaanites over the power and courage of Zelophehad's daughters, yet without eliminating the importance of the latter. In a conflicted society, she concludes, two readings may be rightfully held in tension. Claassens adopts a different strategy for negotiating the potential conflict between the daughters and the Canaanites when it comes to the question of justice, bringing to bear contemporary discussions of human dignity and the recognition of the vulnerability of Others as the basis for transformative conversation between such competing claims.

I shall return to postcolonialism in due course, but my interest in feminist and gender-critical biblical interpretation does not fundamentally lie in assessing whether a given text is good for women, bad for women, or both. The answer to that question too often lies in the desire of the interpreter for a "usable" text. I seek instead to locate the gender discourse of a given text within the larger ideological system of biblical identity construction and social control mechanisms, an enterprise that often renders the question of a text's "usability" for women moot: the book of Numbers, certainly, is bad for everyone, except for those men who are in control. In what follows, then, I offer a couple of different angles for examining the intersection of Numbers' gender ideology, especially as it is evident in Chapters 27 and 36, with other interests hidden in the biblical cards.

Feminist and Geographical Interpretations: An Intersection

It will come as no surprise that conventional biblical interpreters in the twentieth century read Numbers with an eye to identifiable geographic locations as well as, especially earlier in the century, an assumption that "history" recounted in the book bore some, if not perfect, resemblance to actual events in the past. Though these perspectives in their naïve form have largely had their day, we cannot discount the possibility that topographical references may have had some meaning to people of the (much later) day in which the book was written. They may also, alternatively or in addition, have represented in literary form the deep structures of other social needs and tensions.

What makes this consideration relevant from a feminist perspective is the fact that some of the daughters' names, as well as those of others connected to them, match those of towns or geographic areas. As is often noted, the name of one daughter, Tirzah, is well-attested as the name of a town in the region of Samaria, and their grandfather's name, Hepher, is as well. Other daughters' names, Noah and Hoglah, are used as toponyms in the Samaria Ostraca, as are four of the Manassite clan names listed in Numbers 26:30–31, Abiezer, Asriel, Shechem, and Shemida.[40] Eskenazi further notes that the daughter's name Mahlah is a place name in 1 Kings 19:16, and Milcah may be a northern regional name as well.[41] One question, then, is why these toponyms were personalized and drawn into a story dealing with a problematic question of inheritance.[42]

Baruch Levine takes a politics of geography approach that is representative of the twentieth-century work on this question.[43] "The naming of clans by toponyms in this case reveals the hidden agenda of Numbers 26–27, which is the substantiation of the claim of the tribe of Manasseh to territory west of the Jordan."[44] This agenda is a postexilic priestly one in his view, and "the legal innovation associated with the family of Zelophehad must be understood in the context of the plan for the settlement of Canaan put forth in several versions by the priestly school." Put in another way: "The clan of Zelophehad truly belonged west of the Jordan."[45] But the *towns* (erstwhile daughters) of "Zelophehad" also truly belonged to Manasseh and no other tribe.

David Jobling, while affirming the importance of the Jordan boundary as a problem for Israelite identity, proposes a different methodological approach, using structuralist analysis to tease out the less transparent aspects of the textual ideology and clarify the role of gender ideology as part and parcel of it. He asks: "What viewpoint does the Bible reveal towards the idea of Israelites living east of Jordan?"[46] Jobling focuses first on Numbers 32 and Joshua 22, which contain two separate but sequentially linked stories of conflict and resolution related to the issues of land allotment and settlement east and west of Jordan. The first story (Num 32; Josh 22:1–8) deals with the desire of the Transjordanian tribes to remain east of Jordan and the negotiated settlement that these tribes will lead the way into Cisjordan as long as they may first build their homes and settle their families. The second story, in Joshua 22:9–34, follows the successful invasion, when the two and a half Transjordanian tribes, on their way home, build an altar to Yhwh on the west bank of the Jordan. The other tribes accuse them of rebelling against Yhwh and encourage them to move west "if your land is unclean" (Josh 22:19). The Transjordanians, however, express their fear that the children of the westerners might exclude their children from a "portion in Yhwh," viewing the Jordan as a boundary (Josh 22:25). The Cisjordanians accept the explanation, and the altar is called Witness, as testimony to their faithfulness.

Jobling's argument is far too dense to summarize briefly, so I will simply highlight elements of it that are relevant to my argument. First, these two episodes are evidence of the Cisjordanian anxiety of the disunifying effect on Israel of having some tribes live east of Jordan, where the danger of apostasy seems (at least to the Cisjordanians) to lurk—these were, after all, the lands of Moab and Ammon.[47] The fact that there are two stories in this vein suggests an ongoing conflict rather than one once and for all resolved—a reality underlined by the recurring nature of the Transjordanians' obligation to cross and recross the Jordan toward the west, first to aid in the conquest and later to properly serve Yhwh in the sanctuary.[48] Ideologically, moreover, the bipartitioned northern tribe of Manasseh—less problematic as Transjordanians because they are also Cisjordanians—"recapitulates and *mediates* the bipartition of Israel."[49]

While the problematic identity of Transjordanian men is provided an ongoing solution—they will evermore travel to serve at the sanctuary in the west—the

Transjordanian *women* remain "a potentially dangerous anomaly, dealt with, in these texts at least, largely by silence."[50] The identity problem posed by women is also highlighted by the nine and a half tribes' appeal to "the sin of Peor" (Josh 22:17) in their verbal attack on the altar built by the Transjordanians.[51] The Transjordanian Israelite women are thus implicitly but perniciously tarred by the brush of foreignness, by implicit association with those foreign, sexual, apostate women who tempted Israelite men to remain east of Jordan.

While the Jordan *as* a boundary is clearly a multifaceted, and gendered, concern, problems also arise when the boundary is blurred, not only by Israelites living to the east, but also by non-Israelites in the west, who must be exterminated along with all signs of their apostate worship.[52] This identity-threatening boundary-blurring again receives a gendered expression, this time in the genealogies of Zelophehad's daughters, which appear differently in Numbers 26:29–33 and in Joshua 17:1–2. The former runs from Manasseh through Machir and Gilead to Hepher (who also has five brothers), then to Zelophehad, and finally to the daughters.[53] The "strong implication" here is that the daughters are from the Transjordan, part of which is known as Gilead. In Joshua 17:1–2, however, Hepher (with his five brothers) appears in the same generation as Machir, rather than as his grandson. In this case Hepher is included among the Cisjordanian clans of Manasseh, making his son, Zelophehad, and granddaughters "unambiguously Cisjordanian."[54] In verse 3, though, the genealogy reverts to the standard form.

Insofar as they are first introduced in Numbers as Transjordanian and then painted in Joshua as Cisjordanian, the daughters of Zelophehad function as a prime example of the problem of Transjordanian women: as it were, "the text makes them marry and move west, and this is felt to solve an urgent problem."[55] It also brings together the issue of the Transjordanian women with that of the inheritance of the land. The solution is analogous to that effected for the Transjordanian men, with their commitment to ongoing service at the western sanctuary, and also similar to the way that the virgin Midianite (i.e., "really" foreign Transjordanian) women were married into Israel after the Midianite war of Chapter 31.[56] The identity of true Israelites resides in the west. Interesting too, though, is the way this case recapitulates the problem of Jordan-divided Israel, within the very tribe that "solved" it by straddling the boundary. The daughters of Zelophehad threaten the singleness of Manasseh itself.

Jobling's analysis thus reveals that Numbers' overt concern for land claims, articulated through stories of territory-seizing wars and disputes over inheritance, is as much or more a matter of conflicts over identity boundaries as it is about land claims as such. There is a double-sided problem of identity boundaries—here concretized by the fact and symbol of the Jordan river—in which the problem of the stranger within is both paralleled and overlain with the problem of the (still very close) stranger without. Consistent with a good deal of the book of Numbers, this identity discourse—who is "us" and who is "them"—is carried out significantly by means of gender discourse, with women representing both the stranger without and the stranger within.[57] As Jobling concludes, "At a deep level, Cisjordan and Transjordan are coded simply as male and female. Nothing so bald as this ever appears on the surface, for many other semantic elements overlie it; nonetheless, the hypothesis is worth framing that this is the semantic force most deeply charging the manifest texts."[58]

We can further extend Jobling's complex and astute analysis. First, I return to his observation that the problem of Israel's division, east and west of Jordan, is recapitulated in the threat to the unity of Manasseh by the possible exogamous marriages of the daughters. Overtly, the text constrains their choices in defense of its androcentric tribalism. At the same time, it leaves them in a textually deconstructive role. For the requirement for their intra-tribal marriages represents a solution to a problem that their very existence creates. Like the need for the Transjordanian men to cross and recross the Jordan to perform service to YHWH, the proper husbands for inheriting daughters will have to be found over and over again: the threat of disunity they represent is omnipresent. Like the wife whose very status as wife creates the fear of her possible adultery (Num 5), like the sister whose priestly lineage must be suppressed (Num 12), the inheriting daughter is one more challenge to a "national" unity that is fundamentally male-defined. We could imagine a text in which the narrative solution to Israel's geographical division, which was provided by Manasseh's Jordan-straddling, was simply left intact, without being undermined by a story like this. We could also imagine such undermining taking place in any number of other ways. The choice in this case, however, was to use female characters, acting in a powerful and authoritative way, to do the job. This textual strategy shows again, as was true of Miriam, both that women are the problem and that de-authorizing them is the solution. But the presence of the stranger within is never fully suppressed, and it is telling that the claim of Transjordanian Manasseh, not just to territory in the west, but to *identity with an Israel defined by its west*, is made through its women. Like the altar built by the Transjordanians, itself in Cisjordan, the women whose story concludes the book of Numbers are witness to both the fact of and the anxiety about the stranger within.

Priests, Law, and Community Leadership in Postexilic Yehud

Though source criticism of the book of Numbers continues apace, there is broad agreement among recent scholars that much of the book is postexilic, and certainly its final form is.[59] With that sociopolitical setting in mind, David Aaron has argued that the apparent "revision" of the Chapter 27 ruling in Chapter 36 is precisely that: an appearance only.[60] In fact, he argues, both chapters were composed by the same hand and textually placed as they are to create the impression of ruling and revision, when what we have in fact is a fiction created for a larger ideological purpose. Aaron picks up on Baruch Levine's point that "it is hard to accept that Torah legislators would not have anticipated the consequences of allowing daughters to inherit family land, initially."[61] As Aaron observes, the idea is so hard to accept that we in fact should not take the bait: the priestly composer of Numbers knew perfectly well that the "solution" of Chapter 27 would create the "new" problem of Chapter 36.

Following Zefrira Ben-Barak's extensive discussion of the evidence for both the fluidity and the "ubiquity of the concern for female inheritance" in the ancient Near East,[62] Aaron contends that it was highly likely that the Israelites followed similar practices.[63] Indeed, Numbers 27:8–11 "captures many of the practices reflected in documents culled from other cultures," with daughters inheriting based on "patriarchal stipulation."[64] For Aaron, "this brief passage *is the starting point* for the author; and it is its content that the author seeks to undermine."[65] What appears in Chapter 36 as "a 'revision' is actually a self-serving invention."[66] The story of the daughters is a fabrication designed "to facilitate the invention of a countersuit (Num 36) that directly undermines the practices described in 27:8–11," which derived from a time when "women sustaining a father's name may, indeed, have been a structure in place," a practice now replaced by "a more rigid patriarchalism in postexilic Israel."[67] "The author's engagement of storytelling to couch a legal precedent is motivated by the *emotional effect* only this kind of narrative can have on the intended audience."[68] And the association with Moses and the wilderness period of both the initial articulation of daughters' rights in Numbers 27:8–11 and its subsequent revision—or, perhaps more in line with the textual ideology, its "interpretation"—in Chapter 36 lent authority to the later author's agenda in "a world that was apparently keenly concerned with land ownership, the role of women, and using divine authority to situate its policies."[69]

Again we might take some further steps in parsing the power dynamics that come to expression in this literature. Aaron's argument reminds me, first, of one that I have previously made on a possible relationship between the Sotah ritual in Numbers 5 and the story of Miriam and Aaron's rebellion in Numbers 12.[70] These episodes clearly share with Numbers 27 and 36 signs of what Aaron regards as a particularly "rigid patriarchalism" in the postexilic period.[71] What strikes me about the Sotah text, however, is not simply the rather extreme subordination of a wife to her husband, but also *that of her husband to the priest*. The law does not merely *offer* the husband a ritual remedy for his suspicion of jealousy, but in fact *requires* that he avail himself of it: if he even suspects adultery, "he shall bring her to the priest" (Num 5:15). So all this is not really, or not simply, "about the husband"; the law ignores, for example, the shame that would inevitably accompany public confirmation of his having been cuckolded. The larger purpose of the law, rather, is to assert priestly authority over the identity-defining patrilineal system. It establishes the priest, rather than the husband, as master of the workings of patrilineage, preempting the husband's right to make decisions about sexual matters in his own household.

Numbers 12 also uses a female figure, in this case the sister, Miriam, to leverage priestly authority. What is noteworthy about this story is not simply that Miriam is held guilty of rebellion against Moses, while her equally blameworthy brother Aaron is not. Equally striking is the seemingly illogical narrative sequence that *first* bonds Miriam with Aaron and *then* separates her from him, while aligning him with Moses instead. There is, I think, a method to this apparent madness, for Aaron's priestly authority—a degree of authority close to if not equal to Moses's—is thereafter assumed. The effect is not simply a devaluation of women, but the effective estrangement of sisters from the priestly lineage, narratively constituting a female-free identity for the priests.[72] Not once, but repeatedly then in Numbers the authority of particular priestly men is established over *all* Israel by means of gender discourse. Something quite related appears to be happening in Numbers 27 and 36, although, curiously, the priest is less of an actor here: Eleazar appears among the other leaders in Chapter 27 but not at all in Chapter 36. This fact may indicate some assertion of control by the lay leaders of the community over against the authority of the priests, but that control is established using the same narrative strategy used for devaluing the status of Miriam; first, by creating an illusion of the daughters' status and control, and then undercutting it in an arbitrary way.

My previous work also discusses cross-cultural studies that suggest that a rigid system of patrilineal inheritance becomes the norm in political-economic contexts of state-formation, in which there is a shift from and "struggle between kinship-based, autonomous communities and a nonproducing class or classes."[73] At the same time, previously existing patterns of heteronomous authority for women are eliminated, while male sexual control over them increases. Although it would be anachronistic to speak of state formation in Second Temple Yehud, the direct connection between ritualized sexual control of women (ch. 5) and the devaluation of the authority of the sister (ch. 12) with the elevation of priestly control are suggestive of a similar sort of process at the time Numbers was put in its present form. Thus, David Aaron's argument that Chapter 36 is a rhetorical move attempting to eliminate a prior custom of daughters inheriting seems coherent with the larger ideological implications of the passages dealing with the wife and the sister. The issue here goes beyond even what Aaron identifies as "a concern for land ownership [and] the role of women." It has to do with control of the mechanisms of patriliny itself in the interests of a (very likely nonproducing) centralized leadership group, namely a particular (and relatively late) faction of priests whose identity was cast in definitively gendered terms.

I will conclude with a prospect for further investigation that would engage yet another critical perspective: postcolonialism. One question that has nagged at me as I have worked on the story of the daughters of Zelophehad is the question of why the priests themselves, whose characters and status are crucial through most of the book, play such a small role in this ending. The book of Numbers is set in the liminal space of the wilderness, and imagines no outside power over the people other than that of Egypt, from which they have been ostensibly liberated. Numbers thus does not obviously lend itself to a postcolonial reading.[74] Yet the unsaid speaks loudly, for the composer of the book lives in a settled land, not the wilderness, a land controlled by Persia. And the local priestly leadership, despite its claim to power over non-priestly Israelites, is beholden to Persian overlords.

What role might the daughters' story, told at the cusp of entry into the land, be playing in this literary masking game, where such obvious power issues are suppressed? Does the focus on the women who will live in the land distract our view from the intent to dispossess the land's inhabitants (whomever they may be in the time of this priestly writing)? Does the structural connection, as argued by

Jobling, between the Israelite daughters, who are "rightfully" dispossessed, and the "foreign" daughters, whose fathers are about to be, help justify the act of conquest? Why do the priestly editors, so prominent elsewhere in the book, hide themselves behind the women's story, channeling the voice of male authority through the heads of the fathers' houses, who object to Moses's and YHWH's initial ruling? Is it to mask the real source of their power, which is *not* YHWH but Persia? If so, then the patrilineal feint exposed by David Aaron, in which the illusion of legal revision distracts the eye from the overpowering of the daughters' inheritance rights, is at the same time a political feint, in which the assertion of those patrilineal rights on behalf of the heads of the fathers' houses covers for the (priestly) power vested in the (Persian) throne. Gender ideology is a powerful tool used for many purposes!

Conclusion

At the heart of feminist interpretation of the story of the daughters of Zelophehad has been the old reformist vs. revolutionary tension among feminist scholars of religion.[75] While most interpreters in this mode have had to acknowledge the glass-half-empty aspect of the text, most have also clung to the part of the glass half-full. It is not my place to deny anyone the strength or comfort they might find in enjoying the strong, skilled, and public performance of the daughters. Though I believe the story is fictional, I suspect there is some measure of verisimilitude here; that is, very likely the author knew, or at least was able to imagine, real women capable of speaking up for themselves in such a way, and he did not begrudge them their strength and voice, though he also turned it against them. But readers seeking models for exercising their own strength and voice have a right to find them anywhere they can. It is what stories are for.

Yet I also believe that it is dangerously naïve to accord such stories in the Bible an authority beyond what any other story would hold. The gender ideology that constructs Woman as the dangerous Other is pervasive in the Bible; as Esther Fuchs argued long ago,[76] even the most positive views of women tend to serve some other, less empowering purpose. And, even when a text challenges authority, it does so in male terms and in the interests of other men. A critical focus on this ideology means there is simply no way to draw a line between texts that one wants to hold as authoritative and others one wants to reject. To do so is simply to assert the authority of the reader over the text. I'm all for that, but one must own the responsibility.

The project I have undertaken here has a different aim, to tease out the various ways that this gender ideology is entwined in other aspects of biblical thought. In the case of Numbers, this involves, most obviously, the question of what it means to be an Israelite and also, especially earlier in the book, what it means to be a true (read: Aaronite) priest, identities constructed and authorized here by means of gender ideology. A structuralist approach to the geographical indicators in Numbers and Joshua added another dimension to the gender-ideological picture, by tying together two different, identity-constructing symbolic domains, one marked on the body, the other on the land. In the story of the daughters, moreover, these identity issues dovetail with others, of land claims and the manipulation of the law. Along the way, a cross-cultural lens focused on political economics uncovered the possibility, masked by stories about women in Numbers, that *real* women's previous rights were being abrogated while, at the same time, the consolidation of power by a few men at the expense of others was taking place in the context of imperial domination. If the book of Numbers has a message for the present day, it might be that gender is never just about gender.

Notes

1. Norman K. Gottwald, *The Tribes of Yahweh: A Sociology of Religion of Liberated Israel, 1250–1050 B. C. E.* (London: SCM, 2013), first published in 1979.
2. Meyers's classic work is, of course, *Discovering Eve: Ancient Israelite Women in Context* (New York: Oxford University Press, 1988). Cf. also Carol Meyers, *Rediscovering Eve: Ancient Israelite Women in Context* (New York: Oxford University Press), 2013.
3. Claudia V. Camp, *Wisdom and the Feminine in the Book of Proverbs*, BLS 11 (Decatur, GA: Almond Press, 1985).
4. Claudia V. Camp, "Wise and Strange: An Interpretation of the Female Imagery in Proverbs in Light of Trickster Mythology," in *Reasoning with the Foxes: Female Wit in a World of Male Power*, ed. J. Cheryl Exum and Johanna W. H. Bos, *Semeia* 42 (Atlanta: Scholars Press, 1988), 14–36.
5. Robert D. Pelton, *The Trickster in West Africa: A Study of Mythic Irony and Sacred Delight*, HSHR (Berkeley: University of California Press, 1980).
6. Claudia V. Camp, *Wise, Strange and Holy: The Strange Woman and the Making of the Bible*, JSOTSup 320, GCT 9 (Sheffield: Sheffield Academic, 2000).
7. Postcolonial and other intersectionalist interpretations have, of course, connected gender to other discourses such as imperialism, race, and class, but typically with an eye to matters of political power rather than to the rhetoric through which one discourse becomes infused with the other. See later in this essay for reference to feminist postcolonialist analyses of Zelophehad's daughters' story.
8. Camp, *Wise, Strange and Holy*, 191–226.
9. Ken Stone, "Gender Criticism," in *Judges and Method: New Approaches in Biblical Studies*, ed. Gale A. Yee, Second Edition (Minneapolis: Fortress, 2007), 183–201; Deryn Guest, *Beyond Feminist Biblical Studies*, BMW 47 (Sheffield: Sheffield Phoenix, 2012).
10. Camp, *Wise, Strange and Holy*; Claudia V. Camp, "The Problem With Sisters: Anthropological Perspectives on Priestly Kinship Ideology in Numbers," in *Embroidered Garments: Priests and Gender in Biblical Israel*, ed. Deborah W. Rooke, HBM 25 (Sheffield: Sheffield Phoenix, 2009), 119–30; Claudia V. Camp, "Gender and Identity in the Book of Numbers," in *Imagining the Other and Constructing Israelite Identity in the Early Second Temple Period*, ed. Ehud Ben-Zvi and Diana Edelman, LHBOTS 591 (London: Bloomsbury T&T Clark, 2014), 105–21; Claudia V. Camp, "Numbers 5:11–31: Women in Second Temple Judah and the Law of the Controlling Priest," in *Celebrate Her for the Fruit of Her Hands: Studies in Honor of Carol L. Meyers*, ed. Susan Ackerman et al. (Winona Lake, IN: Eisenbrauns, 2015), 111–32.

11. For another such review of the feminist literature, which usefully highlights some different points, see Juliana Claassens, "'Give us a portion among our father's brothers': The Daughters of Zelophehad, Land, and the Quest for Human Dignity," *JSOT* 37 (2013): 319–37 (323–7).
12. For discussions pointing to a range of rabbinic sources, see Josiah Derby, "The Daughters of Zelophehad Revisited," *JBQ* 25 (1997): 169–71; Zvi Ron, "The Daughters of Zelophehad," *JBQ* 26 (1998): 260–2; Tal Ilan, "The Daughters of Zelophehad and Women's Inheritance: The Biblical Injunction and Its Outcome," in *Exodus to Deuteronomy*, ed. Athalya Brenner, FCB Second Series 5 (Sheffield: Sheffield Academic, 2000), 176–86; Yael Shemesh, "A Gender Perspective on the Daughters of Zelophehad: Bible, Talmudic Midrash, and Modern Feminist Midrash," *BibInt* 15 (2007): 80–109; Tamara Cohn Eskenazi, "Numbers," in *The Torah: A Women's Commentary*, ed. Tamara Cohn Eskenazi and Andrea L. Weiss (New York: URJ, 2008), 971–74, 1025–9.
13. Elizabeth Cady Stanton and the Revising Committee, *The Woman's Bible* (New York: The European Publishing Company, 1895–1898), 123–4.
14. Michelle Ellis Taylor, "Numbers," in *The Africana Bible: Reading Israel's Scriptures from Africa and the African Diaspora*, ed. Hugh A. Page, Jr. (Minneapolis: Fortress, 2010), 94–9.
15. Jione Havea, "Numbers," in *Global Bible Commentary*, ed. Daniel Patte (Nashville: Abingdon, 2004), 43–51.
16. Taylor, "Numbers," 96.
17. Sue Levi Elwell, "Numbers," in *The Queer Bible Commentary*, ed. Deryn Guest et al. (London: SCM Press, 2006), 105–21 (119).
18. Elwell, "Numbers," 118.
19. Katharine Doob Sakenfeld, "Zelophehad's Daughters," *PRSt* 15/4 (1988): 37–47 (41); Katharine Doob Sakenfeld, "Numbers," in *Women's Bible Commentary: Expanded Edition with Apocrypha*, ed. Carol A. Newsom and Sharon H. Ringe (Louisville, KY: Westminster John Knox, 1998), 49–56 (54); Shemesh, "A Gender Perspective," 80; Dora Rudo Mbuwayesango, "Can Daughters Be Sons? The Daughters of Zelophehad in Patriarchal and Imperial Society," in *Relating to the Text: Interdisciplinary and Form-Critical Insights on the Bible*, ed. Timothy J. Sandoval and Carleen Mandolfo, JSOTSup 384 (London: T&T Clark, 2003), 251–62; Dennis T. Olson, *Numbers*, IBC (Louisville, KY: John Knox, 1996), 167.
20. Sakenfeld, "Zelophehad's Daughters," 55.
21. Jacob Milgrom, *Numbers: The Traditional Hebrew Text with the New JPS Translation*, JPSTC (Philadelphia: Jewish Publication Society, 1990), 298.
22. Ankie Sterring, "The Will of the Daughters," in *A Feminist Companion to Exodus to Deuteronomy*, ed. Athalya Brenner, FCB 6 (Sheffield: Sheffield Academic, 1994), 94.
23. Mbuwayesango, "Can Daughters Be Sons?," 262.
24. Elwell, "Numbers," 118.
25. Ilan, "The Daughters of Zelophehad," 178–9; Eskenazi, "Numbers," 971.
26. Shemesh, "A Gender Perspective," 80.
27. Elwell, "Numbers," 120.
28. Katharine Doob Sakenfeld, "In the Wilderness, Awaiting the Land: The Daughters of Zelophehad and Feminist Interpretation," *PSB* 9 (1988): 179–96 (195).
29. Whether Chapter 27 is actually as feminist friendly as it appears is questionable, as we shall see later in this essay.

30. Dean R. Ulrich, "The Framing Function of the Narratives about Zelophehad's Daughters," *JETS* 41 (1998): 529–38; John D. Litke, "The Daughters of Zelophehad," *CurTM* 29 (2002): 207–18.
31. Eskenazi, "Numbers."
32. Eskenazi, "Numbers," 971.
33. Eskenazi, "Numbers," 972.
34. Eskenazi, "Numbers," 1,027.
35. Eskenazi, "Numbers," 1,026–7.
36. So with Baruch A. Levine, who suggests that the revision of the ruling in Chapter 36, effectively calling for cousin-marriage in this situation, functions as an alternative to (perhaps historically a replacement for) the levirate law, "merely moving the process forward by one generation," Baruch A. Levine, *Numbers 21–36: A New Translation with Introduction and Commentary*, AB 4A (New York: Doubleday, 2000), 358. There is, in any event, the same net outcome as if a man had had neither sons nor daughters, his property going to (the descendants of) his brothers (Num 27:9), with the daughters functioning merely as temporary placeholders.
37. Judith McKinlay, "Playing an Aotearoa Counterpoint: The Daughters of Zelophehad and Edward Gibbon Wakefield," in *Postcolonialism and the Hebrew Bible: The Next Step*, ed. Roland Boer, SemeiaSt 70 (Atlanta: SBL, 2013), 11–34.
38. Claassens, " 'Give us a portion,' " 319–37.
39. McKinlay, "Playing an Aotearoa Counterpoint," 30.
40. Martin Noth, *Numbers: A Commentary*, OTL (Philadelphia: Westminster, 1968), 207; Levine, *Numbers 21–36*, 321–2, 344.
41. Eskenazi, "Numbers," 972.
42. Eskenazi ("Numbers," 973) holds the toponymic daughters' names as evidence that the daughters were significant figures in early Israel, perhaps among the other ancestors whose names became toponyms. It seems to me more likely that the reverse is the case, namely, that individual female characters were imagined from the names of towns that had a feminine form.
43. See also, e.g., Norman Henry Snaith, "Daughters of Zelophehad," *VT* 16 (1966): 124–7.
44. Levine, *Numbers 21–36*, 322.
45. Levine, *Numbers 21–36*, 344.
46. David Jobling, *The Sense of Biblical Narrative: Structural Analyses in the Hebrew Bible II*, JSOTSup 39 (Sheffield: JSOT Press, 1986), 91.
47. Jobling, *Biblical Narrative*, 101, 104–5. Cf. the inconsistent rhetoric of relationship between tribes on the Jordan's two sides: sometimes it is that of "you" and "your brothers" (Num 32:6; Josh 22:1–8). Elsewhere the Cisjordanians are called "the people of Israel," without a corresponding referent for the Transjordanians. Structurally, of course, the missing term would be *non-Israelites*, foreigners, yet another indication that the easterners are not really part of Yhwh's people (101).
48. Jobling, *Biblical Narrative*, 103–6.
49. Jobling, *Biblical Narrative*, 116. Emphasis in original.
50. Jobling, *Biblical Narrative*, 106.
51. Jobling, *Biblical Narrative*, 104, 106.
52. The combination of repetition and omission in the two accounts of Yhwh's instructions for dividing the land in Numbers 26:52–56 and 33:54—the latter "injected into a section (vv. 51–56) about the issue of *non-Israelites in the west*,"— creates "an important link … between two issues which are superficially unrelated,

but very straightforwardly related in mythic logic—the (continued) existence of non-Israelites in Cisjordan, and the existence of Israelites in Transjordan," Jobling, *Biblical Narrative*, 115.

53. Jobling, *Biblical Narrative*, 118.
54. Jobling, *Biblical Narrative*, 119.
55. Jobling, *Biblical Narrative*, 119.
56. Cf. Jobling, *Biblical Narrative*, 114.
57. Camp, *Wise, Strange and Holy*, 278.
58. Jobling, *Biblical Narrative*, 122.
59. With Reinhard Achenbach, *Die Vollendung der Tora: Studien zur Redaktionsgeschichte des Numeribuches im Kontext von Hexateuch und Pentateuch*, BZABR 3 (Wiesbaden: Harrassowitz, 2002), I take the present form of Numbers to be fundamentally the work of post-Priestly (in the sense of P source) redactors. The textual ideology of these final revisers—namely the construal of "Israel" as a theocratic community governed by a high priest—Achenbach dates to the early fourth century. To this "theological reviser" Achenbach credits Numbers 1–10 and 26–36, as well as a reworking of 11–25.
60. David Aaron, "The Ruse of Zelophehad's Daughters," *HUCA* 80 (2009): 1–38.
61. Levine, *Numbers 21–36*, 357; Aaron, "Ruse of Zelophehad's Daughters," 11.
62. Aaron, "Ruse of Zelophehad's Daughters," 7, following Zafrira Ben-Barak, *Inheritance by Daughters in Israel and the Ancient Near East: A Social, Legal and Ideological Revolution* (Jaffa: Archaeological Center Publications, 2006).
63. Aaron, "Ruse of Zelophehad's Daughters," 7–8.
64. Aaron, "Ruse of Zelophehad's Daughters," 28.
65. Aaron, "Ruse of Zelophehad's Daughters," 28. Emphasis in original.
66. Aaron, "Ruse of Zelophehad's Daughters," 31.
67. Aaron, "Ruse of Zelophehad's Daughters," 33–4.
68. Aaron, "Ruse of Zelophehad's Daughters," 22. Emphasis in original.
69. Aaron, "Ruse of Zelophehad's Daughters," 26–7.
70. Camp, "Problem With Sisters"; Camp, "Numbers 5:11–31."
71. Aaron, "Ruse of Zelophehad's Daughters," 34.
72. Camp, *Wise, Strange and Holy*, 227–78.
73. Christine Ward Gailey, *Kinship to Kingship: Gender Hierarchy and State Formation in the Tongan Islands*, Texas Press Sourcebooks in Anthropology 14 (Austin: University of Texas Press, 1987), xii.
74. Writing from the perspective of their own contexts, Mbuwayesango and, especially, McKinlay and Claassens have explored important interpretive possibilities in this vein, as noted earlier. I seek here to include a more historical dimension as well.
75. See, e.g., Rita Gross, *Feminism and Religion: An Introduction* (Boston: Beacon, 1996).
76. Esther Fuchs, "Status and Role of Female Heroines in the Biblical Narrative," *Mankind Quarterly* 23 (1982): 149–60.

Chapter 13

"I WILL TAKE NO BULL FROM YOUR HOUSE": FEMINIST BIBLICAL THEOLOGY IN A CREATIONAL CONTEXT

Jacqueline E. Lapsley

Creational Dignity and Psalm 50

Human beings are animals. Yet, we think we are gods. To be sure, we are unique among other animals in our ability to shape our environment—which is, of course, not our environment alone, but the one we share with all other living beings. This power to shape the world we live in has been matched only by the hubris with which we wield it. In this essay, I take up some of these questions from the perspective of Christian biblical theology. After acknowledging the contours of the problem of anthropocentrism, I will explore a feminist hermeneutic of creational dignity through which I will then read Psalm 50, with special attention to the central section of the psalm (vv. 7–15).

Human and Nonhuman Animals in Cosmic Context

Some decades ago, the scientist and educator Carl Sagan envisioned a Cosmic Calendar to make comprehensible the vast history of the universe. On the Cosmic Calendar, the 13.8-billion-year lifetime of the universe is condensed into a single year. In this visualization, the Big Bang took place at the beginning of January 1 at midnight, and the current moment is mapped onto the end of December 31 at midnight. Life appears on September 21, multicellular life on December 5, land plants on December 20, mammals on December 26, and humans late in the evening on December 31. A human life lasts a quarter of a second, literally, the blink of an eye. Sagan also offered a spatial image: if the Cosmic Calendar is scaled to the size of a football field, then all of human history would occupy an area the size of a human hand.[1]

The Cosmic Calendar puts us human beings in our place: very late to a party that has been going on for a long time. Cosmically speaking, human beings are not at the center of the world, with the rest of creation—everything that appears on the calendar before us—as resources for our use. How could we be at the center when we are a kind of footnote in the cosmic story?

Christian Anthropocentrism

The view set forth in the Cosmic Calendar is not, of course, the traditional Christian view, which is decidedly anthropocentric in its perspective. The historian Lynn White is now famous for having forcefully argued in the mid-1960s that Christianity was largely to blame for environmental degradation due to its anthropocentric worldview. White lays the blame for the modern environmental crisis squarely on "orthodox Christian arrogance toward nature." He says:

> In sharp contrast [to Greco-Roman thought], Christianity inherited from Judaism not only a concept of time as nonrepetitive and linear but also a striking story of creation. By gradual stages a loving and all-powerful God had created light and darkness, the heavenly bodies, the earth and all its plants, animals, birds, and fishes. Finally, God had created Adam and, as an afterthought, Eve to keep man from being lonely. Man named all the animals, thus establishing his dominance over them. *God planned all of this explicitly for man's benefit and rule: no item in the physical creation had any purpose save to serve man's purposes.*[2]

White makes two basic claims here: first, the Bible asserts human domination over nature, establishing an anthropocentric worldview. And in a related, second move, Christianity makes a distinction between human beings (formed in God's image) and the rest of creation, which has no soul or reason and is thus inferior.

Ever since the publication of this essay, scholars have been debating: is what Lynn White says true? Does Christianity bear the bulk of the responsibility for our current environmental crisis due to centuries of depredation brought about by industrialization? Yes and no. Yes, he hit a nerve: the integration of Christianity and industrialization has led to many of our environmental problems. But White also oversimplifies the issue. Some writers, for example, have argued that White does not take account of the non-Christian influences on Western thought.[3] Furthermore, scholars have argued that what the Bible actually says about creation and the world must be carefully distinguished from the ways in which dominant Christianity *has interpreted* the Bible and which have been destructive for the environment.[4]

Lynn White was generally correct that most dominant strains of the Judeo-Christian tradition have in fact placed human beings at the clear center of the cosmos (even if the theologies espoused sometimes resist that perspective in theory): we do live in an anthropocentric society, and our Christian heritage bears some responsibility for it. Christians, and the societies that Judeo-Christian traditions have fostered, tend to view the created world as objects for our exclusive, human use. There are too many examples of this attitude to name, but the ways in which animals are treated in the agri-industrial complex—not as living, sensate creatures, but as objects that can be treated like any inanimate object—are horrific. Yet the deep irony is that the Scriptures warn against precisely this temptation: the biblical witness is clear that we live in a theocentric universe, and our failure to properly situate ourselves vis-à-vis the deity, as creatures embedded within creation, leads to violence, suffering, and oppression. Accordingly, in recent years biblical scholars and theologians have returned to the biblical witness, seeking to recover that lost perspective.

The anthropocentrism characteristic of traditional Christian theology is not supported by much of the biblical witness. A careful reading of the creation accounts in Genesis, of many psalms (e.g., especially, Pss 104, 148, 150), most of the wisdom material,[5] and many other biblical texts reveal that much of the biblical witness *explicitly* holds a theocentric worldview in which human beings have an important role to play, but not as the center of value (and this perspective is implicit in many other biblical texts).

A Cosmocentric Hermeneutic of Creational Dignity

I will argue for a way of reading—a feminist hermeneutic—that emphasizes the dignity of all creation while embedding human dignity within the larger context. Why is such a hermeneutic feminist, one might ask? Many feminist readers find that concern for others—the vulnerable, the impoverished, the powerless—goes beyond issues of gender. Rosemary Radford Ruether, for instance, rejects the binaries in which so much of Christian theology is mired, and instead posits relationality as the key. She explains:

> Autonomy is a delusion based on denial of the others on whom one depends. Rather one seeks to become ever more deeply aware of the interconnections on which one's own life depends, ultimately the whole network of relations of the whole cosmos … To be is to *be related*; shaping the quality of those relations is the critical ethical task.[6]

And it has become abundantly clear that we are related to the world in ways that go far beyond our intra-human relations. Human beings possess authentic self-knowledge only when we understand our embeddedness within, and interconnectedness to, creation as a whole.

God is both the One who creates and sustains a world in which we humans are infinitesimally unimportant (as suggested by Sagan's images) and the One who nonetheless cares for the most vulnerable among us (as suggested by the biblical witness). Biblical texts, properly interpreted, provide us sharper lenses for understanding who we are: we are not as important as we traditionally have thought ourselves, but are more important than the Cosmic Calendar alone would suggest. A feminist hermeneutic committed to flourishing and creational dignity frees us from the tyranny of thinking ourselves the center of the universe and comforts us that our fate and the fate of our fellow creatures are of deep concern to the maker of such a vast cosmos. We are thus liberated from our self-involvement, and our self-deception: our hope does not lie in ourselves, but in God. A life saturated in praise to this God both flourishes and enables the flourishing of others.

Flourishing and Cosmocentrism

For the theologian Chris Cuomo, the concept of flourishing is large enough to encompass both humans and nonhumans without sentimentalizing the natural world or humanity's relationship to it. Flourishing, for Cuomo, refers to that which promotes the integrity, stability, and beauty of both human and nonhuman communities.[7] Such flourishing will look different for each community within creation, but the crucial feature is that for any to truly thrive, all must thrive. The emphasis in such an ethic is on assessing "actions, practices, institutions, attitudes, and values in terms of their impact on ecological and human flourishing."[8] The feminist hermeneutic with which I read the Bible entails a commitment to the flourishing and dignity of all creation.

Such a perspective may seem obvious to some, but in my experience even some progressive communities of faith are still working out of a hermeneutic of *human* flourishing. I found myself stumbling over the Affirmation of Faith in a recent worship service in a local progressive congregation of the Presbyterian Church (USA). The source of the affirmation varies week-to-week, and on this particular Sunday morning the affirmation came from the Confession of 1967. The selected section of the confession speaks of the implications of the life, death, and resurrection of Jesus Christ for the way the church is to be in the world. The life, death, and resurrection of Jesus "set the pattern for the church's mission." The confession continues:

> His *human* life involves the church in the common life of all *people.*
>
> His service to *men and women* commits the church to work for every form of *human* well-being.
>
> His suffering makes the church sensitive to all *human* suffering so that it sees the face of Christ in the faces of *persons* in every kind of need.
>
> His crucifixion discloses to the church God's judgment on the inhumanity that marks *human* relations, and the awful consequences of the church's own complicity in injustice.
>
> In the power of the risen Christ and the hope of his coming the church sees the promise of God's renewal of *human* life in society and of God's victory over all wrong.[9]

I appreciate the Confession of 1967 for its earnestness, and I even appreciate the wonky need to explain everything in detail that characterizes this confession compared to the more compact, restrained style of others, written at different moments of the church's life. Set against the backdrop of the turmoil of the 1960s, the confession speaks faithfully into the context from which it arose. Yet, I am struck by this confession's relentless attention to human beings to the exclusion of the rest of God's world, as revealed by my highlighting of language for humans in the portion cited above. It is as though the rest of the world is outside of God's, and therefore the church's, concern. More troubling to me than the wording of the original confession, which is understandable given that it was written in the mid-1960s, is my suspicion that almost no one else around me in the worshiping congregation that day was likely troubled by the anthropocentric language.

If I were to rewrite the confession from a less anthropocentric, and more theocentric, or perhaps even *cosmocentric*, focus, it might look something like this:

> His life involves the church in the life of the world.
>
> His service to God's creation commits the church to work for every form of well-being among God's creatures.
>
> His suffering makes the church sensitive to the suffering of all creation, so that it sees the face of Christ in the faces of creatures in every kind of need.
>
> His crucifixion discloses to the church God's judgment on the inhumanity that marks human relations with one another and with the world, and the awful consequences of the church's own complicity in injustice.
>
> In the power of the risen Christ and the hope of his coming the church sees the promise of God's renewal of all life in society and the world and of God's victory over all wrong.

Typically, theological discourse has offered a choice between an *anthropocentric* worldview (the dominant one) and a *theocentric* one (more biblical, but not *actually* widely represented in theological practice).[10] But perhaps a third possibility might be useful: a *cosmocentric* reading, which is more biblical than the anthropocentric model. In a way, a cosmocentric reading leads us astray: the biblical material does *not* posit the world as the *center* of value—God is almost always at the center in the biblical material—but heuristically it may be useful because talking about *theocentrism* has not sufficiently curbed our tendency toward, and preference for, the anthropocentrism that has historically had such a firm grip on the Christian theological imagination. Not that new terminology ever fostered transformation, but scholars live in hope, and so in the hope that it might add to the growing scholarly efforts to decenter human beings for the good of the world, I espouse a *cosmocentric* reading.[11]

The conversation about the consequences of anthropocentrism is, however, not confined to scholars, but is now reaching a broader audience. A recent Op-Ed by Frans de Waal in the *New York Times* speaks of the pervasive, deep-seated nature of Western anthropocentrism. The very existence of such an opinion piece in the *Times* suggests that the problem of human exceptionalism has risen to a fairly widespread level of consciousness. De Waal shows how scientists, and even the general public, do linguistic gymnastics to avoid anthropomorphizing animal behavior. For example: "Animals don't have 'sex,' but engage in breeding behavior. They don't have 'friends,' but favorite affiliation partners." He concludes: "In our haste to argue that animals are not people, we have forgotten that people are animals, too."[12] De Waal traces the problem in part to Aristotle (though he is not the only guilty party, to be sure), with his hierarchical chain of being:

The great philosopher put all living creatures on a vertical Scala Naturae, which runs from humans (closest to the gods) down toward other mammals, with birds, fish, insects and mollusks near the bottom. Comparisons up and down this vast ladder have been a popular scientific pastime, but all we have learned from them is how to measure other species by our standards. Keeping Aristotle's scale intact, with humans on top, has been the unfailing goal.[13]

The long conversation that many trace back to Lynn White (and no doubt one might posit earlier sources) continues, but the audience for such discussions has broadened considerably beyond academic journals. More and more people are wondering whether what makes human beings distinct from other animals is not their rationality, or their toolmaking abilities, or their special status as loved by God, but their hubris, and their capacity to act on that hubris. Much of the public discourse on these matters either assumes or concludes that Christian theology is part of the problem of anthropocentrism, and *de facto* cannot be part of a solution.

I included earlier in this essay, however, a revised section of a confession from the Reformed tradition to show that traditional Christian theology can, when adapted to our current context, still be a powerful way of interpreting God and the world. One does not need to abandon historic Christianity to advocate for a cosmocentric/theocentric worldview. Though some Christians no doubt slap the derogatory label of ecofeminist (which is necessarily pagan, et cetera, in this way of thinking) onto the kind of interpretation I offer here, I see myself as drawing on the strengths of the Christian tradition (and more specifically in my case, the Reformed tradition, "Reformed and Always Reforming"), and indeed standing within that tradition, as I seek to hear the voices from our world that can provide a corrective to some of theology's more anthropocentric tendencies.

Even the recent renewed attention in Christian theological circles to human dignity can have unintended negative repercussions for the nonhuman world. Attention to human dignity is not a recent innovation; indeed, when it comes to dignity and the Bible, human beings have long been the focus of concern. The assertion found in Genesis 1:26 that human beings are made in the image and likeness of God has been a powerful affirmation of human worth and dignity for millennia in both Jewish and Christian traditions.[14] Principalities and powers may make distinctions, but in the eyes of God all persons have inherent dignity. The dignity of every human being has been no less important in more recent history when it has again been threatened, as in the battle over slavery in the United States, to say nothing of more recent political discourse in the United States and elsewhere, such as in South Africa, where human dignity has been the focus of scholarly reflection.[15] Thus the importance of reaffirming human dignity, as in the 1979 *Book of Common Prayer* of the Episcopal Church, in the baptismal covenant ("Will you uphold the dignity of every human being?") should not be underestimated.[16]

Yet the emphasis on human dignity in theological and political discourse does not stem the tide of negative consequences for the dignity of other living creatures, and for creation as a whole, because, as it has been traditionally conceived, human dignity relies on the *theoretical* degradation of everything in creation that is nonhuman. Emphasizing human dignity means emphasizing the inherent importance of human beings *over against* someone else. And that someone else is every nonhuman creature. Philosophically nonhuman lives are not creatures at all, but objects, and thus possess no dignity. And I wonder to what extent the construction of human dignity is not in some ways to blame for this problem. After all, the question is: human dignity over against what? Just as constructions of Whiteness rely on constructing opposing, denigrated identities of Blackness, so it seems that some discourses of human dignity may have inadvertently exacerbated the way our culture views animals as lacking basic dignity.[17]

And theoretical degradation entails real, lived consequences. The solution to this problem is not to deny the dignity of human beings, but to reconfigure human dignity so that it does not rely on the inferior Otherness of nonhuman creation as its conceptual foundation.[18] In the rest of this essay, I will consider Psalm 50 through a cosmocentric lens, or better, a theocentric lens that sets the cosmos, not human beings in particular, as the focus of divine concern. The psalm, I argue, is more concerned with nonhuman creatures than most interpreters allow.

"I Will Take No Bull from Your House": Psalm 50

To show how this feminist hermeneutic of creational dignity works on a particular text, I will reflect on Psalm 50, and mainly on the central section in verses 7–15, with some attention to the beginning of the psalm. The psalm as a whole focuses on the covenantal relationship between YHWH and Israel, with a beginning section that announces the identity of YHWH (vv. 1–6); a central section engaging questions of sacrifice (vv. 7–15); and the last section taking up the ethical implications of covenantal relationship (vv. 16–23). In my reading I look briefly at the identity of YHWH as the one who has authority to judge God's people on their covenantal faithfulness, before looking more closely at the central section on the merits of sacrifice. First, my translation of the relevant portions of the psalm:

God, GOD, YHWH—speaks,
and summons Earth
from the rising of the sun
to its setting.
Out of Zion, the perfection of beauty,
God radiates. (vv. 1–2)
[…]
"Hear, O my people, and I will speak,
O Israel, I will testify against you.
God, your God, am I.
Not for your sacrifices do I rebuke you—
for your burnt offerings [*'olot*] are continually before me.
I will take no bull from your house,
nor goats from your paddocks.

For every living creature of the forest is mine,
(and) domestic animals [*behemot*] on a thousand hills.[19]
I know all the birds of the hills,
and every creature that moves in the field is mine.
If I were hungry, I would not tell you,
for the world and its fullness are mine.
Do I eat the flesh of mighty animals,
or drink the blood of goats?
Offer to God thanksgiving,
and fulfill your vows to the Most High.
Call on me in the day of trouble;
I will deliver you, and you shall glorify me." (vv. 7–15)

The psalm begins with names of God piled up: "God ['*el*], GOD ['*elohim*], YHWH—speaks and calls upon the earth from the rising of the sun to its setting" (v. 1). The repetition with variation of the divine name intensifies the effect of divine power over the cosmos, even as verse 2 connects this God-of-the-cosmos to Zion, to the particularity of Israel's covenantal partner. Setting the particular (the God of Israel) within the universal (the God of the cosmos) is a consistent dynamic throughout the Hebrew Bible and the New Testament—God, the creator of the universe, operates in particular ways.

In the verses I did not translate here (vv. 3–6), God is presented as the judge of the covenantal partners, with the heavens testifying to the deity's role and right to judge. In a style not unusual in the ancient Near Eastern context, God calls upon heaven and earth (v. 4) to witness to the divine judgment of the covenantal partners while the psalmist declares that the heavens testify to the righteousness of God (v. 6). The overall effect of the introductory section is to establish the God who is in covenant with Israel as the same God who summons all creation, and to whom all creation responds.

Then in verse 7 the testimony against Israel begins with the declaration of the covenantal relationship ("I am God, your God"). The psalm follows at least some of the conventions of the *rib*—the covenantal lawsuit. For my purposes in this essay, what follows is the heart of the matter: Israel is not criticized for engaging in sacrifices per se; that is, the Israelites are implementing the sacrificial system just fine. The '*olot* (burnt offerings) are being offered as prescribed; God finds no fault in the Israelites' attentiveness in making the system work.

All of which makes the verses that follow (vv. 8–13) seem puzzling at first: God asserts that all animals,[20] from pesky critters that cause farmers headaches (the *ziz* in v. 11 include "the small creatures that ruin the fields")[21] to every wild and domestic animal, already belong to the deity. Thus the idea of human beings offering them to God, as though the animals somehow belonged to human beings in the first place, is absurd, a deep theological misunderstanding of the structures of the cosmos. It seems self-contradictory: is animal sacrifice to be encouraged (as suggested by vv. 14 and 23) or condemned (so vv. 8–13)? Johanna W. H. Bos notes the problem: "Yet we have before us an intriguing text, one that seems to condemn sacrifice, to condone it, and even to call for it, all at once."[22]

Scholars generally resolve the problem by speaking of the disordered perspective of the one sacrificing: s/he is not approaching animal sacrifice in the right spirit. J. Clinton McCann's reading is not atypical:

> The issue of the misuse of the sacrificial system (see vv. 8–15) need not be viewed as a call to abolish the system. In fact, "a sacrifice of thanksgiving" (v. 14) still involved the slaughter of animals. Rather, the call is to put sacrifice in proper perspective ... Instead of bringing their sacrificial offerings out of gratitude to God, the people were doing so as a means of asserting their own merit and self-sufficiency, as if God needed them instead of their needing God (vv. 12–13).[23]

The argument here is that verse 14 calls on the Israelites to offer their sacrifices of thanksgiving, which is, according to tradition, an animal sacrifice.[24] Therefore the sacrificial system per se is not in question. It is all about attitude when sacrificing. The difficulty with this argument is that the text does not actually say this. It may or may not be true in other texts (McCann lists Pss 40:6–8, 51:16–19; Isa 1:12–17; Hos 6:6; Amos 5:21–24), but this text suggests that such a reading is strained. The text does not suggest that there is a problem in the Israelites' internal perception of the sacrifices—there is no language to support this. A preponderance of the verses is about how the Israelites should not sacrifice animals. That is the plain meaning of the text.

One could argue just as, or perhaps more, persuasively that the phrase offer to God thanksgiving (*zebach l'elohim todah*) provides, in this text, a reinterpretation of the verb *zabach*—where traditionally it was understood to mean slaughter an animal in sacrifice, perhaps it is meant to take on new resonances? Perhaps the phrasing suggests that thanksgiving can be offered in ways other than slaughtering the animals that do not belong to human beings anyway. I am not making an argument that *zebach* necessarily has such a new meaning here—that would require a much longer argument focused on the many other texts in which the word appears—but I am suggesting that we should not accept *prima facie* that it necessarily entails an animal sacrifice just because that is the prevailing scholarly assumption based on reading precisely that reading into every text. The presence of the same phrasing in verse 23 (*zobeach todah*) does not answer the question. The emphasis on *not* sacrificing animals in verses 7–15 suggests that reading *zebach* as sacrifice an animal renders the psalm self-contradicting and incoherent.

Even McCann ends up close to the idea that the point of the section is "thanksgiving": "Thus the proper sacrifice is really the thanksgiving itself ... which is often associated with the payment of vows ... In short, the proper approach to God begins with gratitude."[25] Ellen Charry argues along similar lines that the psalmist does not "criticize the sacrificial system as such" but that the psalmist is positing a moral chasm between the performance of the correct sacrifices and the behaviors of the people, who do not follow the commandments, as suggested by the indictment beginning in verse 16: "But to the wicked[26] God says: How can you recite my statutes, and take my covenant on your lips?"[27]

Yet it is also equally plausible that the psalmist's indictment has two parts: in verses 7–15 she criticizes the sacrificial system itself because in it human beings have failed to understand who God is in relation to nonhuman animals, and in verses 16–21 the psalmist criticizes the people's failures vis-à-vis the covenant stipulations. Indeed, Charry moves in this direction:

> Whatever the dating of this poem, sacrifices were problematic by the time of its composition. God's point in this speech is that sacrifices are redundant; he neither wants nor needs them. Further, given that they are readily misunderstood and misused, what is the reason for retaining them in Jerusalem's public worship?[28]

Indeed. While verse 23 sums up the two-part indictment,[29] verse 21 most accurately reflects the broader charge: "you thought that I was one just like yourself" (*dimmiytah heyot-'ehyeh kamokah*). Human beings are animals more like nonhuman animals than they are like God. This is true scientifically, and it is true theologically.

We have not taken seriously enough God's statement in verse 9 of the psalm: "I will take no bull from your house." The translation is intentionally humorous, to be sure, yet it also conveys a sharp edge.[30] Human beings have in fact been dealing in bullshit in their treatment of God's world. Thus the psalm asserts that not only are animal sacrifices unnecessary, but that God, and the whole creation, have no tolerance for the "bull" in which human beings traffic. Our capacity for anthropocentrism—a form of human exceptionalism—is matched only by our capacity to inflict its consequences on the rest of the cosmos that God also loves.

Notes

1. The calendar appears in Carl Sagan, *The Dragons of Eden: Speculations on the Evolution of Human Intelligence* (New York: Random House, 1977), but variations of it have appeared in a wide variety of sources since then.
2. Lynn White, "The Historical Roots of Our Ecological Crisis," *Science* 155 (1967): 1,203–7 (1,206).
3. See Richard Bauckham, *Living with Other Creatures: Green Exegesis and Theology* (Waco, TX: Baylor University Press, 2011), 20–9.
4. Bauckham, among others, points to Francis Bacon and other Enlightenment thinkers of his ilk, who interpret a divine right to dominate nature and make it their slave, Bauckham, *Living with Other Creatures*, 49.
5. Many scholars see Job and Ecclesiastes as significant voices that undermine anthropocentrism. William Brown says of the animals appearing in the whirlwind speeches in Job: "Each creature is an alien endowed with inalienable dignity, for whom God is their provider." God in Job is a "biophile," as Brown says, "a creator who delights in all these various creatures, who live and move and have their being in God as God intended, free and fearless," William P. Brown, "The Comforting Cosmos: God,

Creation, and Job in the Light of Astrobiology," William Witherspoon Lecture on Theology and the Natural Sciences, Center of Theological Inquiry, Princeton, New Jersey, March 10, 2016.

6. Rosemary Radford Ruether, *Integrating Ecofeminism, Globalization, and World Religions* (Lanham: Rowman & Littlefield, 2005), 113, emphasis added.

7. Chris J. Cuomo, *Feminism and Ecological Communities: An Ethic of Flourishing* (London: Routledge, 1998), 73.

8. Cuomo, *Feminism and Ecological Communities*, 65.

9. Confession of 1967, section 9.32–3, emphasis added.

10. Some recent efforts to decenter human beings include David H. Kelsey, *Eccentric Existence: A Theological Anthropology*, two volumes (Louisville, KY: Westminster John Knox, 2009); Celia Deane-Drummond and Agustin Fuentes, "Human Being and Becoming: Situating Theological Anthropology in Interspecies Relationships in an Evolutionary Context," *Philosophy, Theology and the Sciences* 1 (2014): 251–75; Lucas John Mix, "Life-Value Narratives and the Impact of Astrobiology on Christian Ethics," *Zygon* 51 (2016): 520–35. Mix, in arguing against human exceptionalism, sees both hierarchical narratives and romantic and existential narratives present in the Bible, and rightly notes it is what we do with these narratives that counts.

11. Lucas John Mix notes that in some scholarly discourse *geocentrism* is contrasted to homocentrism (anthropocentrism), and both are contrasted to Christocentrism, Mix, "Life-Value Narratives," 12. *Cosmocentrism* is a more expansive term, though one could make a good argument for *geocentrism* as well. *Cosmocentrism* is used in some circles to mean the rejection of human intervention in the cosmos (space travel, colonization of other planets, etc.), but in others it signifies making "the universe a priority in a worldview, perhaps along with other priorities," M. L. Lupisella, "Cosmocentrism and the Active Search for Extraterrestrial Intelligence," *Astrobiology Science Conference 2010: Evolution and Life: Surviving Catastrophes and Extremes on Earth and Beyond*, available at: http://adsabs.harvard.edu/abs/2010LPICo1538.5597L, accessed March 15, 2016.

12. Frans de Waal, "What I Learned from Tickling Apes," *New York Times* (April 8, 2016), available at: https://www.nytimes.com/2016/04/10/opinion/sunday/what-i-learned-from-tickling-apes.html?_r=0 , accessed April 9, 2016.

13. De Waal, "What I Learned from Tickling Apes."

14. For example: "The Christian apologist Lactantius (240–320) memorably addressed the dignity that comes to humans by God's work of creation when he declared that God had created humankind as a 'sacred animal' (*sanctum animal*). For this reason, he declared, God had prohibited that humans be killed, not only in those instances also recognized by public law, such as wanton murder, but in any case whatsoever, including warfare, and the exposure of infants (*Divine Institutes* 6.20)," R. Kendall Soulen and Linda Woodhead, eds., *God and Human Dignity* (Grand Rapids, MI: Eerdmans, 2006), 3–4.

15. The excellent volume emerging from a conference in South Africa is one example: *Restorative Readings: The Old Testament, Ethics, and Human Dignity*, ed. L. Juliana Claassens and Bruce C. Birch (Eugene, OR: Pickwick, 2015).

16. *The Book of Common Prayer and Administration of the Sacraments and Other Rites and Ceremonies of the Church Together with The Psalter or Psalms of David According to the use of The Episcopal Church* (New York: Church Publishing Incorporated, 1979), 292. *The Book of Alternative Services of the Anglican Church of Canada* was recently amended to add this question to the baptismal covenant: "Will you strive to

safeguard the integrity of God's creation, and respect, sustain and renew the life of the Earth?" Available at: http://jointassembly.ca/delegates/acc/cc/resolutions/c001.html and http://c2892002f453b41e8581-48246336d122ce2b0bccb7a98e224e96.r74.cf2. rackcdn.com/BAS.pdf, accessed March 31, 2016.

17. The National Religious Campaign Against Torture, for example, has done extremely valuable work in combating torture as an acceptable governmental and military practice. But it is dismaying that torture can be opposed only on the theological grounds of the sacredness of *human* life; "Torture violates the basic dignity of the human person that all religions, in their highest ideals, hold dear" ("Torture Is a Moral Issue," available at: http://nrcat.org/sign-the-statement, accessed February 23, 2016), because such an argument implies a chasm between human and nonhuman animals that allows, by implication, brutal treatment (torture?) of the latter. (However, that is no doubt *not* the intent, and was perhaps necessary to bring on board diverse groups. I am not impugning motives, only pointing to the way underlying assumptions have real consequences.) Why does nonhuman life have to be desacralized for human beings not to be tortured? Since animals are routinely legally tortured in our sanctioned industrial systems of food production, the point is not merely theoretical.

18. How does one construct human dignity without compromising the dignity of other living beings, through a biblical lens? Much of that work remains to be done.

19. The end of verse 10 is not clear. The word *'eleph* has been interpreted in several different ways: the word can mean "oxen," which is the direction the Greek takes (τὰ θηρία τοῦ δρυμοῦ κτήνη ἐν τοῖς ὄρεσιν καὶ βόες; "the cattle on the mountains, and oxen"), or "thousand," reflected in the NRSV, NIV, KJV, JPS, and other translations as well as my own. "A thousand hills" suggests the comprehensive scope of God's owning of the animals—*they all belong to God.*

20. Richard Whitekettle offers a taxonomy of the animals listed, concluding: "The juxtaposition of a sacrificial animal with the broad sweep of divine zoological holdings made it clear to the Israelites that God did not need their sacrificial animals," Richard Whitekettle, "Forensic Zoology: Animal Taxonomy and Rhetorical Persuasion in Psalm 1," *VT* 58 (2008): 404–19 (419).

21. See the entry *ziz* in *HALOT* (Vol. 1, 268). Even locusts are in view here. The psalmist is not just including in this section the domestic animals that humans use for their benefit, and certainly not just the *attractive* animals that may be the beneficiaries of compassion today, but *all* life that skitters on the earth.

22. Johanna W. H. Bos, "Oh, When the Saints: A Consideration of the Meaning of Psalm 50," *JSOT* 24 (1982): 65–77 (65).

23. J. Clinton McCann, "The Book of Psalms," in *NIB: A Commentary in Twelve Volumes,* Volume 4, ed. Leander E. Keck (Nashville: Abingdon, 1994), 641–1,280 (882). See also C. Peter Craigie, *Psalms 1–50,* WBC 19 (Waco, TX: Word, 1983), 365–6; Hans-Joachim Kraus, *Psalms 1–59: A Commentary,* trans. Hilton C. Oswald, CC (Minneapolis: Fortress, 1988), 493–4.

24. See, e.g., Leviticus 7:12–15.

25. McCann, "Psalms," 882.

26. That those addressed in verses 7–15 might be equated with the "wicked" is a bit strange (and BHS suggests the phrase is a gloss); after all, in verse 5 there is reference to "my faithful ones" (*ḥasiyday*), but the matter is beyond the scope of this essay.

27. Ellen T. Charry, *Psalms 1–50: Sighs and Songs of Israel* (Grand Rapids, MI: Brazos, 2015), 251.

28. Charry, *Psalms 1–50*, 254.

29. Verse 23 is problematic at the end, but I suggest: "The one who offers thanksgiving honors me; there is a path I will show him/it by the deliverance of God."

30. I am indebted to the late Old Testament scholar John Haralson Hayes for the translation.

PART V
POSTSCRIPT

FEMINIST BIBLICAL INTERPRETATION: HOW FAR DO WE YET HAVE TO GO?

Elna Mouton

Agency, Resistance, Discernment

Feminist Frameworks and the Bible is a collective work—a rich, delightfully diverse collage of contributions from various (biblical and present-day) sociocultural contexts, personal biographies, intellectual convictions, and pastoral-ethical concerns. These essays simultaneously reclaim and criticize the voices of women in Old Testament narratives—from Naomi and Ruth (Sharp; Masenya), Abigail (Claassens), Esther (Wacker), Dinah (Dube), Jael (Van der Walt), Miriam (Olojede), and Jezebel (McKinlay), to the "foreign" women in Ezra-Nehemiah (Maier) and the brotherless daughters of Zelophehad (Camp).

We are grateful to each author for sharing her wisdom in the process of exploring and (re)creating intelligible, sense-making, restorative frameworks for ongoing discussions on the multifaceted theme of feminism and the well-being of creation. As noted in the introduction to this book, the origin of the *Feminist Frameworks and the Bible* volume was the occasion of Juliana Claassens's inaugural lecture as the first female professor in Old Testament at the Faculty of Theology in Stellenbosch on March 10, 2015. This offered the backdrop for the Feminist Frameworks conference and the ensuing book project.

What immediately strikes one about the essays and their varied ideological-critical perspectives are the remarkable analogies among them. In general, they are all committed to the core vision and values represented by Claassens's essay namely, recognition and (critical) affirmation of *female agency* in both the patriarchal biblical documents and contemporary interpretive contexts, *resistance* of "all conditions that hamper the human ability to flourish," and the *discernment* to understand "that survival is rooted in the ability to share goods rather than to hoard them for oneself."[1] Or, put differently, as coeditor Carolyn Sharp phrases it in terms of the three goals of her feminist hermeneutics, the essays collectively aim to "honor all subjects struggling against commodification of their bodies and labor," to "interrogate distorted relations of power," and to reform and "reconfigure community as a place of resistance against the exploitative predations of imperialism."[2]

In an even more encompassing sense the project explores "a feminist (or rather cosmocentric) hermeneutic of creational dignity" (Lapsley) that promotes "the integrity, stability, and beauty of both human and nonhuman communities" (quoting Chris Cuomo).[3] It rejects the binaries that often (still) characterize Christian theology, and chooses *relationality* as its primary hermeneutical key instead.[4] "The crucial feature is that for any to truly thrive, all must thrive ... The feminist hermeneutic with which I read the Bible entails a commitment to the flourishing and dignity of all creation".[5]

A first analogy that these essays bring to the fore is an awareness of the need for clarification regarding the *what, who/with whom, why/whose interests are served*, and *how* questions involved in the feminist project. Together they reflect basic elements of what Claassens called an Abigail Optic: a continuing need for (a) informed and empathetic moral agency, (b) critical-constructive epistemologies and methodologies of inquiry, and (c) imaginative hermeneutical theories and spiritualities that will nurture and sustain such a vision. All the contributions are characterized by profound respect for the nature and rhetorical purposes of the ancient texts of the Old Testament, while being "especially sensitive to female characters and issues that are hidden in liminal spaces of Scripture" (Olojede).[6] Authors are particularly mindful of the contexts from which these scriptures originated and "the specific struggles hidden in the texts" (Wacker),[7] as well as present-day contexts in which their often devastating effects in terms of the inferiority of women are felt.

As far as methodology is concerned, it is a great asset that authors chose to read the biblical texts with "multiple, intersecting reading lenses," at the intersections of discernable yet intertwined dimensions of both the texts and their life experiences.[8] Such modes of reading "in more than one key" (McKinlay) have become a pivotal feature of recent feminist literature (Sakenfeld). By reading Old Testament narratives *intersectionally*, the authors seek to account for the subtle, complex sociological, hermeneutical, and ethical relations displayed among issues related to power hierarchy and values of (male) honor and (female) shame. This includes the many expressions of injustice distorting the integrity of creation—be it ecological or cultural imperialism, anthropocentrism, ethnocentrism, classism, ageism, sexism, -isms with regard to ability, as well as endemic poverty. As Christl Maier puts it, "intersectionality explores how these systems mutually construct one another."[9]

In this regard, Musa Dube unequivocally declares: "Together with the feminist guild, I subscribe to the paradigm that recognizes that gender oppression is always in tandem with other categories of oppression and domination ... My feminist practice also takes a closer interest in understanding how and why biblical texts are linked to imperial and colonial domination, resistance, and collaboration ... As a postcolonial feminist ... being ever so conscious of the West's claim to the center of knowledge, theory, and philosophy, I also employ indigenous and contextual ways of reading such as storytelling ... In sum, my feminist reading is, more often than not, multifaceted and multidisciplinary in engaging the colonial and patriarchal oppression and in relation to all forms of oppression."[10] After her intriguing analysis of the story of the daughters of Zelophehad, Claudia Camp likewise concludes: "If the book of Numbers has a message for the present day, it might be that gender is never just about gender."[11]

According to the many voices represented here, this situation is mainly due to the often unconscious or unspoken presuppositions underlying patriarchy as it (still) functions as a hypernorm in well-meaning people's ordinary interactions. As Katharine Sakenfeld's introductory essay aptly recalls: "We have come far, but there is still a long way to go."[12] The lingering picture of distorted representations of bodies and voices continues to invite courageous responses from individual believers and faith communities—be it through seeing (understanding) differently, telling our stories and naming injustice, claiming our identities and footprints, resisting evil and superficial remedies for it, or reforming community.[13] In the words of Carolyn Sharp: "It remains an urgent feminist mandate to uncover practices of exploitation, especially the exploitation of those whose marginalized social status may diminish their capacity for resistance."[14]

At the same time the book poses a subtle yet potentially powerful challenge to its audiences. By creating implied readers "with empathy and moral imagination" (Van der Walt),[15] these reflections clearly reveal their anticipated rhetorical effects. In the words of Jacqueline Lapsley, "As a rule, the kind of ethical reflection I propose here asks the reader to allow herself to be drawn into a complex moral world evoked by the narrative."[16] The challenge entails that all this may happen not in a destructive and alienating manner, but with discernment,[17] in "a sensitive and relational way that takes into account other characters in such stories" (Olojede),[18] and in "a spirit of generosity" (Sharp).[19]

A second analogy among the essays, closely related to the first, is the implicit and explicit identification of the *exigence* (crisis, conflict, trauma) underlying the incident, phenomenon, or context under discussion. Authors write passionately about what they experience and observe as the result of broken identities, communities, and families and/or marriages in crisis. Madipoane Masenya summarizes the core of this exigence as follows: "Above all, I feel that the real challenge will come about when women can say—with or without husbands, with or without children—that the most important fact is that women are *human*."[20] The contexts in which the discussed narratives are embedded resemble complex stratified social realities, within which the "dominant patriarchal discourse is that men are mainly defined within a binary relationship to women ... Within this binary construction men ... become everything that is superior to women" (Van der Walt).[21] As Sakenfeld states with reference to the Bible's histories of reception, "It has been used historically to circumscribe and control the place of women in the family, in the religious sphere, and in society generally."[22]

According to the values of the feminist project, these hierarchical (often oppressive) structures reveal a serious flaw in the thought framework of the institutions and relations involved. This explains Carolyn Sharp's emphasis on cultural *processes* when appropriating biblical perspectives to present-day contexts: "In feminist interpretation of the Hebrew Scriptures, my focus is not on figures to emulate but, rather, on cultural processes of contestation and deconstruction."[23] So also Judith McKinlay: "It is the textual and interpretive processes and their long-term effects that interest me."[24] It is therefore no wonder that the need for rigorous interdisciplinary (and intradisciplinary theological) studies runs like a golden thread through the contributions.

A third analogy among the essays concerns the dearth of problem-solving, community-building strategies in the institutions and discourses of which they give account, where the Bible still functions as an authoritative text. The personal narratives reflected in the book tragically show how piety and charismatic leadership often go hand in hand with a life-threatening ethos when boundaries and dominating structures are reasserted. This ambivalence reflects the danger of exhibiting "good" moral leadership while neglecting one or more aspects of the dignity of creation. In my view, the greatest challenge in this respect is posed by restricting God images that often function as foundational in arguments for human dignity and the integrity of creation. Instead of imagining a compassionate, self-giving, the other-receiving God, a God of exclusion, partiality, and dominating power is presented, be it unwittingly.[25]

According to the biblical witness, the intersections of gender, race, class, et cetera are to be seen as primarily *theological* in nature, and not (only) as *ethical*, even when they present themselves as such. These intersections belong to the core of people's identities. They embody our profoundly relational nature. They express who we are and where we belong. They remind us of the bigger picture of a *theocentric* universe (Lapsley).

There is a fundamental yet often neglected side to the covenant God of the Hebrew Scriptures that needs to be emphasized here. As part of Moses's speech to the Israelites before their entry into the promised land, Deuteronomy 10:17 describes YHWH's greatness in terms of YHWH's impartiality. The expression "For YHWH your God ... is not partial" (NRSV) literally means "God does not lay hold of someone's face"; that is, "God does not esteem anyone according to outward appearance."[26] The image probably derived from a judicial context in which disputes were settled before judges, and in which God's impartiality would mean that God cannot be bribed, even by the virtue of human beings.[27] In Deuteronomy 10:17 the phrase occurs in a context that emphasizes God's sovereignty and power ("The LORD your God is mighty and awesome ... Fear the LORD your God"—NIV; see Exod 34:6–10). In contrast to the often abusive power of contemporary authorities (Exod 1:8–22), the essence of YHWH's power is defined in terms of loving care and concern for people, particularly those who are marginalized socioeconomically.[28]

According to the New Testament accounts, Jesus' impartial, unconditional, nonjudgmental love and compassion for people would be the primary expression of God incarnated in a Roman imperial context. As a radical response to the human condition of vulnerability and alienation, the concept of *shalom* in the Hebrew Scriptures (well-being and wholeness in terms of people's relation with God, others, themselves, and creation) is translated in the New Testament with various terms such as εἰρήνη (peace), σωτηρία (salvation, deliverance from danger, well-being), ἄφεσις (forgiveness, freedom, wholeness), and δικαιοσύνη (righteousness, justice). These are all-encompassing terms characteristic of life in God's new kingdom, referring to reconciliation, liberation, and healing related to physical health, peace of mind, human relations, social justice, peace with God, and ecological well-being. Jesus' entire ministry is characterized by this radical and all-inclusive manifestation of God's presence in the world.

To understand the God of the Bible as relational, impartial, and compassionate would have radical ethical and pastoral implications. Creation and human ethos would then, likewise, have to be regarded in terms of dignity, harmony, and relationality (total neighborhood). Yet, instead of nurturing a sense of belonging and mutuality, allowing for porous boundaries at the intersections of our shared realities, binary positions are often strengthened and justified by an essentialist view of God, humanity, and the rest of creation. Instead of discerning and recognizing God-given opportunities "to show solidarity with other individuals and groups who find themselves in a situation of precarity,"[29] we pass by on the other side. Instead of welcoming liminal, hybrid positions, we miss precious chances to explore the rich yet complex relational nature of creation and thereby inhibit the dynamic of "infinite possibilities" of interpretation (Sharp).

Embracing Ambiguity, Celebrating Intersectionality

The essays in this volume assist feminist biblical interpreters in taking stock of what we have gained and that for which we need to be grateful, that which we may continue to do, and that which we may need to improve and/or avoid in the future. The journey continues while (changing) landscapes remain complex. So, where and how do we hope to be going from here?

While navigating between old and new frameworks and shifting perspectives, what kind of instruments (vision, agency), fuel and energy (nourishment, life-protecting habits, methods, theories) would we need not only to survive the journey, but to change the direction and even innovate and build new roads where necessary, while keeping our co-travelers motivated and engaged? What will it take "for individuals and societies to become compassionate in nature, moving beyond disgust to truly seeing the face of the other?"[30] In the words of Charlene van der Walt, with reference to Jael and Winnie Madikizela-Mandela: "How does my resistance against violence and dehumanization not succumb to the allure of a subtly violent response, but instead open up the fragile possibility of compassion, care, and community—essential elements for the vulnerability of life together?"[31] And further, how do we "construct human dignity without compromising the dignity of other living beings, through a biblical lens?" (Lapsley).[32] How do we move from empire language to kingdom of God language, using gender as a primary lens? What kind of rhetoric would be needed to transform households into microcosms of God's peaceable kingdom (Sakenfeld)?[33] What kind of a framework, exegetical method, and hermeneutical theory would be capable of producing life-giving answers to such complex challenges and dire needs? It is clear that much work remains to be done!

Let me share some of the motivation that helps sustain my focus amid the necessary clutter of such a task. In my own inaugural lecture at the Faculty of

Theology in Stellenbosch twelve years ago, on March 22, 2005 (being the first woman to give an inaugural address in the institution's 146 years of existence), I referred to liminality as a useful concept in describing the richness and complexity of the early Christians' interpretation of Jesus of Nazareth.[34] I still find the paradoxical dynamic of liminality helpful in terms of intersectional discourse, particularly with regard to the work of the Circle of Concerned African Women Theologians.[35] These notions also characterize the life and work of Denise M. Ackermann, doyenne of South African feminist scholarship, whose eightieth birthday we celebrated at the University of the Western Cape on March 13, 2015— just after the Feminist Frameworks conference.

The concept of liminality was introduced by French anthropologist Arnold van Gennep, who used the term rites of passage in connection with the ceremonies and rituals performed at different stages in the life cycle of individuals and groups (birth, puberty, marriage, parenthood, retirement, and death). He distinguished three types of rites, namely, rites of separation from a previous world, rites of transition, and rites of incorporation into a new world.[36] Using the Latin word *limen* (threshold), he respectively calls these rites preliminal, liminal, and postliminal.

In the fields of cultural anthropology, sociology, and even theology, the notion of liminality has since been adapted and appropriated by many scholars. For example, Mark Lewis Taylor, systematic theologian at Princeton Theological Seminary, develops it—together with admiration—as a Christian reconciliatory strategy for dealing with human differences.[37] He observes, "*liminality* is the term I reserve for the kind of life known 'betwixt and between' differentiated persons, groups or worlds. This is an experience of the *wonder*, the *disorientation* and *discomfort* that can rise when one is suspended between or among different groups or persons."[38] Taylor describes the liminal space between cultural (including gender) boundaries as a difficult, fragile, risky, and trying experience, of which the ambiguities and strains are not easily tolerated. At the same time the liminal encounter represents a dynamic and dialectic process wherein no one remains static. As new alliances are constructed in the interaction between different worlds, people's moral identities and lifestyles are reconstituted by it.[39]

In short, liminality involves experiences of both the wonder and the discomfort when one is suspended between different groups, persons, or viewpoints. The choice for intersectionality, complexity, vulnerability, and tension is thus not self-inflicted martyrdom. Rather, it is a choice to experience and account for both the richness and the complexity, both the admiration (awe, trust, hope) and the discomfort in the struggle for gender and cosmic justice.

This dynamic is exemplified in the work of several authors in the *Feminist Frameworks and the Bible* volume. Claassens—like Dube, Sharp, and several others—deliberately situates herself on the threshold of various intersections: "If I have to summarize my own feminist framework that over the years has been shaped to inform the way I read the Old Testament, it would involve the ongoing quest of embracing intersectionality ... An important part of my ... framework ... relates to the approach of using Old Testament texts as a means for the reader to engage his/her context more deeply."[40] So also Carolyn Sharp:

I bring two feminist strategies to my interpretive work in the academy and my political work in communities, including communities of teaching and learning. First, I embrace dissensus as vital for authentic dialogue in groups, honoring spirited and irreducible disagreement as a way of welcoming the Other ... Second, I explore ambiguity in biblical texts as a potentially subversive resource with which to dismantle oppressive structures and ideological distortions. The Hebrew Scriptures offer many marvelous examples of ellipsis, ironic misdirection, unexpected juxtaposition, and freighted silence. All these modes underscore the fragility and infinite possibilities of language understood as both the spoken and the unspoken.[41]

In this regard, several authors build on and affirm the work of coauthors in the volume. For example, referring to Musa Dube's Rahab prism of appropriating postcolonial theory to biblical studies (informed by Homi Bhabha's concepts of a third space and hybridity), Marie-Theres Wacker welcomes these as concepts that may do justice to "the increasing complexity of situations, needs, and challenges people ... face."[42]

While reading through these essays, I was saddened by the many incidents of inhumanity and injustice described by the authors. Yet, I was saddened even more by the simplistic, unnuanced, one-dimensional solutions referred to, which are often offered as responses to these complex issues. That forced me to step back to remember the beauty of the multifaceted sunsets that Carolyn Sharp describes at the beginning of her essay, and to allow myself to appreciate the privilege of living and working on the intersections, the thresholds (not the margins!) of an awesome universe, a "wonderful world" (Louis Armstrong). And since beauty is in the eye of the beholder/receiver, these essays invite and challenge me to be open to being surprised by new connections, new expressions of God's grace, new opportunities to see through the eyes of others, and to help make these liminal intersections the very safe space in which I may experience abundant life together with the rest of God's creation—risky and fragile as it may be.

So, what would the implied rhetorical effect of these essays be for inhabitants of the twenty-first century? What would it mean to be Yhwh's covenantal community in contexts across the globe—intelligibly, mindfully, imaginatively? With *Ehrfurcht vor dem Leben* (Albert Schweitzer), with reverence for God's gift of sacred life in all its expressions, for the integrity and wholeness of creation— caring for mothers, fathers, sisters, brothers, and other family members, for needy neighbors and foreigners, including refugees, for the poor and marginalized, for human and nonhuman animals, for the plants and the trees?

If I may then respond to the question "how far do we as feminist biblical interpreters yet have to go?" I would say that this book ultimately invites us to give priority to the imaginative possibilities of God's liberating, healing love over the broken realities of our lives and the world. "Our hope does not lie in ourselves, but in God" (Lapsley).[43] With Juliana Claassens we believe that the future landscape of feminist discourse will be fundamentally determined by a fine balance between compassionate moral agency, prophetic resistance to life-denying practices, and prayerful discernment. In the process, the art of listening with discernment—"hearing the inner movements of God's Spirit"—will be crucial.[44] It is ultimately about nurturing trust in a presence and power beyond ourselves.

This, however, remains a never-ending struggle—an ongoing battle between perspectives. What we need is to create a radically new narrative, a new symbolic world, a language home, a "third space" that *all* may inhabit—a space not merely meant for human survival, but for the flourishing of all creation. The feminist project is, therefore, about homemaking and homecoming. It is about love and hospitality. It is about mothering salvation to all. Ironically, it is necessarily to be characterized by liminality and hybridity, ambiguity and contradiction, mystery and paradox, fragility and tension, yes, by intersectionality and inter(con)-textuality. It is a space that invites us to respect and account for the richness and complexity of life together in God's cosmos.

What kind of an optic, hermeneutical framework, theology, and spirituality would be needed to protect, nourish, and sustain such a vulnerable process? This book inter alia enables us to name the feminist frameworks from within which we operate in terms of the delicate combination of *wonder and discomfort*. Both have to be nurtured to keep the bifocal feminist-cosmocentric vision alive. Perhaps Letty Russell's famous saying may help us to understand this as simultaneously "remembering forward and hoping backward." While we eagerly yearn for the fulfilment of God's promises of well-being and justice for all, for the abundant relational covenantal life of the Hebrew Scriptures and Second Testament, we continue to tell our stories and encourage one another to live boldly with paradox and risk.

Notes

1. L. Juliana Claassens, "An Abigail Optic: Agency, Resistance, and Discernment in 1 Samuel 25," in *Feminist Frameworks and the Bible: Power, Ambiguity, and Intersectionality*, ed. L. Juliana Claassens and Carolyn J. Sharp (London: Bloomsbury T&T Clark, 2017), 21–37 (31).
2. Carolyn J. Sharp, "Is this Naomi? A Feminist Reading of the Ambiguity of Naomi in the Book of Ruth," in *Feminist Frameworks and the Bible*, 152.
3. Jacqueline E. Lapsley, "'I Will Take No Bull From Your House': Feminist Biblical Theology in a Creational Context," in *Feminist Frameworks and the Bible*, 198.
4. As Richard Rohr, OFM from the Center of Action and Contemplation in Albuquerque, New Mexico explains in his daily online meditation of September 19, 2016, "The energy in the universe is not in the planets, nor in the atomic particles, but very surprisingly in *the relationship between them*. It's not in the cells of organisms but in the way the cells feed and give feedback to one another through semi-permeable membranes. The energy is not in any precise definition or in the partly arbitrary names of the three persons of the Trinity as much as in *the relationship between the Three*! This is where all the power for infinite renewal is at work," available at: https://cac.org/a-relational-universe-2016-09-19/, accessed October 11, 2016.

5. Lapsley, "'I Will Take No Bull from Your House," 198.

6. Funlola Olojede, "Miriam and Moses's Cushite Wife: Sisterhood in Jeopardy?" in *Feminist Frameworks and the Bible*, 133.

7. Marie-Theres Wacker, "The Violence of Power and the Power of Violence: Hybrid, Contextual Perspectives on the Book of Esther," in *Feminist Frameworks and the Bible*, 100.

8. Claassens, "An Abigail Optic," 21.

9. Christl M. Maier, "The 'Foreign' Women in Ezra-Nehemiah: Intersectional Perspectives on Ethnicity," in *Feminist Frameworks and the Bible*, 80.

10. Musa W. Dube, "Dinah (Genesis 34) at the Contact Zone: 'Shall Our Sister Become a Whore,'" in *Feminist Frameworks and the Bible*, 47.

11. Claudia V. Camp, "Daughters, Priests, and Patrilineage: A Feminist and Gender-Critical Interpretation of the End of the Book of Numbers," in *Feminist Frameworks and the Bible*, 190.

12. Katharine Doob Sakenfeld, "Feminist Biblical Interpretation: How Far Have We Come?" in *Feminist Frameworks and the Bible*, 13.

13. For but a few examples, see Musa W. Dube, *Postcolonial Feminist Interpretation of the Bible* (St. Louis: Chalice, 2000); Jacqueline E. Lapsley, *Whispering the Word: Hearing Women's Stories in the Old Testament* (Louisville, KY: Westminster John Knox, 2005); Denise M. Ackermann, *Surprised by the Man on the Borrowed Donkey: Ordinary Blessings* (Cape Town: Lux Verbi, 2014); Elna Mouton et al., eds., *Living with Dignity: African Perspectives on Gender Equality* (Stellenbosch: Sun Press, 2015).

14. Sharp, "Is this Naomi?," 158.

15. Charlene van der Walt, "'Is There a Man Here?': The Iron Fist in the Velvet Glove in Judges 4," in *Feminist Frameworks and the Bible*, 119.

16. Lapsley, *Whispering the Word*, 11.

17. Claassens, "An Abigail Optic," 31.

18. Olojede, "Miriam and Moses's Cushite Wife," in *Feminist Frameworks and the Bible*, 133.

19. Sharp, "Is this Naomi?," 151.

20. Madipoane Masenya, "Stuck Between the Waiting Room and the Reconfigured Levirate Entity? Reading Ruth in Marriage-Obsessed African Christian Contexts," 171 (citing Mercy A. Oduyoye; emphasis added).

21. Van der Walt, "'Is There a Man Here?,'"122.

22. Sakenfeld, "Feminist Biblical Interpretation," 16.

23. Sharp, "Is this Naomi?," 151.

24. Judith E. McKinlay, "Jezebel and the Feminine Divine in Feminist Postcolonial Focus," in *Feminist Frameworks and the Bible*, 71.

25. See Miroslav Volf, *Exclusion and Embrace: A Theological Exploration of Identity, Otherness, and Reconciliation* (Nashville: Abingdon, 1996), 99–190. Regarding Christians' God language, Robert Rohr—with reference to Thomas Kuhn—proposes nothing less than a paradigm shift. For him, changing our foundational view of God has the potential to change everything else too. He succinctly states, "History has so long operated with *a static and imperial image of God*—as a Supreme Monarch who is mostly living in splendid isolation from what he—and God is always and exclusively envisioned as male in this model—created … We always become what we behold; the presence that we practice matters. That's why we desperately need a worldwide paradigm shift in Christian consciousness for how we relate to God," online meditation, September 14, 2016, available at: https://cac.org/spiritual-paradigm-shift-2016-09-14/, accessed October 11, 2016.

26. See Leviticus 19:15–8, 33–4; Deuteronomy 16:19; 2 Chronicles 19:7; Matthew 22:16; Mark 12:14; Luke 20:21.

27. See Luke T. Johnson, *Sharing Possessions: What Faith Demands*, second edition (Grand Rapids, MI: Eerdmans, 2011), 75, 85, 93.

28. See Elna Mouton, *Reading a New Testament Document Ethically* (Atlanta: SBL, 2002), 72.

29. Claassens, "An Abigail Optic," 31.

30. Claassens, "An Abigail Optic," 22, with reference to Martha Nussbaum.

31. Van der Walt,"Is There a Man Here?," 127.

32. Lapsley, "'I Will Take No Bull From Your House,'" 206n.18.

33. Katharine Doob Sakenfeld, *Ruth*, IBC (Louisville, KY: John Knox, 1999), 10.

34. Elna Mouton, "The Pathos of New Testament Studies," *Th Viat* 30 (2006): 50–86. On p. 58, I argue that the early Jesus followers "were forced to interpret new experiences and changing circumstances in the light of a pluralistic first-century Mediterranean symbolic world, constituted by diverse and complex combinations *inter alia* of Roman rule, Greco-Roman (specifically Hellenistic) culture, and the religious symbols of Judaism (the torah, prophets and 'writings')."

35. See Dube, *Postcolonial Feminist Interpretation of the Bible*; Mouton, "Pathos of New Testament Studies," 67–76; Mouton et al., *Living with Dignity*, 13–4.

36. Arnold van Gennep, *The Rites of Passage*, trans. M. B. Vizedom and G. L. Caffee (London: Routledge & Kegan Paul, 1960), 15–25, 192–4. See also Mouton, "Pathos of New Testament Studies," 64–6.

37. Mark Lewis Taylor, *Remembering Esperanza: A Cultural-Political Theology for North American Praxis* (Maryknoll, NY: Orbis, 1990), 199–208.

38. Taylor, *Remembering Esperanza*, 200, emphasis added.

39. Mouton, "Pathos of New Testament Studies," 65.

40. Claassens, "An Abigail Optic," 21.

41. Sharp, "Is this Naomi?," 151.

42. Wacker, "The Violence of Power and the Power of Violence," 102.

43. Lapsley, "'I Will Take No Bull From Your House,'" 197.

44. Ackermann, *Surprised by the Man on the Borrowed Donkey*, 179. For Ackermann's personal journey in discovering the gift of discernment, see pp. 177–208. On p. 201 she summarizes: "Awareness of God's gracious self-giving, coupled with our commitment to openness and change, makes for discernment."

BIBLIOGRAPHY

Aaron, David H. "The Ruse of Zelophehad's Daughters." *HUCA* 80 (2009): 1–38.

Achenbach, Reinhold. *Die Vollendung der Tora: Studien zur Redaktionsgeschichte des Numeribuches im Kontext von Hexateuch und Pentateuch.* BZABR 3. Wiesbaden: Harrassowitz, 2002.

Ackermann, Denise. *Tamar's Cry: Re-reading an Ancient Text in the Midst of an HIV/AIDS Pandemic.* Johannesburg: Ecumenical Foundation of Southern Africa, 2001.

Ackermann, Denise M. *Surprised by the Man on the Borrowed Donkey: Ordinary Blessings.* Cape Town: Lux Verbi, 2014.

Albertz, Rainer. *Israel in Exile: The History and Literature of the Sixth Century B. C. E.* Translated by David Green. SBLStBL 3. Atlanta: SBL, 2003.

Alexander, Pat, ed. "Genesis." Pages 127–54 in *The Lion Handbook to the Bible.* Berkhamsted, UK: Lion Publishing, 1978.

Alter, Robert. *The Art of Biblical Narrative.* Revised and updated. New York: Basic Books, 2011.

Amit, Yairah. "Judges 4: Its Contents and Form." *JSOT* 39 (1987): 89–111.

Bach, Alice. "The Pleasure of Her Text." Pages 25–44 in *The Pleasure of Her Text: Feminist Readings of Biblical and Historical Texts.* Edited by Alice Bach. Philadelphia: Trinity Press International, 1990.

Bahemuka, Judith M. "Social Changes in Women's Attitudes toward Marriage in East Africa." Pages 119–34 in *The Will to Arise: Women, Tradition, and the Church in Africa.* Edited by Mercy A. Oduyoye and Musimbi R. A. Kanyoro. Maryknoll, NY: Orbis, 2006.

Bailey, Randall. "They're Nothing but Incestuous Bastards: The Polemical Use of Sex and Sexuality in Hebrew Canon Narratives." Pages 121–38 in *Reading from This Place: Social Location in the USA.* Volume 1. Edited by Fernando Segovia and Mary Ann Tolbert. Minneapolis: Fortress, 1994.

Bal, Mieke. *Femmes imaginaires. L'Ancien testament au risque d'une narratologie critique.* Collection ES/Écrire les Femmes 1. Utrecht: HES Publishers, 1986.

Bal, Mieke. *Lethal Love: Feminist Literary Readings of Biblical Love Stories.* ISBL. Bloomington: Indiana University Press, 1987.

Ballantyne, Tony. *Webs of Empire: Locating New Zealand's Colonial Past.* Wellington: Bridget Williams Books, 2012.

Ballantyne, Tony. *Entanglements of Empire: Missionaries, Māori, and the Question of the Body.* Auckland: University of Auckland Press, 2014.

Bandstra, Barry. *Reading the Old Testament.* Belmont, CA: Thomson Wadsworth, 2004.

Baratieri, Daniela. "'More than a Tree, Less than a Woman.' Sex and Empire: The Italian Case." *Australian Journal of Politics and History* 60 (2014): 360–72.

Barton, Mukti. "The Skin of Miriam Became as White as Snow: The Bible, Western Feminism and Colour Politics." *Feminist Theology: The Journal of the Britain and Ireland School of Feminist Theology* 27 (2001): 68–80.

Bauckham, Richard. *Living with Other Creatures: Green Exegesis and Theology.* Waco, TX: Baylor University Press, 2011.

Ben-Barak, Zafrira. *Inheritance by Daughters in Israel and the Ancient Near East: A Social, Legal and Ideological Revolution.* Jaffa: Archaeological Center Publications, 2006.

Berlin, Adele. *Poetics and the Interpretation of Biblical Narrative.* Winona Lake, IN: Eisenbrauns, 1999.

Berlin, Adele. *Esther. The Traditional Hebrew Text with the New JPS Translation.* JPS Bible Commentary. Philadelphia: JPS, 2001.

Bhabha, Homi K. "DissemiNation: Time, Narrative, and the Margins of Modern Nation." Pages 291–322 in *Nation and Narration.* Edited by Homi Bhabha. London: Routledge, 1990.

Bhabha, Homi K. *The Location of Culture.* London: Routledge, 1994; with a new preface by the author, 2006.

Bhabha, Homi K. *Über kulturelle Hybridität. Tradition und Übersetzung.* Edited by Anna Babka and Gerald Posselt. Translated by Kathrina Menke. Vienna: Turia & Kant, 2012.

Bhabha, Homi K., ed. *Nation and Narration.* London: Routledge, 1990.

Biddle, Mark E. "Ancestral Motifs in 1 Samuel 25: Intertextuality and Characterization." *JBL* 121 (2002): 617–38.

Binney, Judith. *The Legacy of Guilt: A Life of Thomas Kendall.* Auckland: Published for the University of Auckland by the Oxford University Press, 1968.

Binney, Judith. "Christianity and the Maoris to 1840: A Comment." *New Zealand Journal of History* 3 (1969): 143–65.

Bird, Phyllis A. *Missing Persons and Mistaken Identities: Women and Gender in Ancient Israel.* OBT. Minneapolis: Fortress, 1997.

Bird, Phyllis A. *Faith, Feminism, and the Forum of Scripture: Essays on Biblical Theology and Hermeneutics.* Eugene, OR: Cascade, 2015.

Bird, Phyllis A. "Old Testament Theology and the God of the Fathers: Reflections on Biblical Theology from a North American Perspective." Pages 69–107 in *Biblische Theologie: Beiträge des Symposiums "Das Alte Testament und die Kultur der Moderne."* Altes Testament und Moderne 14. Edited by Bernd Janowski, Michael Welker, and Paul Hanson. Münster: LIT, 2005. Reprinted pages 1–44 in P. A. Bird, *Faith, Feminism, and the Forum of Scripture: Essays on Biblical Theology and Hermeneutics.* Eugene, OR: Cascade, 2015.

Blenkinsopp, Joseph. *Ezra-Nehemiah: A Commentary.* OTL. London: SCM, 1988.

Block, Daniel I. *Judges, Ruth.* NAC 6. Nashville: Broadman & Holman, 1999.

Boehmer, Elleke. *Colonial and Postcolonial Literature.* Oxford: Oxford University Press, 1995.

Booth, Wayne C. *The Company We Keep: An Ethics of Fiction.* Berkeley: University of California Press, 1988.

Bos, Johanna W. H. "Oh, When the Saints: A Consideration of the Meaning of Psalm 50." *JSOT* 24 (1982): 65–77.

Bos, Johanna W. H. "Out of the Shadows, Genesis 38; Judges 4:17–22; Ruth 3." *Semeia* 42 (1988): 37–67.

Bottéro, Jean. *Everyday Life in Ancient Mesopotamia.* Translated by Antonia Nevill from *Initiation à l'Orient ancien* (Paris: Editions du Seuil, 1992). Baltimore: Johns Hopkins University Press, 2001.

Brah, Avtar. "Diaspora, Border and Transnational Identities." Pages 613–34 in *Feminist Postcolonial Theory: A Reader.* Edited by Reina Lewis and Sara Mills. New York: Routledge, 2003.

Brenner, Athalya. "Ruth as a Foreign Worker and the Politics of Exogamy." Pages 158–62 in *Ruth and Esther: A Feminist Companion to the Bible*. Edited by Athalya Brenner. FCB Second Series. Sheffield: Sheffield Academic, 1999.

Brenner, Athalya and Carole Fontaine, eds. *A Feminist Companion to Reading the Bible: Approaches, Methods and Strategies*. London and Chicago: Fitzroy Dearborn, 1997.

Britt, Brian. "Death, Social Conflict, and the Barley Harvest in the Hebrew Bible." *JHebS* 5 (2005).

Brown, William P. "The Comforting Cosmos: God, Creation, and Job in the Light of Astrobiology." William Witherspoon Lecture on Theology and the Natural Sciences. Princeton, NJ: Center of Theological Inquiry, March 10, 2016.

Brueggemann, Walter. *Texts Under Negotiation: The Bible and Postmodern Imagination*. Minneapolis: Fortress, 1993.

Brueggemann, Walter. *Theology of the Old Testament: Testimony, Dispute, Advocacy*. Minneapolis: Fortress, 1997.

Budd, Philip J. *Numbers*. WBC 5. Waco, TX: Word, 1984.

Buell, Denise Kimber. *Why This New Race: Ethnic Reasoning in Early Christianity*. New York: Columbia University Press, 2005.

Buller, James. *Forty Years in New Zealand*. London: Hodder & Stoughton, 1878.

Bush, Frederic W. *Ruth/Esther*. WBC 9. Dallas: Word, 1996.

Butler, Judith P. *Bodies that Matter: On the Discursive Limits of "Sex."* New York: Routledge, 1993.

Butler, Judith. *Precarious Life: The Powers of Mourning and Violence*. London: Verso, 2004.

Butler, Judith. *Frames of War: When Is Life Grievable?* London: Verso, 2009.

Butler, Judith. "Performativity, Precarity and Sexual Politics." *AIBR. Revista de Antropología Iberoamericana* 4/3 (2009): i–xiii. Available at: http://www.aibr.org/antropologia/04v03/criticos/040301b.pdf. Accessed January 27, 2015.

Butler, Judith. *Gender Trouble: Feminism and the Subversion of Identity*. New York: Routledge, 2011.

Butting, Klara. *Die Buchstaben werden sich noch wundern. Innerbiblische Kritik als Wegweisung feministischer Hermeneutik*. Berlin: Alektor-Verlag, 1994.

Butting, Klara. "Ester: About Resistance against Anti-Judaism and Racism." Pages 207–20 in *Feminist Biblical Interpretation: A Compendium of Critical Commentary on the Books of the Bible and Related Literature*. Edited by Luise Schottroff and Marie-Theres Wacker. Translated by Martin Rumscheidt et al. Grand Rapids, MI: Eerdmans, 2012.

Byron, Gay L. and Vanessa Lovelace. *Womanist Interpretations of the Bible: Expanding the Discourse*. Atlanta: Society of Biblical Literature, 2016.

Camp, Claudia V. *Wisdom and the Feminine in the Book of Proverbs*. BLS 11. Decatur, GA: Almond Press, 1985.

Camp, Claudia V. "Wise and Strange: An Interpretation of the Female Imagery in Proverbs in Light of Trickster Mythology." Pages 14–36 in *Reasoning with the Foxes: Female Wit in a World of Male Power*. Edited by J. Cheryl Exum and Johanna W. H. Bos. *Semeia* 42. Atlanta: Scholars Press, 1988.

Camp, Claudia V. *Wise, Strange and Holy: The Strange Woman and the Making of the Bible*. JSOTSup 320. GCT 9. Sheffield: Sheffield Academic, 2000.

Camp, Claudia V. "The Problem with Sisters: Anthropological Perspectives on Priestly Kinship Ideology in Numbers." Pages 119–30 in *Embroidered Garments: Priests and Gender in Biblical Israel*. Edited by Deborah W. Rooke. HBM 25. Sheffield: Sheffield Phoenix, 2009.

Camp, Claudia V. "Feminist and Gender-Critical Perspectives on the Biblical Ideology of Intermarriage." Pages 303–15 in *Mixed Marriages: Intermarriage and Group Identity in the Second Temple Period*. Edited by Christian Frevel. LHBOTS 547. New York: T&T Clark, 2011.

Camp, Claudia V. "Gender and Identity in the Book of Numbers." Pages 105–21 in *Imagining the Other and Constructing Israelite Identity in the Early Second Temple Period*. Edited by Ehud Ben-Zvi and Diana V. Edelman. LHBOTS 591. London: Bloomsbury T&T Clark, 2014.

Camp, Claudia V. "Numbers 5:11–31: Women in Second Temple Judah and the Law of the Controlling Priest." Pages 111–32 in *Celebrate Her for the Fruit of Her Hands: Studies in Honor of Carol L. Meyers*. Edited by Susan Ackerman, Charles E. Carter, and Beth Alpert Nakhai. Winona Lake, IN: Eisenbrauns, 2015.

Carey, Hilary M. *God's Empire: Religion and Colonialism in the British World, c.1801–1908*. Cambridge, UK: Cambridge University Press, 2011.

Charlesworth, Hilary. "Martha Nussbaum's Feminist Internationalism." *Ethics* 111 (2000): 64–78.

Charry, Ellen T. *Psalms 1–50: Sighs and Songs of Israel*. Grand Rapids, MI: Brazos, 2015.

Chernin, Kim. *The Hungry Self: Women, Eating, and Identity*. New York: Harper & Row, 1985.

Christianson, Eric S. "The Big Sleep: Strategic Ambiguity in Judges 4–5 and in Classic *Film Noir*." *BibInt* 15 (2007): 519–48.

Claassens, L. Juliana M. "The God Who Feeds: A Feminist Theological Analysis of Key Pentateuchal and Intertestamental Texts." PhD dissertation, Princeton Theological Seminary, 2001.

Claassens, L. Juliana M. "Biblical Theology as Dialogue: Continuing the Conversation on Bakhtin and Biblical Theology." *JBL* 122 (2003): 127–44.

Claassens, L. Juliana M. *The God Who Provides: Biblical Images of Divine Nourishment*. Nashville: Abingdon, 2004.

Claassens, L. Juliana M. "Isaiah." Pages 209–22 in *Theological Commentary of the Bible*. Edited by Gail R. O'Day and David L. Petersen. Louisville, KY: Westminster John Knox, 2009.

Claassens, L. Juliana M. "Calling the Keeners: The Image of the Wailing Woman as Symbol of Survival in a Traumatized World." *JFSR* 26 (2010): 63–78.

Claassens, L. Juliana M. *Mourner, Mother, Midwife: Reimagining God's Delivering Presence in the Old Testament*. Louisville, KY: Westminster John Knox, 2012.

Claassens, L. Juliana M. "Resisting Dehumanization: Ruth, Tamar, and the Quest for Human Dignity." *CBQ* 74 (2012): 659–74.

Claassens, Juliana. "'Give Us a Portion among Our Father's Brothers': The Daughters of Zelophehad, Land, and the Quest for Human Dignity." *JSOT* 37 (2013): 319–37.

Claassens, L. Juliana M. "Like a Woman in Labor: Gender, Queer, Postcolonial and Trauma Perspectives on Jeremiah." Pages 117–132 in *Prophecy and Power: Jeremiah in Feminist and Postcolonial Perspective*. Edited by Christl M. Maier and Carolyn J. Sharp. LHBOTS 577. London: Bloomsbury T&T Clark, 2013.

Claassens, L. Juliana. "An Abigail Optic: Reading the Old Testament at the Intersections." Inaugural Lecture, Faculty of Theology, Stellenbosch University, March 10, 2015.

Claassens, L. Juliana M. "Violence, Mourning, Politics: Rizpah's Lament in Conversation with Judith Butler." Pages 19–36 in *Restorative Readings: The Old Testament, Ethics, and Human Dignity*. Edited by L. Juliana M. Claassens and Bruce C. Birch. Eugene, OR: Wipf & Stock, 2015.

Claassens, L. Juliana M. *Claiming Her Dignity: Female Resistance in the Old Testament.* Collegeville, MN: Liturgical Press, 2016.

Claassens, L. Juliana M. "Trauma and Recovery: A New Hermeneutical Framework for the Rape of Tamar (2 Samuel 13)." Pages 177–192 in *Bible through the Lens of Trauma.* Edited by Christopher Frechette and Elizabeth Boase. Atlanta: SBL, 2016.

Claassens, L. Juliana M. "Cultivating Compassion? Abigail's Story (1 Samuel 25) as Space for Teaching Concern for Others." In *Considering Compassion: Global Ethics, Human Dignity, and the Compassionate God.* Edited by Frits de Lange and L. Juliana M. Claassens. Eugene, OR: Wipf & Stock, forthcoming.

Claassens, L. Juliana and Bruce C. Birch, eds. *Restorative Readings: The Old Testament, Ethics, and Human Dignity.* Eugene, OR: Pickwick, 2015.

Claassens, L. Juliana M. and Klaas Spronk, eds. *Fragile Dignity: Intercontextual Conversations on Scriptures, Family, and Violence.* SemeiaSt 72. Atlanta: SBL, 2013.

Cody, Philip. *Seeds on the Word: Ngā Kākano o te Kupu.* Wellington: Steele Roberts, 2004.

Cohen Shaye J. D. *The Beginnings of Jewishness: Boundaries, Varieties, Uncertainties.* Berkeley: University of California Press, 1999.

Collins, John J. *Introduction to the Hebrew Bible.* Minneapolis: Fortress, 2004.

Collins, Patricia Hill. "It's All in the Family: Intersections of Gender, Race, and Nation." *Hypatia* 13/3 (1998): 62–82.

Conczorowski, Benedict J. "All the Same as Ezra? Conceptual Differences between the Texts on Intermarriage in Genesis, Deuteronomy 7, and Ezra." Pages 89–108 in *Mixed Marriages: Intermarriage and Group Identity in the Second Temple Period.* Edited by Christian Frevel. LHBOTS 547. New York: T&T Clark, 2011.

Craig, Kenneth M. *Reading Esther. A Case for the Literary Carnivalesque.* Louisville, KY: Westminster John Knox, 1995.

Craigie, C. Peter. *Psalms 1–50.* WBC 19. Waco, TX: Word, 1983.

Crenshaw, Kimberlé W. "Demarginalizing the Intersection of Race and Sex: A Black Feminist Critique of Antidiscrimination Doctrine, Feminist Theory, and Antiracist Politics." *University of Chicago Legal Forum* (1989): 139–67.

Cuomo, Chris J. *Feminism and Ecological Communities: An Ethic of Flourishing.* London: Routledge, 1998.

Daly, Mary. *Beyond God the Father: Toward a Philosophy of Women's Liberation.* Boston: Beacon Press, 1973.

Day, Linda M. *Esther.* AOTC. Nashville: Abingdon, 2005.

De Beauvoir, Simone. *The Second Sex.* Translated by H. M. Parshley. New York: Vintage Books, 1973.

De Troyer, Kristin and Marie-Theres Wacker. "Esther (Das Buch Ester)." Pages 593–618 in *Septuaginta Deutsch. Das griechische Alte Testament in deutscher Übersetzung.* Edited by Martin Karrer and Wolfgang Kraus. Stuttgart: Deutsche Bibelgesellschaft, 2009.

De Troyer, Kristin and Marie-Theres Wacker. "Das Buch Ester." Pages 1253–96 in *Septuaginta Deutsch. Erläuterungen und Kommentare Vol. I: Genesis bis Makkabäer.* Edited by Martin Karrer and Wolfgang Kraus. Stuttgart: Deutsche Bibelgesellschaft, 2011.

De Waal, Frans. "What I Learned from Tickling Apes." *New York Times* (April 8, 2016). Available at: http://www.nytimes.com/2016/04/10/opinion/sunday/what-i-learned-from-tickling-apes.html. Accessed April 9, 2016.

Deane-Drummond, Celia and Agustin Fuentes. "Human Being and Becoming: Situating Theological Anthropology in Interspecies Relationships in an Evolutionary Context." *Philosophy, Theology and the Sciences* 1 (2014): 251–75.

Derby, Josiah. "The Daughters of Zelophehad Revisited." *JBQ* 25 (1997): 169–71.

Deutsch, Celia. "Jesus as Wisdom: A Feminist Reading of Matthew's Wisdom Christology." Pages 88–113 in *A Feminist Companion to Matthew*. Edited by Amy-Jill Levine. Sheffield: Sheffield Academic, 2001.

Diamant, Anita. *The Red Tent: A Novel*. New York: Picador, 1997.

Donaldson, Laura. *Decolonising Feminisms: Race, Gender, and Empire Building*. Chapel Hill: University of North Carolina Press, 1992.

Donaldson, Laura E. "The Sign of Orpah: Reading Ruth through Native Eyes." Pages 130–44 in *Ruth and Esther: A Feminist Companion to the Bible*. Edited by Athalya Brenner. FCB Second Series. Sheffield: Sheffield Academic, 1999. Also: Pages 159–70 in *The Postcolonial Biblical Reader*. Edited by R. S. Sugirtharajah. Oxford: Blackwell; 2006.

Dor, Yonina. "The Composition of the Episode of the Foreign Women in Ezra IX–X." *VT* 53 (2003): 26–47.

Dor, Yonina. "From the Well in Midian to the Baal of Peor: Different Attitudes to Marriage of Israelites to Midianite Women." Pages 150–69 in *Mixed Marriages: Intermarriage and Group Identity in the Second Temple Period*. Edited by Christian Frevel. LHBOTS 547. New York: T&T Clark, 2011.

Douglas, Mary. *In the Wilderness: The Doctrine of Defilement in the Book of Numbers*. JSOTSup 158. Sheffield: JSOT Press, 1993.

Douglas, Mary. "Responding to Ezra: The Priests and the Foreign Wives." *BibInt* 10 (2002): 1–22.

Du Preez Bezdrob, Anné Mariè. *Winnie Mandela: A Life*. Cape Town: Zebra Press, 2004.

Du Toit, Louise. "Rumours of Rape: A Critical Consideration of Interpretations of Sexual Violence in South Africa." Stellenbosch Forum Lecture, February 25, 2013.

Du Toit, Megan and Michael Quayle. "Multiracial Families and Contact Theory in South Africa: Does Direct and Extended Contact Facilitated by Multiracial Families Predict Reduced Prejudice?" *South African Journal of Psychology* 41 (2011): 540–51.

Dube, Musa W. "Reading for Decolonization (John 4:1–42)." *Semeia* 75 (1996): 37–59.

Dube, Musa W. "Towards a Postcolonial Feminist Interpretation of the Bible." *Semeia* 78 (1997): 11–26.

Dube, Musa W. "*Batswakwa*: Which Traveler Are You? (John 1:1–18)." Pages 150–62 in *The Bible in Africa: Transactions, Trajectories and Trends*. Edited by Gerald O. West and Musa W. Dube. Leiden: Brill, 2000.

Dube, Musa W. *Postcolonial Feminist Interpretation of the Bible*. St. Louis: Chalice, 2000.

Dube, Musa W. "Divining Ruth for International Relations." Pages 179–98 in *Other Ways of Reading: African Women and the Bible*. Edited by Musa W. Dube. Atlanta: SBL, 2001.

Dube, Musa W., ed. *Other Ways of Reading: African Women and the Bible*. Atlanta: SBL, 2001.

Dube, Musa W. "Rahab Says Hello to Judith: A Decolonizing Feminist Reading." Pages 142–58 in *The Postcolonial Biblical Reader*. Edited by R. S. Sugirtharajah. Oxford: Blackwell, 2006.

Dube, Musa W. "The Subaltern Can Speak: Reading the Mmutle (Hare) Way." *Journal of Africana Religions* 4 (2016): 54–75.

Dube, Musa W., Andrew M. Mbuvi, and Dora Mbuwayesango, eds. *Postcolonial Perspectives in African Biblical Interpretations*. Atlanta: SBL, 2012.

Dutcher-Walls, Patricia. *Jezebel: Portraits of a Queen*. Interfaces. Collegeville, MN: Liturgical Press, 2004.

Eagleton, Terry. *Criticism and Ideology: A Study in Marxist Literary Theory*. London: New Left Books, 1976.

Edelman, Diana. "Huldah the Prophet—of Yahweh or Asherah?" Pages 231–50 in *A Feminist Companion to Samuel and Kings*. Edited by Athalya Brenner. Sheffield: Sheffield Academic, 1994.

Ego, Beate. *Esther*. BKAT. Neukirchen-Vluyn: Neukirchener, forthcoming.

Elsmore, Bronwyn. *Like Them That Dream: The Maori and the Old Testament*. Second edition. Auckland: Libro International, 2011.

Elwell, Sue Levi. "Numbers." Pages 105–21 in *The Queer Bible Commentary*. Edited by Deryn Guest et al. London: SCM Press, 2006.

Erickson, Kai. "Notes on Trauma and Community." Pages 183–99 in *Trauma: Explorations in Memory*. Edited by Cathy Caruth. Baltimore: Johns Hopkins University Press, 1995.

Eskenazi, Tamara Cohn. "The Missions of Ezra and Nehemiah." Pages 509–29 in *Judah and the Judeans in the Persian Period*. Edited by Oded Lipschits and Manfred Oeming. Winona Lake, IN: Eisenbrauns, 2006.

Eskenazi, Tamara Cohn and Andrea L. Weiss, eds. *The Torah: A Women's Commentary*. New York: URJ, 2008.

Eskenazi, Tamara Cohn and Eleanore P. Judd. "Marriage to a Stranger in Ezra 9–10." Pages 266–85 in *Second Temple Studies 2: Temple and Community in the Persian Period*. Edited by Tamara Cohn Eskenazi and Kent H. Richards. JSOTSup 175. Sheffield: JSOT Press, 1994.

Eskenazi, Tamara Cohn and Tikva Frymer-Kensky. *Ruth*. JPS Bible Commentary. Philadelphia: Jewish Publication Society of America, 2011.

Everhart, Janet. "Women Who love Women Reading Hebrew Bible Texts: About a Lesbian Biblical Hermeneutics." Pages 188–204 in *Feminist Interpretation of the Hebrew Bible in Retrospect. Volume II: Social Locations*. Edited by Susanne Scholz. Sheffield: Sheffield Phoenix, 2014.

Exum, J. Cheryl. "The Centre Cannot Hold: Thematic and Textual Instabilities in Judges." *CBQ* 52 (1990): 410–29.

Exum, J. Cheryl. *Fragmented Women. Feminist (Sub)Versions of Biblical Narratives*. JSOTSup 163. Sheffield: JSOT Press, 1993.

Exum, J. Cheryl. "Second Thoughts about Secondary Characters: Women in Exodus 1.8–2.10." Pages 75–87 in *A Feminist Companion to Exodus and Deuteronomy*. Edited by Athalya Brenner. FCB 6. Sheffield: Sheffield Academic, 1994.

Exum, J. Cheryl. "Feminist Criticism: Whose Interests Are Being Served?" Pages 65–90 in *Judges and Method: New Approaches in Biblical Studies*. Edited by Gale A. Yee. Minneapolis: Fortress, 1995.

Exum, J. Cheryl. "Developing Strategies of Feminist Criticism/Developing Strategies for Commentating the Song of Songs." Pages 206–49 in *Auguries: The Jubilee Volume of the Sheffield Department of Biblical Studies*. Edited by David J. A. Clines and Stephen D. Moore. JSOTSup 269. Sheffield: Sheffield Academic, 1998.

Fanon, Frantz. *Peau noir, masques blancs*. Paris: Editions de Seuil, 1952.

Fanon, Frantz. *Les damnés de la terre*. Paris: Maspéro, 1961. Translated by Constance Farrington: *The Wretched of the Earth*. New York: Grove Weidenfeld, 1963.

Fanon, Frantz. *Black Skin, White Masks*. Translated by Charles Lam Markmann. New York: Grove Press, 1967.

Feder, Stephanie. "Esther Goes to Africa. Rezeptionen des Esterbuches in Südafrika." Pages 41–55 in *Esters unbekannte Seiten. Theologische Perspektiven auf ein vergessenes biblisches Buch*. Edited by Stephanie Feder and Aurica Nutt. Festschrift Marie-Theres Wacker. Ostfildern: Grünewald-Verlag, 2012.

Fewell, Danna N. and David M. Gunn. "Controlling Perspectives: Women, Men, and the Authority of Violence in Judges 4 & 5." *JAAR* 58 (1990): 389–411.

Fewell, Danna Nolan and David M. Gunn. *Gender, Power, and Promise: The Subject of the Bible's First Story*. Nashville: Abingdon, 1993.

Finkelstein, Israel. *The Forgotten Kingdom: The Archaeology and History of Northern Israel*. ANEM 5. Atlanta: SBL, 2013.

Fischer, Irmtraud. "The Book of Ruth: A 'Feminist' Commentary to the Torah?" Pages 24–49 in *Ruth and Esther: A Feminist Companion to the Bible*. Edited by Athalya Brenner. FCB Second Series. Sheffield: Sheffield Academic, 1999.

Fischer, Irmtraud. *Rut*. HThKAT. Freiburg im Breisgau: Herder, 2001.

Fischer, Irmtraud. *Women Who Wrestled with God: Biblical Stories of Israel's Beginnings*. Collegeville, MN: Liturgical Press, 2005.

Fodor, Jim. "Reading the Scriptures: Rehearsing Identity, Practicing Character." Pages 141–55 in *The Blackwell Companion to Christian Ethics*. Edited by Stanley Hauerwas and Samuel Wells. Oxford: Blackwell, 2004.

Fretheim, Terence E. "Genesis." Pages 319–674 in *NIB: A Commentary in Twelve Volumes*. Volume 1. Edited by Leander E. Keck. Nashville: Abingdon, 1994.

Frevel, Christian. "Introduction: The Discourse on Intermarriage in the Hebrew Bible." Pages 1–14 in *Mixed Marriages: Intermarriage and Group Identity in the Second Temple Period*. Edited by Christian Frevel. LHBOTS 547. New York: T&T Clark, 2011.

Fried, Lisbeth S. *Ezra: A Commentary*. Sheffield: Sheffield Phoenix, 2015.

Fuchs, Esther. "Status and Role of Female Heroines in the Biblical Narrative." *Mankind Quarterly* 23 (1982): 149–60.

Fuchs, Esther. *Sexual Politics in the Biblical Narrative: Reading the Hebrew Bible as a Woman*. LHBOTS 310. Sheffield: Sheffield Academic, 2000.

Fuchs, Esther. "Biblical Feminisms: Knowledge, Theory and Politics in the Study of Women in the Hebrew Bible." *BibInt* 16 (2008): 205–26.

Gafney, Wilda C. "Ruth." Pages 398–403 in *The Peoples' Bible: New Revised Standard Version with the Apocrypha*. Edited by Curtiss P. DeYoung et al. Minneapolis: Fortress, 2009.

Gailey, Christine Ward. *Kinship to Kingship: Gender Hierarchy and State Formation in the Tongan Islands*. Texas Press Sourcebooks in Anthropology 14. Austin: University of Texas Press, 1987.

Gibbons, Peter. "Cultural Colonization and National Identity." *New Zealand Journal of History* 36 (2002): 5–17.

Glover, Neil. "Elijah versus the Narrative of Elijah: The Contest between the Prophet and the Word." *JSOT* 30 (2006): 449–62.

Goldman, Stan. "Narrative and Ethical Ironies in Esther." *JSOT* 47 (1990): 15–31.

Gottwald, Norman K. *The Tribes of Yahweh: A Sociology of Religion of Liberated Israel, 1250–1050 B. C. E.* London: SCM, 2013.

Grabbe, Lester L. "Reflections on the Discussion." Pages 331–41 in *Ahab Agonistes: The Rise and Fall of the Omri Dynasty*. Edited by Lester L. Grabbe. LHBOTS 421. London: T&T Clark, 2007.

Gray, John. *I & II Kings*. Second edition. OTL. Philadelphia: Westminster, 1970.

Green, Barbara. "Enacting Imaginatively the Unthinkable: 1 Samuel 25 and the Story of Saul." *BibInt* 11 (2003): 1–23.

Greene, Gayle. "Feminist Fiction and the Uses of Memory." *Signs: Journal of Women in Culture and Society* 16 (1991): 290–321.

Gross, Rita. *Feminism and Religion: An Introduction*. Boston: Beacon, 1996.

Gruber, Mayer I. Review of *Inheritance by Daughters in Israel and the Ancient Near East: A Social, Legal and Ideological Revolution* by Zafrira Ben-Barak. *IEJ* 59 (2009): 123–5.

Gruen, Erich S. *Diaspora: Jews amidst Greeks and Romans*. Cambridge: Harvard University Press, 2002.

Guardiola-Sáenz, Leticia A. "Borderless Women and Borderless Texts: A Cultural Reading of Matthew 15:21–28." *Semeia* 78 (1997): 69–81.

Guardiola-Sáenz, Leticia A. "Border-Crossing and Its Redemptive Power in John 7:53–8:11: A Cultural Reading of Jesus and the Accused." Pages 129–52 in *John and Postcolonialism: Travel, Space, and Power*. Edited by Musa W. Dube and Jeffrey L. Staley. Sheffield: Sheffield Academic, 2002.

Guest, Deryn. *When Deborah Met Jael: Lesbian Feminist Hermeneutics*. London: SCM Press, 2005.

Guest, Deryn. *Beyond Feminist Biblical Studies*. BMW 47. Sheffield: Sheffield Phoenix, 2012.

Guest, Deryn, Robert E. Goss, Mona West, and Thomas Bohache, eds. *The Queer Bible Commentary*. London: SCM, 2006.

Ha, Kien Nghi. "Crossing the Border? Hybridity as Late-Capitalistic Logic of Cultural Translation and National Modernisation." *Transversal Texts* 11/2006. Available at: http://eipcp.net/transversal/1206/ha/en. Accessed January 27, 2016.

Habel, Norman C. *The Land Is Mine: Six Biblical Land Ideologies*. OBT. Minneapolis: Fortress, 1995.

Hadjiev, Tchavdar S. "Elijah's Alleged Megalomania: Reading Strategies for Composite Texts, with 1 Kings 19 as an Example." *JSOT* 39 (2015): 433–49.

Hadley, Judith M. "From Goddess to Literary Construct: The Transformation of Asherah Into Hokmah." Pages 360–99 in *A Feminist Companion to Reading the Bible: Approaches, Methods and Strategies*. Edited by Athalya Brenner and Carole Fontaine. Sheffield: Sheffield Academic, 1997.

Halpern, Baruch. *David's Secret Demons: Messiah, Murderer, Traitor, King*. The Bible in Its World. Grand Rapids, MI: Eerdmans, 2001.

Hanauer, Cathi. *The Bitch in the House: 26 Women Tell the Truth about Sex, Solitude, Work, Motherhood, and Marriage*. New York: HarperCollins, 2002.

Hauerwas, Stanley. "Christians in the Hands of Flaccid Secularists: Theology and 'Moral Inquiry' in the Modern University." *Ethical Perspectives* 4 (1997): 32–47.

Hauser, Alan J. "Yahweh versus Death—the Real Struggle in 1 Kings 17–19." Pages 9–89 in *From Carmel to Horeb: Elijah in Crisis*. Edited by Alan J. Hauser and Russell Gregory. JSOTSup 85. Sheffield: Almond Press, 1990.

Havea, Jione. "Numbers." Pages 43–51 in *Global Bible Commentary*. Edited by Daniel Patte. Nashville: Abingdon, 2004.

Hazleton, Lesley. *Jezebel: The Untold Story of the Bible's Harlot Queen*. New York: Doubleday, 2007.

Heimbach-Steins, Marianne. "Subjekt werden—Handlungsmacht gewinnen. Eine Glosse zu Est 4,13–14." Pages 189–92 in *Esters unbekannte Seiten. Theologische Perspektiven auf ein vergessenes biblisches Buch*. Edited by Stephanie Feder and Aurica Nutt. Festschrift Marie-Theres Wacker. Ostfildern: Grünewald-Verlag, 2012.

Herman, Judith. *Trauma and Recovery: The Aftermath of Violence—from Domestic Abuse to Political Terror*. New York: Basic Books, 1997.

Hiepel, Ludger. "Ester das ist auch Ištar. Eine Lesebrille für die hybride Esterfiguration vor dem Hintergrund der altorientalischen Kriegs- und Liebesgöttin." *BN* 163 (2014): 53–71.

Hoglund, Kenneth G. *Achaemenid Imperial Administration in Syria-Palestine and the Missions of Ezra and Nehemiah.* SBLDS 125. Atlanta: Scholars Press, 1992.

hooks, bell. *Ain't I a Woman? Black Women and Feminism.* Boston: South End Press, 1981.

Hornsby, Teresa J. and Ken Stone. "Already Queer: A Preface." Pages ix–xiv in *Bible Trouble: Queer Reading at the Boundaries of Biblical Scholarship.* Edited by Teresa J. Hornsby and Ken Stone. SemeiaSt 67. Atlanta: SBL, 2011.

Hornsby, Teresa J. and Ken Stone, eds. *Bible Trouble: Queer Reading at the Boundaries of Biblical Scholarship.* SemeiaSt 67. Atlanta: SBL, 2011.

Howard, Cameron B. R. "1 and 2 Kings." Pages 164–83 in *The Women's Bible Commentary: Revised and Updated.* Edited by Carol A. Newsom, Sharon H. Ringe, and Jacqueline E. Lapsley. Louisville, KY: Westminster John Knox, 2012.

Huber, Wolfgang. "Why Ethics?" Inaugural Lecture as Honorary Professor of Stellenbosch University. February 19, 2015.

Hyslop, Jonathan. *The Representation of White Working Class Women in the Construction of a Reactionary Populist Movement: "Purified" Afrikaner Nationalist Agitation for Legislation against "Mixed" Marriages, 1934–1939.* Johannesburg: African Studies Institute, University of the Witwatersrand, 1993.

Ilan, Tal. "The Daughters of Zelophehad and Women's Inheritance: The Biblical Injunction and its Outcome." Pages 176–86 in *Exodus to Deuteronomy.* Edited by Athalya Brenner. FCB Second Series 5. Sheffield: Sheffield Academic, 2000.

Ipsen, Avaren. *Sex Working and the Bible.* London: Equinox, 2009.

Isasi-Díaz, Ada María. "The Bible and *Mujerista* Theology." Pages 261–9 in *Lift Every Voice: Constructing Christian Theologies from the Underside.* Edited by Susan Brooks Thistlethwaite and Mary Potter Engel. Maryknoll, NY: Orbis, 1998.

Jackson, Melissa A. *Comedy and Feminist Interpretation of the Hebrew Bible: A Subversive Collaboration.* Oxford Theological Monographs. Oxford: Oxford University Press, 2012.

Jacobson, Diana. "Jesus as Wisdom in the New Testament." *WW* Supplement Series 3 (1997): 72–93.

Japhet, Sara. "The Expulsion of the Foreign Women (Ezra 9–10): The Legal Basis, Precedents, and Consequences for the Definition of Jewish Identity." Pages 141–61 in *"Sieben Augen auf einem Stein" (Sach 3,9): Studien zur Literatur des Zweiten Tempels. Festschrift Ina Willi-Plein.* Edited by Friedhelm Hartenstein and Michael Pietsch. Neukirchen-Vluyn: Neukirchener Verlag, 2007.

Jaynes, Claire. "The Influence of *The Family* on Interracial Intimate Relationships in Post-apartheid South Africa." *South African Journal of Psychology* 40 (2010): 396–413.

Jobling, David. *The Sense of Biblical Narrative: Structural Analyses in the Hebrew Bible II.* JSOTSup 39. Sheffield: JSOT Press, 1986.

Jobling, David. "The Dead Father: A Tragic Reading of 1 Samuel." Pages 250–81 in *Berit Olam: Studies in Hebrew Narrative and Poetry: 1 Samuel.* Collegeville, MN: Liturgical Press, 1998.

Johnson, Luke T. *Sharing Possessions: What Faith Demands.* Second edition. Grand Rapids, MI: Eerdmans, 2011.

Johnson, Willa M. *The Holy Seed Has Been Defiled: The Interethnic Marriage Dilemma in Ezra 9–10.* Sheffield: Sheffield Phoenix, 2011.

Jordan, Yolanda. "Single, Saved—and Having Sex." *Ebony* (May 2, 2012).

Junior, Nyasha. *An Introduction to Womanist Biblical Interpretation.* Louisville, KY: Westminster John Knox, 2015.

Kamaara, Eunice. "Family in Eastern Africa." Page 410 in *The Cambridge Dictionary of Christianity*. Edited by Daniel Patte. Cambridge, UK: Cambridge University Press, 2010.

Kampen, Melanie. *Unsettling Theology: Decolonizing Western Interpretations of Original Sin*. MThS dissertation, University of Waterloo, Ontario, 2014.

Kanyoro, Musimbi R. A. *Introducing Feminist Cultural Hermeneutics: An African Perspective*. Sheffield: Sheffield Academic, 2002.

Kareem, Peter K. "A Critical Examination of Naomi's and Ruth's Use of Feminine Insight and Wisdom for Survival as a Tool for Solving Widowhood Socio-Economic Problems in Africa." Pages 229–47 in *Biblical Studies and Feminism in the African Context: In Honour of the Late Dr. Dorcas Olubanke Akitunde*. Edited by Olabiji A. Adewale. National Association for Biblical Studies 3. Ibadan: NABIS Western Zone, 2012.

Karrer-Grube, Christiane. "Ezra and Nehemiah: The Return of the Others." Pages 192–206 in *Feminist Biblical Interpretation: A Compendium of Critical Commentary on the Books of the Bible and Related Literature*. Edited by Luise Schottroff and Marie-Theres Wacker. Grand Rapids, MI: Eerdmans, 2012.

Kelsey, David H. *Eccentric Existence: A Theological Anthropology*. 2 volumes. Louisville, KY: Westminster John Knox, 2009.

Kelso, Julie. *O Mother, Where Art Thou? An Irigarayan Reading of the Book of Chronicles*. London: Equinox, 2007.

Kessler, Rainer. "Die Juden als Kindes- und Frauenmörder? Zu Est 8,11." Pages 337–45 in *Die Hebräische Bibel und ihre zweifache Nachgeschichte*. Edited by Erhard Blum, Christian Macholz, and Ekkehard W. Stegemann. Festschrift Rolf Rendtorff. Neukirchen-Vluyn: Neukirchener, 1990.

Kessler, Rainer. *The Social History of Israel: An Introduction*. Translated by Linda M. Maloney. Minneapolis: Fortress, 2008.

Kessler, Rainer. "Die interkulturellen Ehen im perserzeitlichen Juda." Pages 276–94 in *Moderne Religionsgeschichte im Gespräch: Interreligiös—interkulturell—interdisziplinär. Festschrift Christoph Elsas*. Edited by Adelheid Hermann-Pfandt. Berlin: EB-Verlag, 2010.

Kgalemang, Malebogo. "Sex and the Single Pentecostal Christian in Botswana." *JTSA* 149 (2014): 90–110.

Klapheck, Elisa. "Ester und Amalek. Ein jüdisch-feministisches Selbstverständnis nach der Shoa." Pages 242–56 in *Von Gott reden im Land der Täter. Theologische Stimmen der dritten Generation seit der Shoa*. Edited by Katharina von Kellenbach, Björn Krondorfer, and Norbert Reck. Darmstadt: Wiss. Buchgesellschaft, 2001.

Kottsieper, Ingo. "'And They Did Not Care to Speak Yehudit': On Linguistic Change in Judah during the Late Persian Era." Pages 95–124 in *Judah and the Judeans in the Fourth Century B. C. E.* Edited by Oded Lipschits, Gary N. Knoppers, and Rainer Albertz. Winona Lake, IN: Eisenbrauns, 2007.

Kraus, Hans-Joachim. *Psalms 1–59: A Commentary*. Translated by Hilton C. Oswald. CC. Minneapolis: Fortress, 1988.

Krog, Antjie. *Country of My Skull: Guilt, Sorrow, and the Limits of Forgiveness in the New South Africa*. New York: Broadway Books, 2007.

Kupenga, Vapi, Rina Rata, and Tuki Nepe. "Whāia te Iti Kahurangi: Māori Women Reclaiming Autonomy." Pages 304–9 in *Te Ao Mārama. Regaining Aotearoa: Māori Writers Speak Out*. Volume 2. Edited by Witi Ihimaera. Auckland: Reed Books, 1993.

Kwok, Pui-lan. *Discovering the Bible in the Non-Biblical World*. Maryknoll, NY: Orbis, 1995.

Kwok, Pui-lan. *Postcolonial Imagination and Feminist Theology*. Louisville, KY: Westminster John Knox, 2005.

Kwok, Pui-lan. "Making the Connections: Postcolonial Studies and Feminist Biblical Interpretation." Pages 45–64 in *The Postcolonial Biblical Reader*. Edited by R. S. Sugirtharajah. Oxford: Blackwell, 2006.

LaCocque, André. *Ruth: A Continental Commentary*. Translated by K. C. Hanson. CC. Minneapolis: Fortress, 2004.

Lapsley, Jacqueline E. *Whispering the Word. Hearing Women's Stories in the Old Testament*. Louisville, KY: Westminster John Knox, 2005.

Lee, Oo Chung, ed. *Women of Courage: Asian Women Reading the Bible*. Seoul: Asian Women's Resource Center for Culture and Theology, 1992.

Leveen, Adriane. *Memory and Tradition in the Book of Numbers*. Cambridge, UK: Cambridge University Press, 2008.

Levine, Baruch A. *Numbers 21–36: A New Translation with Introduction and Commentary*. AB 4A. New York: Doubleday, 2000.

Liew, Tat-Siong Benny. "Echoes of a Subaltern's Contribution and Exclusion." Pages 211–31 in *Mark & Method: New Approaches in Biblical Studies*. Second edition. Edited by Janice Capel Anderson and Stephen D. Moore. Minneapolis: Fortress, 2008.

Linafelt, Tod. *Ruth*. Berit Olam. Collegeville, MN: Liturgical Press, 1999.

Litke, John D. "The Daughters of Zelophehad." *CurTM* 29 (2002): 207–18.

Lubetski, Edith and Meir Lubetski. *The Book of Esther. A Classified Bibliography*. Bible Bibliographies. Sheffield: Sheffield Phoenix, 2008.

Lupisella, M. L. "Cosmocentrism and the Active Search for Extraterrestrial Intelligence." Astrobiology Science Conference 2010: Evolution and Life: Surviving Catastrophes and Extremes on Earth and Beyond. Available at: http://adsabs.harvard.edu/abs/2010LPICo1538.5597L. Accessed March 15, 2016.

Macule, Salvador Armando and Sarojini Nadar. "Women Oppressing Women: The Cultivation of *Esprit de Corps* in Xirilo (Women's Association) of the UCCSA in Mozambique." *The Ecumenical Review* 64 (2012): 357–65.

Magen, Yitzhak. "The Dating of the First Phase of the Samaritan Temple on Mount Gerizim in Light of the Archaeological Evidence." Pages 157–93 in *Judah and the Judeans in the Fourth Century B. C. E.* Edited by Oded Lipschits, Gary N. Knoppers, and Rainer Albertz. Winona Lake, IN: Eisenbrauns, 2007.

Maier, Christl M. "Conflicting Attractions: Parent Wisdom and the 'Strange Woman' in Proverbs 1–9." Pages 92–108 in *Wisdom and Psalms: A Feminist Companion to the Bible*. Edited by Athalya Brenner and Carole Fontaine. FCB Second Series. Sheffield: Sheffield Academic, 1998.

Maier, Christl M. *Daughter Zion, Mother Zion: Gender, Space, and the Sacred in Ancient Israel*. Minneapolis: Fortress, 2008.

Maier, Christl M. and Carolyn J. Sharp, eds. *Prophecy and Power: Jeremiah in Feminist and Postcolonial Perspective*. LHBOTS 577. London: Bloomsbury T&T Clark, 2013.

Maluleke, Tinyiko S. "African Ruths, Ruthless Africas: Reflections of an African Mordecai." Pages 237–51 in *Other Ways of Reading: African Women and the Bible*. Edited by Musa W. Dube. Atlanta: SBL, 2001.

Mandela, Nelson. *Long Walk to Freedom*. London: Abacus, 1995.

Masenya, Madipoane J. "A Feminist Perspective on Theology with Particular Reference to Black Feminist Theology." *Scriptura* 49 (1994): 64–74.

Masenya, Madipoane J. "Ngwetši (Bride): The Naomi-Ruth Story from an African-South African Woman's Perspective." *JFSR* 14 (1998): 81–90.

Masenya (ngwana' Mphahlele), Madipoane. "Esther and Northern Sotho Stories: An African-South African Woman's Commentary." Pages 27–49 in *Other Ways of Reading: African Women and the Bible*. Edited by Musa W. Dube. GPBS 2/2. Atlanta: SBL, 2001.

Masenya (ngwana' Mphahlele), Madipoane. "What Differences Do African Contexts Make for English Bible Translations?" *OTE* 14 (2001): 281–96.

Masenya (ngwana' Mphahlele), Madipoane. "'A Small Herb Increases Itself (Makes Impact) by a Strong Odour': Re-imagining Vashti in an African-South African Context." *OTE* 16 (2003): 332–42.

Masenya (ngwana' Mphahlele), Madipoane. *How Worthy Is the Woman of Worth? Rereading Proverbs 31:10–13 in African-South Africa*. Bible and Theology in Africa 4. New York: Peter Lang, 2004.

Masenya (ngwana' Mphahlele), Madipoane. "Teaching Western-Oriented Old Testament Studies to African Students: An Exercise in Wisdom or in Folly?" *OTE* 17 (2004): 455–69.

Masenya (ngwana' Mphahlele), Madipoane. "An African Methodology for South African Biblical Sciences: Revisiting the Bosadi (Womanhood) Approach." *OTE* 18 (2005): 741–51.

Masenya (ngwana' Mphahlele), Madipoane. "Their Hermeneutics Was Strange! Ours Is a Necessity! Reading Vashti in Esther 1 as African Women in South Africa." Pages 179–94 in *Her Master's Tools? Feminist and Postcolonial Engagements of Historical-Critical Discourse*. Edited by Caroline van der Stichele and Todd Penner. GPBS 9. Atlanta: SBL, 2005.

Masenya (ngwan'a Mphahlele), Madipoane. "'For Better or for Worse?': The (Christian) Bible and Africana Women." *OTE* 22 (2009): 126–50.

Masenya, Madipoane. "Is Ruth the 'Ēšet Hayil for Real? An Exploration of Womanhood from African Proverbs to the Threshing Floor (Ruth 3:1–13)." *Studia Historiae Ecclesiasticae* 36 Supplement (2010): 253–72.

Masenya, Madipoane. "Biblical Studies in South(ern) Africa: An Overview." Pages 454–65 in *Handbook of Theological Education in Africa*. Edited by Isabel I. Phiri and Dietrich Werner. Pietermaritzburg: Cluster Publications, 2013.

Masenya (ngwan'a Mphahlele), Madipoane. "Engaging with the Book of Ruth as Single African Christian Women: One African Christian Woman's Reflection." *Verbum et Ecclesia* 34 (2013), doi: 10.4102/ve.v34i1.771.

Masenya (ngwan'a Mphahlele), Madipoane and Hulisani Ramantswana. "Anything New under the Sun of South African Old Testament Scholarship? African Qoheleth's Review of OTE 1994–2010." *OTE* 25 (2012): 598–637.

Mbiti, John S. *African Religions and Philosophy*. Second edition. Oxford: Heinemann, 1989.

Mbuwayesango, Dora Rudo. "Can Daughters Be Sons? The Daughters of Zelophehad in Patriarchal and Imperial Society." Pages 251–62 in *Relating to the Text: Interdisciplinary and Form-Critical Insights on the Bible*. Edited by Timothy J. Sandoval and Carleen Mandolfo. JSOTSup 384. London: T&T Clark, 2003.

McCann, J. Clinton. "The Book of Psalms." Pages 641–1280 in *NIB: A Commentary in Twelve Volumes*. Volume 4. Edited by Leander E. Keck. Nashville: Abingdon, 1996.

McKinlay, Judith E. "A Son Is Born to Naomi: A Harvest for Israel." Pages 151–7 in *Ruth and Esther: A Feminist Companion to the Bible*. Edited by A. Brenner. FCB Second Series. Sheffield: Sheffield Academic, 1999.

McKinlay, Judith E. "To Eat or Not to Eat: Where Is Wisdom in This Choice?" *Semeia* 86 (1999): 73–84.

McKinlay, Judith E. "Negotiating the Frame for Viewing the Death of Jezebel." *BibInt* 10 (2002): 305–323.

McKinlay, Judith E. *Reframing Her: Biblical Women in Postcolonial Focus.* BMW 1. Sheffield: Sheffield Phoenix, 2004.

McKinlay, Judith E. "Challenges and Opportunities for Feminist and Postcolonial Biblical Criticism." Pages 19–37 in *Prophecy and Power: Jeremiah in Feminist and Postcolonial Perspective.* Edited by Christl M. Maier and Carolyn J. Sharp. LHBOTS 577. London: Bloomsbury T&T Clark, 2013.

McKinlay, Judith, E. "Playing an Aotearoa Counterpoint: The Daughters of Zelophehad and Edward Gibbon Wakefield." Pages 11–34 in *Postcolonialism and the Hebrew Bible: The Next Step.* Edited by Roland Boer. SemeiaSt 70. Atlanta: SBL, 2013.

McKinlay, Judith E. *Troubling Women and Land: Reading Biblical Texts in Aoteara New Zealand.* BMW 59. Sheffield: Sheffield Phoenix, 2014.

Meyers, Carol. *Discovering Eve: Ancient Israelite Women in Context.* New York: Oxford University Press, 1988.

Meyers, Carol. "Miriam the Musician." Pages 207–30 in *A Feminist Companion to Exodus and Deuteronomy.* Edited by Athalya Brenner. Sheffield: Sheffield Academic, 1994.

Meyers, Carol, ed. *Women in Scripture: A Dictionary of Named and Unnamed Women in the Hebrew Bible, the Apocryphal/Deuterocanonical Books, and the New Testament.* Boston: Houghton Mifflin, 2000.

Meyers, Carol. *Exodus.* The New Cambridge Bible Commentary. Cambridge, UK: Cambridge University Press, 2005.

Meyers, Carol. *Rediscovering Eve: Ancient Israelite Women in Context.* New York: Oxford University Press, 2013.

Milgrom, Jacob. *Numbers: The Traditional Hebrew Text with the New JPS Translation.* JPSTC. Philadelphia: Jewish Publication Society, 1990.

Miller, J. Maxwell. "Introduction to the History of Ancient Israel." Pages 244–71 in *NIB: A Commentary in Twelve Volumes.* Volume 1: General and Old Testament Articles. Edited by Leander E. Keck. Nashville: Abingdon Press, 1994.

Miller, Tricia. *Three Versions of Esther. Their Relationship to Anti-Semitic and Feminist Critique of the Story.* CBET. Leuven: Peeters, 2014.

Miller, Tricia. *Jews and Anti-Judaism in Esther and the Church.* Cambridge, UK: James Clarke, 2015.

Mix, Lucas John. "Life-Value Narratives and the Impact of Astrobiology on Christian Ethics." *Zygon* 51 (2016): 520–35.

Mojapelo-Batka, Emily Mapula. "Interracial Couples within the South African Context: Experiences, Perceptions and Challenges." PhD dissertation, University of South Africa, 2008.

Moore, Stephen D. "A Modest Manifesto for New Testament Literary Criticism: How to Interface with a Literary Studies Field that is Post-Literary, Post-Theoretical, and Post-Methodological." *BibInt* 15 (2007): 1–25.

Mosala, Itumeleng J. "The Implications of the Text of Esther for African Women's Struggle for Liberation in South Africa." *Semeia* 59 (1992): 129–37.

Mouton, Elna. *Reading a New Testament Document Ethically.* Atlanta: SBL, 2002.

Mouton, Elna. "The Pathos of New Testament Studies." *Th Viat* 30 (2006): 50–86.

Mouton, Elna, Gertrude Kapuma, Len Hansen, and Thomas Togom, eds. *Living with Dignity: African Perspectives on Gender Equality.* Stellenbosch: Sun Press, 2015.

Mwaura, Philomena N. "Family in African Instituted Churches." Page 410 in *The Cambridge Dictionary of Christianity*. Edited by Daniel Patte. Cambridge, UK: Cambridge University Press, 2010.

Myers, Jacob M. *Ezra. Nehemiah*. AB 14. Garden City, NY: Doubleday, 1965.

Nadar, Sarojini. "A South African Indian Womanist Reading of the Character of Ruth." Pages 159–75 in *Other Ways of Reading: African Women and the Bible*. Edited by Musa W. Dube. Atlanta: SBL, 2001.

Nadar, Sarojini. "Gender, Power, Sexuality and Suffering Bodies in the Book of Esther: Reading the Characters of Esther and Vashti for the Purpose of Social Transformation." *OTE* 15 (2002): 113–30.

Nadar, Sarojini. "'Texts of Terror' Disguised as the 'Word of God': The Case of Esther 2:1–18 and the Conspiracy of Rape in the Bible." *Journal of Constructive Theology* 10 (2004): 59–79 = "'Texts of Terror': The Conspiracy of Rape in the Bible, Church, and Society: The Case of Esther 2:1–18." Pages 77–95 in *African Women, Religion, and Health: Essays in Honour of Mercy Amba Oduyoye*. Edited by Isabel Apawo Phiri and Sarojini Nadar. Maryknoll, NY: Orbis, 2006.

Nadar, Sarojini. "The Politics of Reconciliation: Re-inscribing the Wounded Body through a Feminist Body Hermeneutic." *Concilium: International Journal of Theology* (2013): 35–41.

Nasimiyu-Wasike, Anne. "Polygamy: A Feminist Critique." Pages 101–18 in *The Will to Arise: Women, Tradition, and the Church in Africa*. Edited by Mercy A. Oduyoye and Musimbi R. A. Kanyoro. Maryknoll, NY: Orbis, 2006.

Ndebele, Njabulo S. *The Cry of Winnie Mandela: A Novel*. Cape Town: David Philip, 2003.

Nemet-Nejat, Karen Rhea. *Daily Life in Ancient Mesopotamia*. Westport, CT: Greenwood, 1998.

Newsom, Carol A. "Bakhtin, the Bible, and Dialogic Truth." *JR* 76 (1996): 290–306.

Newsom, Carol A. and Sharon H. Ringe, eds. *Women's Bible Commentary: Expanded Edition with Apocrypha*. Louisville, KY: Westminster John Knox, 1998.

Newsom, Carol A., Sharon H. Ringe, and Jacqueline E. Lapsley, eds. *Women's Bible Commentary: Revised and Updated*. Louisville, KY: Westminster John Knox, 2012.

Niditch, Susan. "Genesis." Pages 10–25 in *The Women's Bible Commentary*. Edited by Carol Newsom and Sharon H. Ringe. Louisville, KY: Westminster, 1992.

Niditch, Susan. "Eroticism and Death in the Tale of Jael." Pages 305–16 in *Women in the Hebrew Bible: A Reader*. Edited by Alice Bach. New York: Routledge, 1999.

Niditch, Susan. *Judges: A Commentary*. Louisville, KY: Westminster John Knox, 2008.

Nielsen, Kirsten. *Ruth: A Commentary*. OTL. Louisville, KY: Westminster John Knox, 1997.

Nihan, Christophe. Review of *Die Vollendung der Tora: Studien zur Redaktionsgeschichte des Numeribuches im Kontext von Hexateuch und Pentateuch* by Reinhold Achenbach. *RBL* 2006.

Njoroge, Nyambura J. "A Spirituality of Resistance and Transformation." Pages 67–76 in *Talitha Cum: Theologies of African Women*. Edited by Nyambura J. Njoroge and Musa W. Dube. Pietermaritzburg: Cluster, 2001.

Njoroge, Nyambura J. and Musa W. Dube, eds. *Talitha Cum! Theologies of African Women*. Pietermaritzburg: Cluster, 2001.

Noth, Martin. *Numbers: A Commentary*. OTL. Philadelphia: Westminster, 1968.

Nussbaum, Martha C. *Love's Knowledge: Essays on Philosophy and Literature*. Oxford: Oxford University Press, 1990.

Nussbaum, Martha C. *Sex and Social Justice*. Oxford: Oxford University Press, 1999.

Nussbaum, Martha C. *Upheavals of Thought: The Intelligence of Emotions*. Cambridge, UK: Cambridge University Press, 2001.

Nussbaum, Martha C. *The New Religious Intolerance: Overcoming the Politics of Fear in an Anxious Age*. Cambridge: Harvard University Press, 2012.

Nussbaum, Martha C. *Political Emotions: Why Love Matters for Justice*. Cambridge: Harvard University Press, 2013.

O'Collins, Gerald, S. J. and David Braithwaite , S. J. "Tradition as Collective Memory: A Theological Task to Be Tackled." *TS* 76 (2015): 29–42.

O'Connor, Kathleen. M. *Jeremiah: Pain and Promise*. Minneapolis: Fortress, 2011.

Oduyoye, Mercy Amba, ed. *The Will to Arise: Women, Tradition, and the Church in Africa*. Maryknoll, NY: Orbis, 1992.

Oduyoye, Mercy A. *Daughters of Anowa: African Women and Patriarchy*. Maryknoll, NY: Orbis, 1995.

Oduyoye, Mercy Amba. *Introducing African Women's Theology*. Sheffield: Sheffield Academic, 2001.

Oh, Irene. "The Performativity of Motherhood: Embodying Theology and Political Agency." *Journal of the Society of Christian Ethics* 29/2 (2009): 3–17.

Okure, Teresa. "Invitation to African Women's Hermeneutical Concerns." *AJBS* 19 (2003): 71–95.

Olson, Dennis T. *Numbers*. IBC. Louisville, KY: John Knox, 1996.

Oppenheim, A. Leo. *Ancient Mesopotamia: Portrait of a Dead Civilization*. Revised edition completed by Erica Reiner. Chicago: University of Chicago Press, 1977.

Ostriker, Alicia Suskin. *Feminist Revision and the Bible: The Unwritten Volume*. Oxford: Blackwell, 1993.

Otto, Susanne. *Jehu, Elia und Elisa. Die Erzählung von der Jehu-Revolution und die Komposition der Elia-Elisa-Erzählungen*. BWA(N)T 152. Stuttgart: Kohlhammer, 2001.

Page, Hugh, Jr., ed. *The Africana Bible: Reading Israel's Scriptures from Africa and the African Diaspora*. Minneapolis: Fortress, 2010.

Pardes, Ilana. *Countertraditions in the Bible: A Feminist Approach*. Cambridge: Harvard University Press, 1992.

Park, Sung Jin. "The Cultic Identity of Asherah in Deuteronomistic Ideology of Israel." *ZAW* 123 (2011): 553–64.

Patte, Daniel, ed. *Global Bible Commentary*. Nashville: Abingdon, 2004.

Pelton, Robert D. *The Trickster in West Africa: A Study of Mythic Irony and Sacred Delight*. HSHR. Berkeley: University of California Press, 1980.

Phiri, Isabel A. "Ruth." Pages 319–24 in *Africa Bible Commentary*. Edited by Tokunboh Adeyemo. Nairobi: World Alive Publishers, 2006.

Phiri, Isabel. "Major Challenges for African Women Theologians in Theological Education (1989–2008)." *Studia Historiae Ecclesiasticae* 34 (2008): 63–81.

Phiri, Isabel and Sarojini Nadar, eds. *African Women, Religion, and Health: Essays in Honor of Mercy Amba Ewudiziwa Oduyoye*. Pietermaritzburg: Cluster Publications, 2000.

Phiri, Isabel A. and Sarojini Nadar. "Introduction: 'Treading Softy but Firmly.'" Pages 1–16 in *African Women, Religion, and Health: Essays in Honor of Mercy Amba Ewudziwa Oduyoye*. Edited by Isabel A. Phiri and Sarojini Nadar. Pietermaritzburg: Cluster, 2006.

Plaatjie, Gloria K. "Toward a Post-Apartheid Black Feminist Reading of the Bible: A Case of Luke 2:36–38." Pages 114–42 in *Other Ways of Reading: African Women and the Bible*. Edited by Musa W. Dube. Atlanta: SBL, 2001.

Plaut, W. G. "Genesis, Book of." Pages 436–42 in *Dictionary of Biblical Interpretation*. Edited by John Hayes. Nashville: Abingdon, 1999.

Polzin, Robert. *Samuel and the Deuteronomist: A Literary Study of the Deuteronomic History. Part Two: 1 Samuel.* San Francisco: Harper & Row, 1989.

Pratt, Mary Louise. *Imperial Eyes: Travel Writing and Transculturation.* New York: Routledge, 1992.

Premnath, D. N. "Margins and Mainstream: An Interview with R. S. Sugirtharajah." Pages 153–65 in *Border Crossings: Cross-Cultural Hermeneutics.* Edited by D. N. Premnath. Maryknoll, NY: Orbis Books, 2007.

Pressler, Carolyn. "The 'Biblical View' of Marriage." Pages 200–11 in *Engaging the Bible in a Gendered World: An Introduction to Feminist Biblical Interpretation in Honor of Katharine Doob Sakenfeld.* Edited by Linda Day and Carolyn Pressler. Louisville, KY: Westminster John Knox Press, 2006.

Pruin, Dagmar. "What Is in a Text? Searching for Jezebel." Pages 208–35 in *Ahab Agonistes: The Rise and Fall of the Omri Dynasty.* Edited by Lester L. Grabbe. LHBOTS 421. London: T&T Clark, 2007.

Punt, Jeremy. "Intersections in Queer Theory and Postcolonial Theory, and Hermeneutical Spin-Offs." *Bible and Critical Theory* 4.2 (2008).

Reiss, Moshe. "Miriam Rediscovered." *JBQ* 38 (2010): 183–90.

Robertson Farmer, Kathleen A. "The Book of Ruth: Introduction, Commentary, and Reflections." Pages 889–946 in *NIB: A Commentary in Twelve Volumes.* Volume 2. Edited by Leander E. Keck. Nashville: Abingdon, 1998.

Rom-Shiloni, Dalit. *Exclusive Inclusivity: Identity Conflicts Between the Exiles and the People Who Remained (6th–5th Centuries BCE).* LHBOTS 543. New York: Bloomsbury T&T Clark, 2013.

Ron, Zvi. "The Daughters of Zelophehad." *JBQ* 26 (1998): 260–2.

Rowlett, Lori. "Disney's Pocahontas and Joshua's Rahab in Postcolonial Perspective." Pages 68–75 in *Culture, Entertainment and the Bible.* Edited by George Aichele. JSOTSup 309. Sheffield: Sheffield Academic, 2000.

Ruddick, Sara. *Maternal Thinking: Toward a Politics of Peace.* New York: Ballantine Books, 1989.

Ruether, Rosemary Radford. *Integrating Ecofeminism, Globalization, and World Religions.* Lanham: Rowman & Littlefield, 2005.

Russell, Letty M., Kwok Pui-lan, Ada María Isasi-Díaz, and Katie Geneva Cannon, eds. *Inheriting our Mothers' Gardens: Feminist Theology in Third World Perspective.* Louisville, KY: Westminster, 1988.

Rutherford, Jonathan. "The Third Space. Interview with Homi Bhabha." Pages 207–21 in *Identity. Community, Culture, Difference.* Edited by Jonathan Rutherford. London: Lawrence & Wishart, 1990.

Sagan, Carl. *The Dragons of Eden: Speculations on the Evolution of Human Intelligence.* New York: Random House, 1977.

Said, Edward W. *Orientalism.* New York: Pantheon, 1978.

Said, Edward W. *Culture and Imperialism.* London: Chatto & Windsor, 1993.

Sakenfeld, Katharine Doob. "In the Wilderness, Awaiting the Land: The Daughters of Zelophehad and Feminist Interpretation." *PSB* 9 (1988): 179–96.

Sakenfeld, Katharine Doob. "Zelophehad's Daughters." *PRSt* 15/4 (1988): 37–47.

Sakenfeld, Katharine Doob. *Numbers: Journeying with God.* ITC. Grand Rapids, MI: Eerdmans, 1995.

Sakenfeld, Katharine D. "Deborah, Jael, and Sisera's Mother: Reading the Scriptures in Cross-Cultural Context." Pages 13–22 in *Women, Gender, and Christian Community.* Edited by Jane D. Douglass and James F. Kay. Louisville, KY: Westminster John Knox, 1997.

Sakenfeld, Katharine Doob. *Ruth*. IBC. Louisville, KY: John Knox, 1999.

Sakenfeld, Katharine Doob. *Just Wives? Stories of Power and Survival in the Old Testament and Today*. Louisville, KY: Westminster John Knox, 2003.

Sakenfeld, Katharine Doob. "Numbers." Pages 79–87 in *Women's Bible Commentary*. Third edition: revised and updated. Edited by Carol A. Newsom et al. Louisville, KY: Westminster John Knox Press, 2012.

Sands, Kathleen M. "Tragedy, Theology, and Feminism in the Time after Time." *New Literary History* 34 (2004): 41–61.

Schäfer, Peter. *Judeophobia. Attitudes toward the Jews in the Ancient World*. Cambridge: Harvard University Press, 1998.

Schaumberger, Christine. "Verschieden und vereint. Frauen der Dritten und Frauen der Ersten Welt." *Schlangenbrut: Zeitschrift für feministisch und religiös interessierte Frauen* 3 (1983): 40–2.

Scholz, Susanne. "Through Whose Eyes? A 'Right' Reading of Genesis 34." Pages 150–71 in *Genesis: A Feminist Companion to the Bible*. Edited by Athalya Brenner. FCB Second Series. Sheffield: Sheffield Academic, 1998.

Schroer, Silvia and Sophia Bietenhard, eds. *Feminist Interpretation of the Bible and the Hermeneutics of Liberation*. JSOTSup 374. Sheffield: Sheffield Academic, 2003.

Schüssler Fiorenza, Elisabeth. *But She Said: Feminist Practices of Biblical Interpretation*. Boston: Beacon, 1992.

Schüssler Fiorenza, Elisabeth. "Transforming the Legacy of the Woman's Bible." Pages 1–24 in *Searching the Scriptures. Vol. 1: A Feminist Introduction*. Edited by Elisabeth Schüssler Fiorenza. New York: Crossroad, 1993.

Schüssler Fiorenza, Elisabeth. *Sharing Her Word: Feminist Biblical Interpretation in Context*. Boston: Beacon, 1998.

Schüssler Fiorenza, Elisabeth. *Wisdom Ways: Introducing Feminist Biblical Interpretation*. Maryknoll, NY: Orbis Books, 2001.

Schwartz, Regina M. *The Curse of Cain: The Violent Legacy of Monotheism*. Chicago: University of Chicago Press, 1997.

Schweickart, Patrocinio P. "Reading Ourselves: Towards a Feminist Theory of Reading." Pages 31–62 in *Gender and Reading: Essays on Readers, Texts, and Contexts*. Edited by Elizabeth A. Flynn and Patrocinio P. Schweickart. Baltimore: Johns Hopkins University Press, 1986.

Scully, Pamela. "Rape, Race, and Colonial Culture: The Sexual Politics of Identity in the 19th Century Cape Colony, South Africa." *The American Historical Review* 100 (1995): 335–59.

Segovia, Fernando F. "Mapping the Postcolonial Optic in Biblical Criticism: Meaning and Scope." Pages 23–78 in *Postcolonial Biblical Criticism: Interdisciplinary Intersections*. Edited by Stephen D. Moore and Fernando F. Segovia. New York: T&T Clark, 2005.

Sharp, Carolyn J. *Irony and Meaning in the Hebrew Bible*. ISBL. Bloomington: Indiana University Press, 2009.

Sharp, Carolyn J. "'Are You for Us, or for Our Adversaries?' A Feminist and Postcolonial Interrogation of Joshua 2–12 for the Contemporary Church." *Int* 66 (2012): 141–52.

Sharp, Carolyn J. "Feminist Queries for Ruth and Joshua: Complex Characterization, Gapping, and the Possibility of Dissent." *SJOT* 28 (2014): 229–52.

Shectman, Sarah. *Women in the Pentateuch: A Feminist and Source-Critical Analysis*. HBM 23. Sheffield: Sheffield Phoenix, 2009.

Shemesh, Yael. "A Gender Perspective on the Daughters of Zelophehad: Bible, Talmudic Midrash, and Modern Feminist Midrash." *BibInt* 15 (2007): 80–109.

Sherman, Rebecca and Melissa Steyn. "E-race-ing the Line: South African Interrelationships Yesterday and Today." Pages 55–81 in *The Prize and the Price: Shaping Sexualities in South Africa*. Edited by Melissa Steyn and Mikki van Zyl. Cape Town: HSRC Press, 2009.

Shields, Mary. "A Feast Fit for a King: Food and Drink in the Abigail Story." Pages 38–54 in *The Fate of King David: The Past and Present of a Biblical Icon*. Edited by Tod Linafelt, Timothy Beal, and Claudia V. Camp. LHBOTS 500. London: T&T Clark, 2010.

Simic, Charles. *That Little Something: Poems*. Boston: Mariner, 2009.

Simpson, Jane. "Io as Supreme Being: Intellectual Colonization of the Māori?" *History of Religions* 37 (1997): 50–85.

Smith, Anthony D. *The Ethnic Revival in the Modern World*. Cambridge, UK: Cambridge University Press, 1981.

Smith, Mark S. *The Early History of God: Yahweh and the Other Deities in Ancient Israel*. San Francisco: Harper & Row, 1990.

Smith, Mitzi J., ed. *I Found God in Me: A Womanist Biblical Hermeneutics Reader*. Eugene, OR: Cascade, 2015.

Smith-Christopher, Daniel. "The Mixed Marriage Crisis in Ezra 9–10 and Nehemiah 13: A Study of the Sociology of the Post-Exilic Judean Community." Pages 243–65 in *Second Temple Studies 2: Temple and Community in the Persian Period*. Edited by Tamara Cohn Eskenazi and Kent H. Richards. JSOTSup 175. Sheffield: JSOT Press, 1994.

Smith-Christopher, Daniel L. *A Biblical Theology of Exile*. OBT. Minneapolis: Fortress, 2001.

Snaith, Norman Henry. "Daughters of Zelophehad." *VT* 16 (1966): 124–7.

Snyman, Gerrie. "'Ilahle Elinothuthu'? The Lay Reader and/or the Critical Reader—Some Remarks on Africanisation." *Religion & Theology* 6 (1999): 140–67.

Snyman, Gerrie. "Identification and the Discourse of Fundamentalism: Reflections on a Reading of the Book of Esther." Pages 160–208 in *Rhetorical Criticism and the Bible*. Edited by Stanley E. Porter and Dennis L. Stamps. JSOTSup 195. Sheffield: Sheffield Academic, 2002.

Snyman, Gerrie. "Narrative Rationality, Morality and Readers' Identification." *OTE* 15 (2002): 179–99.

Snyman, Gerrie. "Race in South Africa: A Hidden Transcript Turned Public? The Problem of Identifying with Esther/Mordecai or Haman in the Book of Esther." *Scriptura* 84 (2003): 438–52.

Soulen, Kendall R. and Linda Woodhead, eds. *God and Human Dignity*. Grand Rapids, MI: Eerdmans, 2006.

Southwood, Katherine. "The Holy Seed: The Significance of Endogamous Boundaries and Their Transgression in Ezra 9–10." Pages 189–224 in *Judah and the Judeans in the Achaemenid Period: Negotiating Identity in an International Context*. Edited by Oded Lipschits, Gary N. Knoppers, and Manfred Oeming. Winona Lake, IN: Eisenbrauns, 2001.

Sperling, S. David. "Miriam, Aaron and Moses: Sibling Rivalry." *Hebrew Union College Annual* 70 (2000): 39–55.

Spivak, Gayatri Chakravorty. "Can the Subaltern Speak?" Pages 271–313 in *Marxism and the Interpretation of Culture*. Edited by Cary Nelson and Lawrence Grossberg. Urbana: University of Illinois Press, 1988.

Spivak, Gayatri Chakravorty. *A Critique of Postcolonial Reason: Toward the History of the Vanishing Present*. Cambridge: Harvard University Press, 1999.

Stafford, Jane and Mark Williams, eds. *Anthology of New Zealand Literature*. Auckland: Auckland University Press, 2012.

Stanton, Elizabeth Cady and the Revising Committee. *The Woman's Bible*. New York: European Publishing Company, 1895–1898.

Sternberg, Meir. *The Poetics of Biblical Narrative: Ideological Literature and the Drama of Reading*. ISBL. Bloomington: Indiana University Press, 1985.

Sterring, Ankie. "The Will of the Daughters." Pages 88–99 in *A Feminist Companion to Exodus to Deuteronomy*. Edited by Athalya Brenner. FCB 6. Sheffield: Sheffield Academic, 1994.

Stiebert, Johanna. *Fathers and Daughters in the Hebrew Bible*. Oxford: Oxford University Press, 2013.

Stone, Ken. "Gender Criticism." Pages 183–201 in *Judges and Method: New Approaches in Biblical Studies*. Second edition. Edited by Gale A. Yee. Minneapolis: Fortress, 2007.

Sugirtharajah, R. S. *The Bible and Empire: Postcolonial Explorations*. Cambridge, UK: Cambridge University Press, 2005.

Sugirtharajah, R. S. "Charting the Aftermath: A Review of Postcolonial Criticism." Pages 7–32 in *Postcolonial Biblical Reader*. Edited by R. S. Sugirtharajah. Malden, MA: Blackwell, 2006.

Tamez, Elsa, ed. *Through Her Eyes: Women's Theology from Latin America*. Maryknoll, NY: Orbis, 1989.

Taylor, Marion Ann, ed. *Handbook of Women Biblical Interpreters: A Historical and Biographical Guide*. Grand Rapids, MI: Baker Academic, 2012.

Taylor, Marion Ann and Heather E. Weir, eds. *Let Her Speak for Herself: Nineteenth-Century Women Writing on Women in Genesis*. Waco, TX: Baylor University Press, 2006.

Taylor, Mark L. *Remembering Esperanza: A Cultural-Political Theology for North American Praxis*. Maryknoll, NY: Orbis, 1990.

Taylor, Michelle Ellis. "Numbers." Pages 94–9 in *The Africana Bible: Reading Israel's Scriptures from Africa and the African Diaspora*. Edited by Hugh A. Page Jr. Minneapolis: Fortress, 2010.

Taylor, Richard. *Te Ika a Maui, or New Zealand and Its Inhabitants*. London: Wertheim and Macintosh, 1855.

Thon, Johannes. "Sprache und Identitätskonstruktion: Das literarische Interesse von Neh 13,23–27 und die Funktion dieses Textes im wissenschaftlichen Diskurs." *ZAW* 121 (2009): 557–76.

Tinker, George E. "Reading the Bible as Native Americans." Pages 174–80 in *NIB: A Commentary in Twelve Volumes*. Volume 1. Edited by Leander E. Keck. Nashville: Abingdon Press, 1994.

Tolbert, Mary. A. "Gender." Pages 99–105 in *Handbook of Postmodern Biblical Interpretation*. Edited by Andrew K. M. Adam. St. Louis: Chalice, 2000.

Tongue, Samuel. *Between Biblical Criticism and Poetic Rewriting: Interpretative Struggles over Genesis 32:22–32*. BibInt 129. Leiden: Brill, 2014.

Trible, Phyllis. *God and the Rhetoric of Sexuality*. OBT 2. Philadelphia: Fortress, 1978.

Trible, Phyllis. "Five Loaves and Two Fishes: Feminist Hermeneutics and Biblical Theology." *TS* 50 (1989): 279–95.

Trible, Phyllis. "Bringing Miriam out of the Shadows." Pages 166–86 in *A Feminist Companion to Exodus and Deuteronomy*. Edited by Athalya Brenner. FCB 6. Sheffield: Sheffield Academic, 1994.

Trible, Phyllis. "Exegesis for Storytellers and Other Strangers." *JBL* 114 (1995): 3–19.

Trible, Phyllis. "Naomi" and "Ruth." Pages 130–1 and 146–7 respectively in *Women in Scripture: A Dictionary of Named and Unnamed Women in the Hebrew Bible, the Apocryphal/Deuterocanonical Books, and the New Testament*. Edited by Carol Meyers. Grand Rapids, MI: Eerdmans, 2000.

Tuhiwai Smith, Linda. *Decolonizing Methodologies: Research and Indigenous Peoples*. Second edition. New York: Zed Books, 2012.

Tull, Patricia K. and Jacqueline E. Lapsley, eds. *After Exegesis: Feminist Biblical Theology*. Essays in Honor of Carol A. Newsom. Waco, TX: Baylor University Press, 2015.

Ulrich, Dean R. "The Framing Function of the Narratives about Zelophehad's Daughters." *JETS* 41 (1998): 529–38.

Van Gennep, Arnold. *The Rites of Passage*. Translated by MB Vizedom and GL Caffee. London: Routledge & Kegan Paul, 1960.

Van Wolde, Ellen. "Yaʿel in Judges 4." *ZAW* 107 (1995): 240–6.

Van Wolde, Ellen. *Ruth and Naomi: Two Aliens*. Translated by John Bowden. London: SCM Press, 1997. Originally *Ruth en Naömi, twee vreemdgangers*. Baarn: Ten Have, 1997.

Van Wolde, Ellen. "A Leader Led by a Lady: David and Abigail in 1 Samuel 25." *ZAW* 114 (2002): 355–75.

Vialle, Cathérine. *Une analyse comparée d'Esther TM et LXX: Regard sur deux récits d'une même histoire*. BETL 233. Leuven: Peeters, 2012.

Volf, Miroslav. *Exclusion and Embrace: A Theological Exploration of Identity, Otherness, and Reconciliation*. Nashville: Abingdon, 1996.

Wacker, Bernd and Marie-Theres Wacker. *… verfolgt, verjagt, deportiert. Juden in Salzkotten 1933–1942. Eine Dokumentation aus Anlaß des 50. Jahrestages der "Reichskristallnacht."* Salzkotten: Private Publication, 1988.

Wacker, Bernd and Marie-Theres Wacker. *Ausgelöscht. Erinnerung an die jüdische Gemeinde Salzkotten*. Salzkotten: Judentum in Salzkotten, 2002.

Wacker, Marie-Theres. *Weltordnung und Gericht. Studien zu 1 Henoch 22*. FB 45. Würzburg: Echter-Verlag, 1982 (second edition, 1985).

Wacker, Marie-Theres. "Feministische Theologie." Pages 535–60 in *Neues Handbuch theologischer Grundbegriffe*. Volume 1. Edited by Peter Eicher. München: Kösel-Verlag, 1984.

Wacker, Marie-Theres. "Feministische Theologie." Pages 45–51 in *Neues Handbuch theologischer Grundbegriffe*. Volume 1. Second reworked edition. Edited by Peter Eicher. München: Kösel-Verlag, 1991.

Wacker, Marie-Theres. "Feministische Theologie und Antijudaismus. Diskussionsstand und Problemlage in der BRD." *Kirche und Israel* 5 (1990): 168–76 = "Theologie Féministe et Anti-judaïsme. Mise à Jour et Évaluation de la Situation en R.F.A." *Recherches Féministes* 3 (1990): 155–65 = "Feminist Theology and Anti-Judaism: The Status of the Discussion and the Context of the Problem in the FRG." *JFSR* 7 (1991): 109–17.

Wacker, Marie-Theres. "Traces of the Goddess in the Book of Hosea." Pages 219–41 in *The Latter Prophets: A Feminist Companion to the Bible*. Edited by Athalya Brenner. FCB First Series. Sheffield: Sheffield Academic, 1995.

Wacker, Marie-Theres. "Mit Toratreue und Todesmut dem einen Gott anhangen. Zum Esther-Bild der Septuaginta." Pages 312–32 in *Dem Tod nicht glauben. Sozialgeschichte der Bibel*. Edited by Frank Crüsemann et al. Festschrift Luise Schottroff. Gütersloh: Gütersloher Verlagshaus, 2004.

Wacker, Marie-Theres. "Tödliche Gewalt des Judenhasses—mit tödlicher Gewalt gegen
    Judenhass? Hermeneutische Überlegungen zu Est 9." Pages 609–37 in *Das Manna fällt
    auch heute noch. Beiträge zur Geschichte und Theologie des Alten, Ersten Testaments*.
    Edited by Frank-Lothar Hossfeld and Ludger Schwienhorst-Schönberger. Festschrift
    Erich Zenger. Herders Biblische Studien 44. Freiburg: Herder, 2004.

Wacker, Marie-Theres. "Ester im Bild." Pages 78–87 in *Ester*. Edited by Klara Butting,
    Gerard Minnard, and Marie-Theres Wacker. *Die Bibel erzählt ...* Wittingen: Erev
    Rav, 2005.

Wacker, Marie-Theres. *Von Göttinnen, Göttern und dem einzigen Gott. Studien zum
    biblischen Monotheismus aus feministisch-theologischer Sicht*. Second edition.
    Theologische Frauenforschung in Europa 14. Münster: LIT, 2005.

Wacker, Marie-Theres. "Widerstand—Rache—verkehrte Welt Oder: Vom Umgang
    mit Gewalt im Esterbuch." Pages 35–44 in *Ester*. Edited by Klara Butting, Gerard
    Minnaard, and Marie-Theres Wacker. Die Bibel erzählt ... Wittingen: Erev Rav, 2005.

Wacker, Marie-Theres. "'... ein großes Blutbad'. Ester 8–9 und die Frage nach Gewalt im
    Esterbuch." *Bibel Heute* 167 (2006): 14–6.

Wacker, Marie-Theres. *Ester: Jüdin, Königin, Retterin*. Stuttgart: Katholisches
    Bibelwerk, 2006.

Wacker, Marie-Theres. "Wann ist der Mann ein Mann? Oder: Geschlechterdisput
    vom Paradies her." Pages 93–114 in *Mannsbilder. Kritische Männerforschung
    und Theologische Frauenforschung im Gespräch*. Edited by Marie-Theres Wacker
    and Stefanie Rieger-Goertz. Theologische Frauenforschung in Europa 21.
    Münster: LIT, 2006.

Wacker, Marie-Theres. "Seresch." Pages 140–51 in *Lieblingsfrauen der Bibel und der Welt.
    Ausgewählt für Luise Metzler zum 60. Geburtstag*. Edited by Christina Duncker and
    Katrin Keita. Norderstedt: BoD, 2009.

Wacker, Marie-Theres. "'Three Faces of a Story': Septuagintagriechisches und
    pseudolukianisches Estherbuch als Refigurationen der Esther-Erzählung."
    Pages 64–89 in *La Septante en allemagne et en France/Septuaginta Deutsch und
    Bible d'Alexandrie*. Edited by Wolfgang Kraus and Olivier Munich. OBO 238.
    Fribourg: Universitätsverlag, 2009.

Wacker, Marie-Theres. "Feldherr und Löwensohn. Das Buch Josua—angeeignet durch
    David Ben-Gurion." Pages 609–47 in *The Book of Joshua*. Edited by Ed Noort. BETL
    250. Leuven: Peeters, 2012.

Wacker, Marie-Theres. "Das biblische Esterbuch zwischen Palästina und Israel. Zum
    Film 'Esther' von Amos Gitai (1985) und seiner Kontextualisierung." Pages 39–59 in
    Religion und Gewalt im Bibelfilm. Edited by Reinhold Zwick. Film und Theologie 20.
    Marburg: Schüren, 2013.

Wacker, Marie-Theres. "Homme sauvage et femmes Étrangères. Le Cycle d'Élie (1 Rois
    17–2 R 2) selon les perspectives de 'genre'/Gender (I–II)." *Lectio Difficilior* 2 (2014).
    Available at: http://www.lectio.unibe.ch/14_2/wacker_marie_theres_homme_sauvage_
    et_femmes_etrangeres.html. Accessed January 27, 2016.

Wacker, Marie-Theres. "Innensichten und Außensichten des Judentums im
    septuagintagriechischen Estherbuch (EstLxx)." Pages 55–92 in *Gesellschaft und Religion
    in der spätbiblischen und deuterokanonischen Literatur*. Edited by Friedrich V. Reiterer,
    Renate Egger-Wenzel, and Thomas R. Eißner. DCLS 20. Berlin: De Gruyter, 2014.

Wacker, Marie-Theres. "Von der Wurzel getragen. Feministische Exegese und
    jüdisch-christliches Gespräch in biographischer Brechung." Pages 97–111 in
    Der jüdisch-christliche Dialog veränderte die Theologie. Ein Paradigmenwechsel

aus ExpertInnensicht. Edited by Edith Petschnigg and Irmtraud Fischer. Vienna: Böhlau, 2016.

Wacker, Marie-Teres and Elaine Wainwright, eds. *Land Conflicts, Land Utopias.* Concilium 2007/2. London: SCM, 2007.

Wacker, Marie-Theres and Stefanie Rieger-Goertz, eds. *Mannsbilder. Kritische Männerforschung und Theologische Frauenforschung im Gespräch.* Theologische Frauenforschung in Europa 21. Münster: LIT, 2006.

Walker, Alice. *In Search of Our Mothers' Gardens.* San Diego: Harcourt Brace Jovanovich, 1983.

Walker, Ranginui. *Ka Whawhai Tonu Matou: Struggle without End.* Auckland: Penguin Books, 1990.

Walsh, Carey. "Why Remember Jezebel?" Pages 311–31 in *Remembering Biblical Figures in the Late Persian and Early Hellenistic Periods: Social Memory and Imagination.* Edited by Diana Vikander Edelman and Ehud Ben Zvi. Oxford: Oxford University Press, 2013.

Walther, Daniel J. "Racializing Sex: Same Sex Relations, German Colonial Authority, and *Deutschtum.*" *Journal of the History of Sexuality* 17 (2008): 11–24.

Walther, Daniel J. "Sex, Race and Empire: White Male Sexuality and the 'Other' in Germany's Colonies, 1894–1914." *German Studies Review* 33 (2010): 45–71.

Warrior, Robert Allen. "A Native American Perspective: Canaanites, Cowboys, and Indians." Pages 235–41 in *Voices from the Margin: Interpreting the Bible in the Third World.* Revised and expanded third edition. Edited by R. S. Sugirtharajah. Maryknoll, NY: Orbis, 2006.

Washington, Harold C. "Violence and the Construction of Gender in the Hebrew Bible: A New Historicist Approach 1." *BibInt* 5 (1997): 324–63.

Washington, Harold C. "Israel's Holy Seed and the Foreign Women of Ezra-Nehemiah: A Kristevan Reading." *BibInt* 11 (2003): 427–37.

Weems, Renita J. *Just a Sister Away: A Womanist Vision of Women's Relationships in the Bible.* San Diego: LuraMedia, 1988.

Weems, Renita J. *Battered Love: Marriage, Sex and Violence in the Hebrew Prophets.* Minneapolis: Fortress Press, 1995.

Weems, Renita J. "Re-reading for Liberation: African American Women and the Bible." Pages 27–39 in *Voices from the Margin: Interpreting the Bible in the Third World.* Revised and expanded third edition. Edited by R. S. Sugirtharajah. Maryknoll, NY: Orbis, 2006.

Weingreen, Jacob. "The Case of the Daughters of Zelophehad." *VT* 16.4 (1966): 518–22.

White, Judith S. "Pipeline to Pathways: New Directions for Improving the Status of Women on Campus." *Liberal Education* 91 (2005): 22–7.

White, Lynn. "The Historical Roots of Our Ecological Crisis." *Science* 155 (1967): 1,203–7.

Whitekettle, Richard. "Forensic Zoology: Animal Taxonomy and Rhetorical Persuasion in Psalm 1." *VT* 58 (2008): 404–19.

Whybray, R. N. "Genesis." Pages 53–91 in *The Pentateuch.* Edited by John Barton and John Muddiman. Oxford: Oxford University Press, 2010.

Williams, Dolores. "Hagar in African American Appropriation." Pages 171–84 in *Hagar, Sarah, and Their Children: Jewish, Christian, and Muslim Perspectives.* Edited by Phyllis Trible and Letty M. Russell. Louisville, KY: Westminster John Knox, 2006.

Williamson, H. G. M. *Ezra, Nehemiah.* WBC 16. Nashville: Nelson, 1985.

Winslow, Karen S. "Mixed Marriage in Torah Narratives." Pages 132–49 in *Mixed Marriages: Intermarriage and Group Identity in the Second Temple Period.* Edited by Christian Frevel. LHBOTS 547. New York: T&T Clark, 2011.

Wright, Jacob L. *David, King of Israel, and Caleb in Biblical Memory*. New York: Cambridge University Press, 2014.

Yancey, George and Richard Lewis Jr. *Interracial Families: Current Concepts and Controversies*. New York: Routledge, 2009.

Yate, William. *An Account of New Zealand; and of the Formation and Progress of the Church Missionary Society's Mission in the Northern Island*. Second edition. London: Seeley and Burnside, 1835.

Yates-Smith, G. R. Aroha. *Hine! e Hine! Rediscovering the Feminine in Maori Spirituality*. PhD dissertation, University of Waikato, Hamilton, 1998.

Yee, Gale. A. "By the Hand of a Woman: The Metaphor of the Woman Warrior in Judges 4." *Semeia* 61 (1993): 99–134.

Yee, Gale A. "Ideological Criticism and Woman as Evil." Pages 9–28 in her *Poor Banished Children of Eve: Woman as Evil in the Hebrew Bible*. Minneapolis: Fortress, 2003.

Yee, Gale A. "Yin/Yang Is Not Me: An Exploration into Asian American Biblical Hermeneutics." Pages 152–63 in *Ways of Being, Ways of Reading: Asian American Biblical Interpretation*. Edited by Mary F. Foskett and Jeffrey Kah-Jin Kuan. St. Louis: Chalice, 2006.

Zacharia, Katerina. "Herodotus' Four Markers of Greek Identity." Pages 21–36 in *Hellenisms: Culture, Identity, and Ethnicity from Antiquity to Modernity*. Edited by Katerina Zacharia. Aldershot: Ashgate, 2008.

Zenger, Erich. "Das Buch Ester." Pages 376–86 in *Einleitung in das Alte Testament*. Eighth edition. Edited by Christian Frevel. Stuttgart: Kohlhammer, 2012.

Ziarek, Ewa Płonowska. *An Ethics of Dissensus: Postmodernity, Feminism, and the Politics of Radical Democracy*. Stanford, CA: Stanford University Press, 2001.

Zierler, Wendy. "'On Account of the Cushite Woman that Moses Took': Race and Gender in Modern Hebrew Poems about Numbers 12." *Nashim: A Journal of Jewish Women's Studies and Gender Issues* 19 (2010): 34–61.

CONTRIBUTORS

Claudia V. Camp
John F. Weatherly Professor Emerita of Religion
Texas Christian University
Fort Worth, Texas
USA

L. Juliana Claassens
Professor of Old Testament
Director of Gender Unit
Faculty of Theology
Stellenbosch University
Stellenbosch, South Africa

Katharine Doob Sakenfeld
Professor Emerita of Old Testament
Princeton Theological Seminary
Princeton, New Jersey
USA

Musa W. Dube
Professor of New Testament
Department of Theology and Religious Studies
University of Botswana
Gaborone, Botswana

Jacqueline E. Lapsley
Associate Professor of Old Testament
Princeton Theological Seminary
Princeton, New Jersey
USA

Judith E. McKinlay
Former Senior Lecturer in Biblical Studies
University of Otago
Dunedin, New Zealand

Christl M. Maier
Professor of Old Testament
Philipps-Universität Marburg
Marburg, Germany

Madipoane Masenya (ngwan'a Mphahlele)
Professor of Old Testament
Department of Biblical and Ancient Studies
University of South Africa
Pretoria, South Africa

Elna Mouton
Professor of New Testament
Faculty of Theology
Stellenbosch University
Stellenbosch, South Africa

Funlola Olojede
Research Fellow, Gender Unit
Beyers Naudé Centre for Public Theology
Stellenbosch University
Stellenbosch, South Africa

Carolyn J. Sharp
Professor of Hebrew Scriptures
Yale Divinity School
New Haven, Connecticut
USA

Marie-Theres Wacker
Professor of Old Testament
Katholisch-Theologische Fakultät
Münster Universität
Münster, Germany

Charlene van der Walt
Research and Program Coordinator
Gender Unit
Faculty of Theology
Stellenbosch University
Stellenbosch, South Africa

INDEX OF MODERN AUTHORS

INDEX OF SCRIPTURE TEXTS

Lightning Source UK Ltd.
Milton Keynes UK
UKHW011336130519
342578UK00003B/299/P